ECONON

A New Approach

new edition

A·G·ANDERTON

Collins Educational

An imprint of HarperCollins*Publishers*

First published 1986 by Unwin Hyman Ltd

This edition 1992 by
Collins Educational
An imprint of HarperCollins*Publishers*
77–85 Fulham Palace Road
London W6 8JB

Reprinted 1993, 1995, 1996, 1998

British Library Cataloguing in Publication Data

Anderton, A. G. (Alain G)
    Economics: a new approach.–New ed.
    I. Title
    330

    ISBN 0 00 322240 3

Cover photograph by courtesy of Lloyd's of London
Cover design by Geoff Wadsley
Typeset and originated in Great Britain by
August Filmsetting, Haydock, St Helens
Printed and bound in Great Britain by
Scotprint Ltd, Musselburgh

Preface

Economic theory has developed rapidly in recent years. Despite this, disagreement amongst economists has increased. It is possible to look back to the 1950s and 1960s and see a certain consensus—sometimes called the neo-classical Keynesian consensus. The rise of monetarism and neo-Keynesianism, and the disturbing economic events of the 1970s shattered that consensus. Since 1979 the British Government has openly rejected Keynesian economics and has been strongly influenced by monetarist thought.

This textbook attempts to reflect the new climate in British economics. It provides a course in economic theory at A level. Competing theories are contrasted throughout. Inevitably, as in any textbook, theories have had to be simplified and it has been impossible to include some major schools of thought, such as the Marxist School.

The book is designed not only as a text for study, but also as a workbook. Each chapter contains various items of data (including press reports, and graphs covering major UK variables) with questions on them. Cartoons and photographs also have questions attached, the photographs being selected for their value as stimulus rather than as general illustrations. Each chapter ends with essay questions.

The data response questions, cartoons and photographs have been included to encourage students to apply their economic theory to particular situations. In this way economic theory should not be seen as an arid discipline but as a genuine help towards understanding our economy.

The book follows a macro-micro approach. Elementary price theory is introduced before the macro-economic chapters because price theory is used to analyse macro-economic topics. The nature of economics and economic methodology is left until the end, in the belief that students can only fully understand these topics after having studied a fair amount of economics. However, the book may be used flexibly. A more traditional approach might be to start at chapters 31 and 32, and then work through chapters 2, 21 to 30, 10, 6 to 9, 11, 3 to 5 and 12 to 20.

In this second edition nearly all the data has been revised and updated. The text has been rewritten where necessary and in particular the whole of chapter 13 has been set aside for a treatment of aggregate demand and aggregate supply analysis.

I would particularly like to thank Peter Chapman, Steve Hurd, David Whitehead and Ronald Bramham who helped so much in the preparation of the first edition; my editor Rosie Ward for skilfully preparing the second edition; and not least my wife and children for putting up with the stresses and strains of living with an author husband.

A. G. Anderton
January 1990

Acknowledgements

The author and publisher would like to express their thanks to the following for the use of photographs: pp. **26, 29, 80** (bottom right), **173, 205, 224** (bottom), **246** (bottom left) George Williams; p. **25** Bank of England; p. **58** (bottom left) BMW Ltd.; pp. **58**, (top left) Canon Uk Ltd; p. **58** (right) Hitachi UK; p. **69** Tony Stone Photolibrary – London; p. **80** (top, bottom left) Co-operative Wholesale Society Ltd.; pp. **92** IFL/Report, photographer: Eamonn O'Dwyer; **105** (top) The Royal Air Force; p **105** (bottom) Unwin Hyman; p. **136** (top) BBC Hulton Picture Library; p. **36** (bottom) IFL/Report, photographer: John Smith; p. **152** (top) Spanish National Tourist Office; p. **152** (bottom left) Food & Wine from France; p. **152** (bottom right) Bruno de Hamel; p. **199** Peter Stalker, *New Internationalist;* p. **212** (top right) Honda; p. **312** (bottom left) Unwin Hyman p. **212** (bottom right) Unwin Hyman; p. **212** (top left) Hitachi UK; p. **220** R. Griggs & Co. Ltd; p. **224** (top) J. Sainsbury plc.; p. **233** a Shell photograph; p. **236** (top) The Sales Promotion Agency; p. **236** (bottom left) The Outspan Organisation; p. **236** (bottom right) Bastable-Dailey Advertizing & Marketing International; p. **246** (top) Tesco; p. **246** (bottom right) © Ian Cook with permission of J. Sainsbury plc; p. **253** (both) Unwin Hyman; p. **258** Shilland & Company Ltd, with permission of Levi's; p. **268** United Kingdom Atomic Energy Authority; p. **282** The Image Bank, © F Gundlach; pp. **292, 301** Oxfam; p. **50** Barnaby's Picture Library, photographer: Bill Coward; p. **277** University of Cambridge Committee for Aerial Photography.

They are also grateful to all those who permitted them to use copyright material in this book; due acknowledgement has been made to each underneath the relevant data/diagrams/graphs.

Cartoons by Trevor Vincent Graphics, Cambrige. Graphs by Chartwell Illustrators.

Contents

1 Introduction 1

2 Price theory—an introduction 3

3 The money supply and the rate of interest 14

4 The demand for money 29

5 Controlling monetary variables 34

6 Consumption 45

7 Saving 53

8 Investment 58

9 The public sector 67

10 National income measurement 79

11 Growth 86

12 Income determination—the Keynesian multiplier model 97

13 Aggregate demand and aggregate supply 107

14 Inflation 116

15 Unemployment 129

16 The trade cycle 141

17 The balance of payments and exchange rates 151

18 International trade 166

19 Government macro-economic policy 177

20 Development economics 193

21 Prices and markets 201

22 Demand theory 211

23 The theory of costs 219

24 The goals of firms 230

25 The firm and its industry 235

26 The neo-classical theory of the firm 241

27 Other theories of the firm 252

28 Markets and efficiency 260

29 Factors of production—the neo-classical approach 274

30 Factors of production—the classical and neo-Keynesian approaches 282

31 The economic problem 289

32 Economic methodology 299

Index 306

1

Introduction

Thomas Carlyle, writing in the first half of the nineteenth century, called economics 'the dismal science'. He was referring to the gloomy predictions made by economists of the day. Economists can still make gloomy forecasts today. Moreover, economics may be thought to be a 'dismal' science because economists frequently are unable to agree and recommend opposite and conflicting courses of action. It is no wonder that the man in the street is left bewildered by economic matters.

Can a study of economics be of any value? The answer is definitely 'Yes'. Firstly, there is much that economists do agree upon. Secondly, it is important to establish what is still uncertain, so that one can treat with scepticism the economist (or politician) who claims he has the answers to all our most pressing economic problems.

Economic theory is concerned with making sense of economic reality. It attempts to gather facts and to classify them. More importantly, it seeks to build **models** or **theories** which attempt to explain chains of economic events. A powerful model or theory provides one explanation for a large number of sequences of events found in the real world and is able to offer predictions of future events.

This book is concerned with outlining such models or theories. These tend to be grouped together into 'schools of thought'. This is because different models or theories may start out with common assumptions which link economists of the same school of thought. An economic school is like a political party. No two members agree completely with each other, but their disagreements are far less important than their shared underlying philosophy.

Capitalist economics is usually considered to have started with Adam Smith who worked in Scotland in the late eighteenth century. He was interested in how a country could become economically prosperous. In his most famous book, *The Wealth of Nations* (1776), he dealt with specialisation, mechanisation, the role of agriculture and government, and how the free enterprise market system could bring about an optimal allocation of resources. The school of thought of which he is

regarded as the father-figure is called the **classical** school.

About 1860, a new school of thought emerged called the **neo-classical** school. Its proponents were interested in mathematical applications and in particular the application of calculus to the study of economics. They believed that economic decision-making could, in part at least, be explained by studying the behaviour of economic units at the **margin**—a concept which is explained later in this book. Much of today's **micro-economics**—the study of individual parts of the economy, such as firms and consumers—is based upon the ideas which they put forward. Many economists today would consider themselves 'neo-classical' in their approach.

However, neo-classical economics failed to present a solution to one of the great economic disasters of this century—the great depression of the 1930s. Between 1929 and 1933, and beyond, most western economies went through a period of extremely high unemployment. At times as many as one in four males of working age were unemployed in some countries. This caused much misery and hardship. Government policy at the time, based upon current neo-classical thinking, seemed to do little to alleviate the situation. In 1936, John Maynard Keynes published a book entitled *The General Theory of Employment, Interest and Money*. It revolutionised economic theory at the macro-economic level (**macro-economics** being the study of the whole economy, which deals with topics such as levels of employment and consumption). Keynes died in 1946, but a group of economists developed his ideas and became known as **Keynesians.** Keynesian thinking dominated economic policy making in the UK throughout the 1950s and 1960s.

The 1960s saw the emergence of a 'new' school of thought directly challenging the Keynesian viewpoint. 'New' is perhaps not the right word because **monetarism** has a long history. It is far older even than one of the best early expositions written by David Hume in 1752. At its simplest it says that changes in the quantity of money in the economy can affect the rate of inflation. If Keynesianism seemed the answer to the unemployment problem of the 1930s, the new monetarism presented a plausible explanation of inflation in the 1970s. The new monetarism was far more sophisticated than that which both classical and neo-classical economists believed in. It presented an alternative view, with alternative policy prescriptions to Keynesianism. Today, one of the great economic debates is between monetarists and Keynesians.

Little attempt is made in this book to judge competing theories. If the greatest economists of the day cannot agree it would be wrong to imply that there is one correct set of economic models or theories. The truth of a model or theory can only be judged by looking at evidence. It is left to readers to judge for themselves which models or theories best explain today's world.

Terms for review

economic model or theory

macro-economics

micro-economics

Price theory—an introduction

Water is essential for man's existence. Diamonds are beautiful but not essential. Yet normally the price of water is very low and the price of diamonds very high. This paradox puzzled economists for many generations. Adam Smith, often regarded as the founder of modern-day economics, was unable to provide a satisfactory answer. It was not until the last half of the nineteenth century, with the rise of neo-classical economics, that a solution was found. Neo-classical economists put forward the theory that price was fixed by demand and supply for that good.

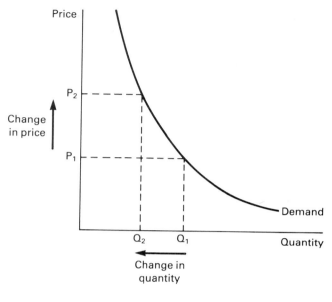

Fig. 2.1

Demand

It is usual to pick out three main variables which affect the quantity demanded for a product.

1 Price The higher the price of a product, the lower will be the demand for it. A rise in price will cause some, if not all, consumers to consume less of the product. For instance, if the price of a chocolate bar goes up in the shops, and everything else remains the same, consumers will buy fewer of those chocolate bars. If a shop cannot sell an item, it will reduce its price. This is the principle behind New Year sales. A firm might be able to sell 50 fur coats at £6 000 each. If it reduced the price to £5 000 it might sell 70 fur coats.

The relationship between price and quantity demanded can be shown diagrammatically (Fig. 2.1). Price is put on the vertical y axis, quantity demanded on the horizontal x axis. The demand curve shows the quantity which would be demanded by consumers at any particular price. The higher the price, the lower the quantity demanded. So a rise in price from P_1 to P_2 will reduce quantity demanded from Q_1 to Q_2. Equally a shop could not sell quantity Q_1 of a product if it charged price P_2. It would have to charge price P_1. The demand curve shows **effective**

demand because it shows how much consumers will buy at each price.

2 Income The greater the income of consumers, the more will be demanded of a normal good. On average, households earning £15 000 a year will demand more clothes, more cars and more holidays than households earning £8 000 a year. However, there are some goods and services for which demand falls as incomes increase. These are known as **inferior goods.** (The term 'inferior goods' is an example of the way in which economists use common words and give them a precise economic meaning.) Commonly given examples of inferior goods are bread and bus services. With rising incomes, consumers buy less bread and demand more expensive foods such as meat. Equally they switch from buses to cars. For an inferior good, an increase in income will decrease the demand for the product at any given price.

This relationship between quantity demanded

and income can be represented on a price–quantity diagram. Initially (Fig. 2.2), the demand curve is given by the curve D_1. Hence, at price P_1, demand is Q_1. There is now a rise in incomes such that at the same price P_1, more is demanded (i.e. the good is a normal good rather than an inferior good). Assume that this increase results in quantity Q_2 being demanded at price P_1. Then we know that the new demand curve D_2 must pass through the point A. Similarly, at every price, the new quantity demanded is found until the exact position of the new demand curve D_2 can be plotted on the graph. So, an increase in income has caused the demand curve (showing the price–quantity relationship) to shift to the right from D_1 to D_2.

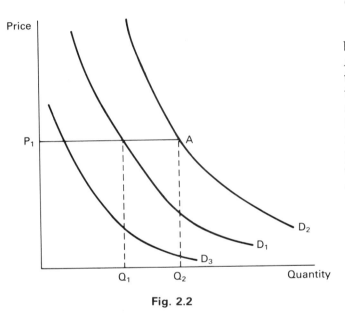

Fig. 2.2

If the good had been inferior, then less would have been demanded at every price when income rises. Hence, the demand curve would have shifted to the left as a result of the income increase: for instance, from D_1 to D_3. Note that these demand curves need not necessarily be parallel with each other when they shift. How far they shift depends entirely on how consumers react to their change in income—and consumers do not necessarily react in parallel shifts!

3 The price of other goods An increase in the price of cement is unlikely to have much effect on the demand for chocolate bars. However, an increase in the price of one chocolate bar might have con-

siderable impact on the demand for other chocolate bars. This may lead to an increase in the demand for other bars as consumers switch some of their demand from the higher priced bar to the other products. In terms of Fig. 2.2, assume the graph represents the price–quantity relationship for a chocolate bar. When the price of a competing product increases, the demand curve for the original chocolate bar will shift to the right, from D_1 to D_2 for instance. That is, more will be demanded at any given price. On the other hand, a fall in price of competing chocolate bars will make the original bar less attractive in terms of price. Hence, the demand curve for it will shift to the left, from D_1 to D_3 for instance. In general, then, demand for a good will be affected to some extent by the relative price of other goods.

It was said above that three major variables could be singled out as affecting the demand for a product. All other factors are collected together and called **tastes**. This is a common feature of many economic theories. Major causal factors are singled out, and all other factors in the relationship are put together in a last variable. With regard to demand theory, tastes could mean that consumers get bored with a product and hence switch to others, as is the case with perfume brands or certain types of fashion clothes. It could be that the need for the product simply disappears, e.g. horse-drawn carriages being replaced by motor cars. It could be that changes in the structure of the population might alter patterns of demand, e.g. an increase in the birth rate is likely to increase the demand for baby products. Just as with income and prices of other products, these changes in tastes can be represented by shifts in the demand curve. For instance, if Fig 2.2 represents the market for squash rackets, an increase in popularity of the game will shift the demand curve to the right from D_1 to D_2.

It is very important to distinguish between movements **along** a demand curve and **shifts** in that demand curve. If quantity demanded changes due to a change in any other variable apart from price, i.e. **income, price of other goods**, or **tastes**, then there would be a **shift** in the demand curve.

For instance, a drop in income results in a shift in the demand curve from D_1 to D_2 in Fig. 2.3. As a result of this shift, price may change too. Originally consumers bought Q_1 of the product and paid price P_1. As a result of a drop in income, the consumers' demand curve shifts from D_1 to D_2. It is unlikely that consumers will continue to either buy Q_1 of the product or indeed pay P_1 for it. For, if price remained

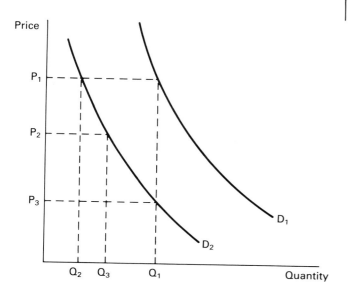

Fig. 2.3

at P_1, firms would only sell Q_2 of the product—a massive cut-back in production. If consumers continued to buy Q_1, this would mean that price had now dropped to P_3—a massive drop in price by the producers. The most likely occurrence is that producers will drop their price and also accept a cut-back in production and consumption, for instance, to price P_2 and quantity Q_3. The drop in income has resulted in a shift to the left in the demand curve, which in turn has led to a fall in the price and quantity demanded.

Movements along a demand curve and shifts in the demand curve cause much confusion because a change in price is usually involved in both. If a change in price causes the change in quantity demanded, then a movement along the demand curve is the result. However, a change in incomes, the price of other goods or tastes will result in a shift in the demand curve, even if price then changes as a result.

In summary, we can say that quantity demanded Q_X of good X is a function of (i.e. depends upon or varies with) the price of that good P_X, the price of all other goods P_Z, income Y and tastes T. Put in mathematical form (where f means 'is a function of' or depends upon or varies with):

$$Q_X = f(P_X, P_Z, Y, T)$$

Data 2.1

Dirt and high prices 'threaten growth of UK tourist industry'

By David Churchill

HIGH PRICES, poor domestic transport and dirty leisure facilities threaten the growth of tourist industries in the 1990s, the British Tourist Authority warned yesterday.

"Britain is in danger of both pricing and dirtying itself out of its place among the world's top five tourist countries," Mr Michael Medlicott, the BTA's chief executive, said....

The Channel tunnel – with a forecast 15m users in its first year – was likely to "have a swift and enormous impact on British tourism," the BTA suggested.

But, Mr Medlicott said, "unacceptable levels of litter and pollution" could lead to a lower growth rate.

He also strongly criticised domestic transport facilities. "Many trains on the routes from seaports are inferior. Often there is no co-ordination between ferry and rail services and there is a drastic lack of baggage handling and passenger reception facilities at some of our seaports."

Airport delays, together with expensive fares on domestic flights and the high cost of entry visas, were also causes of concern.

The Financial Times. 1.2.89

1 Using diagrams, explain how and why demand for tourist services in the UK is likely to change in the future.

Supply

The amount supplied to the market by firms and other organisations is also dependent upon a number of factors.

1 Price The higher the price the supplier can get, the more will be supplied to the market. For instance, assume that total market sales are one million and that the price increases from £2 to £3. Firms in the industry will now find it far more attractive to sell goods in view of the extra profit they can make. Other firms outside the industry will also be attracted into the market because of the large profits available. The result will be increased supply at the higher price. In Fig. 2.4, at price P_1 the industry will supply Q_1. If prices now rise to P_2 there will be an increase in supply to Q_2.

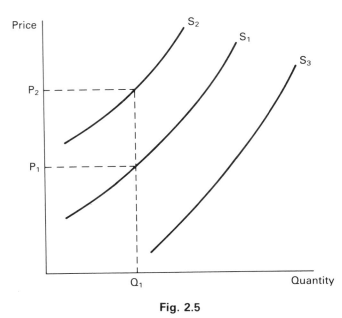

Fig. 2.5

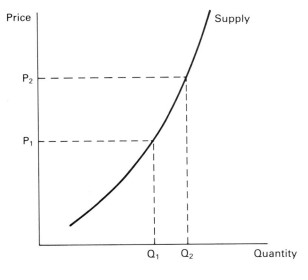

Fig. 2.4

2 Costs A rise in costs will mean that a producer will want to charge a higher price for his output. Thus in Fig. 2.5, assuming that he raises prices from P_1 to P_2, at output Q_1, the supply curve will shift upwards and to the left from S_1 to S_2. In other words, to supply the same quantity, the producer will charge a higher price.

3 Price of other goods and services A rise in the price of other goods and services, particularly goods which are very close substitutes, will allow producers to make larger profits on those goods. As a

result producers will switch production to the higher priced goods in order to secure greater profit. Thus less will be produced of the original good, causing its supply curve to shift downwards and to the right, from S_1 to S_3 in Fig. 2.5.

4 The state of technology This will affect the sort of goods offered to the consumer, their cost and many other variables. For instance, if a new technology allows lower cost production, then the supply curve for the product will shift downwards and to the right.

5 Other factors Taxes, business climate, the workforce and many other factors will affect how much producers will put on to the market at any given price.

Putting it mathematically, we can say that

$$Q_X = f(P_X, P_Z, C, T, F)$$

where Q_X is the quantity supplied of good X, f means 'is a function of', P_Z is the price of all other goods, C are costs, T is the state of technology, and F is all other factors. As with demand curves, there is a movement **along** the curve on a price–quantity diagram if there is a change in **price** causing a change in quantity supplied. If **any other variables** change apart from price, then the result is a **shift** in the supply curve.

Price

Price is determined by the interaction of demand and supply. In Fig. 2.6 assume that price is initially set at P_1, in which case consumers will demand Q_1 of the product. Producers however decide to supply Q_2 to the market. Now producers are supplying far more than consumers want—Q_1Q_2 too much in fact. Standard economic theory states that the glut of produce on the market will result in a lowering of price, a reduction in production and a rise in consumption. This process will continue until there is no glut or indeed until there is a shortage. **Equilibrium** (defined as a point where there is no tendency to change) will occur where quantity demanded and quantity supplied at a particular price are equal. As can be seen from the diagram, there is only one point at which this occurs, the point P_E, Q_E, where the two curves cross.

Returning to the initial paradox of water and diamonds, although the demand for water in terms of volume is much greater than the demand for

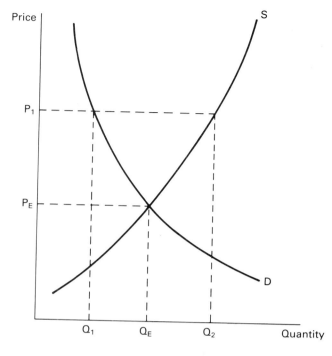

Fig. 2.6

Use the concepts of demand and supply to explain what is going on in this photograph.

Data 2.2

Cocoa falls on talk of rising Ivory Coast supply

By David Blackwell

COCOA PRICES fell to their lowest levels for nearly six months in London yesterday as the fundamental world over-supply re-asserted itself.

On the London Futures and Options Exchange (Fox) the July contract lost £22 a tonne to close at £772 on talk that more Ivory Coast beans are becoming available.

The Ivory Coast, the world's biggest producer, has for 15 months been withholding its top quality cocoa because it believes prices have been too low. It has been refusing to sell below FFr 1,200 a kilogram (£1,100 a tonne), but an Economist Intelligence Unit report last week said there was evidence that its minimum price was being less rigidly applied.

There was talk yesterday of a premium of only £100 a tonne for Ivory Coast cocoa. This compares with premiums of more than £250 a tonne at times last year.

While the Ivory Coast has had some success in keeping prices up, forecasts of excess supply over demand have risen. Both Gill & Duffus and the International Cocoa Organisation recently put the surplus at 199,000 tonnes for the year.

The Financial Times. 13.4.89

1 Using the cocoa market as an example, outline what is meant by the term 'market' in economics.

2 Illustrating your answer with a diagram, explain the changes in cocoa prices described in the article.

diamonds at any given price, so is the supply. In Fig. 2.7, S_D and D_D are the supply and demand curves respectively for diamonds. The equilibrium price for diamonds will be P_D, with Q_D being produced and consumed. The equilibrium price of water, arising from its supply and demand curves S_W and D_W, is much lower at P_W and consumption is consequently greater at Q_W. Diamonds are high in price because they are scarce in relation to their demand.

What will happen if the cost of labour used in

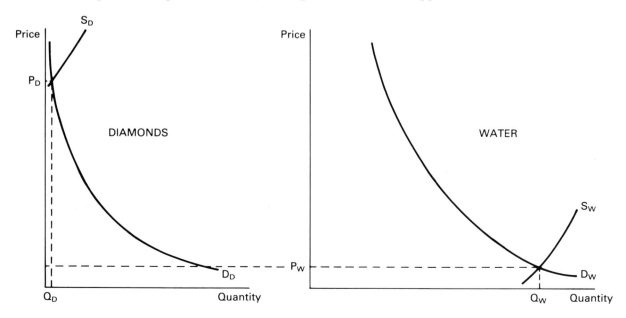

Fig. 2.7

mining diamonds increases? If costs increase, producers will put up their prices. But if prices go up, consumers will want to buy less. So, a rise in labour costs will increase price but reduce production and consumption. This is illustrated in Fig. 2.8. Initially price and quantity are in equilibrium at P_1 and Q_1. A rise in the cost of labour will mean that producers will try to charge a higher price for the same output. Hence, the supply curve will shift upwards to S_2. A new equilibrium price of P_2 is now set, and a new equilibrium quantity Q_2 is produced and consumed. The rise in costs has resulted in a rise in price (but notice not by as much as P_1P_3, the initial rise in costs of producing the original output Q_1), and a fall in the equilibrium quantity produced and consumed.

are engaged in buying and selling food in many places.

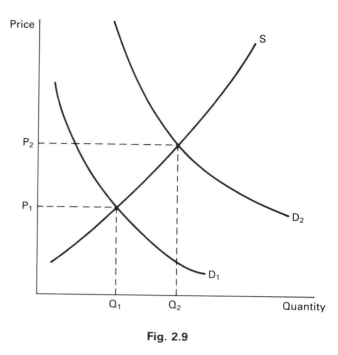

Fig. 2.9

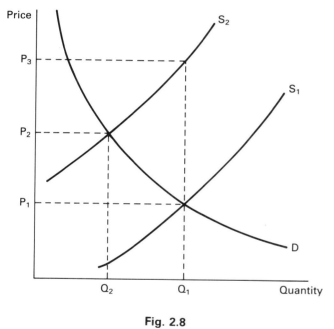

Fig. 2.8

If income rises, this will result in a shift in the demand curve for a normal good to the right—from D_1 to D_2 in the case of Fig. 2.9. As a result, the price will increase from P_1 to P_2 and the quantity supplied and consumed will increase too from Q_1 to Q_2.

The price of the product is fixed in a market. A market is any arrangement by which goods or services are exchanged for money. A market may be physically visible—such as a street market, but most markets are not 'visible' in this sense. The food market for instance is made up of millions of consumers and many producers and middlemen. They

Elasticities

Demand and supply theory is essential for any understanding of economics. Without it, economists would lose one of their most powerful tools of analysis. There is, however, one more aspect which must be considered at this stage. It has been argued that certain relationships exist between price and quantity demanded. But if price changes, by how much does quantity demanded change? It could be that a large price increase will have little effect on quantity demanded. On the other hand, a small price increase might result in massive falls in demand. Theoretically it is not possible to say exactly what will happen in cases like these. Each product and each point along its demand curve may have a different price–quantity reaction. It is a matter for economists to try to collect evidence and calculate this relationship.

However, theoretical economics does provide a useful means of studying this. **Elasticity** is a measure of the relationship between quantity demanded or supplied and another variable, such as price or income, which affects the quantity demanded or supplied. Exact formulations are as follows:

$$\text{Price elasticity} = \frac{\text{percentage change in quantity}}{\text{percentage change in price}}$$

$$= \frac{\Delta Q/Q}{\Delta P/P} = \frac{\Delta Q}{\Delta P} \times \frac{P}{Q}$$

$$\text{Income elasticity} = \frac{\text{percentage change in quantity}}{\text{percentage change in income}}$$

$$= \frac{\Delta Q/Q}{\Delta Y/Y} = \frac{\Delta Q}{\Delta Y} \times \frac{Y}{Q}$$

Cross elasticity of good X =

$$\frac{\text{percentage change in quantity of X}}{\text{percentage change in price of other goods}}$$

$$= \frac{\Delta Q/Q}{\Delta Z/Z} = \frac{\Delta Q}{\Delta Z} \times \frac{Z}{Q}$$

where Q is quantity, Y is income, Z is the price of other goods, P is price and Δ means 'change in'. Note that the percentage change in quantity always appears on the top of the formula and the related variable (price, income, etc.) always appears on the bottom. Elasticity may be demand or supply elasticity. Thus, price elasticity of demand is the percentage change in quantity demanded divided by the percentage change in price. Equally, other elasticities may be calculated depending upon what relationship the economist may be interested in. Cost elasticity of supply for instance would be the percentage change in quantity supplied divided by the percentage change in costs.

Elasticity is not an easy concept to grasp, but it is a very important one and is used again and again in every field of study in economics. The most frequently used elasticity concept is price elasticity of demand. It is nearly always negative because in general a price increase (+) leads to a quantity decrease (−), or a price decrease (−) is associated with a quantity increase (+). Putting these signs in the formula for price elasticity of demand will always lead to a minus sign mathematically. The minus sign is often omitted—mathematically inaccurate of course, but convenient for the economist. Special names are attached to various values (or ranges) of price elasticity of demand as in Table 2.1.

What value of cross elasticity of demand do you think there would be between different breeds of dog?

Table 2.1

Price elasticity of demand	Term
0	perfectly inelastic
between 0 and (−)1	inelastic
(−)1	unitary elasticity
between (−)1 and (−) infinity	elastic
(−) infinity	perfectly elastic

Thus, if a good goes up in price by 10% and this results in a drop in quantity demanded of 20% then price elasticity of demand is (−)20/10 or (−)2. Hence, demand is here said to be elastic. If on the other hand, a 10% rise in price resulted in no change in quantity demanded, price elasticity of demand is (−)0/10 or 0. Here, demand is said to be perfectly inelastic.

Looking at elasticity diagrammatically, a straight line demand curve has a different elasticity all along the line ranging from infinity at one end (point A in

Fig. 2.10), to zero at the other end (point C in Fig. 2.10), with an elasticity of (−)1 half way along the line (point B in Fig. 2.10). A perfectly inelastic demand curve is a vertical straight line (Fig. 2.11). A horizontal straight line is perfectly elastic (Fig. 2.12). A demand curve of unitary elasticity is a rectangular hyperbola (Fig. 2.13). All of this can be proved by simple manipulations of the price elasticity formula.

One application of the concept of elasticity relates to revenue. Total revenue from sales can be calculated by multiplying price and quantity sold:

$$\text{Revenue} = \text{Price} \times \text{Quantity}$$

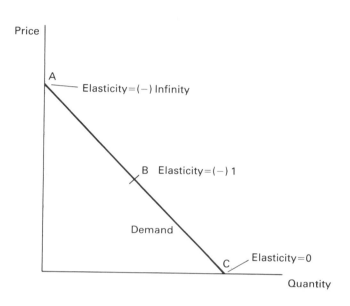

Fig. 2.10

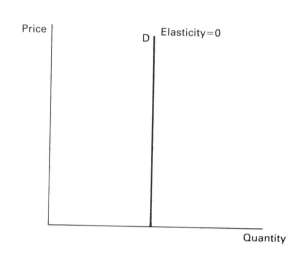

Fig. 2.11

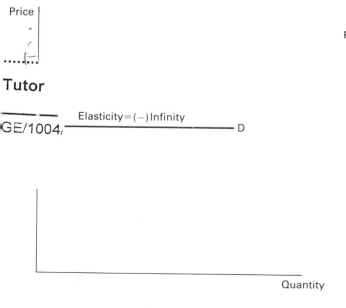

Fig. 2.12

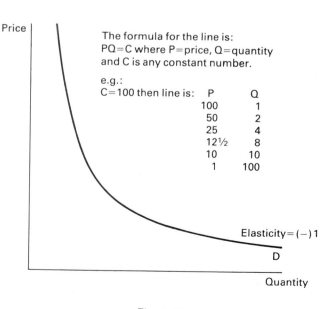

The formula for the line is:
PQ=C where P=price, Q=quantity
and C is any constant number.

e.g.:
C=100 then line is:

P	Q
100	1
50	2
25	4
12½	8
10	10
1	100

Fig. 2.13

For example, a shopkeeper sells 3 apples at 4p each: his total revenue is therefore 12p from the sale. Price and quantity appear in the formula for price elasticity. If, for instance, price goes up by 10% and quantity demanded goes down by 20% as a result, then elasticity is (−)20/10 or (−)2. It is therefore elastic. The seller meanwhile will have seen his total revenue fall. He might get an extra 10% on everything he sells, but he sells 20% fewer goods. The higher price does not compensate for the lower sales volume. If instead the 10% increase in price has resulted in a drop in quantity demanded of 10%, elasticity would be (−)10/10 or (−)1. Therefore, elasticity is unitary. Here revenue remains constant because the 10% drop in sales volume is exactly countered by the 10% increase in the price of the remaining goods sold. A 10% rise in price with a 5% drop in volume (inelastic demand of (−)5/10 or (−)$\frac{1}{2}$) would result in a rise in sales revenue. Hence if the elasticity of demand for a product is known, the effect on revenue of a fall or rise in price can be calculated. To take a more realistic example, suppose British Rail wishes to gain increased revenue from a commuter line. If the demand is inelastic, then the correct pricing policy to adopt is to raise the price and suffer some drop in demand. On the other hand, if demand is elastic, British Rail would do better to cut prices in order to gain extra revenue. A summary of the relationship between elasticity and revenue is given in Table 2.2.

Table 2.2

Price elasticity of demand	Price	Effect on revenue
inelastic	rise	rise
	fall	fall
unitary	rise	remains constant
	fall	remains constant
elastic	rise	fall
	fall	rise

Elasticity is not an intuitive concept. It is not possible to imagine a good with an elasticity of (−)2.65 as one does a 'tall' building or a 'brown' cow. When the concept is encountered, it is always best to go back to first principles—the formulae—and work out the significance of the statement from that. It is only with continual use that elasticity becomes an easy concept to use.

Data 2.3

Restaurant trade growth 'will slow this year'

By Christopher Parkes

THE fastest-growing sectors of the food industry will soon start to feel the effects of the economic squeeze, according to a study published today by Charterhouse, the merchant and investment banking arm of the Royal Bank of Scotland.

The restaurant trade can expect growth to slow this year and next, and snack makers are warned of "significant variations in demand."

However, underlying trends are strong. Rapid growth in eating out is forecast to resume between 1991 and 1993, and the perception of eating snacks as "a substitute for good solid meals for many in the low-income groups... could prevent demand from falling off too dramatically," the study says.

The study forecasts above-average annual growth of around 3 to 4 per cent for confectionery, bread and biscuits, snacks, cereals, and fruit and vegetables.

The food industry will face increasing cost pressures, the authors say, including the likely dampening of consumption when value added tax is charged on food " some time in the 1990s".

The Financial Times. 23.5.89

1 What factors, according to the article, are likely to affect the demand for snacks over time?
2 Given that real incomes increase on average at about $2\frac{1}{2}$ per cent a year, what is the likely income elasticity of demand for snacks in the 1990s?

It was pointed out earlier that every commodity has a different price elasticity of demand and that it was not possible to predict from economic theory the exact value of elasticity for the product. However, economic theory does suggest that there are two main factors which tend to make a product relatively price elastic.

1 The availability of substitutes A substitute product is one which buyers can replace for the existing product. For instance, a Ford car is a good substitute for a Vauxhall car. On the other hand, a Ford car is not a good substitute for a holiday. If the price of a product which has good substitutes increases, consumers can easily switch to the substitute product. So a small rise in price can result in a large fall in quantity demanded.

2 Time If the price of a product goes up, the immediate reaction by consumers may be to buy the same quantity as before. Spending decisions often take time to change. It may take time for consumers to find substitute products. It may take time for substitute products to be produced by manufacturers. So the price elasticity of demand in the short term is likely to be lower than in the long term.

Summary

In this chapter we have seen that price is determined by demand and supply in the market. The level of demand is determined by the price of the product, the income of buyers, the price of other goods, and by a number of other factors which are combined together and called 'tastes'. The level of supply is determined by the price of the product, its costs of manufacture, and the price of other goods and services, i.e. the state of technology and other factors. Elasticity is the way in which we measure the responsiveness of quantity demanded or supplied to changes in variables affecting that quantity. For instance, price elasticity of demand measures the responsiveness of changes in quantity demanded to changes in price. Lastly, we saw that revenue and elasticity were connected.

Terms for review

price

effective demand

inferior goods

shift in demand or supply curve

tastes

supply

state of technology

price elasticity of demand

income elasticity of demand

cross elasticity of demand

price elasticity of supply

elastic, inelastic and unit elasticity

revenue

Essay questions

1 What is meant by 'effective demand' for a good? What factors would affect the demand for a company's range of home computers?

2 Distinguish between price elasticity of demand and cross elasticity of demand. Would you expect the price elasticities of demand for potatoes and smoked salmon to differ from the cross elasticities for each other?

3 How would you explain the different prices of a gallon of petrol and a gallon of champagne?

3

The money supply and the rate of interest

Money has been a magic word for economists down the centuries. Three important questions about it need to be answered: Why do we have money? What is money? What effect does it have on the economy?

What is money and why is it necessary?

These two questions are interrelated, because we cannot decide what money is without defining it in terms of its functions. Four functions of money have been put forward by economists.

Money is a medium of exchange Before money existed, man traded by bartering. However, arranging a swap can often prove very difficult. Imagine one farmer who wants ten chickens. He is willing to give one cow in return. Another farmer might have ten chickens to sell, but he does not want a cow. He wants a horse. The two will not exchange unless there is some prospect that someone who has horses will accept cows, or unless there is someone who will accept cows in return for a commodity that the horse owner wants, and so on. Paying teachers with the products that their pupils' parents make would be a frustrating experience for all concerned! Money makes exchange a great deal easier. A consumer with money can go and buy a wide range of different articles whatever the work he or she does in order to get that money. Certain features of money help it to serve as a good medium of exchange. Money should not be too heavy or too bulky. If it were, it would be inconvenient to carry around. It should not perish or deteriorate easily. It should not be easy to forge or obtain for less than the supposed value of the money. These are desirable characteristics of money, but they are not essential. In the past, sea shells, cows, and wives have all been used as money!

Money is a measure of value All goods and services can be priced in terms of money. By comparing the price of two goods with money, one can compare their respective values. If a shirt is priced at £5 and a pair of jeans at £10, then one pair of jeans is worth two shirts. An example of money which is used as a measure of value rather than as a medium of exchange is the European Unit of Account (EUA)—a form of money used by the European Community (EC) in its spending policies, but which has to be converted into the currencies of individual member countries when money is actually spent.

Money is a store of value People are unlikely to accept money in payment for their services if they think that they will be unable to exchange that money for goods and services. For instance, this might happen if money devalues (i.e. loses its value) considerably between the time of receipt and the time it is used for purchasing items. In the German hyper-inflation of 1923, workers refused money for payment because they knew that within hours it would lose most of its value. Money **can** lose value over a period of time and still remain money. But when the loss from holding money starts to exceed the usefulness it gives in acting as a medium of exchange, then that money will cease to be accepted.

Money is a standard for deferred payments Many purchases are made on credit—that is, payment is made at some future date for goods and services obtained now. Money must be able to bridge that time period. If the value of money is constantly changing, it starts to lose its role as money. In the money markets around the world, big lenders often try to stabilise monetary values by lending in terms of a currency which does not lose value, or indeed in terms of an average of several currencies where losses made by one currency are likely to be cancelled out by gains made by another. In this way, big

Data 3.1

Land where looting is a form of survival

Gary Mead

For Argentines, hyper-inflation running at over 1000% per annum strikes with different weight, but it hits most of them.

"Three weeks ago my baby was going to have disposable nappies. After the birth I was going to have six months at home and a domestic, to help with the housework and shopping. All that's changed. Now there won't be a maid, the nappies won't be disposable and I will have to go back to work after one month. And my baby is going to be privileged – at least I can still afford nappies."

Claudia and her husband, both in their thirties, are part of Argentina's sinking middle class. They would not dream of ransacking supermarkets, as did many of their fellow Argentines last week in desperation at the growing gulf between the money they earned and what that money would buy. She runs her own business and her husband – a qualified physician – is training to be a psychiatrist. She is the breadwinner. His salary is in australs, Argentina's terminally sick currency. She gets paid in US dollars.

Private tutors, lawyers, opinion pollsters, builders, furniture makers – everyone who can, demands dollars as payment. Argentina is now a dollarized economy.

Hyper-inflation of more than 70 per cent has widely disparate effects on Argentina's citizens. The upper class (which has always thought in terms of dollars anyway) has helped to spirit over $200 million a week out of the country in flight capital. Middle-class people such as Claudia face being forced down into poverty. Below them the already poor who took to looting last week are finding it impossible.

Simply trying to sort out the relative price distortions brought about by hyper-inflation calls for great mental dexterity. When a one-week course of anti-biotics (2,000 australs) costs half as much as a month's rent on a small Buenos Aires apartment (4,000 australs), which also translates into the price of five jars of instant coffee, the market – and the austral – have become meaningless.

The Financial Times. 3.6.89

1 To what extent is the Argentinian austral a perfect form of money?

2 What problems are caused by hyper-inflation?

lenders hope to get back the real value of what they lent out. This would be in addition to any interest received.

Any money must combine all these functions to some degree. In the past, a whole host of items has been used as money. The idea of paper money is a relatively recent invention, and it is only money because the community is prepared to accept it as money. If large sections of that community started to refuse it, it would cease to be a medium of exchange, a store of value, etc. In a modern economy, however, notes and coins form only a very small part of the total amount of money in circulation. The total amount of money in the economy is called **the money supply.**

The greater part of the money supply is in the form of money deposited in various financial institutions. There are two types of deposit. In the case of **sight** deposits, the money lent is available on de-

mand (i.e. immediately). In the case of **time** deposits, the money is only available at some future time, e.g. 7 days or 3 months. Sight deposits held with banks or building societies pay little or no interest. However, depositors are normally given cheque books. Cheques are not quite as widely accepted as notes and coins, but in the vast majority of transactions a cheque will be acceptable. Hence, the money which lies behind the cheque—that is, the amount of money in a sight deposit account (often known as a current account)—can be counted as part of the money supply. After all, the money possesses the other three characteristics of money. One definition of the money supply is notes and coins in circulation together with the value of sight deposits held by the private sector (i.e. not including the public or government sector). This is officially known as sterling M_1 in the UK.

There are, however, numerous other items which possess some, but not all, of the functions of money.

Consider money placed in time (or deposit) accounts at banks. Notice of anything from one week to six months must be given in order to withdraw money from a deposit account. In practice, often some fixed amount is allowed on demand. Furthermore, banks are often prepared to waive their rules if the cash is available at the bank on that day, or if the customer is prepared to accept a cheque. However, no cheque book is given on time accounts. The customer must go in person to the bank to obtain the money. Here, the money is certainly a measure and store of value and a standard for deferred payments, but is it a medium of exchange? It is money because money in the account can be obtained at fairly short notice, and the cash obtained can be spent. At what point the money in time accounts ceases to be money is debatable. If ten years' notice of withdrawal had to be given, economists would say definitely that it was not money. But if only 7 days' notice need be given, many economists would want to include deposit accounts in the money supply. There are many other financial institutions offering time deposit facilities, such as building societies and the Government. It is sometimes argued that these too should be included as part of the money supply. Going further afield, companies issue stocks and shares, whilst governments issue stocks. These vary in value according to a number of factors, but they can be sold at fairly short notice through stock exchanges. They are not pure money, but possess some of the characteristics of money.

Assets can be viewed as a spectrum, as in Fig. 3.1, ranging from items such as notes and coins which possess the properties of money almost perfectly, through to items which possess only some of the characteristics of money, and poorly at that. At some point along the spectrum, a cut-off point needs to be made. The assets just to the right and left of that cut-off point will be similar and some will strongly argue that if one asset is to be included then that another very similar asset should be included too. However, this argument applies all along the spectrum, and an arbitrary decision has to be made on other grounds.

In the UK, the Bank of England now calculates a number of measures of the money supply, 6 of which are defined in the panel below. The **narrow** measures of the money supply, M_0, M_1 and M_2, show the money supply which is used primarily for transaction purposes (i.e. as a medium of exchange). **Broad money**, M_3, M_4 and M_5, is narrow money plus money which is sometimes used for transaction purposes but is mainly used as short term fairly liquid savings (i.e. as a store of wealth).

Money supply

Narrow money

M_0 (monetary base): consists mainly of notes and coin.

M_1: is M_0 plus private sector sterling sight bank deposits.

M_2: is M_0 plus retail deposits (money in accounts with less than £100 000 deposited and where savers have to give notice of withdrawal of one month or less) at banks, building societies or the National Savings Bank Ordinary Account.

Broad money

M_3: is M_1 plus interest bearing time deposit accounts at banks.

M_4: is M_3 plus money in building society share and deposit accounts.

M_5: is M_4 plus private sector holdings of money market assets (e.g. Treasury Bills, certificates of tax deposits and national savings such as Premium Bonds).

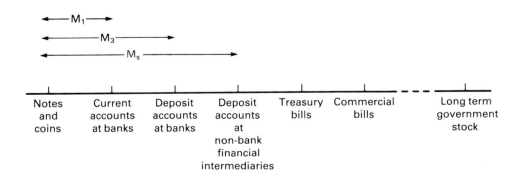

Fig. 3.1 Money as a part of a spectrum of assets

Data 3.2

Change in money stock (M_0)

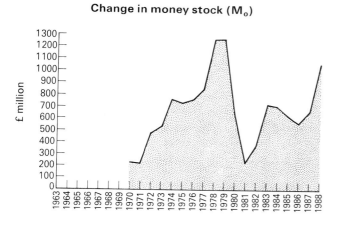

Change in money stock (M_1)

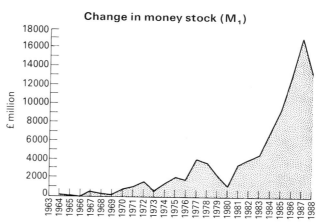

Change in money stock (M_3)

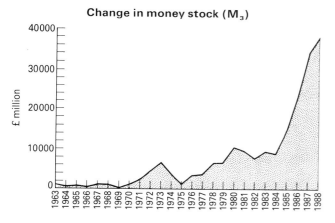

Change in money stock (M_4)

Change in money stock (M_5)

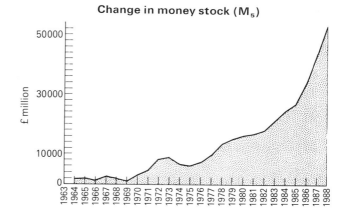

1 Describe the main changes in the growth in the money supply shown in the data.

2 To what extent would you expect the rates of growth of the different measures of the money supply to be the same over time? Illustrate your answer from the data.

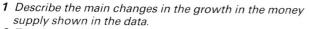

Source: CSO, Economic Trends, Annual Abstract of Statistics

Defining what is and what is not money is not only important for the sake of the study of money. The money supply and its growth has today become of vital interest to all economists studying major problems facing the economy, such as inflation and unemployment. Hence, measuring its growth from an agreed definition becomes a vital task for those, particularly in Government, who are trying to foresee what path the economy is taking and what corrective measures are needed.

The banking system and the creation of money

The banking system has the power to create money. Its power to do this is rooted in the fact that all bank depositors are unlikely to want to withdraw all their money at the same time.

Consider an economy with only one bank operating. Customers have deposited £100 million in the bank and it is going to make a profit by lending out that money to its customers. Not all of the £100 million will be lent out. From experience, the bank knows that its depositors will from time to time withdraw some of the deposits and expect cash. Over long years the bank in our economy has come to know just what proportion it needs to cope with even quite exceptional withdrawals. Let us assume that it needs to keep £1 in cash for every £10 of deposits. Hence, it can lend out £90 million of the £100 million originally deposited, keeping £10 million in cash. That £90 million in cash is unlikely to remain for long in the real economy. It will turn up as new deposits in the banking system, placed by customers who have received the money from the original borrowers. Hence the bank can now lend out another 90% of £90 million, keeping £9 million in cash to cover possible cash withdrawals. That £81 million lent out will also reappear as new deposits in the banking system. Ninety per cent of that will be lent out, and this process carries on until the sums are too small to be worth mentioning. If all of the money deposited is added up (£100 million + £90 million + £81 million + ...) it will come to £1 000 million. The bank will have all of the original £100 million of cash (£10 million + £9 million + £8.1 million + ...), but that will be supporting another £900 million of book entry money. It will owe £1 000 million to its customers who have deposited money.

To balance that, it will have £100 million in cash and £900 million owing to it in the form of loans.

The creation of money by banks is always considered quite extraordinary to those meeting it for the first time. This is partly because they wrongly assume that anybody who can create money will become rich very quickly. The banks' creation of money is not at all like that. The money they create does not belong to them, although they do get extra customers as a result. The money belongs to the customers of the banks.

Two features of our simple example need to be altered to make the **model** (a model is an explanation of reality) more realistic. Firstly, most economies have a multibank system. Imagine a three-bank system, with the three banks being A, B and C. Each bank must balance its books at the end of each day—that is, the amount a bank owes to its customers (its **liabilities**) must be covered by the amount of money that the bank has in its possession or is owed by other bank customers (its **assets**). Assume that the three banks only hold cash or loan out money to customers. Each bank has an equal share of the market. Each bank also needs to keep 10% of its assets in the form of cash, with total assets and liabilities for each bank being £100 million. The balance sheet for each bank will then look like this:

	Assets £m		Liabilities £m
Cash	10		
Loans	90	Deposits	100
Total	100		100

Now assume that an extra £10 million cash is suddenly deposited in the banking system, and that Bank A is twice as successful at attracting new deposits as Banks B and C. Initially the new balance sheets will look like this:

Bank A
£m

Cash	15		
Loans	90	Deposits	105
Total	105	Total	105

Bank B or Bank C
£m

Cash	12.5		
Loans	90	Deposits	102.5
Total	102.5	Total	102.5

Notice that cash held by the banks rises from £30 million to £40 million, but their liabilities have also gone up by £10 million. The banks are now able to expand their loans. Bank A, for instance, with deposits of £105 million needs only to keep £10.5 million in cash to meet the 10% cash ratio. It has £15 million in cash. Hence, it will lend out £4.5 million, which will reappear within the banking system as new deposits, placed there by customers who have received the money from the original borrowers. The banks will then need to keep 10% of that £4.5 million in the form of cash to satisfy the 10% cash ratio. The rest, £4.05 million, can be lent out. That too will reappear as new deposits within the banking system, and so on. The final balance sheet will look like this:

Bank A
£m

Cash	15		
Loans	135	Deposits	150
Total	150		150

Bank B or Bank C
£m

Cash	12.5		
Loans	112.5	Deposits	125
	125		125

It was assumed that Bank A had captured £5 million of the initial cash deposit whereas Bank B and Bank C had only captured £2.5 million each. Assuming that Bank A continues to be twice as successful at attracting new deposits as Bank B and Bank C, then Bank A will have been able to increase its total deposits and liabilities by £50 million to a new total of £150 million. At this point, Bank A is just maintaining its 10% cash ratio—£15 million of cash supporting £150 million of assets. Loans of £135 million make up the difference between its cash assets and its total assets. Banks B and C, however, did less well, managing only to build up their assets to £125 million. The total new assets and liabilities created out of the £10 million cash with a 10% cash reserve requirement was £100 million. Bank A will have gained a greater share of the market due to a variety of factors such as more aggressive advertising, management skill in recognising the new market, more branch offices, etc.

The second feature of our model which needs altering is the assumption that banks need to keep 10% of their assets in the form of cash.

The money multiplier

It was argued in the above example that an increase in cash of £10 million with a cash reserve ratio of 10% would finally raise the assets and liabilities of the banking system by £100 million. The proof of this is mathematical. Each time the money is deposited in the banking system, the banks keep 10% and lend the rest. Therefore if £X are initially deposited, the final increase in deposits will be:

$$(X) + (0.9X) + (0.9 \times 0.9X) + (0.9 \times 0.9 \times 0.9X) + \ldots$$

Students of mathematics will recognise this as a geometric progression whose final sum works out as $10X$.

There is a simple formula for calculating the amount of money created by banks from new deposits. It is called the **money multiplier** (sometimes also called the **bank or credit multiplier**). In our simple example, banks had to keep 10% of their total assets in the form of cash. Cash then becomes a **reserve asset** or **high powered money**—an asset which the banks have to keep to be able to create credit. 10% then becomes the **reserve ratio** or **reserve asset ratio** (R)—the proportion of reserve assets which a bank has to keep in relation to its total assets. The money multiplier is given by the following formula:

$$\text{Money Multiplier} = \frac{1}{R}$$

The money multiplier is a simple concept in principle. For instance, if the reserve ratio is 10% the money multiplier is 1/0.1 or 10. If the banks can obtain £10 million of extra reserve assets, then eventually £100 million of new assets and liabilities can be created. Taking another example, if the banks have to keep a

Data 3.3

Bank lending rises more quickly than expected

By Peter Norman

BRITISH BANK and building society lending grew more strongly than expected last month while M0, the narrow measure of money supply targeted by the Treasury, expanded faster than its 1 to 5 per cent annual target range.

The Bank of England reported a £6.7bn seasonally adjusted increase in bank and building society lending in May compared with growth of £7bn in April and an average monthly increase of £6.9bn over the past six months.

The figure is higher than the £5.8bn to £6bn consensus forecast of City analysts. However, information released yesterday by the Committee of London and Scottish Bankers suggests that personal-sector borrowing from banks was subdued, with corporate borrowing accounting for the bulk of the bank lending in May.

According to Mr Nigel Richardson, an economist with Warburg Securities, the figures are consistent with the building societies' regaining market share in a depressed home loans market and industry's continuing to borrow to finance capital investment and the purchase of raw materials from abroad. Mr Robinson said: "The company side of the economy is not yet feeling the pinch" of high short-term interest rates.

The Bank announced that M0, which consists almost entirely of notes and coins in circulation, increased by an unadjusted 1.6 per cent in May and by 6.5 per cent in the year to May.

However, broader measures of money supply also continued to show strong growth, with M4, which includes bank and building society deposits, growing a seasonally adjusted 0.9 per cent last month. M4 grew a seasonally adjusted 18.6 per cent in the year to May after 18.1 per cent in the 12 months to April.

The Financial Times. 21.6.89

---

1 By how much did the money supply increase in May 1989 according to the article?

2 How would economic theory explain the link between the growth in credit and the increase in the money supply?

---

reserve ratio of 2% then the money multiplier is 1/.02 or 50. If a bank can obtain an extra £1 million of reserve assets it will be able to increase its deposits by £50 million. Some further examples are given in Table 3.1.

In the UK today, cash is the only asset which acts as a reserve asset. Banks have to keep $\frac{1}{2}$% of their total assets in cash at the Bank of England. They also keep some cash to satisfy the withdrawal needs of their account customers—typically about 4% for high street banks. The supply of cash is measured by M_0. This is called the **monetary base** of the economy (or high powered money) because all types of bank money are built upon the foundation of cash in the system. This leads us to the very important conclusion that

Table 3.1

Reserve ratio (R) %	Bank multiplier (1/R)	Increase in bank holdings of high powered money ($\triangle H$) £m	Final increase in bank deposits (1/R × $\triangle H$) £m
20	5	50	250
25	4	25	100
5	20	20	400
1	100	10	1 000
33	3	40	120

increases in the monetary base, i.e. increases in the cash issued by the Bank of England, is necessary for any increase in the money supply. Any increase in cash will lead to a multiple increase in the total money supply in the economy.

So far it has been assumed that any increase in the monetary base of the economy ends up in bank vaults supporting bank money such as money in current accounts. However, this is obviously untrue. Some of the cash will be kept by households and firms who demand money to keep for spending or even for saving. Not everyone has a bank account; many people literally keep their savings under the bed or in tins; and people in the black economy wanting to avoid tax, estimated at 7% of the total value of spending in the UK, will only use cash to avoid detection. In the simple example above, it was assumed that all the money lent out by a bank was redeposited with it. In practice in the UK today, only about 60% of the money comes back in new deposits. The general public keep about 40% of the money in cash. That means that banks create less money from new deposits than the simple example implies. In general, the higher the proportion of cash kept by the general public and not deposited with banks, the lower will be the money multiplier.

The quantity theory of money

Economists differ in their assessment of the importance of the money supply. Central to this debate is the quantity theory of money. The quantity theory of money has several different formulations. Only one, the 'Fisher' formulation after the economist who derived it, will be considered here. The Fisher formula is:

$$M V \equiv P T$$

where M is the money supply, V is the velocity of circulation, P is the average price of each transaction and T is the number of transactions. The '$\equiv$' sign denotes that the expression is an identity, i.e. it is true simply by definition.

The velocity of circulation of money is the average number of times money circulates round the economy. For instance, if the only money in the economy is two £5 notes and if £30 worth of goods and services were bought, then on average that £10 must have flowed three times round the economy. A transaction occurs each time money changes hands. For instance, there might have been 4 transactions involving the £30 spent on goods and services: two at

£5 and two at £10. The average price per transaction therefore must have been:

$$\left(\frac{(2 \times £5) + (2 \times £10)}{4}\right) \text{ i.e. £7.50.}$$

Logically, it must be true that the amount of money in circulation in the economy (£10) multiplied by the average number of times that money circulates round the economy (3) is equal to the average price per transaction (£7.50) multiplied by the total number of transactions (4).

The quantity theory of money only becomes of serious economic interest when assumptions are made about the relationship between the variables

What implications does this have for economists who argue that increases in the money supply cause inflation?

in the identity and their likely value. For instance if V and T are constant then changes in M must be linked to changes in P. Changes in P, i.e. changes in average prices, can either be inflationary or disinflationary. Increases in M could increase inflation. On the other hand, the causality may be the reverse: increases in inflation could cause increases in the money supply. Equally, if we assume V and P to be constant, then changes in M will be associated with changes in T. The number of transactions in an economy is closely linked to the value of total income in the economy. Assuming constant prices, the more income there is, the more goods and services will be bought and therefore the more transactions will take place. So, either a change in the money supply might cause changes in income, or the causality might flow from increases in income to increases in the money supply.

The rate of interest

Economic theory often deals with the rate of interest as if there were only one rate of interest in a country. Quite the opposite is true. There are many different interest rates. Nor do they all move together, in terms either of time or direction.

Some interest rates might go up when others are coming down. Interest rates represent the price of money—the amount that has to be paid in order that a borrower may obtain the use of that money over a certain time-period. Money markets are markets where money is bought and sold. There is not just one money market but many, each serving the needs of a particular group of borrowers and lenders. The building societies, for instance, serve the needs of small private savers and private borrowers who wish to purchase property. The interbank market in London serves the needs of banks in London who wish to borrow and lend for very short periods of time.

Price is determined by demand and supply. Hence, the individual demand and supply conditions in each market will determine the rate of interest in that market. Banks, for instance, cannot open an account at a building society and lend it £1 million for two days. A private borrower wishing to buy a house is unable to use the interbank market in London to borrow money for two days to finance his purchase. Hence, there is a limit to the amount of money which can be transferred from market to market, to bring all interest rates into line. Building

societies may be finding it difficult to attract savings to finance potential loans and so they may raise interest rates. At the same time, there may be falling interest rates in the interbank market as banks have larger than normal sums to lend out.

On the whole, however, over a period of time interest rates will tend to move together in a recognisable pattern. Three important factors explain much of the difference in interest rates in the long term:

1 Risk The riskier the loan, the higher will be the rate of interest prevailing in the market. For instance, hire purchase carries a much higher rate of interest than a normal bank loan. This is largely due to the fact that consumers using hire purchase tend to default on their debts to a greater extent that consumers taking out bank loans.

2 Time The shorter the time period on the investment, the lower will be the rate of interest. Short term investments are in fact far less risky. A lender can obtain the full value of his money quickly to reinvest at the best available interest rates. On a long term investment he may be unable to realise his money for a long period of time. This reduces his freedom of choice. He might suddenly find that he needs the cash. Or interest rates might rise, and he is unable to move his cash to an asset earning the higher rate of interest. Even if he can get his money back quickly by selling his long term asset to someone else, he may discover that he has suffered a capital loss. The easier it is to turn a financial asset into money, the more **liquid** it is said to be. In our economy cash is perfectly liquid because it is money. An assurance policy however, is highly illiquid because it is nearly impossible to turn it into money at its full value in a short period of time.

3 Administrative cost If the cost of administration (e.g. bank employees, paper, computer time, offices) is high in comparison with the amount borrowed, the rate of interest charged will tend to be high too. All other things being equal, it is proportionally cheaper to borrow £1 million than to borrow £100. The big clearing banks in the UK, for instance, borrow money at 0% interest rate through current accounts. But the administrative cost of the system is so high that it is not a cheap form of borrowing for the banks.

One key interest rate in the money market is the rate at which the central bank is willing to act as lender of last resort. Virtually every industrialised country today has some mechanism whereby the banking system can obtain money from the central bank to tide it over a crisis when it does not have enough money to pay for all its short term obliga-

tions. Without this safety-valve, banks would have to declare themselves bankrupt when they could not pay out in the short term, even though they were basically financially sound in the long term. Recurrent bank failures would harm individuals, industry and the economy.

Data 3.4

Building Societies interest rate on ordinary shares: last Friday of the year

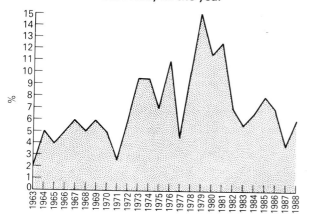

London clearing banks deposit account (7 days' notice) rate of interest: last Friday of the year

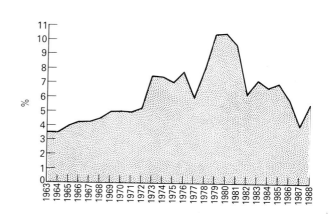

British government securities long dated (20 years): Percentage yield average of working days

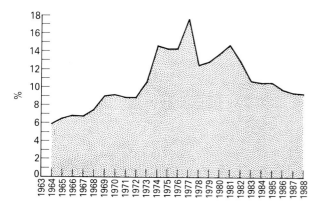

Treasury bill yield: Last Friday of the year

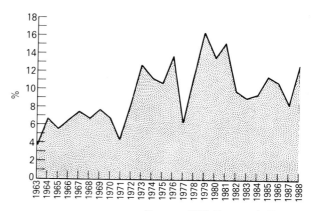

Source: CSO, Economic Trends

1 Describe the major changes in interest rates shown in the data.

2 Why does economic theory suggest that interest rates are likely to move broadly in line with each other? Does the evidence support this?

Data 3.5

LONDON MONEY RATES

April 11	Overnight	7 days notice	One Month	Three Months	Six Months	One Year
Interbank Offer	12	$11\frac{1}{2}$	$12\frac{5}{8}$	$13\frac{1}{4}$	$13\frac{5}{16}$	$13\frac{1}{4}$
Sterling Certificates of Deposits	—	—	$12\frac{5}{8}$	$13\frac{1}{8}$	$13\frac{1}{8}$	$13\frac{1}{16}$
Local Authority Deposits	10	$11\frac{1}{8}$	$12\frac{1}{2}$	$13\frac{1}{16}$	$13\frac{1}{8}$	$12\frac{7}{8}$
Local Authority Bonds	—	—	—	—	—	—
Discount Market Deposits	12	$11\frac{1}{4}$	$12\frac{3}{8}$	$12\frac{3}{4}$	—	—
Company Deposits	—	—	$12\frac{9}{16}$	$13\frac{1}{4}$	$13\frac{1}{4}$	$13\frac{1}{8}$
Finance House Deposits	—	—	$12\frac{1}{2}$	$13\frac{3}{16}$	$13\frac{3}{16}$	$13\frac{1}{8}$
Treasury Bills (Buy)	—	—	$12\frac{7}{16}$	$12\frac{25}{32}$	—	—
Bank Bills (Buy)	—	—	$12\frac{15}{32}$	$12\frac{13}{16}$	$12\frac{1}{2}$	—
Fine Trade Bills (Buy)	—	—	$13\frac{3}{32}$	$13\frac{7}{16}$	$13\frac{1}{8}$	—

The Financial Times. 12.4.89

1 Account for the differences in interest rates shown in the data.

Bonds, bills and the rate of interest

A **bond** is a type of financial asset in the form of a loan. The borrower, in return for the loan of the money, promises to pay interest. There is usually a time limit on the loan, at the end of which the borrower will repay the money. The rate of interest may be fixed (e.g. 10% a year), or it may vary (e.g. increasing with the length of time the bond is held, or linked with the rate of inflation or linked with the movements in other interest rates). The time limit, or date of **maturity**, may also vary considerably from just a few years to 20 years or more. One very important feature of a bond is that it may be bought and sold during its 'lifetime'. The new owner will receive interest payment due following the purchase and be able to receive the sum of money originally lent out when the bond finally matures. However, the price at which the bond changes hands before maturity may well differ from the value of the money originally lent (the sum of money to be paid back at the end of the loan is called the **nominal value** of the bond).

Take an example of a bond whose nominal value is £100. It carries a yearly rate of interest at $2\frac{1}{2}$%; that is, the borrower has promised to pay £2.50 interest a year to the holder of the bond. Assume furthermore that the bond is irredeemable—that is, the borrower has not set a time limit for maturity on the bond. The borrower need never pay the money back, although he would need to go on paying £2.50 interest a year forever in this case. Interest rates now rise to 10% a year. Somebody investing £25 would now be able to earn £2.50 interest a year. Hence, he would only be prepared to pay £25 for a bond which gave interest of £2.50. The holder of such a bond would not be able to sell his bond at the nominal price of £100 but only for £25. In other words, if the bond was originally bought for £100 then the seller has made a capital loss on his bond of £75. Generalising from this example, it is true to say that a rise in the rate of interest will cause bond prices to fall. Bond holders will suffer capital losses. A fall in the rate of interest will cause bond prices to rise. This is equally true of bonds which are paid back or **redeemed** after a certain period of time. The bond can be seen as giving a number of interest payments over its lifetime, with one final large payment at the end (the nominal value of the bond). Interest rate rises will depress the prices of bonds because a similar investment of the nominal value of the bond will yield a higher interest rate.

There are a number of different types of bond which are worth specifically mentioning in the UK context. All carry a fixed rate of interest and mature after a fixed period of time unless otherwise stated.

1 Long term Government stocks They mature between 5 and 20 years after purchase. They can be bought new either from the Government broker on the Stock Exchange, or through a direct bid, or from various financial institutions such as the Post Office. They can be bought and sold second-hand on the Stock Exchange. These bonds are often called **gilts**.

2 Irredeemable Government stock—a type of gilts often known as **Consols** or **War Loan**. Issued by the Government mainly during the first and second world wars, they are unlikely ever to be repaid. They pay a fixed rate of interest and can be bought and sold second-hand on the Stock Exchange.

What is this certificate? What is its nominal value? What rate of interest does it carry?

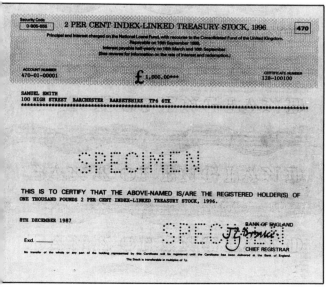

The design of the stock certificate is the copyright of the Bank of England and is reproduced here at less than its actual size with the permission of the Bank of England.

3 Company stocks or debentures These are bonds issued by companies to raise funds for investment. They can be bought and sold second-hand on the Stock Exchange.

4 Local Authority stocks Local Authorities issue bonds to finance capital expenditure, e.g. the building of schools and offices.

5 Certificates of deposit (CDs) They are issued by banks to finance loans.

6 Eurobonds Eurobonds are issued by companies or Governments. They are loans made in a foreign currency either to the borrower or to the lender or both. They carry a variety of different rates of interest, some fixed, some variable.

Bills of exchange differ from bonds. A bill is a piece of paper representing a promise to pay the owner (or the bearer) a sum of money at a specified time in the future (say in three months' time). Pound notes used to be a specific type of bill where the bearer could obtain his 'money' at any time from the bank issuing the note. In other words, the specified date was immediately. His 'money' was gold. However, if the bill was due to mature in the future, there was still a way in which the bearer could get his money straight away—he could sell his bill to someone else. The buyer would see the bill as a form of saving. He would want interest on his money. So he would buy the bill, but for less than the amount he would collect at maturity. The difference between what he paid and what he received at maturity represented his interest payment. For example, if a £110 bill were to mature in a year's time, and current rates of interest for similar investments were 10%, then he would only be willing to pay £100 for it today. If the three-monthly rate of interest is 5%, a £105 bill maturing in three months' time is worth £100 today. There are two main types of bill in the UK context.

1 Commercial bills These are issued by private companies. They were initially used to finance trade between countries and regions. A company would send goods off to another country in return for a commercial bill to pay at some fixed date in the future. The selling company could then obtain its money immediately by selling the commercial bill in the City of London—less the discount (i.e. the interest payment) of course.

EXCHANGE FOR £10,750.00   15th February   19

At 91 days date   *pay this* first   *Bill of Exchange*
        second unpaid   *to the Order of*

ourselves

the sum of ten thousand seven hundred and fifty pounds only

Value received   *which place to Account*

To Pierre Brun & Cie   Beaumonts Ltd.
                                A. Fortesque
    Paris   Director

SPECIMEN

What is this certificate? What is its face value? If the rate of interest were 10% how much would it be worth 91 days before maturity?

2 Treasury bills Issued by central government, they are a form of borrowing money on a short term basis. They are issued for 91 days and are sold at a weekly auction or tender. Buyers pay less for them to the Government than they get back in 91 days' time. The less paid for the bill, the higher the current rate of interest on short term assets.

Real and money variables

It was stated earlier that money was a measure of value. This function is impaired if inflation occurs. A dress costing £20 in 1950 would bear no comparison to a dress costing £20 in 1990, because of the vast increase in prices over the period. In order to overcome this problem, economists distinguish between 'real' and 'money' values. The real value of a sum of money is the goods and services that it can purchase. So, the real value of £100 might be a portable television set, or 10 economics textbooks or 150 pints of beer. The money value of money is its face value, for example £100, $200, 2 000 French francs. Over time, money values are unlikely to change. £100

today is the same as £100 ten years ago. But the real value of money declines if there is inflation.

Often the economist is only interested in comparing real values over time. Therefore, he wishes to remove the inflation element from money figures. One way to do this is to express all years figures at **constant prices**. This means that one year is taken as a **base** year and money figures for all other years are adjusted to the price level of the base year.

Consider Table 3.2, giving figures for average yearly wages in an economy. If year 1 is taken as the base year, the wages figure of £12 000 at current (year 2) prices is converted to £10 435 at constant (year 1) prices, given a 15% inflation rate. If year 2 is taken as the base year, the wages figure of £10 000 at current (year 1) prices is converted to £11 500 at constant (year 2) prices, given a 15% inflation rate. The real increase in wages was £435 at year 1 prices, or £500 at year 2 prices. The figure for year 2, is higher than that for year 1 because prices were higher in year 2.

A second way of expressing real values is by **index numbers**. With an index number, the base period value is given the number 100. All years are then converted to comparable index numbers. In

26

Data 3.6

Nominal[1] and real[2] interest rates in the UK: 1963–1988

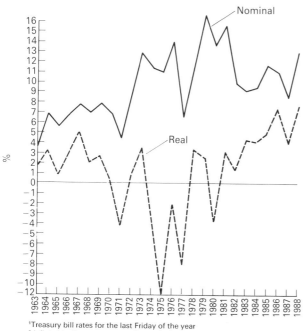

[1]Treasury bill rates for the last Friday of the year
[2]deflated by the year on year change in the Retail Price Index

Source: CSO, Economic Trends

1 *Distinguish between nominal and real interest rates.*

2 *During what period(s) did nominal and real interest rates move in opposite directions? Explain why this might have taken place.*

Table 3.2, if year 1 were the base year, £10 000 would be called '100'. Year 2's real average wage, or the average wage at constant prices would then be 104.35. Year 2's money average wage, or the average wage at current prices would be 120. If year 2 were the base year, £12 000 would be called '100'. Year 1's real average wage or average wage at constant prices would be 95.83. Year 1's average wage at current prices would be 83.33.

Table 3.2

Year	Average yearly wages at current prices	Inflation %	Average yearly wages at constant (Year 1) prices	Average yearly wages at constant (Year 2) prices
1	£10 000	15	£10 000	£11 500
2	£12 000		£10 435	£12 000

Summary

In this chapter we have seen that money has four essential functions—it must be a medium of exchange, a store of value, a measure of value and a standard of deferred payments. In practice, defining the money supply is very difficult because some assets only partially fulfil these functions. Hence a number of different measures of the money supply are computed. In the UK, two such measures are M_1 and M_3. The banking system has the power to create money. The limit on the creation of money is placed by the reserve ratio. To calculate the amount of money created by banks it is useful to use the money multiplier, which is the inverse of the reserve ratio One way of controlling the money supply is for the central bank to control the stock of high-powered money in the economy. The quantity theory of money $MV \equiv PT$ has been outlined and its possible economic significance discussed. The rate of interest has been discussed and it has been argued that in practice there are a large number of different interest rates in the economy, but they tend to move upwards and downwards together in the long term. Bonds and bills were explained. In particular it was seen that the price of bonds and bills varies inversely with the rate of interest. Real and money values were distinguished.

Terms for review

money

the money supply

$M_0, M_1, M_2, M_3, M_4, M_5$.

money multiplier

liquidity

the rate of interest

bonds

bills

the quantity theory of money

index numbers

real and money variables

Essay questions

1 What are the functions of money? To what extent does gold possess these functions in a developed economy such as the UK?

2 What is meant by the 'money supply' in the UK? How can the banking system increase the total money stock in the economy?

3 How is the price of a bill of exchange determined? Why is the rate of interest on bills likely to differ from the rates of interest on other types of assets?

4 The demand for money

When we talk about the demand for money, an immediate question comes to mind: surely everyone wants money? Therefore the demand for money could be assumed to be infinite. However, this is not true. Each economic unit has a limited number of assets. It might, for instance, have £60 000 worth of assets including a house, a car, furniture, stocks and shares and cash. The more non-monetary assets the unit holds, the less money it can own. Holding money has **opportunity costs**. Opportunity cost is defined as what has to be given up in order to gain something else. The opportunity cost of a new pair of jeans might be 3 records. The opportunity cost of a holiday in France might be a video tape recorder. The opportunity cost of holding £500 in cash could be a holiday for two in Spain, a new stereo system or the interest to be gained by placing the money in a time account at a bank. Hence, a person's demand

for money is limited in the same way that his demand for any other good or service is limited. The amount of money that anybody holds is dependent upon the differing satisfactions (or **utilities**) to be gained from holding money as opposed to any other type of asset. Three important reasons for holding or demanding money are traditionally distinguished:

The transactions demand for money

Money holders demand money because it enables them to purchase goods and services. The ordinary householder needs money to buy cornflakes, petrol

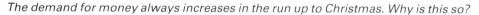

The demand for money always increases in the run up to Christmas. Why is this so?

29

etc. On the whole, the larger the income, the more transactions will take place. A person earning £15 000 a year will on the whole purchase more goods and services than a person only earning £5 000. For this reason the £15 000 income earner will demand more money to finance those transactions than the £5 000 a year person. So, the higher the income, the higher will be the demand for money. Put mathematically:

the transactions demand for money = f(Y)

where Y is income and f means 'function of'.

The precautionary demand for money

Uncertainty may also play an important part in a money holder's decision-making. A money holder does not know necessarily what his financial commitments will be in the future. He may have a car crash, or lose his job, or the central heating may break down. For this reason he will keep money as a precaution. The size of his precautionary balances will depend upon his particular lifestyle. For instance, a poor person will not need to put money aside for problems with his car since he is unlikely to own a car. So the precautionary demand for

Data 4.1

Change in the demand for money (change in M_3)

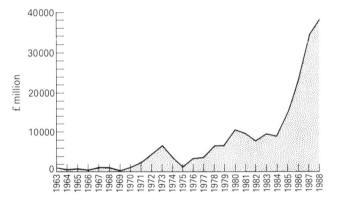

British government securities long dated (20 years): Percentage yield average of working days

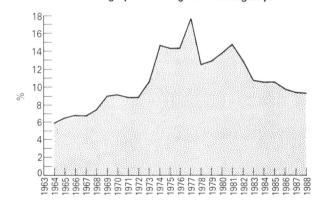

Change in gross domestic product at factor cost (at current prices)

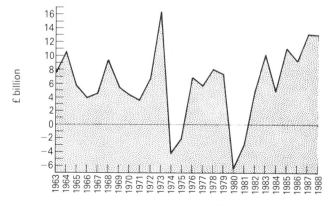

1 Does the data support the hypothesis that the demand for money is a function both of income and of the rate of interest?

Source: CSO, Economic Trends

money is likely to vary with the income of the money holder. It would also depend upon the opportunity cost of holding money. A rise in interest rates would induce some money holders to increase their risk-taking by tying up their money in other types of financial assets. Lowering the rate of interest would lessen the attraction of earning interest and increase their precautionary balances. Expressing this mathematically:

the precautionary demand for money $= f(Y, r)$

where f is 'function of', Y is income and r is the rate of interest.

The speculative demand for money

Money can also be held to make more money. It is not always true that holding money will bring a worse rate of return than holding financial assets. Consider what is happening if Stock Market prices are going down in general. It would be better to sell shares when prices were very high, hold the money thus obtained, and buy back when shares have reached their lowest point rather than hold the shares throughout. This happens because returns on financial assets come from two sources. Firstly, interest (or equivalent) is paid; secondly, the price of the financial asset may change, giving rise to a capital gain or loss.

Assume that the only type of financial asset that a money holder can obtain is bonds. The price of bonds goes up when interest rates fall, and goes down when interest rates rise (see Chapter 3). If money holders expect the rate of interest to fall, then some will speculate and buy into bonds in order to make a capital gain. If bond holders expect the rate of interest to rise, some will sell their bonds in order to avoid making a capital loss. The higher the rate of interest, the more will speculators expect the rate of interest to fall. This is because they will have some idea of what is a 'normal' or 'average' rate of interest on that asset. Large divergencies from that mean will be regarded as abnormal and likely to be of short duration. If the rate of interest is very high, speculators will expect it to fall, and hence bond prices will tend to rise. So speculators at high interest rates will have a high demand for bonds and a low demand for money. If the rate of interest is low, speculators will expect it to rise, and bond

prices to fall. Therefore they will want to sell bonds and the demand for money will be high. The speculative demand for money then is inversely related to the rate of interest:

the speculative demand for money $= f(1/r)$

The demand for money is therefore dependent upon the level of income because money holders want money for transactions and precautionary purposes. It is also dependent upon the rate of interest because earning interest is the opportunity cost of holding money and because of the speculative demand for money.

Figure 4.1 expresses this diagrammatically in a graph plotting the demand for money against the rate of interest. OA represents the transactions and part of the precautionary demands for money. They are constant whatever the level of the rate of interest since they are dependent upon income. The curve relating the demand for money to the rate of interest is known as the **liquidity preference schedule** (or LP schedule). It shows money holders' desire to hold money at given rates of interest.

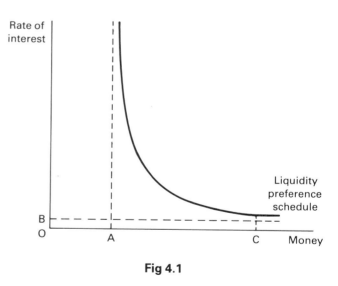

Fig 4.1

At very low rates of interest, it might be the case that all speculators expect the rate of interest to decline no further. The liquidity preference schedule is then perfectly interest-elastic, shown by a horizontal line on the diagram. Increases in the demand for money will have no effect on interest rates. This situation is known as a **liquidity trap**, and is represented by OB on the diagram. At demands for money greater than OC, the demand for money can increase without consequent changes in interest rates.

The monetarist/Keynesian debate

Both monetarists and Keynesians agree that income and the rate of interest affect the demand for money. However, disagreement arises over what asset holders buy when they no longer want money (or vice versa). Keynesians stress that holders either want money or financial assets (represented by bonds). Monetarists argue that holders want money or financial assets or physical assets. The debate is over whether holders of money regard physical assets as a good substitute for holding money.

For instance, if the rate of interest falls, both monetarists and Keynesians predict that the demand for money will rise. Financial interest-bearing assets will be sold because liquidity will now be relatively more attractive, bond holders might fear capital losses, etc. Keynesians predict that the money obtained from the sale of assets will be kept as money. It will not be spent. Monetarists on the other hand argue that some of the money gained by selling financial assets will be used to purchase physical commodities, such as cars and holidays. There will be some increases in the demand for money, but it will be only one small part amongst many increases in demands for a whole range of assets. Hence, on a monetarist assumption, a fall in the rate of interest will not lead to as great an increase in the demand for money as on Keynesian assumptions. To put it another way, Keynesians predict that the liquidity preference schedule is far more interest-elastic than do monetarists.

Figure 4.2 expresses this graphically. A fall in the rate of interest from r_1 to r_2 brings about a much bigger increase in the demand for money on Keynesian grounds than on monetarist assumptions. For monetarists, the rate of interest is only a minor determinant of liquidity preference. The major one is the level of income. This difference in opinion about the influence of the rate of interest upon the demand for money is crucial to the whole monetarist-Keynesian debate.

Monetarists do not believe in the existence of the liquidity trap. For much of the post-war period Keynesians argued that it did exist and that its existence meant that governments could not affect the economy through controlling the money supply. This debate will be considered further in the next chapter. Recently, however, Keynesians too have accepted that it is unlikely that the liquidity trap exists because studies of the UK economy have failed to show its existence.

Testing the theory

This book deals with economic **theory**. Theory attempts to explain the complex workings of the real world. It may at first sight seems relatively easy to decide whether or not the liquidity preference schedule is interest-inelastic or not. Economists would obtain figures for interest rates and the demand for money and see whether changes in interest rates were followed by large or small changes in the demand for money.

Unfortunately, it is not possible to do this in any simple way. For instance, there are no figures in existence which directly measure the demand for money. So, many economists use money supply figures. This is possible because it can be argued that

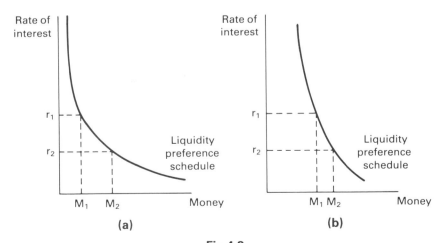

Fig 4.2

...s the demand for money interest-inelastic?

Lastly, there has been much dispute about statistical techniques. Has the statistical technique been applied correctly? Was it the right one to use?

Given all these difficulties, it is no surprise that economists have not yet reached firm conclusions. Monetarist economists claim that the evidence supports their viewpoints. Keynesians point to evidence supporting their own viewpoint. Objectively we can only say that the evidence is not sufficiently clear for a majority concensus view to emerge. The theoretical controversy remains.

...t any point in time the demand for money must ...xactly equal the supply of money. But, which mea-...ure of the money supply should be used? M_1 or M_3, ...r M_4 or M_5, or some other measure? And which ...easure of the rate of interest should be used? Bank ...ase rates, long term government stock rates, com-...ercial bill rates, or some other measure?

Moreover, the economy is not static. Other vari-...bles such as income are likely to change as interest ...ates change. Economists have to try to eliminate ...he effect of those other variables on the demand for ...oney in order to be left with the interest ...ate/demand for money relationship.

Summary

It has been argued that there are three main motives for holding money: a transactions motive, a precautionary motive and a speculative motive. The demand for money is consequently a function of both income and the rate of interest. Monetarists argue that the rate of interest is not an important determinant of the demand for money. Therefore the demand for money is relatively interest-inelastic. Keynesians argue that the rate of interest is a significant determinant and that the demand for money is relatively interest-elastic. The controversy over the interest-elasticity of the demand for money comes about because of a controversy over whether physical assets are a good substitute for holding money. Keynesians argue they are not and that money holders changing their stock of money will substitute primarily financial assets. Monetarists argue that they will substitute both financial and physical assets when altering their stocks of money.

Terms for review

demand for money	**transactions demand for money**
opportunity cost	**precautionary demand for money**
liquidity preference	**speculative demand for money**

Essay questions

What determines the demand for money? To what ...xtent is the demand for money interest-inelastic?

2 What effect would (a) a rise in income and (b) a rise in bond prices have on the demand for money?

5

Controlling monetary variables

The Government may wish to control a number of important monetary variables. It may wish to control the money supply, believing that too much or too little money might particularly affect inflation rates. It may wish to control rates of interest believing that rates of interest may affect how much businessmen will invest and how much consumers will spend. It may wish to control the amounts of money being lent to particular sectors of the economy, wanting for instance to give priority to exporting firms rather than to the consumer who wants to buy a car. It may wish to affect the price of the home currency in relation to other currencies. Two questions arise from this:

1 How many monetary variables can the monetary authorities regulate at any point in time?

2 How effective will that control be?

Monetary policy: a choice of variables

The price of money is the rate of interest. Those who have money may loan it out. The price they charge is expressed as a percentage of the loan and is called the interest rate. Conversely, those who need extra money can obtain it by borrowing, but only at a price—the rate of interest.

Price is determined by demand and supply. So the price of loanable money, the rate of interest, is determined by the demand and supply of loanable money. It has been argued that demand curves for a commodity are normally downward-sloping, whilst supply curves are normally upward-sloping. Money is no different from any other commodity in many respects. As was shown in Chapter 4, the liquidity preference schedule (the demand for money curve) is downward-sloping. It will be assumed here that the supply curve for money also is normal. Later, this assumption will be looked at in more detail.

A demand and supply diagram can be drawn (Fig 5.1) where D and S are the initial demand and supply curves respectively. The equilibrium price or rate of interest is r_E and Q_E of money is demanded and supplied in equilibrium. The monetary authorities might regard Q_E as an undesirable level of money supply and wish to reduce it to Q_1. In order to do this, they attempt to restrict the money supply and succeed in pushing the supply curve back to S'. They have thus achieved their initial objective, for the new equilibrium quantity is indeed Q_1.

But in the process interest rates have been pushed up. This leads to the very important conclusion that the monetary authorities cannot control both the money supply and the rate of interest at the same time. If they decide to fix the money supply at a certain level, they will have to accept whatever rate of interest that entails. Of course they could fix the rate of interest, but that would mean losing control of the money supply. Note also that all other things being equal, reducing the money supply pushes up the rate of interest. This is just common sense. When an item becomes scarcer its price will tend to rise.

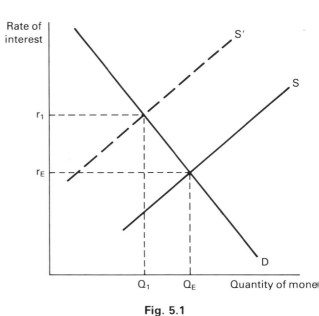

Fig. 5.1

Restricting the supply of money will push up its price, the rate of interest.

The balance of payments further complicates matters. Every day currencies are bought and sold on the foreign exchange markets. The price of each currency is determined by demand and supply. If the demand for the currency increases, its price will tend to rise. If the supply of the currency rises, its price will tend to fall. Governments have the power to affect the price of their own currency. They keep large amounts of gold and foreign currency reserves. For instance, the Bank of England owns large amounts of US dollars, French francs, and so on. On any one day, it can decide to exchange some of these reserves for pounds sterling which are being offered for sale. In other words, the Bank of England increases the amount of pounds sterling demanded at that price. Increasing the demand will push up the price of pounds. On the other hand, if it prints extra pounds and uses those to buy up dollars and francs which are being offered for sale that day, that will increase the supply of pounds at a given price and this will force down the price of the pound.

These dealings can affect the domestic money supply. If, for instance, the monetary authorities are trying to prevent a fall in the value of their currency, they will start to buy up their currency in exchange for foreign currencies kept in their reserves. If they buy up their currency this will reduce the supply of domestic money, as domestic currency bought is neutralised in the central bank.

Diagrammatically, this will push the supply curve of money to the left. In Fig. 5.1 the supply curve shifts from its original position S to S', resulting in a decrease in the money supply from Q_E to Q_1 and a rise in interest rates from r_E to r_1. Conversely, trying to keep the value of a currency at an artificially low level will entail the monetary authorities selling their own currency for foreign currencies and thus increasing the domestic money supply. Hence, the monetary authorities cannot choose to control both the foreign exchange rate and the level of the money supply.

In the long term, persistent pressures on the exchange rate for devaluation and revaluation are caused by balance of payments surpluses or deficits. Devaluation of the currency means that its value against other currencies goes down. Revaluation of the currency means that its value against other currencies rises. Devaluation occurs if the supply of that currency exceeds its demand. Domestic currency is demanded and supplied to finance foreign

Why is the Chancellor not able to control these four variables simultaneously?

trade—such as the purchase of foreign cars, or to finance a loan to a foreign firm. The balance of payments is an account which measures all foreign transactions, both the monies received by a country and the money it has spent. If the balance of payments is in deficit, the country has spent, invested or lent more money than it has received. If this is the case then that country's supply of domestic currency to purchase foreign currency will exceed the demand for domestic currency from holders of foreign currency. As a result, the value of its own currency will decline. The Government can step in to try and keep the price of its currency high by buying it up with the foreign currencies that it holds. But this will have the effect of reducing the money supply. The reverse is also true. If there is a balance of payments surplus, there will be a tendency for the value of the currency to rise. If the Government steps in and sells its currency, this will result in the value of the currency being kept down. But this will also mean that the money supply will rise.

Some economists believe that changes in the money supply resulting from exchange rate dealings and balance of payments transactions should be excluded from the money supply figures. They believe that domestic money supply changes are the important monetary variable. One major institution which believes this is the International Monetary Fund (IMF) which can lend money to countries in difficulty. However, the country must agree to pursue policies laid down by the IMF designed to cure that country of its economic ills. **Domestic Credit Expansion** (DCE) is the name given to this measure of the money supply which excludes balance of payments effects. Roughly speaking DCE is equal to the increase in the domestic money supply minus the balance on the balance of payments. For example, if the domestic money supply rose by £100 million and there was a £60 million deficit on the balance of payments, then DCE would be $100 - (-60)$ or £160 million.

Government borrowing also complicates monetary matters. Governments spend large sums of money, and finance that spending in two ways: firstly, by receiving revenues such as taxes, and secondly by borrowing. Sometimes governments spend less than they receive in taxes, in which case that borrowing is turned into saving. The same principles apply whether it is saving or borrowing that is being discussed. Government borrowing is sometimes called the **Public Sector Borrowing Requirement** (PSBR). The total amount of debt outstanding as a result of often hundreds of years of borrowing is known as the **National Debt**.

If the Government is to borrow, it does so partly by issuing bonds. The mechanism for the selling of these bonds differs from country to country. In the UK, for instance, the bonds are initially bought from the Government by the central bank, the Bank of England. The Bank of England then tries to sell these bonds. They will be sold either to the general public, or to the rest of the banking system, or will be kept by the central bank itself.

Assume that the Government wishes to increase the amount it borrows in the current financial year. All other factors remain constant. If the central bank tries subsequently to sell the bonds either to the general public or to the rest of the banking system, the result will be a rise in the rate of interest. The reason for this is that the supply of money has remained constant, but the demand for money has risen by the amount that the Government wishes to obtain through its borrowing. Thus, demand exceeds supply at the given price (the interest rate), and this price is forced up.

If the central bank does not wishes to see interest rates forced up, it can buy all the bonds itself. But it can only do this by paying money for them to the Government. The result of this is that there is an increase in the supply of money matching the size of extra Government borrowing. So, extra Government borrowing either leads to an increase in the rate of interest, or an increase in the money supply, or some combination of both, i.e. the Government cannot fix the PSBR and both the rate of interest and the money supply.

Monetary objectives in the UK

Over the past 30 years, two objectives of UK government monetary policy have tended to remain the same.

1 Stable short term interest rates The Bank of England has worked to keep short term interest rates (for instance interest rates on Treasury Bills or money at call or short notice) stable from day to day. From time to time, the Bank of England has announced or indicated changes in those interest rates. Before 1981, Bank Rate (later called Minimum Lending Rate) was the rate of interest which the Bank of England controlled, and changes in Bank Rate would almost immediately lead to banks and other financial institutions in the City of London changing their short term interest rates. Since 1981, the Bank of England has only rarely declared a Bank Rate. Instead, it gives 'signals' to the rest of the money markets about the exact interest rate it wants to see prevail in the market. The market always responds to the signals because it knows that the Bank of England can force an interest rate on the markets if it so wishes.

2 Financing the PSBR Up to 1987, the Government almost always needed to borrow money to finance its spending. The Government could have chosen to alter its spending plans if it had not liked the consequences of having to borrow money in the money markets. It never did alter those plans. So the finding of that money was a major objective of government policy. Since 1987, the Government has raised too much money in taxes in relation to its spending. There is now a **public sector debt repayment**. Again, the Bank of England has made it a priority to use that money to pay off the National Debt.

Keeping short term interest rates stable from day to day and financing the PSBR have been the two constants of UK monetary policy. Other objectives have changed.

1 The money supply Traditionally, governments have showed relatively little interest in the money supply. It was only in 1976 that money supply targets were issued. These targets were an indication of the maximum rates of growth of the money supply that the Government wished to see. Initially M_1 and M_3 were targeted. In 1985, M_0 replaced M_1 as the measure of narrow money targeted. In most years, actual increases were larger than the targets. Part of the reason for this must be that controlling the money supply was not seen by governments as being a key objective of monetary policy.

2 Long term interest rates The Government has tended to allow long term interest rates (such as the rate of interest on long term government stock) to fluctuate from day to day. This has been because it has tended to finance the PSBR by the issuing of long term debt and, as explained above, it cannot control both the level of new debt and the interest rate.

3 The exchange rate Up to 1971, the UK operated a fixed exchange rate policy. This meant that the Government was committed to buying and selling currency to keep the level of the pound constant against

---

Data 5.1

Foreign exchange intervention boosts October money supply

Record intervention in foreign exchange markets led to a rapid expansion in the money supply last month.

The Bank said that sterling M_3, the broad monetary aggregate, grew provisionally by 3.4 per cent, seasonally adjusted, in October and by 22.2 per cent over the year.

This fast expansion was attributable to three main factors: the large increase in official reserves in October; the Government's decision not to "sterilise" the effects of this increase in domestic money supply through gilt-edged sales; and the great stock market crash, which was another factor causing the Bank of England to withdraw from selling large amounts of gilts.

Foreign exchange intervention boosted M_3 by £2.9bn after sales of government securities to foreigners of about £750m.

The Financial Times. 20.11.87

1 What effect did open market operations have on the money supply according to the article?
2 Explain why the Bank of England was unable to control both the money supply and the value of the pound during

---

other currencies. Since then, the pound has been allowed to float and its value cha ~~ to day. However, at various times, the C vened to prevent the value of too high or falling too low. buying and selling of pounds, money supply in the economy been used to influence the v 1971, exchange rate policy h month to month, sometimes being seen as very important, at other times as being relatively unimportant.

Instruments of monetary policy

The monetary authorities have a variety of money supply controls available to them which have been used with varying degrees of success over the past 30 years.

1 Open market operations Open market operations is the term used to describe the buying and selling of government debt by the central bank to affect the money supply and the rate of interest. If the Bank of England sells bonds, the bonds are bought with money. So the money supply will decrease and interest rates will tend to rise. If, on the other hand the Bank of England buys bonds, it will pay for those with money. So the money supply will increase and interest rates will tend to fall.

However, the effect of open market operations on the money supply is not as simple as it might at first seem. Firstly, if the Bank of England sells bonds, then the money it receives must be kept by the Bank. It cannot, for instance, use that money to finance government spending, because this would result in there being no impact on the money supply. The private sector would have lost money to pay for the bonds but would then have received an equal amount from government spending, resulting in no change in the money supply. Secondly, if the Bank buys bonds it must print new money. The Government is expanding the money supply by resorting to the printing presses.

Moreover, the effect on the money supply will be greater than the initial change. For instance, assume that the Bank of England sells £100 million of bonds to the banks. The banks will then lose £100 million of cash which they could have lent out to their customers. These customers would have redeposited the money in the banks, money which could have been lent out again. This is the process of credit creation described on page 18. The final fall in the money supply is given by the value of the money multiplier. If the money multiplier is 2, a £100 million loss of cash by the banks to buy bonds will lead to a £200 million fall in the money supply.

Funding Strictly speaking, funding debt is ...d as replacing short term by long term debt. ...can have a number of effects on monetary conditions depending upon the monetary framework existing at the time. For instance, replacing notes and coins (short term government debt) with 25 year bonds (long term government debt) is the same as open market operations described above. Funding can also affect the structure of interest rates. If the Government buys back short term debt and replaces it with long term debt, then short term interest rates will tend to fall whilst long term interest rates will tend to rise. This is because there will be a fall in demand for short term borrowed funds but a rise in demand for long term borrowed funds.

3 Monetary base control As has been argued earlier, the reserve ratio will limit the size of the banking system's deposits. If, for instance, the reserve ratio is 10% and the banks have £1 billion worth of reserve assets, they can only accept £10 billion worth of deposits. If the reserve ratio fell to 1%, the banks could then accept £100 billion of deposits, increasing the money supply by £90 billion. The central bank has the power to set and alter the reserve ratio. Therefore, because the money supply is usually defined as cash (the monetary base of the economy) plus bank deposits, in theory it has a very powerful way of altering the level of the money supply.

To give another example, assume that the money supply is £120, made up of £20 in cash and £100 in bank deposits. The banks have to keep a 10% cash ratio, so £10 of the cash is in the banking system and £10 is held by the general public. The Bank of England decides that it wishes to reduce the money supply to £90. It can do this by ordering the banks to keep a $12\frac{1}{2}\%$ cash ratio. With £10 in cash, the banks can now only hold £80 in deposits ($10/80 = 12\frac{1}{2}\%$). The money supply is now £90—made up of £80 in bank deposits and £10 in cash held by the public.

This example shows one of the problems of monetary base control. There is nothing to stop the banks from trying to persuade their customers to deposit into the bank some of that £10 in cash that they are currently holding. This would then allow the bank to create more money, thus raising the money supply and frustrating the purposes of the central bank.

Monetary base control has never been used in the UK. Apart from the problem of effectiveness just described, the main reason for this is that controlling the money supply in this way would be likely to lead to very large day to day changes in interest rates. Individual banks and other borrowers and lenders in the money markets tend to have either too much cash or too little cash to balance their books at the end of each day. If the market were short of cash, interest rates

Data 5.2

'Overfunding is certainly not a gimmick'

Sir, Mr Samuel Brittan says that he was surprised that I placed "such emphasis" on overfunding in my recent pamphlet, Monetarism Lost, and goes on to describe over-funding as "a gimmick." His remarks are misleading.

In the late 1970s and 1980s broad money targets were set in the belief that reductions in the growth rate of broad money were a necessary and sufficient condition for a reduction in inflation.

Broad money (on the M3 definition) consists almost entirely of bank deposits. Control of broad money is therefore virtually equivalent to controlling the quantity of bank deposits. When a private sector non-bank agent buys a new issue of government debt, it writes out a cheque to the Government and this reduces its bank deposits.

The effect is to cut monetary growth. Because monetary growth is less, the private sector is less eager to spend on goods and services. With demand lower than it would otherwise have been, inflationary pressures are weakened. The inflationary benefits from reducing broad money through government debt sales are much the same as those arising from any other technique of monetary control.

Tim Congdon,
Economic Adviser,
Gerrard & National,
33 Lombard Street, EC3

The Financial Times. 6.6.89

1 Explain how overfunding (often called open market operations) can be used to control the growth of the money supply.

2 Why might a government overfund?

would rise sharply to attract cash from outside the market. At the time this book was written—in 1989—the Bank of England intervenes in the market, buying bonds and bills, thus supplying cash to the market and keeping interest rates constant. As has been argued above, the Bank of England has traditionally placed a very high importance on keeping short term interest rates steady.

4 Other central bank measures Central banks have proved ingenious in devising schemes for controlling money supply growth. Local conditions and local institutions will determine the nature of these schemes and will also determine their success or failure. One such measure, called the **Special Deposit Scheme**, played an important role in UK monetary policy in the 1960s and 1970s. Special Deposits were forced loans from the banks to the Bank of England. The Bank of England had the power to call in a percentage of an individual bank's assets and freeze them. Banks had to sell some of their illiquid financial assets to raise the liquid cash needed to deposit with the Bank of England. This had a multiplier effect reducing the money supply. For instance, if the money multiplier were 2, a calling in of £1 of Special Deposits would, in theory, reduce the money supply by £2.

Another regulation was the **Supplementary Deposit Scheme**, nicknamed 'the corset'. Banks were told to limit the growth of their deposits to a fixed percentage. If they overshot the limit, they were fined by the Bank of England. The idea here was that, given that bank deposits were part of the money supply, restricting the growth of bank deposits would restrict the growth of the money supply.

For many years, credit controls were implemented. These restricted who could borrow money and for how long. In the 1960s, for instance, exporting firms were given preferential treatment for loans. Through the 1960s and 1970s consumers taking out hire purchase agreements were forced to make a minimum percentage deposit and were limited on the maximum number of years over which they could repay the loan. This

Data 5.3

Long-term interest rates 'should be left to rise'

By Simon Holberton, Economics Staff

TO SUPPORT the pound and bear down on inflation, the Treasury should suspend its policy of fully funding the public-sector borrowing requirement and allow long-term interest rates to rise, according to Greenwell Montagu, the UK gilt-edged broker.

Mr Roger Bootle, its chief UK economist, says the current economic situation "is so serious that the time has passed for the arrogant or ideological dismissal of policy options, other than the ones currently employed."

The Government's budget surplus takes money out of the economy and the full fund policy seeks to replace it by the Bank of England buying back from private investors and British government securities, mostly gilt-edged stocks. Mr

Bootle says that gilts purchases have artificially depressed long-term interest rates.

The suspension of the full fund policy would have three beneficial effects, Mr Bootle believes:

● Higher long-term interest rates would attract more stable foreign capital to finance Britain's current-account deficit and support the pound;

● Higher rates would absorb some of the liquidity of domestic institutions while weakening equity prices and raising the cost of capital;

● Higher rates would prevent companies and individuals from avoiding the Chancellor's tight-money policy by borrowing long-term.

The Financial Times. 5.6.89

1 What is meant by a 'full fund' policy?
2 Explain, using a diagram, the effect of this policy on long term interest rates.

3 What should be the effect of higher interest rates on the growth of the money supply?

made deposits and monthly repayments larger, and therefore discouraged borrowing.

The Bank of England has now abandoned these schemes because, on the whole, they did not work. For instance, Special Supplementary Deposits became nicknamed 'the corset' because **disintermediation** took place. A corset does not get rid of fat in the body—it just moves it from one place to another. And

this is what happened with Special Supplementary Deposits. Money was driven out of the banking system which was being controlled. But it did not disappear. Borrowers and lenders became very skilled at linking up outside of the system. Banks are financial intermediaries, linking lenders and borrowers. Hence, when borrowers and lenders are forced out of this sytem, disintermediation is said to take place

Special Supplementary Deposits reduced the official money supply statistics only by driving money underground—it was still there, but it was not being counted any more.

The money supply: exogenous or endogenous?

An exogenous variable is one which is not determined within a model. Its value cannot be determined from other variables in the model. For instance, the exact size of total government spending cannot be determined by economic variables because the level of government spending is a political decision. Different levels of spending will be associated with different governments and with particular chancellors of the exchequer. Similarly, it is very difficult to determine the level of exports for an economy. Exports are determined by the spending decisions of a large number of different economies and economic units within those economies. The exact nature of these relationships is so vague that the economist cannot determine volumes or values. So in nearly all economic models, exports are an exogenous variable.

An **endogenous** variable is one which is determined within a model. The demand for money for instance is determined by income and the rate of interest. Price is determined by the forces of demand and supply. So the demand for money and price are both endogenous variables.

If the money supply is said to be exogenous, this means that it is determined independently by the central bank. This means that the central bank determines the level of the money supply whatever the interest rate, i.e. the money supply is perfectly interest-inelastic. This is shown in Fig. 5.2. The supply curve is vertical because at any interest rate the government can fix the money supply level that it wants. If it is endogenous then the central bank fails to control it and the money supply is determined by free market forces within the banking system. Two distinct questions need to be answered at this stage. Firstly, is the money supply endogenous at a particular moment in time for a particular country? Secondly, can the money supply ever be exogenous?

1 Even if the answer to the second question is yes, it might well be true that at a particular point in time the money supply might be endogenous. If the central bank is pursuing some other monetary aim, such as fixing the level of interest rates or maintaining a certain exchange rate, then it can not fix the money supply. It must accept whatever is determined within the market. Equally the central bank may find the money supply figures quite acceptable as determined by the market. It would hardly bother to intervene if this were the case.

2 What if the central bank did want to control the money supply? Is the money supply then exogenous? Unfortunately, economists still disagree. The central bank can for the most part control the creation of money by the banking system through its battery of monetary weapons.

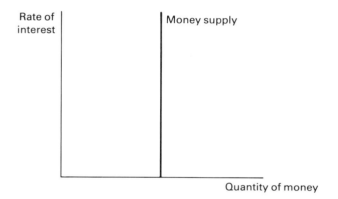

Fig. 5.2

Some economists argue that in a modern economy banks are not the only financial institutions with the ability to create money. A whole host of other institutions, such as fringe banks, savings banks and building societies have a partial ability to create money. It has already been argued that there seems little difference between a time or deposit account at a bank and a similar account at say a building society. Both represent near money in the sense that the saver can withdraw funds usually on demand.

Assume that the banks are subject to restrictive monetary policy. They have discouraged the growth of new deposits by lowering interest rates, raising bank charges, reducing advertising, etc. Potential depositors might well be attracted to building societies. The building society then lends out the money to finance a house purchase. Eventually that money will reappear in the economy either in the pockets of a builder selling a new house or of a person who is selling a house but not buying another

Data 5.4

Anxious analysts watch for debut of M4

This morning at 11.30 traders in the gilt-edged securities and other British money markets will be watching their screens for the release of the money supply figures for March.

The question for many analysts is which figure will be highlighted? The broad money measure known as M_3 which measures deposits in the banking system, or the even broader measure known as M_4 which includes building societies' deposits?

It is not a mere technicality. For the purposes of monetary policy the Treasury watches three indicators closely: M_0, the exchange rate and now M_4 rather than M_3.

M_3, and its counterpart bank lending, is probably the best known of the Ms. It has been the key monetary variable that the present Government and its predecessor had tried (unsuccessfully) to control. A target range for M_3 was dropped formally a little more than a year ago.

M_4 includes all the elements of M_3 but adds to it the deposits held by building societies, less the deposits building societies have with banks.

In the Budget Red Book the Treasury said M_4 was a better measure of broad money, given the changes that have occurred in the financial system which have brought about much greater com-

petition between banks and building societies and blurred the distinction between them.

Bank lending, a counterpart of M_3, has grown rapidly since 1985 but a large measure of growth reflects banks' incursions into traditional building society territory: mortgage lending. Combined bank and building society lending has been growing more modestly.

Although analysts see reason in the Treasury's move to highlight M_4, some note that M_4 is much better behaved than M_3 – its annual rate of growth of about 16 per cent seems much less alarming than M_3's 20 per cent plus – and that may have influenced the move.

The Financial Times. 21.4.88

1 *Explain why the Bank of England has decided to monitor M_4 rather than M_3.*

2 *Does this move support the idea that the money supply is exogenous?*

one at the same time. After a while the money is likely to be redeposited in a non-bank financial institution—remember, the banks are discouraging further deposits. They will lend a proportion of it out again, and so it goes on. Just as with the traditional banking example, there is no reason to suppose that building societies will not receive back a proportion of what they lent out. If that proportion is 50% then for every new £1 that is deposited with them, they will eventually have £2 of new assets and liabilities. They too have created money. The central bank has controlled the banking system, but the result has been that non-bank financial institutions have found it profitable to borrow money in such a way that that money is able to create further money.

In short, the money supply is potentially infinite. Financial institutions outside the control of the central bank will take surplus money from those who want to lend it out, and provide money for those who want to borrow it but can not obtain it from the financial institutions controlled by the central bank. If people want money, they can get it whatever the actions of the central bank.

Keynesians argue that monetary policy can never be made completely effective. Operators in the financial markets, who can afford to employ the best brains in the financial world, will always find ways round central bank control. However, moderate Keynesians would agree that the central bank can exercise some measure of control in the short run. In other words, the money supply is partly exogenous and partly endogenous. Extreme Keynesians argue that the central bank cannot control the money supply, and hence the money supply is completely endogenous.

This viewpoint was best summarised in the Radcliffe Committee Report, 1959. This was a committee set up by the British Government, under the chairmanship of Lord Radcliffe, to investigate the effectiveness of monetary policy. They concluded that monetary policy was totally ineffective because the money supply was potentially infinite. Attempts by the central bank to control one form of money would only result in new forms of money being created. The Radcliffe Committee Report has often been called the highwater mark of Keynesianism,

Data 5.5

Change in money stock sterling M₃

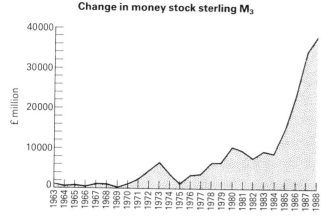

Public sector borrowing requirement

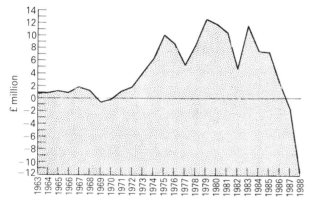

Treasury Bill Yield: last Friday of the year

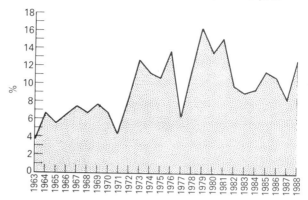

Special deposits, end of year

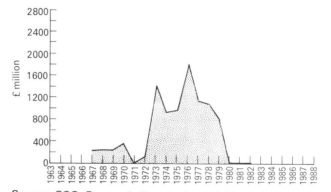

Source: CSO, Economic Trends, Annual Abstract of Statistics

1 What economic arguments are put forward to suggest that:
  (a) high levels of interest rates reduce the growth of the money supply?
  (b) increases in the PSBR increase the money supply?
  (c) increasing Special Deposits reduces the growth of the money supply?

2 To what extent do the data support each of these hypotheses?

representing a viewpoint more extreme than most Keynesians of the day.

Monetarists, on the other hand, argue that the money supply is exogenous. They reject the idea that the central bank can not control the money supply. Obviously, the central bank needs to implement firm monetary controls. The central bank must allow the other monetary variables associated with the money supply—the rate of interest, the foreign exchange rate and the public sector borrowing requirement—to find a level consistent with the money supply target. If it is found that other financial instutitions are creating money, then those financial institutions can simply be drawn into the monetary control net. In the short term, the central bank may find it difficult to keep control as the financial system does its best to get round any controls imposed. In the long run, however, a determined central bank can make its policies stick. Historical evidence, monetarists suggest, proves that central banks with enough willpower can control the money supply.

Summary

The monetary authorities cannot control the money supply, the interest rate, the exchange rate and the public sector borrowing requirement (PSBR) at the same time. They have to choose which variable to control. Techniques of monetary control include monetary base control, open market operations, funding and special deposit schemes. The central bank may also attempt to control the money supply through credit controls. Economists disagree about the effectiveness of these controls. Monetarists argue that the money supply can be controlled by the central bank and is therefore an exogenous variable. Keynesians argue that in the long run it is the financial system which determines the level of the money supply and therefore the money supply is endogenous.

Terms for review

monetary policy

domestic credit expansion

PSBR

National Debt

open market operations

funding

credit policy

exogenous and endogenous variables

Essay questions

1 Explain the relationship between the money supply and the rate of interest. To what extent should a government rely upon control of the PSBR in order to control interest rates?

2 Can governments control the money supply?

3 What is the difference between monetary control and credit controls? How effective are credit controls as a means of affecting expenditure?

6

Consumption

In the previous three chapters, we have considered the role that money plays in an economy. One of the functions of money is as a means of exchange. It is used to pay for goods and services. We will now consider what determines the volume of spending in the economy as a whole over a period of time, i.e. we will consider the determinants of **aggregate consumption**.

What is consumption?

Measured consumption is the value of total expenditure in an economy over a period of time. This includes the value of items as different as cornflakes, paint, cars, Chinese takeaways and bus fares. This expenditure can be subdivided in a number of different ways.

Data 6.1

Distribution of consumers' expenditure

1963

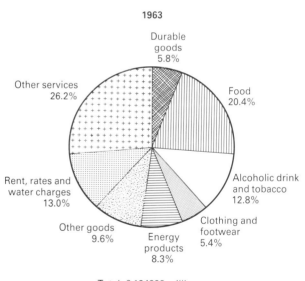

Total £ 134838 million
at 1985 prices

1988

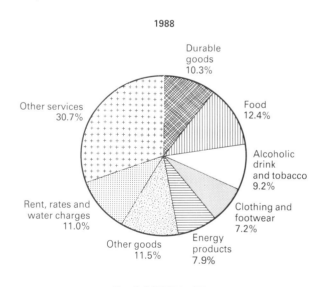

Total £ 255624 million
at 1985 prices

Source: CSO, Economic Trends

1 *Given a 81.5% increase in real personal disposable income over the period 1963 to 1988, account for the changes in consumers' expenditure shown in the data.*

For instance, aggregate consumption could be divided into food, transport, housing, clothing, alcoholic drinks, household durables, fuel and light, services, meals out, tobacco and miscellaneous. These divisions are in fact used to calculate the retail price index (a measure of inflation in the UK).

Another way of subdividing consumption is into durable goods and non-durable goods. A durable good is a product which is not consumed at one point in time. It produces a flow of services over a period of time. Examples are cars, television sets, furniture, kitchen equipment and lawn mowers. The fact that services are derived from these goods over a number of years gives rise to second-hand markets in these goods. If a durable lasts exactly five years and costs £5 000, then conventional statistics will show a measured consumption of £5 000 in the first year and nothing in the other four. But if by its very nature it needs no maintenance or repair over its lifetime, then only £1 000 a year will in fact be consumed.

This gives rise to a different definition of consumption: **permanent consumption**. This is the actual value of goods and services consumed in a particular time period. It contrasts with measured consumption, which is the value of consumer goods and services purchased over a time period.

If the only items purchased in an economy over a time period were 1 million packets of cornflakes (valued at £0.5 million) and 1 000 motorbikes (valued at £1 million and which depreciated over the period by £200 000) then measured consumption would be £1.5 million. The value of permanent consumption however, would only be £700 000.

The propensity to consume

Economists are agreed that one of the major determinants of consumption is the level of income. For instance if a wage earner were to obtain a pay rise of £2 000 a year, it is likely that his consumption would increase too.

This relationship between consumption and income is expressed in terms of the 'propensity to consume'. 'Propensity' means 'willingness' or 'inclination'. The propensity to consume refers to how willing the householder is to spend his income. It is usually expressed as a proportion of 1, e.g. a propensity to consume of 0.6 indicates that a consumer spends 60% of his income. The propensity to consume is usually defined more specifically than this.

The **average propensity to consume** (APC) is defined as total consumption (C) divided by total income (Y). As a mathematical formula:

$$APC = \frac{C}{Y}$$

If total consumption is £500 and total income is £1 000 the APC is $\frac{1}{2}$ or 0.5.

The **marginal propensity to consume** (MPC) is defined as the proportion of additional income which is consumed. It is normal to abbreviate 'change' by using the Greek letter 'delta' (Δ). Thus:

$$MPC = \frac{\Delta C}{\Delta Y}$$

For example, if income goes up by £100 and as a result consumption increases by £70, the MPC is 0.7. Further worked examples are given in Table 6.1.

It is possible to express this relationship between consumption and income mathematically. Assume that the marginal propensity to consume is constant at all levels of income, i.e. the change in consumption as a proportion of the initial change in income remains the same whatever the income level. Assume also that consumers always spend some minimum amount whatever their level of income. If income is less than this minimum consumption level, consumers will dissave (i.e. draw on their savings) or borrow in order to purchase enough goods and services to keep them alive.

Total consumption (C) will equal this minimum consumption level (a) plus the proportion of income that is spent, i.e. the marginal propensity to consume (c) times income (Y):

$$C = a + cY$$

This equation is known as a **consumption function**—a term applied to any equation showing the relationship between consumption and other variables which determine consumption such as income.

Figure 6.1. expresses this relationship graphically. The graph is an income–expenditure graph with the 45° line showing all points where income equals expenditure. If expenditure rises at a slower rate than income (i.e. the MPC is less than 1) then the 45° will be steeper than the consumption line or function. In Fig. 6.1 the consumption function is a straight line since the MPC is assumed to be constant at all levels of income (i.e. the change in consumption divided by the change in income is constant at all points along the line).

Table 6.1

Total income	Increase in income	Total consumption	Increase in consumption	APC	MPC
Y	ΔY	C	ΔC	C/Y	ΔC/ΔY
1 000		900		0.9	
2 000	1 000	1 700	800	0.85	0.8
3 000	1 000	2 400	700	0.8	0.7
5 000	2 000	3 400	1 000	0.68	0.5
10 000	5 000	5 000	1 600	0.5	0.32

However, in Fig. 6.1 the APC declines steadily as income increases. To prove this, compare any two points on the consumption line. The APC would only be constant if the consumption line were linear (straight as opposed to curved) and passed through the origin, as in Fig. 6.2. In this situation the APC also equals the MPC. For instance, the MPC between incomes OA and OB is CD/AB. The APC at income OB is OD/OB. The two fractions are equal. If the consumption line passes through the origin, it must be true that the constant term is zero. Hence the equation is simply:

$$C = cY$$

A consumption function where the MPC changed at different levels of income would be curved. If it is assumed that the MPC tends to decline as income increases, then the consumption function would look as in Fig. 6.3.

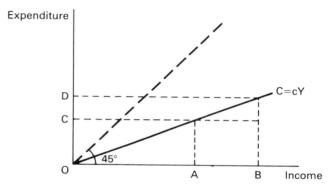

Fig. 6.2

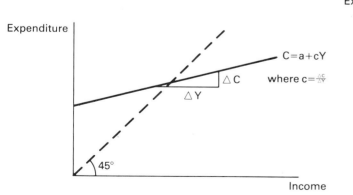

Fig. 6.1

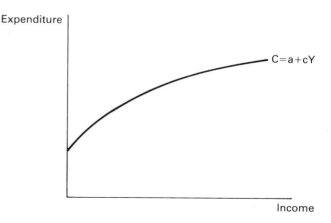

Fig. 6.3

Measures of income

If consumption is a function of income, what definition of income should be used?

Keynesian economists argue that a stable relationship exists between measured consumption and disposable income (i.e. the MPC is constant over time). **Disposable income** is income received by the household, inclusive of any state benefits received, after deductions such as income tax and national insurance contributions have been made. It represents income available for expenditure on consumer goods and services.

However, Milton Friedman, the leading monetarist economist, argues to the contrary. He argues that the APC and MPC, far from being stable as Keynesians maintain, are volatile over time. His theory of the consumption function is known as the Permanent Income Hypothesis.

It is permanent consumption, he argues, which is proportional to **permanent income**. Permanent income is defined as the amount a consumer could consume (or believes that he could) while maintaining his wealth intact. Over a lifetime, an individual will earn and spend a certain sum of money. Most individuals take into account future or past earnings when making spending decisions. It is noticeable, for instance, that young people often have an average propensity to consume of greater than 1. They borrow in order to undertake heavy capital expenditure on their education, their house and its contents. In middle age, consumers pay off accumulated debts and start saving for their old age. After retirement, they run down their savings in order again to spend more than they have earned. Hence major spending decisions are not based on current disposable income, but on expected income in the long term. Permanent income is a measure of this. As an approximation, permanent income could perhaps be seen as a person's lifetime earnings divided by the number of years he expects to be an independent economic unit, e.g. from the age of sixteen onwards.

Why might consumption rise now if consumers revise upwards their expectations of future incomes?

Data 6.2

Reduced growth is seen for home goods

By Alice Rawsthorn

RETAIL groups selling products for the home, such as carpets and furniture, face a slower growth in sales and increased pressure on profits because of the impact of high interest rates on consumer spending.

A study by the Corporate Intelligence Group suggests that home products retailers should muster some sales growth this year, albeit at a far slower pace than last year.

However, Corporate Intelligence disagrees with the pessimistic prediction that sales of "high ticket" items – such as carpets or three-piece suites – will fall because of the slow-down in the housing market and lower disposable incomes.

The study anticipates a 10 per cent increase in furniture shop sales to £5.9bn in 1989, compared with an increase of 14 per cent last year. Carpet sales are also forecast to grow at a slower rate than in 1988.

Both sectors should benefit from the continuing growth of interest in interior design.

The outlook for specialist electrical retailers is less rosy. These groups have been hit not only by the slowdown in consumer spending, but also by the dearth of new products, the lacklustre response to satellite television and a slowdown in compact disc sales.

Nevertheless, Corporate Intelligence expects the market to improve in the autumn and to increase by 7.5 per cent to almost £6bn this year. However, television rental specialists, who are vulnerable to the poor response to satellite TV, face "limited" growth.

The Financial Times. 12.6.89

1 According to the article, what factors affect the level of consumer spending?
2 To what extent does the data support the hypothesis that consumption is a function of disposable income?

Other factors consumption

Consumption

Keynesians argue able for the pur determinant of laxing credit terms, deposit, or allowing repaymᵤ longer period of time, are likely ᵤ volume of credit available and thus increasᵤ sumption.

The permanent income hypothesis, on the other hand, sees the price of money (the rate of interest) as a more accurate predictor of the level of consumption than the volume of credit. A higher rate of interest raises the credit price of consumer durables and results in a fall in expenditure. Higher interest rates will also make saving more attractive, thus lowering expenditure. The ratio of non-human wealth to permanent income is also an important determinant of consumption. If a person gets richer whilst his income remains constant, he will tend to spend more. Other factors could affect levels of consumption such as tastes and population and income distribution.

The size and stability of the MPC and APC

Economists disagree about both the size and the stability of the propensity to consume. Keynesian economists argue that the propensity to consume is stable both in the short and long run. Consumers spend a stable proportion of their current disposable income over time.

Milton Friedman argues that evidence points to the contrary. Although the propensity to consume is stable in the long run, it is unstable in the short run. This is because much of the change in income in the short run is **transitory income**—income which consumers did not expect to earn, such as a large win on the pools, a redundancy settlement or a pay increase from an unexpected promotion. This transitory income, according to Friedman, will initially be saved, as consumers decide what to do with the money. Consumers will then react differently according to whether the extra income is a once and

49

Do the customers and staff of this hotel have different propensities to consume?

for all gain, or a gain likely to continue over a period of time.

Assume a salesman earns £100 000 one year by being extremely lucky with export orders. On Keynesian assumptions, he will base his expenditure for that year on his £100 000 earnings whatever his normal level of earnings. Friedman argues that this will not be the case if the salesman believes that future yearly earnings will be below £100 000. Rather, the salesman will add the difference between £100 000 and his expected annual earnings to his permanent income and consume that extra income over a number of years. He may, for instance, choose to save that extra income in the building society now, and spend the interest earned in future years.

Friedman argues that because the amount of transitory income as a proportion of total income varies from time period to time period, the propensity to consume out of measured income is not constant.

Disagreement also arises over the size of the average and marginal propensities to consume. Keynesians argue that higher income earners have a lower average propensity to consume than lower income earners. A household on the poverty line is likely to have an APC of 1, for instance, whilst a millionnaire is likely to save a large proportion of his income.

Friedman argues that there is no difference between the APC of a high income earner and a low income earner. A millionnaire is just as likely to spend all his income as a pauper. If this were not the case, wealth differentials would increase over time.

50

Data 6.3

Change in consumers' expenditure (at 1985 prices)

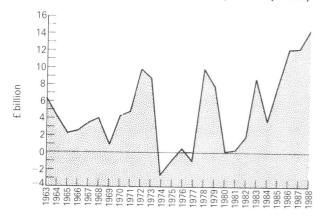

Change in personal disposable income (at 1985 prices)

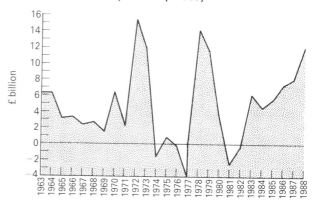

London clearing banks deposit account (7 days' notice) rate of interest

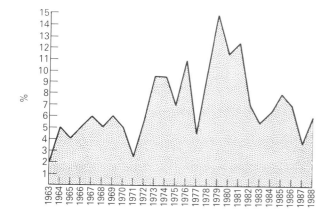

Change in expenditure on durable goods (at 1985 prices)

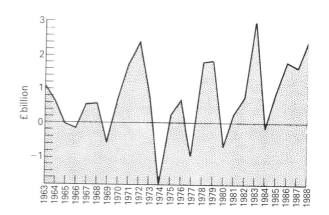

Source: CSO, Economic Trends, Annual Abstract of Statistics

1 *Account for the changes in consumers' expenditure shown in the data.*

2 *Does the data suggest that the marginal propensity to consume is consistent over time?*

High income earners would constantly add to the stock of wealth whilst low income earners would add nothing. But evidence suggests that wealth differentials do not increase over time. Therefore high income earners must save the same proportion (or even less) of their income as low income earners.

Friedman also argues that the long run APC is 1—people aim to spend all they earn over a lifetime, whilst keeping their inherited wealth intact. The implication is that wealth differentials remain constant over time (although high taxes on income and wealth may at times reduce wealth inequalities).

Summary

Measured consumption is the value of aggregate expenditure over a period of time. A major determinant of consumption is the level of income, although credit volumes and the rate of interest may also be important in determining expenditure on consumer durables. The marginal propensity to consume and the average propensity to consume are defined as $\Delta C/\Delta Y$ and C/Y respectively. Economists disagree about both the size and stability of the propensity to consume over time.

Essay questions

1 *What is meant by the 'marginal propensity to consume' of an economy? What effect would you expect (a) a fall of 2% in the standard rate of personal (income) tax and (b) a £200 increase in the Christmas old age pension bonus to have on the economy's marginal propensity to consume?*

2 *What factors affect the level of aggregate consumption? Why might you expect differing income groups to have different propensities to consume?*

Terms for review

aggregate consumption

durable and non-durable goods

measured and permanent consumption

marginal propensity to consume

average propensity to consume

consumption function

disposable and permanent income

7

Saving

A wage earner, having paid his taxes, will not only spend his wages but will also save a part of them. In this chapter, we will define what is meant by **savings**, and then consider why economic units save.

Definitions of savings

Savings represent deferred consumption. The saver chooses to lock away his spending power for a period of time. He may have a number of motives for this. He may wish to save up for an item which could not be purchased at the present moment in time. He may wish to defer consumption because he expects future income to decline (for instance in retirement) and he wishes to supplement that income. He may be tempted to defer consumption because interest will be added to his savings and consequently he will be able to buy more in the future than he can now.

Forms of saving include purchases of stocks and shares on the Stock Exchange, premiums paid for assurance policies, deposits with building societies and contributions to occupational pensions schemes.

Often, in general usage, no clear distinction is made between investment and savings, whereas in economics each word has its own precise meaning. Saving takes place when money is exchanged for other financial assets, such as stocks, shares, and assurance policies. Usually, these financial assets are legally represented by pieces of paper. Investment takes place when money is exchanged for real goods and services of an investment (as opposed to consumption) nature. Examples are factories, machines, offices, schools and houses.

There are two major sources of savings in an economy. Consumers save out of their income. Businesses also save out of their profits. Business units might wish to invest as well, and the balance of advantage between saving and investment will depend upon the firm's individual circumstances and the comparative rewards of both.

Data 7.1

Personal saving: as a ratio of personal disposable income

United Kingdom

Percentage of personal disposable income

[1] 'Other personal saving' consists of saving by unincorporated businesses and private non-profit-making bodies serving persons.

Source: United Kingdom National Accounts, Central Statistical Office

1 Describe the changes in the volume and composition of total savings over the period 1971 to 1986.
2 What might account for the differences in stability of the three component parts of savings shown?

The determinants of saving

Neo-classical economists argued that savings were primarily determined by the rate of interest:

$$S = f(r)$$

where S is the volume of savings and r is the rate of interest.

Savings were undertaken in the hope of making future gains. For instance £100 saved today at 10% interest would be worth £110 in a year's time. By deferring spending £100 for one year, the saver can increase his monetary purchasing power by £10. A rise in the rate of interest would encourage more people to save as postponing present consumption became a more attractive proposition. A fall in the rate of interest would conversely discourage saving. Savers would withdraw money and spend it. Hence in Fig. 7.1 the savings schedule is upward sloping.

Why do people save?

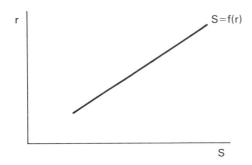

Fig. 7.1

Keynes and his followers argued that the rate of interest was of little importance in determining savings. Keynes pointed out that much of savings is contractual: that is, the saver has promised to save over a fixed period of time, as for instance with an assurance policy, or with a pension fund scheme. Whatever the level of the rate of interest, the saver will continue to save the same amount. So savings are influenced far more by the level of income (Y) than the interest rate. If incomes increase then economic units will tend to save more:

$$S = f(Y)$$

In the simplest Keynesian view, the savings function is given a specific formulation:

$$S = -a + \mathbf{s}\,Y$$

If income is zero, it is assumed that economic units will draw on their savings to maintain some minimum level of consumption (a). This is known as dissaving. In the equation, **s** is the marginal propensity to save (MPS)—that is, the proportion which is saved of a change in income. If income increases by £100, and savings by £30, then the MPS is 0.3. This must be distinguished from the average propensity to save which is defined as the proportion of total income which is saved. Mathematically:

$$MPS = \frac{\Delta S}{\Delta Y}$$

whereas

$$APS = \frac{S}{Y}$$

The simple Keynesian savings function can be represented graphically in Fig. 7.2. Note that the savings function (S) is expressed as a straight line. This reflects the simple Keynesian view that the MPS (given by the slope of the line) is constant. Just

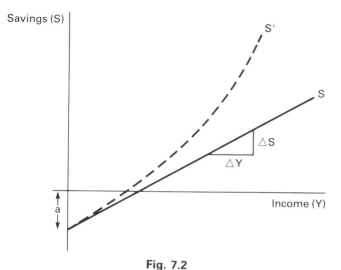

Savings (S)

ΔS
ΔY

Income (Y)

a

Fig. 7.2

as Keynesians believe that consumption is a stable function of income, so too do they believe that savings is a stable function of income.

However, many Keynesians would argue that although the MPS is stable over time, it does increase with income. Economic units with higher income will save more as a proportion of extra income earned than poorer economic units. Graphically, the savings function would then have the shape of S′ in Fig. 7.2.

Friedman's permanent income hypothesis is a theory of savings as well as a theory of consumption. The theory argues that:

1 In the short run, any unplanned increase in income will be saved. This results in the MPS of unplanned income being unity (1). Since unplanned income is not a constant proportion of total income, it also means that the MPS out of total income is not constant.

2 In the very long term, the MPS out of total income is zero. In general, economic units strive to pass on to their inheritors the same amount as they themselves gained from inheritance. Therefore over a lifetime, they will consume all of their income, and their savings will be zero.

3 In the medium term, savings will depend upon such factors as the rate of interest, permanent income, attitudes and habits of saving in the population, the development of means of savings in the economy, etc.

Data 7.2

Fall in people aged 45–64 is 'main cause of decline'

By Simon Holberton

THE DECLINE in the number of people aged 45–64 has been a principal cause of the fall in recorded savings in Britain during the 1980s, according to London Business School economists.

However, they say the level of savings will recover in the 1990s as the number of people in this age group rises.

The authors say the four main reasons cited for a decline in the rate of savings – mismeasurement of savings, financial deregulation, the house price boom and expectations of higher growth – are insufficient to explain the fall.

All have played a part, but the recent tightening in monetary policy should be enough to reverse the trend they started. High interest rates will depress consumption and house price rises and the rate of economic growth, which should help raise savings.

More important, however, is the growth in the numbers of people reaching the age of 45. The group aged between 45 and 64 tends to save more than younger and older groups, and it was this group that fell as a percentage of the population, during the 1980s.

The Financial Times. 27.2.89

1 *Account for the decline in the savings ratio in the UK in the 1980s.*
2 *Does the data support the view that the rate of interest is the most important determinant of savings?*

Savings and inflation

On neo-classical grounds, economists would expect high levels of inflation to reduce the marginal propensity to save. In times of high inflation, interest rates are often below the rate of inflation. This means that the real return is actually negative because the saver could buy more goods and services with his money now than in the future even with interest taken into account. Hence, the individual economic unit should be trying to reduce his savings to a minimum by buying up goods and services which can be stored for future use. However, in the mid 1970s when all industrialised countries experienced a high level of inflation, the propensity to save in these countries actually increased!

One theory put forward to account for this suggests that wealth might play an important part in determining savings. An economic unit is accustomed to holding a fixed proportion of its income in liquid assets—that is, financial assets which can be converted into money very quickly. One possible reason for this is fear of an uncertain future. People or firms like to feel that they have some savings to fall back on if their financial situation deteriorates. In times of high inflation, wages and profits tend to keep pace with the increase in prices. However, the value of their existing financial assets can not keep pace, the real rate of interest being negative; i.e. the

Data 7.3

Personal saving ratio (personal saving as a percentage of personal disposable income)

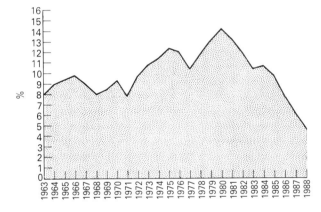

London clearing banks' deposit account (7 days' notice) rate of interest: last Friday of the year

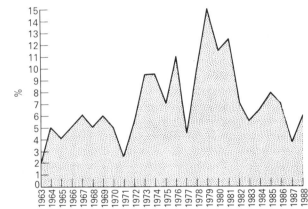

Inflation: Retail price index, percentage change

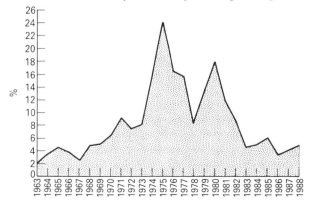

1 What evidence is there to suggest that personal disposable income is the sole determinant of personal saving?

2 To what extent does the data suggest that the rate of interest and inflation affect the average propensity to save?

Source: CSO, Economic Trends

inflation rate is higher than the actual rate of interest. Hence, the ratio of financial assets to income declines. Economic units attempt to remedy this by saving a bigger proportion of their income. They will continue to save more until the ratio returns to some acceptable level. This is unlikely to be as high as the previous ratio because the cost of maintaining this level of savings is now much higher. However, in the adjustment period the propensity to save will be much higher than normal. Economic units have to save doubly hard to make up for their losses due to inflation, as well as maintaining their existing savings commitments. Hence, the higher the rate of inflation, the higher will be the propensity to save.

Terms for review

savings

marginal and average propensities to save

Summary

Saving represents deferred consumption. Neoclassical economists argue that the rate of interest is the primary determinant of the level of savings, whilst Keynesians argue that its primary determinant is income. Keynesians see the marginal propensity to consume as being constant over time. Milton Friedman's permanent income hypothesis argues that this is not the case, because saving is a function not of measured income but of permanent income. There is strong evidence to suggest that high levels of inflation, leading to the erosion of the liquid wealth of economic units, result in a higher average propensity to save than would otherwise be the case.

Essay questions

1 Distinguish between the average propensity to save and the marginal propensity to save. What effect would a rise in the rate of inflation have on the average propensity to save?

2 What is meant by the 'savings function' of an economy? What effect would you expect (a) an increase in the mortgage interest rate and (b) a 20% cut in the real value of unemployment benefit to have on the level of savings in an economy?

8

Investment

Investment is not to be confused with saving. Economists define investment in terms of the creation of physical assets, whereas savings create financial assets. Therefore, a firm buying a new factory is investing, but a firm buying an existing factory is not investing. A consumer buying a new house is investing, but if he buys stocks and shares he is saving. A local authority building a new school is investing, but only pieces of paper are brought into existence when a government nationalises a company. Investment must also be distinguished from consumption. If investment takes place, it implies that goods have been brought into existence which will allow a stream of other goods and services to be produced in the future: for instance, a new factory manufacturing goods over the next ten years, a new school providing 20 or more years of education.

A further distinction must be made—that between **gross investment** and **net investment**. Investment goods depreciate in value every year. In other words, their market value lessens compared to a brand new replacement item. Eventually the good will wear out and be worthless. Gross investment is the value of total investment over a period of time. Net investment is gross investment less the value of **depreciation** of capital over the time period. Depreciation is sometimes called capital consumption. Investment is sometimes called capital formation.

Under what circumstances would these items be classified as investment rather than consumption?

Capital

Capital is the accumulated physical wealth of economic units. Roads, schools, factories, canals, houses, office blocks and shops are all examples of capital. Net investment is the addition to the capital stock of a country, i.e. investment after the value of the depreciation of the capital stock has been taken away. The desired capital stock of an economy is the value of the capital stock which economic units are prepared to hold. Actual capital is the existing stock of capital in the economy. If actual capital is less than desired capital, economic units will invest until the two are equal.

Sometimes, firms refer to their **working capital**.

This refers to money which a firm uses to pay its day-to-day bills. However, working capital is not capital in an economic sense as it does not represent real physical assets.

Three main groups in the economy undertake investment activity:

1 Private households Strictly speaking, expenditure on consumer durables such as television sets and freezers should be classed as investment expenditure rather than consumption. This is because consumer durables yield a stream of services over a long period of time. Traditionally, however, these items have been included in consumption.

There is one major item of household spending which is recognised as investment, and that is

Data 8.1

UK gross domestic fixed capital formation by asset, 1965 and 1988 (£ million at 1985 prices)

1965

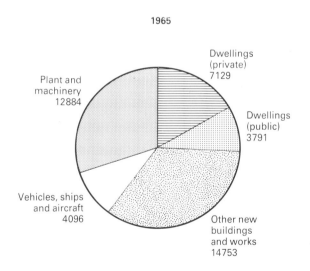

Plant and machinery 12884
Dwellings (private) 7129
Dwellings (public) 3791
Vehicles, ships and aircraft 4096
Other new buildings and works 14753

Total 42689

1988

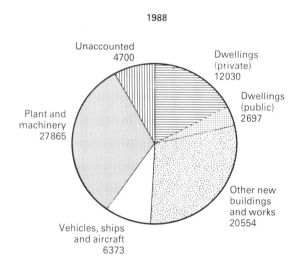

Unaccounted 4700
Dwellings (private) 12030
Dwellings (public) 2697
Plant and machinery 27865
Other new buildings and works 20554
Vehicles, ships and aircraft 6373

Total 74219

Source: CSO, Economic Trends

1 Describe the composition of UK investment in 1988.
2 What factors might have influenced the change in composition of investment between 1965 and 1988?

expenditure on new housing stock. When a second-hand house is bought and sold, no investment takes place because no new assets have been brought into existence. All that has happened is that some pieces of paper have changed hands. When a new house is built and paid for, a real asset has been created and investment has taken place.

Several factors can be singled out which determine the level of investment in new housing stock. Firstly, the rate of interest is important. The higher the rate of interest, the higher the cost of mortgage repayments, and hence the lower will be the demand for home loans. The price of new housing is important too: the higher the price, the lower the demand. If the price of comparable second-hand houses is below that of new houses, buyers will tend to prefer to buy a second-hand home rather than buy a new one. The greater the price difference between existing houses and higher priced new houses, the lower will be the demand for new houses. The reverse is also true if existing houses are dearer than new ones. Consumer incomes will also affect demand: the higher the consumers' income, the higher will be their demand for housing in general and new houses in particular.

2 The public sector The government undertakes considerable investment expenditure itself on such items as new schools, new hospitals and new office blocks. Public sector investment is normally considered to be determined by political factors rather than by economic ones. It can be argued that the level of national income is an important determinant of the level of public sector investment as the higher the level of national income the higher will be the value of taxes bringing revenue to the government. On the other hand, the government could just as well choose to lower taxes or to cut borrowing as to increase public sector investment.

3 Private sector corporate investment The word 'investment' is often used simply to designate investment by firms. As has been shown, investment is much mor~ ~his. However, theories of investment ~ ~ concentrate on trying to ex~ ~porate investment. Two main ~ have been put forward. The ~ s related to the rate of in~ ~y neo-classical economists ~ted by many monetarist ~at investment is a func-~closely associated with

Marginal efficiency of capital theory

If money is lent out, it is normal to expect a return on it. That return is called the rate of interest. Similarly, if a businessman invests, he expects to make a profit on that investment. Before investing, the businessman should attempt to estimate the average rate of return on that investment over its lifetime. For instance, it would make little business sense for him to undertake new investment which only brought a return of 2% a year when he could save his money in a bank deposit account yielding 10% a year. In fact, it would make little sense for him to undertake any investment whose average yield was below the current level of the rate of interest. On the other hand, any investment project which yields more than the current rate of interest could be undertaken profitably. For even if the company did not have the money to pay for the cost, it could always borrow the money, and its true profit would be the difference between the yield on the investment and the interest to be paid on the borrowed money.

Assume that at interest rate r_1 in Fig. 8.1, the desired stock of capital in the economy is C_1. If the rate of interest falls to r_2, then those investment projects which had a rate of return between r_1 and r_2 would now become profitable. Hence, the desired stock of capital would increase, let us assume to C_2. This can be generalised and it can be said that any fall in the rate of interest will raise the desired stock

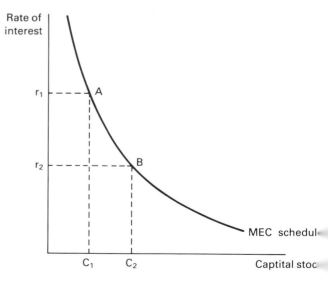

Fig. 8.1

of capital and vice versa. The line showing the relationship between the desired stock of capital and the rate of interest is called the **marginal efficiency of capital schedule** (MEC). As can be seen from Fig. 8.1 it is downward sloping. C_1C_2 represents new investment undertaken when the rate of interest falls from r_1 to r_2. Disinvestment of C_1C_2 would occur if interest rates were to rise from r_2 to r_1—that is, firms would not replace worn-out machinery, buildings, etc., until such time as their actual stock of capital were to match their desired stock of capital at C_1.

However, whilst it is true that changes in the rate of interest can cause changes in investment, other factors influence the location of the MEC schedule. These include:

1 The price of capital If investment goods, such as machines or factory buildings, became cheaper, investment projects would become more profitable, assuming the full value of the reduction were not passed on to the consumer in the form of lower prices. In this case, the MEC schedule would shift to the right (from MEC_1 to MEC_2 in Fig. 8.2). There are now more profitable projects than before at the same rate of interest and hence the desired stock of capital will increase. The reverse is also true. It might pay the company to get rid of workers and replace them by capital, if capital were now relatively cheap compared to labour. This would raise the desired stock of capital at a given interest rate.

There is also a relationship between investment and the price of existing second-hand capital. A firm might wish to expand and has the choice either to build from scratch or take over an existing firm. A good indication of the price of existing firms is given by the value of shares on a stock exchange. Assume that the book value of a firm's assets (that is, the

---

Data 8.2

Shell coaxes star performance from reduced cast

Shell is expected to announce today a number of possibilities for new capital projects at Carrington near Manchester.

The chemical complex at Carrington is one of Britain's biggest chemical production sites. Today it is making a profit but between 1980 and 1984 the site lost £150m.

Many of the moves at Carrington mirror events in the chemicals sector generally. In the early 1980s, demand for many bulk chemicals plummeted. The industry, faced with widespread overcapacity, plunged into a gloomy period of falling sales and wafer-thin profits.

Carrington was no exception to the general pattern. Faced with the decline in fortunes at the site, Shell considered closing it.

Instead, the company cut the workforce and insisted that all remaining employees agreed to work on a highly flexible basis.

Partly because of that – but also because of the better market conditions for many bulk chemicals in the past two years – Carrington now has a bright future. Shell is considering a range of new investments. It is already spending £48m on a new plant at Carrington to make polypropylene. It is now considering building a pipe line to bring ethylene, the main raw material for polyethylene, from Britain's main ethylene production facilities on Teesside and in Scotland.

Carrington currently makes about 100,000 tonnes a year of polyethylene, nearly a fifth of Britain's total output of the material. Any new investment at Carrington could be expected to lead to a substantial increase in the plant's polyethylene output.

In recent years, UK demand for the plastic has risen considerably faster than domestic supply. That has benefited big overseas makers such as Dow Chemical of the US.

However, Mr Stuart Warmsley, a chemicals-industry analyst at Morgan Stanley, said that Shell would be unwise to consider anything more than a small increase in polyethylene capacity.

Polyethylene production capacity worldwide was likely to increase by nearly 30 per cent by 1992. If all those projects went ahead, prices might fall, causing a nosedive in chemicals industry profits, in much the same way as in the early 1980s.

The Financial Times. 27.2.89

1 How can economic theory explain why Shell is considering making investments at its Carrington plant?

2 Use marginal efficiency of capital theory to explain why Shell nearly closed down the plant in the early 1980s.

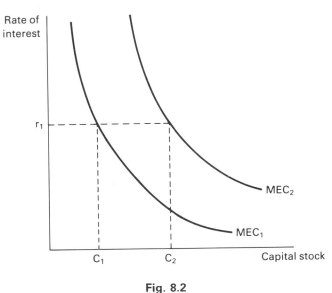

Fig. 8.2

This would mean that some projects would now be shelved, which before would have gone ahead as being profitable. This would be represented by a leftward shift in the MEC schedule, from MEC_2 to MEC_1 in Fig. 8.2 for instance. Increased pessimism might also make businessmen more cautious. Their reward or premium for risk taking would need to be increased. This too would effectively shift the MEC schedule to the left. If business confidence changes constantly in an economy, then the MEC schedule will also shift constantly. As a result, changes in the rate of interest would be only a minor factor in determining investment, and there would be little apparent relationship between interest rates and investment.

3 Technology A change in the level of techno-logy, such as the introduction of the microchip, might affect the MEC schedule too. If it resulted in higher profits for the firm, the MEC schedule would shift to the right.

4 Government policy A fall in company taxation will increase the rate of return on business invest-ment and so increase the desired stock of capital. A rise in investment grants given to industry on new investment projects will increase profitability too, and so increase the desired stock of capital. It will also reduce the price of capital relative to labour and thus encourage firms to substitute capital for labour

value that the company places upon itself) is higher than its stock exchange valuation. Then another firm wishing to expand in that field would do better to buy the existing firm than to invest in new plant and machinery. If the book value were lower than the stock market valuation, it would pay the ex-panding firm to invest in new plant and machinery and ignore the existing company.

The price of shares in a company depends upon a great many factors. Keynes once called the London Stock Exchange a 'casino', emphasising the unpre-dictability of price movements. He very much be-lieved that prices were determined by what inves-tors believed to be true rather than what actually was true. If investors became pessimistic about the future, share prices would fall even if their fears were groundless. Other economists argue that the market value of company shares is more soundly based on reality.

2 'Animal spirits' Keynes believed strongly that businessmen's attitudes and expectations (which he called their 'animal spirits') played a major role in determining the value of key variables in the eco-nomy. When assessing the rate of return on future investment project, a certain amount of guesswork is inevitable. If businessmen became more pessimis-tic about the future, they would downgrade their estimation of future revenue from a project and hence the expected rate of return would decline.

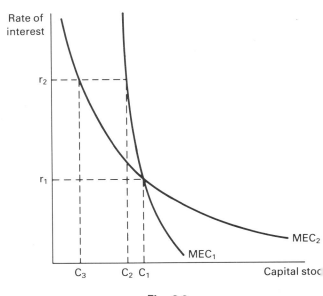

Fig. 8.3

Data 8.3

Interest rates will not hurt underlying growth

BY DAVID LOMAX

The British economy is now in the middle of a major adjustment, with sharp rises in interest rates intended to reduce consumption and bring demand back to a sustainable level. It is natural to fear that this process may damage our long-term prosperity by reducing severely the corporate sector's profits and investment. Is this so? The evidence suggests not.

A major cause of investment and regional expansion is the pressure on companies to move staff, offices and factories away from London and the south east to take advantage of lower costs in the rest of the country. This force is still very powerful.

A second dynamic force is investment by companies in order to do something more efficiently, or to produce new modern products. This incentive still exists, and much of the technological investment down the M4 corridor is of this nature.

Third, revolutions are still happening in two major industries: retailing and leisure. The expansion of superstores and supermarkets is by no means complete, and the leisure industry is being revitalised in much of the country.

Fourth, some investment in the UK is part of the worldwide allocation of assets by major groups, particularly with a view to finding long-term profit opportunities in a stable political environment.

Fifth, only a small proportion of investment in the UK is aimed at the short-term consumer market. A more substantial proportion is for the longer term UK domestic market or for the worldwide or European markets, perhaps with a view to 1992. Much of the investment by foreign companies in the UK would be for a European or global market-place, as for example the investment by Toyota. This investment stream is totally unaffected by UK short-term demand policies. The UK is now the biggest single recipient in Europe of Japanese investment, and this and similar sources have been major contributors to output and jobs in Wales and the north east.

In conclusion, policy is affecting demand much as intended. Consumer spending is being squeezed, but regional and industrial evidence indicates that the dynamic forces acting on the UK economy are still extremely strong and are largely unaffected by the rise in short term interest rates.

The Financial Times. 8.3.89

1 *Using diagrams, explain why the author suggests that investment is 'largely unaffected by the rise in short term interest rates'.*

2 *Do you think his conclusion would have been different if UK interest rates stayed high over a considerable length of time?*

---

5 National income Neo-classical economists would argue that national income might affect the MEC schedule but it is not the major determinant of investment. This will be further discussed below, as Keynesians believe that it is far more important than the rate of interest.

If it is true that the rate of interest is not a major determinant of investment, then investment can be said to be interest-inelastic. In Fig. 8.3, MEC_1 is relatively inelastic, whereas MEC_2 is relatively elastic. If investment is interest-inelastic, then a rise in interest rates from r_1 to r_2 would only reduce investment by C_1C_2; whereas, if it were interest-elastic, investment would be reduced by C_1C_3.

The accelerator theory

Keynesian economists have argued that national income is a more important determinant of investment than the rate of interest because:

1 Fast increases in national income would allow firms to make good profits. Since a majority of funds for company investment come in fact from retained profits (that is, profits which are not given out to shareholders but retained by the firm), high levels of profits are likely to lead to high levels of investment.

2 Fast increases in national income may lead

Investment

businessmen to be more optimistic about the future than slow increases. This will lead them to be optimistic about future returns on investment projects and help increase the level of investment.

3 Often the cost of money, i.e. the rate of interest, is only a very small part of the total cost of an investment project. Hence changes in the cost of money are unlikely to have a major impact on investment expenditure.

4 In calculating the desirability of going ahead with an investment project, businessmen often use other methods than the rate of return method. Hunches

Data 8.4

Gross domestic fixed capital formation: (at 1985 prices)

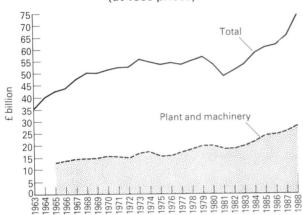

Change in gross trading profits of companies and financial institutions

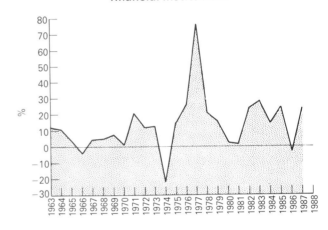

Change in gross domestic product at factor cost (at 1985 prices)

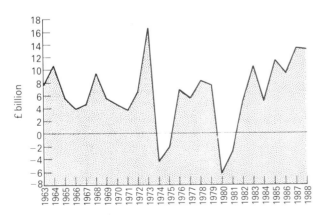

Industrial securities: Debentures: Average yield

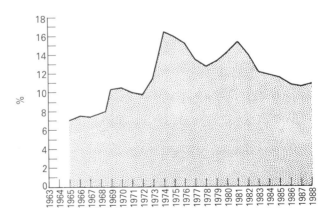

Source: CSO, Economic Trends, Annual Abstract of Statistics

1 What evidence is there that investment is dependent upon:
   a) past changes in income?
   b) the rate of interest?
   c) profitability?

based on the current economic climate and particularly on current national income are far more important, particularly for the small businessman.

The **accelerator theory** argues that investment is a function of past changes in income. The simplest form is:

$$I_t = k(Y_t - Y_{t-1})$$

In other words investment in one time period (I_t where t stands for a time period) is equal to some constant k (often called the accelerator coefficient) times the change in national income over the previous time period ($Y_t - Y_{t-1}$). The equation argues that if national income rises, investment will also have to increase to produce the extra goods and services that consumers are demanding. The accelerator coefficient, k, is the capital–output ratio, i.e. the capital needed to produce a given quantity of output. If for instance it is 2, then an extra £2 000 million of investment goods will be required to help produce a £1 000 million rise in national income.

There are a number of problems with this simple accelerator theory, quite apart from the fact that no real economy seems to repond in the way described:

1 It is not necessarily true that there is some constant relationship between capital (investment) and output (changes in national income). For instance, firms might choose to introduce extra labour shifts rather than buy in extra machines, when they wish to increase output.

2 If the economy is working with spare capacity—that is, not all workers or existing machines are in full use—a rise in income will simply result in existing capital being more fully utilised. No new investment need take place.

3 When businessmen make their investment decisions, e.g. buying plant and machinery which could last for the next 20 years, they are most unlikely to make such decisions on the basis of only one year's change in national income.

4 It is most unlikely that the capital goods industry will be able to meet the surges in demand for new plant and machinery predicted by the accelerator. Desired investment plans could not be realised as delivery dates would be too long.

5 The equation only works when the change in national income is positive. If it is negative—that is, national income actually falls over the period—

businessmen cannot disinvest in the same way that they can invest. Firms can disinvest by not replacing worn-out capital, i.e. depreciation will exceed gross investment. It is rare for industry to destroy capital. Even if a firm goes bankrupt, its capital is more likely to be sold off than to be destroyed.

Keynesian economists would readily admit to all of these criticisms. However, they argue that the problem with this simple accelerator model is just that it is far too simple. More complicated models, with changes in current investment being linked to changes in income over several time periods, are more realistic. Moreover, even if an exact relationship cannot be found, it is still true to say that investment is far more influenced by changes in national income than by changes in the rate of interest.

Summary

Investment and saving are two terms used with precise and different meanings by economists. Investment is the creation of new physical assets. Three sectors in the economy undertake investment: the personal sector in housing, the public sector in hospitals, schools, roads, etc., and the corporate sector in plant, machinery, offices, etc. Two main theories of investment determination have been outlined. The marginal efficiency of capital theory argues that investment is primarily a function of the rate of interest. The accelerator theory argues that investment is determined by past changes in income.

Terms for review

gross and net investment or capital formation

depreciation or capital consumption

capital

marginal efficiency of capital

accelerator theory

Essay questions

1 Outline a theory of investment determination. What effect might you expect a rise in public sector investment to have on private sector investment?

2 What is meant by 'investment' in the UK economy? To what extent can investment be said to be interest–inelastic?

9

The public sector

Introduction

The public sector is that sector of the economy owned and controlled by government. In a typical western developed economy it has three parts:

1 Central Government, taxing and spending across the whole economy.

2 Local Government, taxing and spending in a local area. There are often several tiers of local government, each tier responsible for providing different services in different sized areas.

3 Government-owned enterprises, agencies and bodies. These are accountable to government, either local or central, but to a greater or lesser extent are otherwise free to manage their own affairs. They may provide goods or services free to the public or may price their activities. Equally they may receive their income from government revenues, may charge for their output or may have the power to raise taxes in their own right.

In this chapter we will be particularly concerned with the activities of central and local government. State-owned enterprises are considered in Chapter 28 on 'Markets and Efficiency'.

Types of public spending

No Government in the world provides all goods and services to its citizens. In advanced Western economies, there is a common core of spending in the public sector. This comprises:

1 Defence—army, navy and airforce.

2 Law, order and protective services—including the police, the judiciary, prisons, and fire services.

3 Roads—only motorways and bridges are commonly owned by private interests.

4 Education—although there may be a large private sector education service too.

5 Environmental Services—the provision of parks, coastal protection, water and sewage disposal for example.

6 State Benefits—such as old age pensions, benefits for the handicapped and disabled, unemployment benefits, etc.

7 Health care—even in economies where private health care is the norm, there is always some public health provision, however inadequate this might be.

Government may also be involved in providing goods and services such as electricity, gas, telephone, television and radio, and postal services. In some economies, the public sector owns enterprises in a majority of markets in the economy. Equally there may be public expenditure on grants, subsidies and loans to private sector industry. Other areas of spending might include housing, museums, libraries, industrial training and social services.

Government spending may represent either **current** or **capital** expenditure. Current expenditure is expenditure on goods and services consumed within the accounting time period. For instance teachers' salaries, exercise books and chalk are all classified as current expenditure. Capital expenditure is investment in goods which will yield services over a long period of time. A new motorway, a new school or a new hospital are all items of capital expenditure.

A government needs to establish a correct balance

Data 9.1

Public expenditure, 1963 and 1988/9: £ millions[1]

1963
Total 10 380

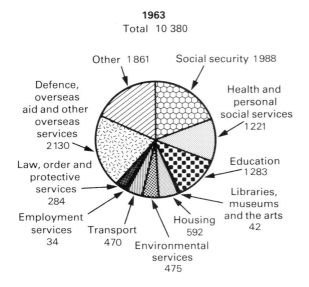

Other 1861
Social security 1988
Defence, overseas aid and other overseas services 2130
Health and personal social services 1221
Law, order and protective services 284
Education 1283
Employment services 34
Transport 470
Environmental services 475
Housing 592
Libraries, museums and the arts 42

1988/89
Total   148400

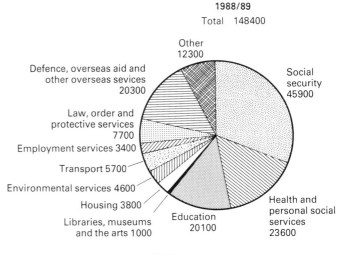

Other 12300
Defence, overseas aid and other overseas sevices 20300
Social security 45900
Law, order and protective services 7700
Employment services 3400
Transport 5700
Environmental services 4600
Housing 3800
Libraries, museums and the arts 1000
Education 20100
Health and personal social services 23600

[1] 1988/9 figures are estimated at 1986/7 prices

Source: CSO, Annual Abstract of Statistics, Social Trends

Change in gross domestic product at factor cost (at 1985 prices)

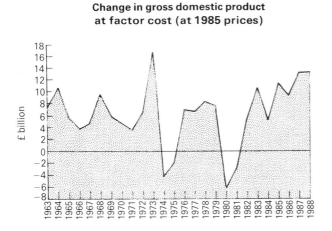

£ billion

Public expenditure as a percentage of GDP

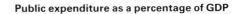
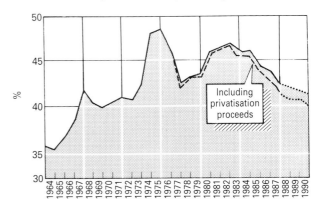

%

Including privatisation proceeds

Source: OECD; CSO, Economic Trends

1 Account for the change in (a) the composition, and (b) the size of public expenditure over the period 1963 to 1988/9.

2 Does the evidence suggest that increases in public spending cause lower economic growth?

between current and capital expenditures. If too few resources are devoted to capital expenditure, it will fail to provide an adequate social infrastructure for future generations. (Infrastructure means the roads, hospitals, sewers, canals, buildings, etc., of any economy, i.e. the man-made environment). This would have an important impact on the quality of the future labour force, the health of a country's citizens and the ability of industries to produce and transport goods efficiently. Too much capital expenditure will either result in undesirable high tax burdens or insufficient current spending. It is senseless to build schools if there is no money to pay for staff; it is senseless to build a new hospital if it stands idle because its operating costs cannot be paid for.

Public goods

All economists agree that governments should provide **public goods** (sometimes also known as **collective consumption goods**). A public good is a good or service which, once provided, benefits all citizens. A citizen cannot opt out of receiving the benefits given by a public good. Nor can his benefiting from the good mean that another citizen loses benefit from it, i.e. it is 'non-exclusive'.

The most clear cut example of a public good is defence. Once provided, no citizen can prevent himself from gaining greater security from foreign attack. The citizen may feel that defence spending puts him at greater risk from damage as a result of

Which of the items in the photograph would be classified as current expenditure and which as capital expenditure?

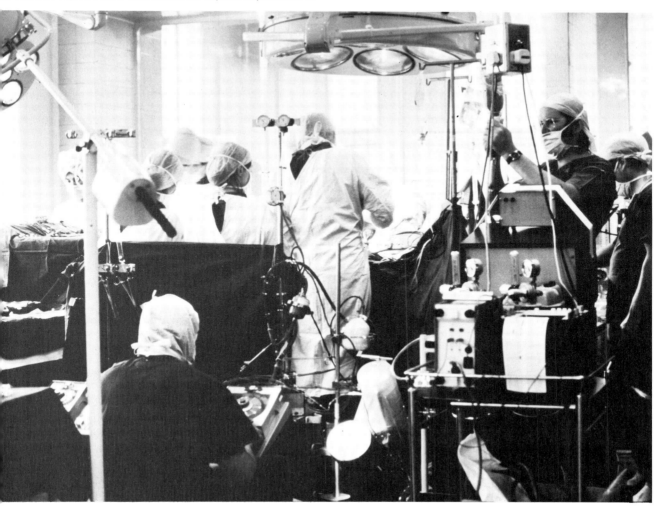

Data 9.2

Tight restraint on spending

CONTROLLING public expenditure is immensely difficult as well as important.

From decisions announced just two weeks ago one can expect more of the same. In the coming public expenditure round, the attempt will be made to keep within the plans for 1990–91 announced last autumn. After inflation of $5\frac{1}{2}$ per cent, "real" public expenditure (excluding privatisation receipts and debt interest payments) would then rise by no more than $1\frac{1}{2}$ per cent.

It appears, however, that the annual inflation rate in general government final consumption runs at almost $1\frac{1}{2}$ percentage points more than in the economy as a whole. This being so, the volume of public expenditure is set to remain static between 1989/90 and 1990/91.

Little Change

This would represent little change from the recent past. Under the present Government, public expenditure peaked as a share of GDP in 1982–83 at $46\frac{3}{4}$ per cent. Remarkably, the ratio fell to $39\frac{1}{2}$ per cent by 1988–89 and is expected to go on falling. It is now 9 percentage points lower than at the peacetime peak reached in 1975–76.

Over the six years, 1982–83 to 1988–89, public spending in real terms, even on the Government's calculations, rose by a mere 5 per cent. Once a more plausible deflator is used, the claimed real increase disappears.

Should this remarkable stringency be continued? Before leaving the Treasury, Mr Major made a speech arguing that "we now need to maintain our policy of restraint in public expenditure in order to produce a sustained reduction in the burden that taxes impose on wealth creating activities."

The argument is weak. Do education, training or public transport impose burdens on wealth creating activities? Are theme parks and casinos more valuable than schools and roads?

Key services

A more valid objection might be to the disincentive created by taxation. For the present Government, one might suppose that the solution to this problem would be to privatise the key services or at least substantially increase the inflow of private resources. But they remain in the public sector precisely because they are too politically sensitive to be left to private provision. It is strange to respond to that national consensus by starving them of resources.

Starved is what they have been. According to the Government's own calculations, expenditure in real terms on the Department of Transport fell by 18 per cent between 1982–83 and 1988–89; that on the Department of Education and Science rose by 9 per cent; and that on the Department of Health rose by 17 per cent. On the basis of more appropriate deflators, the volume of provision fell very sharply in transport, stagnated in education and rose quite modestly in health. Even in supposed priority areas, like education and health, expenditures as a share of GDP last financial year than in 1982–83.

The political system of the UK gives a government extraordinary power. But the power is not unlimited. The Government has been unable to privatise its obligations in health, education or transport, let alone abolish the welfare state. As a result, the UK is getting the worst of both worlds. Key obligations of the state are too sensitive to privatise and too burdensome to meet.

The Financial Times. 26.7.89

---

1 Describe what has happened to government expenditure during the 1980s.

2 Assess the arguments for and against zero growth in the volume of public expenditure.

---

attack, particularly nuclear attack. However, whether one views defence spending as adding to our welfare or detracting from it, no citizen can individually opt out of the benefits (or otherwise) provided. Nor, generally speaking, does providing defence for one citizen mean that there is less defence available for another. Other fairly clear examples of public goods are law, order and protective services.

However, many government-provided goods or services are not pure public goods—only a part of each is a public good. Medical care, for instance, has a direct benefit to individuals. If a hospital is treating one patient, another may have to go on a waiting list. Hence it is not 'non-exclusive'. But although the benefits of medical care directly accrue to individuals, there is a sense in which everybody benefits. In a welfare state, it is accepted that everybody is entitled to a minimum standard of living. If people are allowed to fall seriously or permanently ill through lack of medical attention, they will become burdens upon the state and its taxpayers. Everybody benefits if this is prevented from happening. Equally, everybody benefits if medical care can prevent contagious diseases. Everybody is at risk if people with such diseases are allowed to pass their infection on to others. Better still, if the medical system can vaccinate individuals, everybody benefits.

In education, too, there is a public good element. If everybody in the population can read and write, it means that communication is possible between individuals. Without that ability to communicate, everybody would suffer. However, education is also a private good because the main beneficiary of education is the individual receiving that education.

The state needs to provide public goods because otherwise they would either not be provided at all, or be underprovided. Consider the armed forces. If the state did not provide them, individuals would be most unlikely to pay for them. If a group of individuals did club together to provide resources it would be to the financial advantage of any individual who received the benefit of protection to opt out of payment. This is because the benefit would be there whether or not payment is made. This is known as the **free rider** problem.

Merit goods

Merit goods are goods or services which the government wishes to encourage citizens to consume. At their free market price, the government deems that insufficient would be demanded. So it encourages demand, either by subsidising the good or service or by making no charge for that good.

It has already been argued that part of health and education can be seen as a public good. The rest can be seen as merit goods. Governments tend to take the view that left to their own devices consumers would underconsume these services. This is because for much of their lives, consumers do not demand either medical care or education. They therefore do not set aside monies to pay for these services, and

Why is defence a pure public good? What economic justification might there be for Britain to ban all nuclear weapons?

Data 9.3

GLC makes grant of £700,000 to taxicab maker

BY KENNETH GOODING, MOTOR INDUSTRY CORRESPONDENT

The Greater London Council has made a £700,000 grant to Carbodies, the Coventry-based builder of London taxicabs.

The money will help pay for the design and tooling costs of modifications to a new taxi, due to go into production at the end of next year.

The taxi will be "stretched" to make it big enough to carry nearly all wheelchairs. The original design, based heavily on the Range Rover,

enabled the vehicle to take only standard-sized wheelchairs.

Carbodies has already received a £1.3m Department of Industry grant towards the taxi, known as the CR6. The Department has also offered more backing—the exact amount has not yet been revealed—but this still left part of the cost of "stretching" the taxi uncovered.

Mr Dave Wetzel, chairman of the GLC's Transport Committee, said

yesterday that the GLC stepped in to provide the necessary money because "cabs play a vital public transport role in the capital and it is crucial that disabled Londoners are able to enjoy the benefit of using the next generation of taxis."

Mr Grant Lockhart, managing director of Carbodies, said that the capability to carry most sizes of wheelchairs would add considerably to the CR6's export potential.

Mr Lockhart believes that exports can boost Carbodies' output—1,864 last year—by 20 per cent once the CR6 comes on stream. The company expects that half London's taxi fleet will have been replaced by CR6s by 1988.

The Financial Times. 17.3.83

1 Can taxicabs be classed as merit goods?

when these services are needed they are far too expensive to be met out of current personal income. Unless adequate provision has been made in years when no medical care or education was consumed, then consumers will be unable to pay for these services. Consumers are often short-sighted and are unable to budget over lengthy periods of time. Therefore governments tend either to provide such services themselves or make it compulsory for citizens to join insurance schemes to cover any eventuality.

Transfer payments

A transfer payment is a transfer of resources with no corresponding production of goods or services at the time of payment. A pension paid by the government to an individual is an example. The pensioner does not repay the government with goods or services in exchange for that pension (although they are likely to have made pension contributions when they were working in the past). On the other hand, a salary

paid to a teacher or an army officer is not a transfer payment because both workers have to produce services in order to receive their payments.

Transfer payments are a major component of current public expenditure in the UK economy. For instance, over one-quarter of all government expenditure (both current and capital) is accounted for by transfer payments. Transfer payments are usually given either to support those considered unable to earn a living—the handicapped, the unemployed, pensioners, and children—or to those whose existing incomes are insufficient to give them a minimum acceptable standard of living.

Transfer payments are used by governments to redistribute income within the economy. By taxing those in work, the government can afford to transfer resources to those who are either out of work or low paid. Some types of transfer payment are relatively uncontroversial because they are organised on an insurance principle. The state sets up a national insurance fund to which workers pay contributions and from which in return they receive benefits when they fall ill, or become unemployed or retire. The risks of illness, unemployment or retirement are fairly evenly spread across the working population and therefore contributors can see the need for belonging to such a scheme.

However, some transfer payments can be less popular: for instance those made to the low paid or to parents with children. This is because those who do not fall into those categories will be paying taxes and may never see any direct benefit. For instance, the better paid are unlikely to fall into the low pay category during their working life. Consequently they may find it unacceptable that their income is used to support the less well off.

The most common argument against this redistribution of income is that if an individual has worked to earn a certain sum of money, then that individual should be allowed to keep it. The state has no right to deprive him of his earnings to give to someone who has not earned so much. Whilst this argument has much common sense appeal, it is based on one very important assumption: namely that the workings of the free economy provide a correct and justifiable distribution of income. This is most unlikely to be the case, since the free market throws up a constantly varying pattern of income distribution over time and place. What those in favour of state redistribution need to show, however, is that the distribution of income after redistribution is 'better' (i.e. leads to a higher level of economic welfare) than before.

Types of taxes

In order to finance expenditure, governments need to raise taxes. Taxes may be direct or indirect; or proportional, regressive or progressive.

Today **direct taxes** in developed countries are taxes on income or wealth. They are 'direct' because they are levied directly on economic units who are normally responsible for paying the resulting tax straight to the tax-levying authority. Common direct taxes are taxes on personal income, on capital gains and company profits. Wealth is taxed either as a percentage of wealth owned, or more commonly on transfer to another, usually at death. The UK is unique amongst developed countries in also levying a poll tax—a fixed tax paid by each adult in the population irrespective of income.

An **indirect tax** is a tax on goods or services. In general, the sellers of these goods and services pass on those taxes to the tax-levying authority. However, not all indirect taxes are paid in this way. Property taxes (known as 'rates' in the UK) are

taxes paid by households or firms on their ownership of property directly to government. Expenditure taxes can be 'ad valorem' or 'unit' taxes. An ad valorem tax is one where the tax is calculated as a percentage of the value of the good or service—VAT is an example of such a tax. A unit tax is one where a fixed tax is levied per unit sold. For instance a unit tax on a bottle of wine would be the same whatever the price of the bottle.

Proportional, regressive and progressive taxes are distinguished by the proportion or percentage of income that is paid in tax. A **progressive tax** is one where the proportion of income paid in tax rises as income rises. A **regressive tax** is one where the proportion of income paid in tax declines as income increases. A **proportional tax** is one where the proportion of income paid in tax remains constant at all levels of income. This is illustrated in Fig. 9.1. A common error is to define a progressive tax as one where the more that is earned, the more is paid in tax. This is an incorrect definition, because this rule also applies to nearly all regressive taxes too. A man may earn £10 000 and pay £2 000 of it in tax, i.e. the proportion paid is 20%. If his income doubles to £20 000 and he pays £3 000 in tax, then it is true to say that the more he earns the more he pays in tax. But the tax is actually regressive because the proportion of income paid in tax declines from 20% to 15%.

Taxes on income and wealth tend to be progressive. By giving tax allowances (sums of money on which no tax is paid), and by increasing tax rates at high levels of income or wealth, the tax can be administered so that higher income earners do pay a higher proportion of their income in tax. Indirect taxes, however, tend to be either proportional or

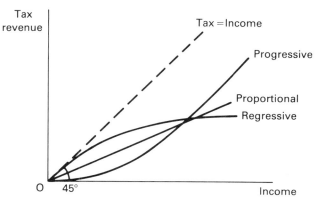

Fig. 9.1

Data 9.4

Poll tax

Figures published by the Environment Department show 53% of households in England will gain under the poll tax system which is due to replace domestic rates from 1990. For the average household with income of less than £50 a week, the average bill will fall from 4.1 per cent of its net income to 3.4 per cent under the new system. In the range £100–£150, the percentage will drop from 4.7 per cent to 4.6 per cent. Among high earners with incomes greater than £500 per week, the proportion will also fall – from 2.1 per cent under the rates system to 1.7 per cent with the community charge.

Financial Times. 14.1.88

The direct impact of the poll tax may be to increase house prices by some 20 per cent relative to earnings between now and 1995. This is because it will significantly reduce the cost of "trading up" in the housing market, particularly at the top end. The impact in London and the south-east will be greater than elsewhere, leading to a further widening in the gap between prices in those areas and the rest of the country.

The Financial Times. 11.6.88

The total cost of collecting the poll tax will be double that of collecting local authority rates according to a report commissioned by the Government. The higher total bill would occur because twice as many people would pay the charge as pay rates. The total cost of collecting the charge in 1990 would be between £379m and £435m, compared with the £200m a year to collect rates, the report continued.

The Financial Times. 24.6.88

Few, apart from members of the Thatcher government, have ever doubted that the poll tax violates accepted canons of fairness, leaving aside its many adverse economic effects. But there is another argument: accountability.

According to Mr Ridley, the Secretary of State for the Environment, "The Community Charge is a sort of pricing mechanism which regulates people's demand for services with their willingness to pay for them. Few argue that it is unfair for high-street shops to charge everyone the same for goods on sale. A Community Charge for local services is fair because we all choose to pay for the policies of the council we vote for." Moreover, "when everyone pays something towards the cost of services, the inefficient and unnecessary will seem far less attractive".

The Financial Times. 10.12.87

---

1 *To what extent would economic theory suggest that the poll tax is a "good" tax?*

---

regressive. This is because it is difficult to raise large sums of revenue except by taxing commodities bought by large sections of the population. It is administratively impossible to charge poor people a lower rate of expenditure tax than higher income earners: low and high income earners cannot be distinguished when they are buying a packet of cigarettes or a television set.

Principles of taxation Adam Smith in his book 'The Wealth of Nations' put forward four 'canons' or principles of taxation. These were:

1 The cost of collection should be low relative to the amount of tax yield.

2 The amount to be paid as well as the timing of collection should be clear and certain to all parties concerned.

3 The means of payment as well as the timing should be convenient to the taxpayer.

4 Taxpayers should pay taxes according to their ability to pay.

In addition modern economists argue that:

5 Taxes should be compatible with tax systems elsewhere in the world, to facilitate world economic co-operation and prevent tax evasion by international companies.

6 Taxes should not interfere with the workings of free markets, where there are no market imperfections present. In particular, high taxation should not discourage workers from working or entrepreneurs from taking risks.

7 Taxes should be able to withstand the effects of inflation. Taxes which automatically adjust in line with inflation are better than those whose tax revenue increases more or less than the inflation rate.

No tax possesses all of these qualities perfectly. In practice many taxes possess all too few of these characteristics. Tax reform is as old a topic as tax itself.

The allocative effects of taxation Taxes can have important effects upon the allocation of resources in the economy. Taxes raise costs. The result is likely to be a fall in demand in the relevant market. In particular:

1 Income taxes raise the cost of earning money and therefore may reduce workers' willingness to work.

2 Income and profit taxes are likely to discourage entrepreneurial activity; ('entrepreneurs' are businessmen willing to risk their financial capital in business ventures).

Data 9.5

The truth about tax cuts

By Michael Prowse

The fact that the share of tax contributed by top earners rose during the 1980s despite substantial cuts in top rates seemed to suggest that tax cuts had a positive impact on work effort, enterprise, risk aversion and so forth. Supply side economics seemed to be working.

History, however, surely casts doubt on this. In the three decades after the Second World War, tax rates in almost all countries were higher than ever before. Yet the world economy enjoyed its longest ever period of sustained prosperity.

Even the evidence in the rise in tax share by top income earners is doubtful.

The 1980s saw a large rise in unemployment, so the share of tax paid by high income earners is bound to have increased. Corporate profitability rose too, again inflating the income figures of the better off without indicating changes in work effort.

Quantitatively far more important, however, is that real earnings at the top of the income pile have increased about six times as fast as those at the bottom. Again this would automatically increase the share of tax paid by top earners.

Ah, but this misses the point, say the supply-siders. The rise in the relative earnings of the rich is a direct consequence of greater enterprise and effort on their part. Really? There is no direct

evidence that chief executives, for example, are working much harder than in the past; there is certainly no evidence that work effort or enterprise has kept pace with their soaring salaries and share bonuses.

It is surely at least as plausible to argue that demand factors (shortage of skills during an economic boom) and changing social norms (less embarrassment about inequality) lie behind the big pay increases awarded top earners.

Note that the 1979 tax changes had relatively little effect on the tax paid by different income groups until 1985–6, when the economic recovery was gaining momentum: this suggests that demand factors and not supply side factors were dominant.

The Financial Times. 2.12.88

1 *Use evidence from the data to suggest how income tax cuts since 1979 have changed the allocation of resources within the UK economy.*

3 Indirect taxes are likely to discourage consumption of particular goods or services. This may be desirable in the case of cigarettes or alcohol. It may be undesirable if it is an ordinary good or service.

A fuller analysis of the above is contained in Chapters 19, 28, 29 and 30.

Redistributing income   One of the major functions of government spending and taxation is to affect the distribution of income and wealth in the economy. Inequalities in income and wealth can have unacceptable consequences. People without income can die of starvation whilst a few miles away those on very high incomes may be enjoying a highly materialistic lifestyle. It is to prevent this sort of situation that all developed economies have sophisticated systems of protecting the poor against the worst aspects of poverty. The extent to which the poor are protected varies. In free market systems (where the public sector is relatively small, such as the USA and Canada) the poor receive far less protection than in mixed economies (where the public sector is nearly as large as the private sector, as in Western Europe). On the other hand, the tax burden on the relatively affluent is lower in North America than it is in Europe.

Economists who favour minimal intervention in income distribution argue that, in the long run, poverty is best alleviated through the free market system. The poor are likely to be better off through receiving the same percentage of a growing national cake than through taking a larger proportion of a fixed national income. The doubling of real incomes in nearly all Western economies between 1949 and 1974, for instance, brought undreamed-of benefits to all in society. Everybody benefited.

A very large assumption is made in this argument. It is that redistributing income in favour of the poor leads to lower growth. It is claimed that higher rates of tax for the better off will reduce their incentive to work and to take risks. Less work, and less risk-taking, results in lower growth. Moreover, it is likely that part of the redistribution will take the form not of extra handouts to the poor, but extra government spending on services. Better medical care, better education and more housing for the poor is all very well, but it is at the expense of private sector spending which includes investment. A loss of investment means fewer jobs, lower growth rates and continued poverty.

Advocates of greater equality dispute this chain of reasoning. They say that there is little evidence to suggest that work and risk incentives are significantly cut by higher taxes. Economies such as Germany, France and Sweden, which have high taxes to pay for their welfare states, have experienced similar or higher growth rates in the post-war period to that of the USA. Redistributing income in favour of the poor does not result in lower economic growth.

Moreover, poverty is not an absolute measure. One can only be poor relative to somebody else. The problem of poverty will always face society. 'Extreme poverty' meant starvation and death in Western Europe a hundred years ago. Today, 'extreme poverty' in Europe may mean living in a house with a shared toilet and other inadequate provisions. A hundred years from today, extreme poverty may mean owning only one car, living in a one-bedroomed flat and having only one continental holiday a year. The point is that the average citizen is able to enjoy a much higher standard of living, a style of living which carries with it prestige and status. Poverty can then be viewed not as some absolute measure (e.g. eating fewer than 1 000 calories a day) but as the inability of a citizen to participate fully in the society in which he lives (Examples of 'poverty' in the UK today might be not being able to afford a week's holiday, not being able to heat your house adequately, not being able to buy books). Economic growth cannot solve this problem. Only reducing inequalities can enable the poor to approach the full participation which is the norm for a society at a particular moment in time.

Governments reduce inequalities through taxation and public spending. A progressive taxation system will allow the government to finance its spending mainly by contributions from the better off. The poor can then receive benefits in the form of transfer payments, free education and free medical care to bring their standard of living up to a minimum acceptable level.

In practice, the redistribution of income works far less well than the above would suggest. Income taxes are progressive but high income earners become adept at evading or avoiding tax. The main burden of income tax tends to fall on the middle range of income earners. Indirect taxes tend to be at best proportional and at worst highly regressive. Value added tax (VAT) at a constant rate, such as 15%, is broadly proportional. Taxes on alcohol and tobacco are broadly regressive. Overall, tax regimes tend to be proportional or mildly progressive.

Government spending benefits the poor far less than one might initially imagine. Many transfer payments are made to households not in need. For instance, child benefits, student grants and old age pensions often go to all in these categories, regardless of income. Equally, government services may well benefit the better off more than the poor. The modern road network is geared to the needs of the private car, but many of the poor cannot afford cars. Expenditure on the police is far more important to those with property to protect than those whose few private possessions are not worth stealing. Equally it is the better off who have more to lose in time of war and possible conquest than the poor. So defence expenditure arguably benefits the rich more than the poor. On the whole, the 'social wage', the value of government spending to a household, forms a larger proportion of the income of the less well off than the better off, but it is not as weighted in favour of the poor as might at first seem the case.

There is no doubt that inequalities would increase in Western economies if governments did not redistribute income through their taxation and public spending programmes. However, some economies such as Sweden have gone much further down the road of equality than other economies such as the USA. Both of these countries enjoy some of the highest per capita incomes in the world today. It is ultimately up to the individual to decide which type of society he or she would prefer.

The economic functions of government

The government, then, has a variety of economic functions to perform. These can be summarised as:

1 Provision of public goods.

2 Provision of merit goods.

3 Provision of other goods and services as it deems fit.

4 Redistribution of income and wealth.

5 Management of the macro-economy. This function will be considered in more detail in Chapter 19.

6 Regulation of individual markets, so that the allocation of resources in each market results in optimum welfare. This point is more fully developed in Chapter 28.

Raising taxes and spending public money are the ways in which governments can achieve some of these aims. Of course, fiscal policy—taxation and public spending policy—is very crude. The sums involved are so large, the room for radical change so small, that governments are more often than not frustrated in achieving their desired objectives. Still, fiscal policy can work, and a policy which achieves some results is better than nothing at all.

Summary

Governments are responsible for providing a wide variety of goods and services in a typical modern economy. These include public goods and merit goods. The Government also provides a wide variety of transfer payments, chiefly to those in need. Taxes need to be raised to finance that expenditure. Taxes can be classified as direct or indirect and as progressive, proportional or regressive. Government spending and taxation help to redistribute income within an economy. However, fiscal policy is so crude that it is not as biased in favour of the poor as many would like or fear.

Terms for review

public sector	transfer payments
current and capital expenditure	direct and indirect taxes
public or collective consumption goods	progressive, proportional and regressive taxes
merit goods	canons of taxation
	distribution of income

Essay questions

1 What is meant by a 'public good'? To what extent is current UK public expenditure devoted to the provision of public goods?

2 Why do governments levy taxes?

3 Is there any economic justification for a government to increase economic inequalities in society? How could it achieve this?

10

National income measurement

Introduction

National income is a measure of the level of economic activity in an economy. It is an aggregate—that is, it is a sum of component parts. It is important for a number of reasons to measure national income. Firstly, economists need national income figures to be able to analyse the workings of the economy and predict future events. Secondly, the Government uses these figures to manage the economy. Management involves manipulating the economy to a more desirable state than it otherwise would have been in. Thirdly, national income is used as a measure of welfare. This will be discussed in more detail in the next chapter.

The circular flow of income

A useful way of considering the workings of the economy is through looking at the circular flow of income. Figure 10.1 shows a simple economy where there are only producers (firms) and consumers (households). Households supply the factors of production which they own, in return for payment. So land, labour and capital are exchanged for rent, wages, interest and profit. Firms in turn supply goods and services to households. Households then pay for those goods and services with the money they have earned from supplying their factors of production.

In this simple economy, money flows round the system. The total flow of money can be measured in three ways.

1 the **expenditure** on goods and services produced by firms;

2 the value of **output** of firms;

3 the **incomes** received by households.

In a real economy, the circular flow is far more complicated. For a start, two other important sectors of the economy are present: government, which spends and taxes; and the foreign sector, which exports and imports. Moreover, households and firms do not spend all of their income—they save. Firms also invest in new plant and machinery. Therefore, a more realistic circular flow of income is such as is given in Fig. 10.2.

As mentioned above, national income can be measured in three ways: as income, expenditure or output. These three methods will now be looked at in more detail.

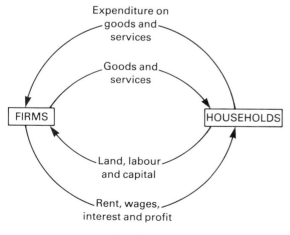

Fig. 10.1

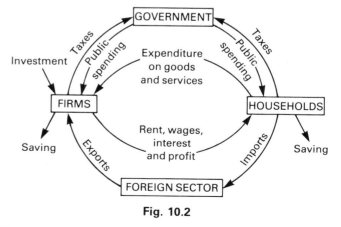

Fig. 10.2

National income measurement

Illustrate the circular flow of income from these photographs.

UNIT CODE	BRANCH WAGE No.	TAX WEEK	WEEK END DATE	
1202	05321	45	11.2.84	**co op**

EMPLOYEE NAME	MR. A. BROWN
UNIT NAME	CREWE TEA & COFFEE CENTRE
GROUP NAME	FOOD MANUFACTURING

STANDING WAGE/RATE 1	OTHER PAYMENTS 1	OTHER PAYMENTS 2	OTHER PAYMENTS 4	HOLIDAY PAY	TAXABLE EXPENSES	NON TAXABLE EXPENSES	STOPPAGES THIS PAY ONLY	NON TAXABLE PAY
84.74								

OVERTIME/RATE 2	RATE 3	RATE 4	RATE	SVNGS/RATE 6	RATE 7	RATE 8	OTHER PAYMENTS THIS PAY ONLY	TOTAL GROSS PAY
18.45				3.60				133.44

INPUT HOURS	TAX CODE	TAX	NATIONAL INSURANCES NUMBER	CODE	AMOUNT	COMPANY PENSION	VAC PENSION	OVER PAY LAST WEEK	OVER PAY THIS WEEK
37.45	0286H	21.5	KB043947C	A	11.99	6.34		0.15	0.20

CODE	AMOUNT	CODE	AMOUNT	CODE	AMOUNT	CODE	AMOUNT	CODE	AMOUNT	CODE	AMOUNT	TOTAL DEDUCTIONS
02	0.01	50	0.05									39.99

TAXABLE GROSS S WEEK	GROSS TO DATE	COMP. PENSION TO DATE	VAC. PENSION TO DATE	TAXABLE GROSS TO DATE	TAX TO DATE		NET PAY
127.10	5990.75	286.30		5704.45	966.30		93.50

CWS READING – 1/81 36665

SPECIMEN

Income

Income can be subdivided into several parts. Firstly, income is generated from labour services: income from employment and income from self-employment. Firms also generate income from the capital they employ. These are called 'profits' if the firms are in the private sector, or 'trading surpluses' if the firms are state-owned. Lastly, rent is received by land and property owners.

Two important points now need to be made. Firstly, many incomes must **not** be included in national income. These incomes are called **transfer payments** which, as we saw in Chapter 9, are payments which are made without any corresponding output. They include pensions, supplementary benefit and unemployment benefit, etc.

Secondly, firms hold stocks of goods either ready to sell or ready to be used in their own production processes. Due to inflation these stocks may well go up in value and this increase in value will be counted as part of the revenue of firms. This in turn will boost their profits. However, this 'stock appreciation' does not produce any corresponding output; after all, the goods have already been produced.

Data 10.1

CSO says figures understate growth

By Simon Holberton, Economics Staff

THE LEVEL of economic activity in Britain during the July to September period appears to have been about $3\frac{1}{2}$ per cent higher than the same period in 1987, according to heavily qualified official figures released yesterday.

The Central Statistical Office said it was unable to produce its usual average measure of Gross Domestic Product, because of "serious under-recording" of growth by one of its key measures of the economy which records national expenditure.

The office took the unusual step of giving a warning that it did not believe the expenditure figures it produced.

They did not "represent what was happening in the economy."

The output measure of the economy was the best guide to short-term trend in growth, it said. That measure, published last month, was revised down to show growth 4 per cent higher in the third quarter than a year ago and 1 per cent up on the second quarter.

The expenditure measure of GDP, which provides the most detailed breakdown of economic activity and is the one most used in economic models of the UK, suggests that Britain entered recession in autumn. According to GDP(E), economic activity in the third

quarter contracted by nearly 3 per cent compared with the March to June period and was 1 per cent lower than the same period in 1987.

The mismatch between the expenditure and income measures of GDP was, at £4bn or nearly 2 per cent of the economy, one of the biggest quarterly statistical discrepancies the CSO has been forced to declare. Theoretically, the three measures of GDP, income, expenditure and output, should equal one another.

Officials said that figures for government expenditure and investment were believed to be reliable, as were those for consumer expenditure. The latter was 6 per cent higher than a year earlier and 2 per cent higher than in the second quarter. That suggests that figures for private-sector investment and stock building – collected on a voluntary basis from a survey of industry – are the main source of the trouble. The survey might have failed to include increases in investment.

The Financial Times. 20.12.88

1 What factors helped GDP(E) to increase in 1987/8?
2 Why do estimates of national income, output and expenditure differ?

Therefore, stock appreciation needs to be subtracted from total income in order to produce an accurate income figure.

Expenditure

Expenditure can be split up into consumers' expenditure, government expenditure and investment. Investment on new plant and machinery is also known as 'fixed capital formation'. In addition, firms may buy stocks from other firms or 'buy' their own goods to put into stock. This expenditure by firms is known as the 'value of physical increase in stocks and work in progress'.

Expenditure by foreigners on our exports must be included in total final expenditure. On the other hand, not all expenditure is on domestically produced goods and services. So, to arrive at an accurate figure for the value of expenditure on domestic output, we must subtract the total value of imports.

Lastly, many goods and services are subject to taxes or subsidies. In the UK the main taxes on goods and services are VAT and excise duties. Some goods may be 'subsidised'—that is the government pays part of the cost of the good. Taxes and subsidies do not correspond to any output. Hence taxes need to be taken away from total expenditure whilst subsidies need to be added on. National income, inclusive of taxes and subsidies, is known as national income **at market prices**. National income exclusive of indirect taxes and subsidies is known as national income **at factor cost**.

Output or product

The final way of calculating national income is to add up the value of all the outputs of firms. **National product** can be calculated in one of two ways. Either it can be calculated by adding up the **value added** at each stage of production; or, the **final values** of goods or services can be added up. This is best understood by means of an example. Consider Sainsbury's plc selling tins of Heinz baked beans. Heinz might pay a total of 3p for items such as raw beans and tins bought in from outside. They process the product and sell it to Sainsbury's, for 12p. Sainsbury's then sells it to the public for 14p. The final value of the output of one tin is 14p. This can either be calculated by taking the final value of the product—

the 14p which Sainsbury's received for it—or it can be gained by adding the value added at each stage of production—3p (Heinz's suppliers) plus 9p (Heinz) plus 2p (Sainsbury's). Adding the total value of production at each stage (3p plus 12p plus 14p) would lead to an overestimation of national product. This is because part of the value of the good would keep on being added on again and again at each stage of production. A vast amount of double counting would take place.

Two provisos must be made. Firstly part of the total value of output will represent imported raw materials and semi-manufactured goods. So, the total value of imports must be subtracted from total output. Secondly, as with expenditure, any increase in the value of stocks must be deducted from total output. Note also that any stocks carried over from a previous accounting period must not be included in the value of the current period's output.

Other factors in national income measurement

So far, we have explained how to measure what is called **gross domestic product at factor cost** via the income, expenditure and output methods. To get a more complete measure of national income several other factors need to be taken into account.

1 Net property income from abroad Foreigners own assets such as factories or office blocks in Britain. Similarly UK residents own assets overseas. These assets earn interest, profits or dividends which belong to the owners. So in order to calculate the total income of an economy, the net property income from abroad must be included. By 'net' we mean the difference between income paid to UK residents, less income paid to foreigners. Hence:

$$\begin{matrix} \text{Gross} \\ \textbf{domestic} \\ \text{product} \end{matrix} \text{ plus } \begin{matrix} \text{net} \\ \text{property} \\ \text{income} \\ \text{from} \\ \text{abroad} \end{matrix} = \begin{matrix} \text{Gross} \\ \textbf{national} \end{matrix} \begin{cases} \text{income} \\ \textbf{expenditure} \\ \text{product} \end{cases}$$

2 Depreciation or Capital Consumption Each year, the value of the nation's existing physical assets declines. This is because physical assets such as factories, machinery, hospitals and houses

Data 10.2

UK National Income, 1987, (£ millions at current prices)

Expenditure		Income		Output	
Consumers' expenditure	258 431	Income from employment	226 343	Agriculture, forestry and fishing	5989
General government final consumption	85 772	Income from self employment	32 959	Production industries	117 999
Gross domestic fixed capital formation	70 767	Gross trading profits of companies	65 596	Construction	21 486
Value of physical increase in stocks and work in progress	627	Gross trading surpluses of public corporations and general government enterprises	6446	Services	206 763
Total domestic expenditure	415 597				
Exports of goods and services	107 506	Rent	24 798		
Total final expenditure	523 103	Imputed charge for consumption of non-trading capital	3235		
		Total domestic income	359 377		
Less imports of goods and services	− 112 030	Less stock appreciation	− 4858		
Gross domestic product at market prices	411 073	Statistical discrepancy	− 2282		
Statistical discrepancy	3382				
Less taxes on expenditure	67 980				
Plus subsidies	5762				
Gross domestic product at factor cost	352 237	Gross domestic product at factor cost	352 237	Gross domestic product at factor cost	352 237
Net property income from abroad	5523				
Gross national product at factor cost	357 760				
Less capital consumption	− 48 238				
National income	309 522				

Source: National Income Blue Book

1 From the data, calculate:
   a) net domestic fixed capital formation;
   b) gross national product at market prices; and
   c) gross domestic product at factor cost assuming that the income method is the most accurate way of measuring national income.

deteriorate in much the same way as do certain consumption items such as cars or television sets. A one-year-old car is almost certain to be of more value than a similar five-year-old car. The value of this decline in assets is known as **depreciation** or **capital consumption**.

Gross national income is income before depreciation has been taken into account. Net national income (or 'national income') shows the figure after depreciation has been deducted. Depreciation represents a fall in the value of a nation's capital stock. If it were not deducted, the nation would be counting as income what is in fact a reduction in its assets. It would be as if an individual included in income for the year a £1,000 withdrawal from his savings. The nation's wealth represents the accumulation of past income. National income is income over the current time period. Therefore deductions in wealth, i.e. depreciation, must be distinguished from what is currently produced and earned:

$$\mathbf{Gross} \begin{Bmatrix} \text{income} \\ \text{expenditure} \\ \text{product} \end{Bmatrix} \mathbf{less} \begin{matrix} \text{capital} \\ \text{consumption} \end{matrix} = \mathbf{Net} \begin{Bmatrix} \text{income} \\ \text{expenditure} \\ \text{product} \end{Bmatrix}$$

The accuracy of national income statistics

In practice national income statistics do not provide an accurate guide to the total level of incomes, output and expenditure in the economy. This is due to a variety of reasons:

1 The basis of the statistics themselves is inaccurate. The government relies for information upon millions of individual returns from a wide variety of sources. Individuals have two good reasons for failing to provide correct information. Firstly, making a return to the Government is itself time-consuming. It represents a time cost to the company or individual. Therefore, they attempt to cut through the 'red tape' by not returning forms or returning them with perhaps inaccurate information hastily jotted down by some junior in the firm. Secondly, returning accurate information may damage the interests of the individual. The main reason is that national income statistics are largely compiled from tax sources. Individuals obviously have an interest in declaring less income, lower sales, or lower output, than they actually have. Measured national expenditure, then, never equals measured national

Data 10.3

The Treasury fish that got away is probably bigger in the story than in the water

Victor Keegan

Few subjects generate such a head of steam from such a paucity of facts as the so-called "black economy" of moonlighting and tax avoidance. It has been estimated to account for anything from 2 to 15 per cent of the entire economy. Some see it as evidence of the moral decline of the nation. Others hail it as the source of ultimate salvation—a resurgence of entrepreneurial activity sheltered from the disincentive influence of the tax man. It is even seen as a harbinger of fundamental economic change—a slow relapse into the "informal economy" of the earlier centuries after 200 years or so of formal activity.

There is only one important ingredient which black economy stories lack: reliable information. Nobody actually knows how big the black economy is at the moment, let alone how large it was 10 or 20 years ago.

Most estimates of its size derive from dubious deductions from national incomes statistics which are themselves prone to errors almost as large as the estimates of the informal economy. Some of the higher estimates are particularly suspect.

Professor Edgar L. Feige, the US economist, reckons that black activity accounts for at least 15 per cent of the UK national income—twice the size of

the guess of 7½ per cent made by the head of the Inland Revenue. If the higher calculation were true it would mean that every household in the UK spent about £1,500 a year on black economy goods. Is that really plausible?

Many people think the black economy is bigger than it is simply because they now own their own houses (and therefore come into contact with the "black" jobs associated with house improvement) whereas 20 years ago they didn't own a house and so hardly ever came across such activity. The black economy may have risen as a proportion of their outgoings but it does not follow that it is growing for the nation as a whole.

As the Institute for Fiscal Studies observed, the black economy can be large enough to yield several billions of pounds of rich anecdotes without adding up to a significant percentage of the economy. The case that higher taxes have produced a sharp growth in the black economy is not yet proven.

The Guardian. 17.5.82

1 Why does the existence of the black economy affect recorded national income?

2 How might one attempt to measure the size of the black economy?

income; neither does it equal national output, even though, theoretically, this is an impossibility. In the UK, an average estimate of income, output and expenditure is produced, and the three measures of national income are made equal by adding or subtracting a 'statistical discrepancy' to each.

The size of the 'hidden' or 'black' economy—the economy which does not show up in the statistics—is naturally difficult to estimate. However, in the UK a possible figure could be about 7% of GNP. In some economies it is much higher. Italy's black economy could well be about 20% GNP. The number of workers and consumers in the black economy is likely to grow as tax and welfare regimes become more onerous and more complicated. The painter who decorates the home in return for £500 by cheque or £400 in notes, or the car mechanic who 'helps' his customers in his spare time at a price, is likely to become a more frequent phenomenon in the future.

2 Much work is done by individuals for themselves. For instance, a man may keep house or a woman may mend her car. This economic activity goes unrecorded. If a woman takes her car to the garage for a service, that should be recorded as part of national income. If she services her car herself, there will be no official record of the work done, and therefore her labour will not appear in the statistics. One of the easiest ways of raising national income overnight would be to pass a law forcing husbands to pay a wage to housewives for the work they do. Yet this rise in national income would not mean that any more goods and services were being produced. In poor third world countries, this problem is very important because so much is produced within the subsistence economy. It is therefore not 'traded' and not included in national income statistics.

3 The individual may also engage in voluntary work. Working for a charity, help with fund raising at school or just repairing the fence for the retired person next door are also examples of services being produced which are not recorded in national income statistics.

Summary

National income can be measured in three main ways. The expenditure method takes into account consumption, investment and public sector current expenditure as well as the net value of foreign trade. The income method uses incomes, profits and rents earned domestically as its basis. The total value of output is measured by the output method. It has been argued that all three measures need to take into account net property income from abroad and capital consumption. Lastly it has been shown that national income statistics present a very incomplete picture of the value of incomes, expenditure and output in the economy.

Terms for review

national income

circular flow of income

factor cost and market prices

value added

property income from abroad

gross domestic product and gross national product

hidden or black economy

Essay questions

1 How is national income measured? Explain how the growth of (a) DIY (do-it-yourself) activities and (b) the 'black' economy affect the various measures of national income.

2 Distinguish between gross domestic product at market prices and national income. Why is it important to measure national income?

11

Growth

Introduction

Economic growth is generally measured in terms of changes in real national income. A constant 2% growth rate would imply that each year 2% more goods and services were available for distribution in the economy. It will be argued later in this chapter that economic growth provides an important way of improving the standard of living within an economy.

Table 11.1 shows five economies growing at different rates. The zero growth economy (A) maintains a constant national income of index number 100. At a modest 2½% growth rate—the average growth rate experienced by the UK economy in the 1950s and 1960s—the economy (C) has over a quarter more goods and services available for distribution at the end of ten years. The 10% 'miracle' growth economy (E)—growth rates achieved by Japan, Taiwan and Singapore at the height of their growth success in the post war period—has increased its national income by a staggering two and a half times. A 2½% growth rate (C) will double national income every 28 years. It only takes 7½ years to double national income at 10% growth rates. So differences in growth rates can seriously affect relative living

standards between countries. The UK had one of the highest national incomes per head of the population in Western Europe in the 1950s. But it also had one of the slowest growth rates. By the early 1980s, it had one of the lowest national incomes per head in Western Europe. On current trends, the UK could have a lower national income by the year 2000 than some of the better-off third world countries. It will certainly be lower than countries such as Spain, Italy and Greece.

Two important questions will be considered in this chapter. Firstly what are the causes of economic growth? Secondly, what is the relationship between economic growth and changes in standards of living?

The causes of economic growth

An increase in the value of output in an economy can come only from one of two sources. Either it must come from an increase in quantity or quality of the factors of production: land, labour and capital. Or it must come from an improvement in the way in which these factors of production are combined. Each will be considered in turn.

Land

Land is defined not only as land itself, but as all natural resources including mineral resources. A country which has scarce natural resources, such as oil or gold, will be able to exploit those resources which will then increase the national income of the economy. A few economies in the world today have grown at spectacular rates due almost entirely to the exploitation of land as a factor of production. Two such economies are Kuwait and Saudi Arabia both oil-producing countries. Other countries, such as South Africa, with its diamonds and gold as well as many other minerals, have derived a good part of

Table 11.1

Economy	A	B	C	D	E
Growth rate	0%	1%	2½%	5%	10%
Year					
0	100	100	100	100	100
1	100	101	103	105	110
2	100	102	105	110	121
3	100	103	108	116	133
4	100	104	110	122	146
5	100	105	113	128	161
6	100	106	116	134	177
7	100	107	119	141	195
8	100	108	122	148	214
9	100	109	125	155	236
10	100	110	128	163	259

their economic growth from their primary industries.

Countries can do little about their factor endowments of land. It is just easier for those lucky enough to be endowed with favourable land factors to grow at a faster rate.

Labour

Labour can be a source of economic growth if it increases either in quantity or in quality. There are various ways in which the stock of labour might grow.

1 The population might grow, thus increasing the number of workers in the population. This might be a result either of an increase in the birth rate or of immigration. The fast development of the USA in the nineteenth century is often ascribed to the growth of population through immigration.

2 The proportion of the population going out to work may rise. In Western economies in recent years there has been a sharp increase in the number of women seeking jobs. GNP should increase as a consequence.

Increases in the stock of labour are less important than increases in the quality of labour as far as welfare is concerned. A fast-increasing population might result in high growth, but it also means that there are many more to feed, clothe and house. A 5% population growth together with a 5% economic growth rate leaves income per head of the population static. Increases in the quality of labour—which represent increases in the stock of human capital—can result from:

1 Education An increase in the quality of education being received by the population should increase their human capital. Raising the school-leaving age, or increasing the number of university places, might secure this. However, it has also been argued that the quality of education is of vital importance. Education in engineering is more important to economic growth than research into ancient South American languages. Comparing the

Is it possible to prove or disprove statements such as 'The Japanese work harder than the British' and 'German workers are more disciplined than Italian workers'?

UK with West Germany, it has been argued that the UK has a lower growth rate because it devotes a larger proportion of educational spending to 'liberal' subjects, such as Latin or Literature, than Germany.

2 Vocational training This type of education is specifically designed to educate a worker to perform a certain task. The task might be very easy, such as operating a simple machine, or it might be complex, such as being a director of a large firm. As an economy grows, the number of complex tasks to be performed increases. Hence there is a greater need for vocational training. Economies such as the UK which have a poor record in vocational training are likely to fall behind their more training-orientated competitors.

3 Social attitudes Different nationalities are often labelled 'hardworking' or 'lazy'. The Chinese, the Japanese and the Germans are amongst the former; the British are all too often amongst the latter. It is very difficult to analyse what makes a particular group of people consistently more economically successful than others. It is certainly bound up with factors such as religion, culture, family and a sense of pride. At the beginning of this century, the sociologist Weber argued that the rise of Western capitalism in the sixteenth and seventeenth centuries was in part caused by the rise of Protestantism. He argued that Protestantism held that work and savings were two fundamental Christian virtues. Working hard, consuming little and investing much, Protestants rapidly came to own an ever-increasing stock of wealth. The system continued to generate an increasing divide between Western Protestant economies and the rest of the world. It was only when the rest of the world started to imitate their Western rivals economically that they too started to grow rapidly. It is easy to criticise theories linking growth to social attitudes because 'social attitudes' are so hard to measure. Yet the work discipline of a nation such as Japan must surely have contributed to its astonishing economic success this century.

4 Labour practices and labour relations Historically, the relations between worker and owner of capital have developed in different ways in different economies. It has been argued that labour practices and relations are better in some economies than in others and that this is a significant determinant in difference in growth rates. An example of a poor labour practice is a rigid demarcation system, i.e. the inability of workers to move flexibly from task to task. Labour relations also might be poor, with workers constantly dissatisfied and taking disruptive action. Some commentators have laid the blame for this squarely on the trade unions. However, empirically there is no correlation at all between growth rates and trade unionism.

Capital

J. K. Galbraith, in his book *The Affluent Society* (1958), said: 'In everyday economic discourse nothing is more frequently taken as an index of economic growth than the volume of capital formation'.

By this, he meant that many economists believe that the main determinant of economic growth is investment. Investment adds to the capital stock of the economy. More investment means that the potential output of the economy is increased. However, to argue that increased investment leads to higher economic growth is rather crude. International comparisons since the second world war show that levels of investment and economic growth are only slightly related. There are a number of reasons why this might be so:

1 The important investment figure to look at is **net** investment. Gross investment is not a true measure of the increase in productive potential, because part of gross investment is used to replace capital which is depreciating and wearing out.

2 The direction of investment is important. Investment in housing adds to the standard of living in the community, but it does not increase the productive potential of the economy. Developed countries making large investments in declining industries such as steel and textiles are less likely to see a high return than countries investing in the industries of the future. The UK has often been criticised for misallocating investment. In particular it has failed to develop its own inventions and has allowed other economies to bring British ideas on to the market.

3 The quality of investment is vital. If industry and government are technologically conservative, they may opt to use tried and tested technologies rather than invest in the technologies of the future. Admittedly there is greater risk in being in the forefront of technological development, but there are greater rewards for success. A firm investing in the latest

Data 11.1

Britain 'may be growth leader'

By Peter Norman, Economics Correspondent

BRITISH economic growth is likely to exceed that in the rest of Europe for most of the next 10 years and UK living standards could overtake those of West Germany by the end of the century, according to the chief economic adviser of the Confederation of British Industry.

Mr Douglas McWilliams said Britain's comparative strength in the services sector should become an increasing advantage while the UK's aggressive financial system and deregulated economy should give it a lead over other countries.

Official figures had considerably underestimated British growth in recent years because of statistical under-recordings associated with the information technology industry and industries using information technology.

UK growth had been about 1.25 per cent per year more than recorded during the 1980s and was now about 1 per cent a year more than in the official figures. As a result Britain had grown more than one fifth faster than the average of the other main industrial economies in the past decade.

Mr McWilliams said "harder, sharper, more robust, more determined and more confident" management had been the key to the "outperformance" of the British economy.

The need to improve financial performance gave a spur to spending on information technology. "There is a clear connection between the UK management renaissance and the spurt in growth in the UK information technology industry in the early to mid-1980s," Mr McWilliams said.

Looking ahead, Mr McWilliams said the further spread of information technology should benefit the UK. Britain already had the largest information technology market place as a proportion of gross national product in Western Europe. It should be able to exploit the shift in this market from being based on the production of electronic hardware to being based on software and services.

The Financial Times. 23.2.89

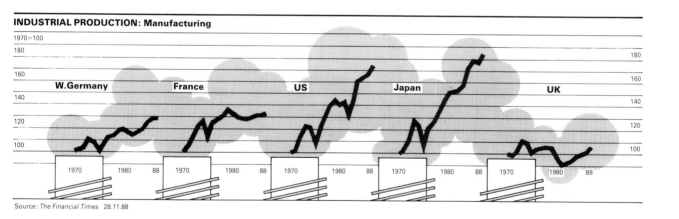

INDUSTRIAL PRODUCTION: Manufacturing

1970=100

W.Germany   France   US   Japan   UK

Source: *The Financial Times* 28.11.88

1 What do the data tell us about the growth of the UK economy in the 1970s and 1980s?

2 Does the relative decline in the manufacturing sector of the UK economy matter?

technology is likely to be able to reduce costs and increase its sales compared to a firm investigating in yesterday's proven, but higher-cost, technology.

An economy's willingness to invest is dependent upon a number of variables. In the private sector, firms need to be able to finance their investment programmes. Investment may be stifled by difficulty in obtaining new share capital, or in finding banks willing to lend over long periods of time. Equally, high corporate taxation will reduce funds available internally (i.e. retained profit), and will reduce a firm's willingness to invest now in order to make future profits. Furthermore, firms will not invest if they believe there will be no market for their goods, whereas high levels of domestic demand should stimulate investment. Finally, high interest rates will also stifle investment.

Combining the factors of production

An economy may have plentiful supplies of high quality land, labour and capital and still have low growth rates, if those factors are poorly combined.

One important determinant of the way in which factors are combined is the level of demand in an economy. If the level of aggregate demand is low, factors of production will remain unused and be wasted. A high level of demand will enable firms in an economy to make the maximum use of available scarce factors.

The availability of a large market also could promote growth. If there is a large market, firms can specialise and grow, thus reducing costs of production and encouraging research and development work. A small market would mean that costs would be higher and the quality of goods inferior. An economy such as the USA is big enough to be classed as a 'large' market. Smaller economies can become part of larger markets either by combining (e.g. The European Community) or by developing 'open' economies—that is economies where foreign trade is actively encouraged (e.g. South Korea, Japan and Singapore).

Of equal importance may be deep-rooted social factors affecting the organising of factors of production. Political and social conflict may be endemic in a society. It may manifest itself in armed conflict, resulting in a large loss of economic wealth, as in Northern Ireland; or it may be expressed in terms of industrial conflict. Constant strife between workers and capitalists may lower production and growth.

Data 11.2

Boiler suit image gives clue to failings in recruitment

By David Thomas, Education Correspondent

Four M.Eng. students at Southampton University have produced an unusually thorough survey of attitudes to engineering among primary school children, secondary school and sixth form pupils, university students and employers.

The research reveals key failings which put large numbers of people off engineering. These include:

● Primary schools. Children aged 7–11 already see engineering as a dirty, greasy profession, to do with mending cars and machinery and carried out by men in boiler suits. This image is reinforced by the failure of primary school children to link technology, which they value, with engineering.

● Six form. Nearly three quarters of sixth-formers said they had no careers advice about engineering. Female sixth-formers dislike the male-dominated image.

● Employers. Many engineering graduates shun the profession because of low pay compared with other professions such as accountancy. The report also found that few engineering employers have tried new ways to recruit engineers, such as advertising in magazines read by students: those that have tried such methods report success.

The Financial Times. 7.3.89

1 How could the data help explain Britain's relative decline in manufacturing?

2 How would economic theory suggest this problem could be reduced in the future?

Data 11.3

Change in Gross domestic product at 1985 prices

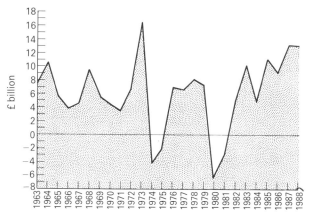

Gross domestic fixed capital formation: Total (at 1985 prices)

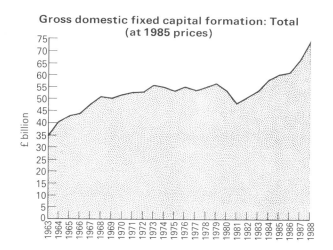

Inflation: Retail price index, percentage change

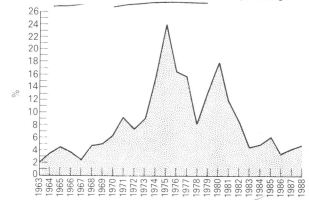

1 Why does economic theory suggest that investment causes economic growth? Does the evidence support this hypothesis?

2 To what extent does inflation impair economic growth?

Source: CSO, Economic Trends

Some economists have seen Britain's class structure as very divisive and a source of conflict in factories and other work-places. On the other hand, they point to countries such as Japan with few social problems, management and workers sharing common aims. The result is said to be low growth in Britain and high growth in Japan.

Equally, a nation may have ambivalent attitudes to economic development. It has been argued that Britain as a society is more interested in leisure, in maintaining traditional values and in preserving its heritage, than in getting rich. In a society where the acquisition of large amounts of goods and money is seen as less important, it is not surprising that factors of production are under-utilised and growth rates are low. Note that this is a different argument from the one which says that workers are inherently 'lazy'. Here it is being argued that the consumption of marketable goods and services is low on the list of priorities for a society.

Why might the troubles in Northern Ireland since 1968 have affected the growth rate for the province?

What causes growth?

In contrast to many other areas of economics, economists tend to agree that there is no one simple answer to this question. For each economy there is a complex set of factors which determines its growth rate. Because the factors are so complex, it is not easy for governments to pursue policies which aim to promote growth. Reforms may take many years to effect. If, for instance, the education system of a country is to blame for poor growth rates, it will take decades to solve this problem and to supply better educated people to the working population.

National income, growth and economic welfare

So far national income and growth have been discussed as if they were positive measures of welfare. A country with a higher national income is seen as

---

Data 11.4

The British character and attitudes towards making money

From Mr H. Parker

Sir,—In his interesting piece "Making money is not quite cricket" (December 30) Ian Davidson makes some fascinating but questionable generalisations about national attitudes to money: "The British are not, in the main, and never have been really interested in making money. By and large the national ethos frowns on making money for its own sake. Japan, Switzerland and America are different, and richer."

It may be true that "the British," or at least some of them, are not too interested in making money, but the ones I have met in 30 years of dealing

with them are just as interested in having money—if not more so—than other nationalities. The national preoccupation with betting on horses, football games and other forms of gambling—not to mention speculation in the stock market, in property and in City institutions like Lloyd's—seems to me to reflect a pretty widespread interest in getting hold of the stuff.

What perhaps is lacking in the British character (if there is such a thing) is the apparent enjoyment of satisfying and productive work that one can observe, say on a building site or in an office or shop, in New York or Zurich or Tokyo. Workers in those places are

probably better paid than their British counterparts, but they invariably seem to do their work with a zest and professional pride in doing the job well and quickly that is rarely seen in London. I believe it is this element of pride in doing a job of work well, rather than just an interest in "making money," that is lacking in many British workers—and I use the term in its widest sense to include those working at all levels and in all sectors of UK society.

Hugh Parker.
McKinsey and Co,
74, St James's Street, SW1

Letter to The Financial Times. January 1983

1 *Does a national desire to 'make money' or 'pride in doing a job well' stimulate economic growth?*

better off than a country with a lower level of national income. Countries with low growth rates are considered to be slipping behind other faster-growing economies. High growth economies are referred to as 'miracle' economies. Countries with low growth rate are seen as 'problem' or 'sick' economies. But to what extent is this a correct value judgement?

The simple answer is that levels of national income are only one measure of welfare for a society. This is because national income is a relatively narrow measurement. It is merely the addition of all marketable output in the economy over a given time period. It will not measure the genuine output of the economy, for a number of reasons:

1 Many goods and services are not marketed. The produce of a subsistence farmer, the DIY activities or domestic work of a householder, are examples of genuine output which goes unrecorded.

2 Many goods and services which are marketed are not recorded—one main reason being the evasion of tax.

But even if all output could be recorded, the resulting measurement would remain only part of the measure of welfare. This is because much welfare is gained outside the production system. The quality of the physical environment is one example. Nearly everyone would agree that a clean and healthy environment affects living standards. Living in leafy suburbia is likely to be more attractive than living next to a noisy factory belching pollutants on to the surrounding houses.

Political liberties, too, are vital to our welfare. Living in a police state, in constant fear of arrest, may be less preferable than living in a democratic state even if one were better off in terms of material goods in the former. Equally, our social environment is important. A society which emphasises the importance of achievement may well grow fast as measured by GNP, but at the same time there may well be tremendous stress put on people in that society. Those who think they fail to achieve will lead blighted lives. One direct outcome may be a higher than average suicide rate. Again, a society where violence is commonplace is unlikely to have as high a level of welfare as a comparable peaceful society.

Equally, increasing material affluence does not necessarily lead to increasing welfare. For instance, a country which spends all of its increased income on building nuclear bombs will record a higher GNP—but its citizens do not directly benefit. But it is not only nuclear bombs which can be a waste of scarce resources. In our modern throw-away consumer society, much is produced that may not be freely demanded by consumers. They buy goods and services because producers, through advertising, tell them that consumption will greatly increase their economic welfare. When they have bought the good or service, they may find that they have gained little or no welfare. Consider all the toys that are bought, demanded by children, and lie unplayed-with in a cupboard; or make up and clothes, used once and eventually thrown out. Many in western society die as a result of over-consumption of food, as they eat their way through heavily promoted, packaged, junk food. Some economists argue that a substantial proportion of our GNP contributes little or nothing to our welfare.

Economic growth, therefore, may or may not lead to increased welfare for the citizens of a country. It is likely that as economic growth takes place, some measures of welfare will increase, whilst others decline. It is the balance between these 'goods' and 'ills' which needs to be considered.

Comparing welfare over time

It is difficult to compare welfare over time. This is not only because measures other than national income are difficult to assess. National income itself is difficult to compare over time.

Firstly, part of an increase in national income is likely to be caused by an increase in prices. If national income increases by 10% but prices also rise by 10% then **real** national income has not changed. Real national income is the measure of how many goods and services are produced in the economy. Money national income measures the total value of goods and services produced over a time period at the prices charged during that time period. In comparing welfare over time, the economist is only interested in measures of real income.

A second problem when comparing income over time is that goods and services produced are not identical. For instance, cars produced today are more comfortable and more reliable than similarly priced cars 50 years ago. Equally, quality may deteriorate over time. Some beer drinkers today think that the beer of 50 years ago was of better

Data 11.5

Inequalities in income widening, study shows

By Ralph Atkins,
Economics Staff

INEQUALITIES in income between rich and poor households have widened in the past decade even after taking account of taxes and benefits, according to official estimates.

The proportion of income going to the poorest 20 per cent of households fell between 1975 and 1986 but the share going to the top 20 per cent rose, figures from the Central Statistical Office show.

This widening of the income gap is particularly pronounced in the original incomes of households, before taxes and benefits. However, the gap has also widened in estimates of final incomes.

These estimates allow for the effect of taxes and state support, including benefits in kind such as state education and school meals.

The results come from a study of the redistributive effect of government spending.

The study shows that state intervention does reduce inequality but that redistribution since the mid-1970s has not kept pace with growing inequality between original incomes.

The original income of a household includes earnings from employment, occupational pensions and investments.

In 1975, original incomes of the poorest fifth of households accounted for 0.8 per cent of total incomes. By 1986 this had fallen to 0.3 per cent. Final incomes of the poorest fifth accounted for 7.1 per cent of the total in 1975, falling to 6.3 per cent in 1986.

At the other extreme the richest fifth of households took 44 per cent of original incomes in 1975 rising to 51 per cent in 1986. The share of final incomes rose from 38 per cent to 42 per cent over the same period.

In 1986, the average original income of the poorest 20 per cent of households was £130 a year. The average original income of the top 20 per cent was £24,790.

Average final incomes, after taxes and benefits, for the two groups were £4,130 a year and £17,260 a year respectively.

The Financial Times. 23.1.89

---

1 Does the data suggest that UK living standards have risen over the period 1975 to 1986?

---

quality than similarly priced beer today. (By 'similarly priced' we are of course referring to real or constant prices.)

Thirdly, population may change. A doubling of the population combined with a doubling of national income leaves the average citizen no better off than before. Consequently, income **per capita** (i.e. per person) must be compared.

Fourthly, national income statistics do not tell us anything about the distribution of income in a country. An economy where 1% of the population received 99% of all income is fairly obviously less well off than an economy with an identical national income but where national income is evenly divided amongst the population. The 'ideal' distribution of income is debatable. Extreme inequalities, however where a small group gains a large share of income are unlikely to maximise welfare.

Data 11.6

GDP per head

Purchasing power parities measure how many pounds, dollars, or francs, for example, people need to buy the same basket of goods and services in the UK, US or France. If people only bought one good, the PPF would simply be the relative price of that item in two countries. (For example, if a loaf of bread costs 50p in the UK and $1 in the US, then the PPP of sterling in relation to the US dollar for this one item would be $2 = £1.)

Source: The Treasury, Economic Progress Report March–April 1987

GDP per head in 1985

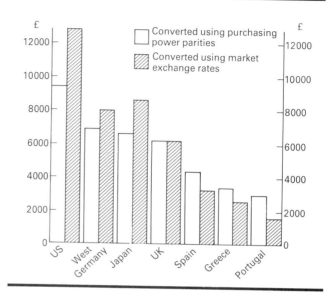

1 Explain the difference between 'GDP per head converted using purchasing power parities' and 'GDP per head converted using market exchange rates'.

2 To what extent are countries such as the US better off than the UK, and countries such as Portugal worse off?

Comparing welfare between economies

Comparing the welfare of different economies is just as difficult as comparing the welfare of one country over time. Firstly, there are the problems associated with measures of welfare not measured by national income statistics (e.g quality of environment, etc.) Secondly, there is the problem that national income statistics measure only part of national output. Each country has its particular way of measuring national income, and what is not included varies widely. Thirdly, there are problems associated with different population and income distributions, and the different quality of goods and services produced.

There are special problems, however, in comparisons between economies. Firstly, different economies have different price and income levels. Translating one economy's national income into the currency of another's at the official exchange rate of the currency would lead to a very misleading comparison. The price of one currency against another is determined by the demand and supply for that currency. Demand and supply in turn are determined by complex forces at work nationally and internationally. Those forces do not accurately reflect differences in price levels between economies. For instance, certain countries such as Sweden and Switzerland, have high per capita incomes at official exchange rates. Yet in part this merely reflects a high cost of living in those countries. Equally, in many developing countries it is perfectly possible to enjoy a reasonable standard of living for US $500 a year, because the cost of locally produced necessities is so low and because so much output is subsistence output. The way to overcome this problem is to compare incomes with the cost of living in an economy.

This leads on to the second problem. The cost of living is generally measured by costing a typical basket of goods and services that a consumer buys.

Growth

The problem is that there is no typical basket of goods bought by consumers in all economies. In some economies, such as Norway and Sweden, expenditure on heating is likely to be greater than in France. We cannot infer, however, that the Norwegians are better off than the French because of this. In fact the Norwegians have to consume a greater part of their national income than the French on heating just to maintain the same real living standards. Different consumption patterns, therefore, make comparisons between economies of national income difficult.

Summary

Economic growth is generally defined as increases in national income. The causes of economic growth are complex. Theoretically it is true that economic growth must come about through increases in land, labour, capital, or an increase in the efficiency of combining these factors. The main causes of growth for some countries may differ markedly from others. There is no consensus view as to why some countries, such as the UK, have poorer growth rates than other very similar economies such as France. Growth is only a partial measurement of the improvement in living standards in an economy. National income statistics are an inaccurate measure of the output of an economy. They cannot take into account other factors vital to welfare such as the quality of the environment and the degree of civil liberty. Making comparisons of welfare using national income statistics is fraught with difficulty both in terms of measurement over time and place.

Terms for review

growth

factors of production

economic welfare

Essay questions

1 What are the main determinants of growth in an advanced industrialised economy? Could it be argued that trade union reform would increase Britain's growth rate?

2 What factors might account for Britain's poor industrial performance in the post war period?

3 To what extent are changes in national income an adequate measure of changes in the standard of living of a nation?

12

Income determination—the Keynesian multiplier model

Introduction

During the Great Depression of the 1930s, neo-classical economists argued that the world economy was in a state of disequilibrium and that it would be only a matter of time before unemployment disappeared and the economy reverted to full employment. There were, however, many dissident economists who argued that existing economic theory failed to explain the workings of the economy. In 1936 John Maynard Keynes, one of the foremost of these dissidents, published a book which was to revolutionise economics. Entitled *The General Theory of Employment, Interest and Money*, it put forward a new radical model of the economy. Its foremost purpose was to explain how an economy could be at less than full employment for long periods of time. There have been many interpretations of Keyne's work, and the traditional textbook view of that theory will be outlined in this chapter.

The circular flow of income

The circular flow of income model was explained in Chapter 10. It portrayed the economy as consisting of four sectors—households, firms, government and the foreign sector—each interconnected by flows of money and corresponding flows of goods and services. This is shown in Fig. 12.1.

Additions to consumption are called **injections**. Monies which are not spent in the economy are called **withdrawals**. At any point in time, withdrawals must equal injections, i.e.:

$$\text{Saving} + \text{Imports} + \text{Taxation} = \text{Investment} + \text{Exports} + \text{Government spending}$$

$$S + M + T = I + X + G$$

$$\text{Withdrawals (W)} = \text{Injections (J)}$$

In a simple Keynesian model it is assumed that injections are 'autonomous' or 'exogenously determined'. This means that the values of I, X and G (investment, exports and government spending) are not determined by any of the other variables in the model. The model does not attempt to explain why I, X and G have the values that they do. This is because:

1 Government spending is determined by political decisions of government.

2 Exports are determined by levels of world income and our competitiveness as regards the rest of the world.

3 Investment is determined by factors such as the rate of interest and levels of business confidence.

None of the above variables, such as levels of

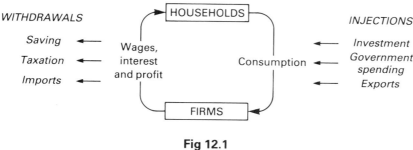

Fig 12.1

world income, are determined in the simple model, because they are either impossible to determine, or the model would need to be more complicated.

Withdrawals, on the other hand, are assumed to be 'induced' or 'endogenously determined'. This means that they are dependent upon variables within the system: in this case the level of income, Y. When Y increases or decreases, S, M and T (savings, imports and taxation) also increase or decrease. This is because, as incomes rise, households and firms:

1 do not spend all of that increase but save part of it;

2 spend part of that increase on imported goods;

3 have to pay part of that increase in taxes to the Government.

What proportion of that income is saved, imported and taxed is given by the value of the respective marginal propensities:

Marginal propensity to save

$$= \frac{\text{Change in total savings}}{\text{Change in income}}$$

Marginal propensity to import

$$= \frac{\text{Change in total imports}}{\text{Change in income}}$$

Marginal propensity to tax

$$= \frac{\text{Change in total taxation}}{\text{Change in income}}$$

Thus: $\text{MPS} = \dfrac{\Delta S}{\Delta Y}, \quad \text{MPM} = \dfrac{\Delta M}{\Delta Y}, \quad \text{MPT} = \dfrac{\Delta T}{\Delta Y}$

In an economy which is **closed**, i.e. which engages in no foreign trade, and where there is no government, the values of the marginal propensities to save and consume must equal 1. This is because households must either spend their money on consumption goods or save their money. Thus:

$$\text{MCP} + \text{MPS} = 1$$

It should be remembered that consumption too is also assumed to be a function of income, with households spending more as their income increases.

In a simple Keynesian model, then, the value of savings, imports and taxation will change only if income changes. For instance, a change in the level of savings will only occur if income has changed. Injections, however, may change independent of a

change in income. In fact, the Keynesian model argues that changes in investment, exports and government spending will themselves cause a change in income via the multiplier process.

The multiplier

Suppose a Japanese firm decides to set up a new car plant in Wales. The effects on the UK economy will be many and varied. Income should go up. Building the factory will mean orders for UK construction companies, for UK machine tool manufacturers, etc. Once the factory is producing cars, there will be orders for everything from car parts for the production line to sausages for the canteen. However, the increase in spending will not be limited to goods and services directly related to car production. The employees of the construction company will spend part of their income on domestically produced goods (the rest of course will be saved, taxed or spent on imported goods). For instance, they might spend part of their income on a Scottish holiday. This will mean extra income for hotels, restaurants and guest houses in Scotland. In turn, these Scottish firms will spend their income on essential supplies and on wages. In turn this will create more income in other parts of the economy, such as the food industry, and so on.

This process of the multiplication of income can be seen on the circular flow model. Consider Fig. 12.2. The Japanese car plant is an example of investment and is therefore an injection into the economy. The income generated starts to flow round the economy. Each time it passes through the hands of households and firms, part is not spent domestically, but is leaked out of the domestic economy. However, each time it changes hands, total income increases. So if the car plant cost £100 million, and half of all income is spent domestically, then the final increase in income will be (in millions of pounds).

$$100 + 50 + 25 + 12.50 + 6.25 + \ldots, \text{ or } 200$$

The initial increase in expenditure on the car plant has lead to a multiple increase in income. The multiplier in this case is 2, because the increase in investment has led to an increase in income of twice that amount. If the multiplier were 3, a £100 million increase in any injection (investment, exports or

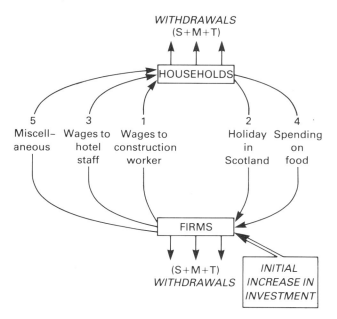

WITHDRAWALS
(S+M+T)

HOUSEHOLDS

5 Miscellaneous
3 Wages to hotel staff
1 Wages to construction worker
2 Holiday in Scotland
4 Spending on food

FIRMS

(S+M+T) WITHDRAWALS

INITIAL INCREASE IN INVESTMENT

Fig 12.2

government spending) would lead to a £300 million increase in income.

In a closed economy the value of the **multiplier** is given by the formulae:

$$\frac{1}{1 - MPC} \quad \text{or} \quad \frac{1}{MPS}$$

The two formulae are equivalent because, as was shown above:

$$1 = MPC + MPS$$

that is, increases in income must either be consumed or saved.

The formula for the multiplier can be derived in one of two ways. The first way is from the circular flow of income model. It was shown in Fig. 12.2 that the increase in income resulting from an increase in injections (ΔJ) was:

$$\Delta J + \frac{1}{1 - MPC} \Delta J + \frac{1}{(1 - MPC)(1 - MPC)} \Delta J + \ldots$$

Mathematically this is known as a geometric progression, whose sum is:

$$\frac{1}{1 - MPC} \times \Delta J$$

A second way is to start from the fact that in equilibrium, planned withdrawals must equal planned

Income determination—the Keynesian multiplier model

injections. In a closed economy with no government, the only injection is investment and the only withdrawal is savings. Therefore, in equilibrium:

$$I = S$$

We know that any increase in S is equal to the marginal propensity to save multiplied by income:

$$\Delta S = MPS \times \Delta Y$$

If planned investment increases, then saving must rise by an equal amount:

$$\Delta I = \Delta S$$

Therefore: $\Delta I = MPS \times \Delta Y$

i.e. $$\Delta Y = \frac{1}{MPS} \times \Delta I$$

where $\frac{1}{MPS}$ is the value of the multiplier.

At this level, it is not too important if the reader cannot remember how the multiplier is derived. What is important is that the basic concept of the multiplier is understood. This is:

1 An increase in the value of injections (investment, exports and government spending) will lead to an increase in income.

2 The increase in income will be greater than the increase in the injection.

3 The value of the multiplier is the ratio between the increase in income and the increase in injections, e.g. an increase in injections of £50 million with a multiplier of 4, will lead to a final increase in income of £200 million.

Equilibrium and disequilibrium

There is **equilibrium** in the circular flow of income when planned expenditure (planned E) and actual income (actual Y) are equal. If E and Y are equal then there is no tendency for the level of income to increase or decrease. Disequilibrium will occur if planned expenditure (or planned **aggregate demand**) differs from actual income. Then income will change. Planned expenditure is defined as the total

Data 12.1

Industry and finance lead Welsh economic recovery

Anthony Moreton

THE DECISION by Bosch, one of the world's leading motor components suppliers, to site its £100m plant outside Cardiff is more than just another piece of inward investment.

It is seen in Wales as recognition by a leading European company that the industrial face of the principality is changing and that one of the most dynamic parts of the UK over the past two years can compete internationally for inward investment.

Recognition that Wales was changing first came with the arrival of US concerns such as Kelloggs. But it was the decision of the Japanese to make Wales an important base that really helped to change the economy.

The first of the arrivals from the Land of the Rising Sun to the land of the falling rain was Takiron in 1972, but it was the second company, Sony, which arrived a few months later that really set the trend in motion. There are now 18 Japanese concerns in Wales, including Matsushita (the Panasonic group), Aiwa, Brother Industries, Orion and Hoya Lens.

Wales has gone out of its way to play host to the Japanese, even setting up a Japanese school and organising a Japanese-Wales golf day.

Bosch has also made it clear that Wales, with its good labour force, easy communications and ample land can compete for the internationally mobile investment decisions that just two years ago most people thought had come to an end. Bosch chose Wales in preference to Spain.

It is not the only motor concern to see advantages in Wales. Ford last year announced the largest single investment in Britain when it decided to spend £750m on its engine plant at Bridgend and components factory at Swansea.

Last year a record £1bn was invested in Wales by incomers. Mr Walker said yesterday that other overseas companies were looking at Wales eagerly and he forecast more announcements in the near future.

One could be an international educational institute which is contemplating a move to Cardiff. In the first quarter of this year 76 companies which had not previously been connected with the country visited Wales to look at sites.

Bosch will be spending heavily on training – probably about £19m – and will also undertake some R & D in the country.

It is no secret that the arrival of the Japanese, with their stringent quality control, has helped put the native technology industry on a higher plane. Bosch is expected to do the same, to the benefit of everyone.

The Financial Times. 18.4.89

1 Explain, using a multiplier model of the economy, how inward investment has led to a 'Welsh economic recovery'.

expenditure (i.e. aggregate demand) which economic units plan or intend to make in the future. Actual income is defined as the level of income which is attained.

Obviously, planned expenditure and actual income need not be the same. One cause of this disequilibrium could be that planned injections are different from actual withdrawals. If this were to be the case then:

(a) actual income would change via the multiplier process leading in turn to

(b) a change in withdrawals (which of course vary with income) such that once again planned injections equal actual withdrawals—the equilibrium position.

For instance, assume the economy in one time period is in equilibrium at an expenditure or income level of £200 billion. The following time period, planned expenditure rises by £20 billion to £220 billion as a result of an increase in planned investment of £10 billion. Then actual income will have to rise to £220 billion to restore equilibrium to the economy. Withdrawals will have risen by £20 billion in the process so that once again planned injections equal actual withdrawals. The value of the multiplier in this example must have been 2 because the increase of £10 billion in investment, the injection, led to a final increase in income of £20 billion.

The second cause of disequilibrium is that marginal propensities may have changed. Economic units may have decided to change the proportion of their income that they consume, save, spend on imported goods or are taxed on. Actual withdrawals cannot change because they must be equal to injections. A change in marginal propensities will not affect the level of injections, $I + X + G$. What will change is the level of income. Consider, for example, an economy with total withdrawals S, M and T, of £100 billion and an income of £400 billion. Economic units decide they want to save an extra £100 billion. Planned withdrawals then rise to £200 billion. But actual withdrawals can only be £100 billion because planned injections have not changed. So income will change. Previously they wanted withdrawals amounting to one quarter of their income. Now they want withdrawals of one half of their income. Their actual withdrawals can only be £100 billion. Therefore the new level of actual income can only be £200 billion.

Keynes called this process the **paradox of thrift**. If people want to save more, they save the same amount but out of a reduced income. What has happened is that the proportion of income saved has increased. The paradox of thrift is very plausible. If people try to save more, they must try to spend less. Less spending means fewer orders for firms. That in turn leads to lower output, greater unemployment and lower incomes. Lower incomes result in lower saving and lower consumption. The extra saving of those who still have incomes is cancelled out by the fall in saving for those now out of work. Total saving remains unchanged but total income has fallen. This paradox applies equally to changes in marginal propensities to tax and import.

A diagrammatic presentation of the Keynesian model

The Keynesian model is normally illustrated in terms of two graphs. One is the 45° diagram of Fig. 12.3. The 45° line shows all points where expen-

---

Data 12.2

Spend for your country's sake

BY SAMUEL BRITTAN

Many misguided people, some of them in very high places, are urging us to "buy British," even where the foreign product has a slight edge.

This is the patriotism of the simple-minded. Apart from anything else, it will simply drive up the sterling exchange rate still further, and lead to a loss of exports comparable in size to the import-saving itself.

Nevertheless, if people want to act patriotically, there is something they can do. This would be not to "buy British," "buy French," or "buy American," but simply to buy. They should make purchases now, which might otherwise have been deferred for a year or two.

Consumer spending is now adding to the forces making for recession. It could be usefully stimulated without rekindling inflation—if it is done without destroying the Government's monetary and fiscal strategy.

The great advantage of a voluntary spending spree is that it is self-correct-ing. For given long-term incomes, if people buy more now, they will buy less later; but in the meantime they will have helped to stem a cumulative downturn. By contrast, a Government fiscal stimulus—say, through the use of a consumer tax regulator—would be far more difficult to reverse. Apart from economic wishful thinking, political pressures would make it extremely difficult to reverse the change sufficiently early.

Of course, higher consumer spending might lead to a slower fall in the cost of borrowing for Government or industry than might otherwise be expected. But at present, the net effect would almost certainly be expansionary. For your country's sake, spend now.

The Financial Times. November 1980

1 *Use a model of income determination to explain why, in the author's opinion, consumers should 'spend now'.*

2 *Would an increase in government spending have the same effect as an equivalent increase in consumer spending?*

Income determination—the Keynesian multiplier model

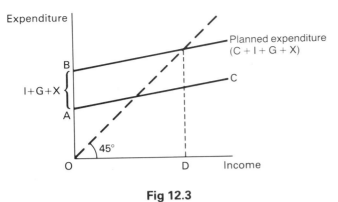

Fig 12.3

diture (on the vertical axis) equals income (on the horizontal axis). The line C is the simple Keynesian function. The line is upward sloping because consumption increases as income increases. To calculate aggregate demand in the economy, we need to add the other components of expenditure—investment, government spending and exports—to consumption. I, G and X are all assumed to be exogenous: that is, these expenditures do not change as income changes. Hence the aggregate expenditure line is parallel to the consumption function. The vertical distance between the aggregate expenditure line and the consumption line is I + G + X.

The aggregate expenditure line, E, is **planned** aggregate expenditure. It shows the amount that households, firms, governments and foreigners plan to spend on goods and services at each level of income. As argued on page 99, the economy is in equilibrium when planned aggregate expenditure equals actual income. Given that the 45° line shows all points where expenditure equals income, the equilibrium level of income must be at OD where E crosses the 45° line.

An alternative graph to illustrate equilibrium income is known as the Keynesian Cross diagram. In Fig. 12.4, J is the planned injection line. It is paral-

lel to the x–axis because injections do not vary with income. Planned withdrawals, however, increase as income rises. Equilibrium income is OD, where planned injections equal planned withdrawals.

If injections (investment, exports or government spending) change, then both the J line and the aggregate expenditure line will change. In Fig. 12.5 an increase in injections (I, G or X) of MN leads to an upward shift of the expenditure line from E to E' and the injections line from J to J'. Equilibrium income changes from D to F. Aggregate expenditure

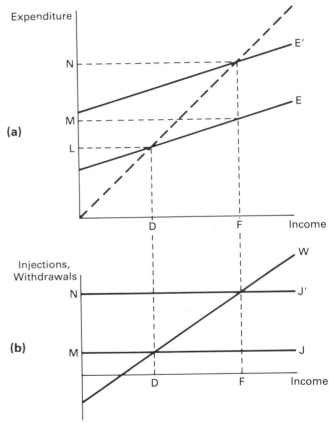

Fig 12.5

rises by LN, where LN = DF since the rise in expenditure must equal the rise in income. MN of that rise was increased injections. The balance, LM, is increased consumption, because as income rises so must consumption. The value of the multiplier is given by the number of times income rises due to increased injections i.e.

$$\frac{DF}{MN}.$$

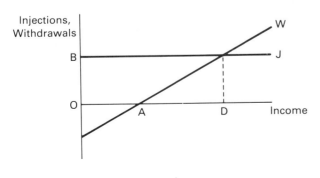

Fig 12.4

102

Full employment, inflationary and deflationary gaps

Full employment in the economy is reached when all factors of production are fully utilised. Often, full employment is used solely in the terms of the full employment of labour but, strictly speaking, land and capital also need to be fully employed for full employment to exist.

In the simple Keynesian model, there is no reason why equilibrium income should be the same as **full employment national income**. The economy could have 20% or 30% unemployment (as happened in some economies during the Great Depression of the 1930s) and there would be no forces which would

Data 12.3

Change in gross domestic product at factor cost (at 1985 prices)

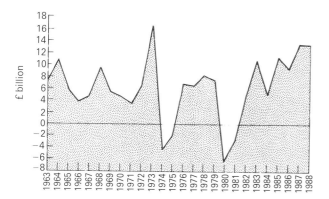

Public sector borrowing requirement (at 1985 prices)

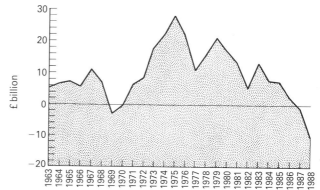

Personal saving ratio (personal saving as a percentage of personal disposable income)

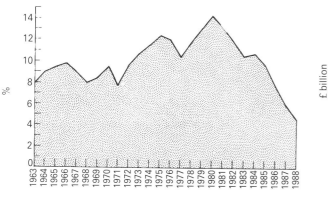

Change in gross domestic fixed capital formation (at 1985 prices)

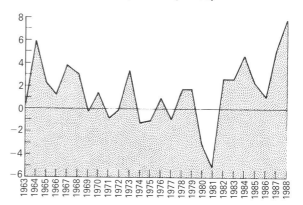

Explain how, in a Keynesian model, changes in a) investment, b) savings, and c) government borrowing affect the level of national income. Illustrate your answer with examples from the data.

Source: CSO, Economic Trends

Income determination—the Keynesian multiplier model

automatically return the economy to full employment. This is a fundamental conclusion of the simple Keynesian model. It would be most unlikely that the economy by itself would settle at full employment income.

If full employment income is greater than equilibrium income, then a **deflationary gap** is said to exist. The size of the deflationary gap is given by the amount that injections (I, X or G) would have to rise for income to reach full employment income. If the multiplier were 3, and income needed to increase by £30 billion to reach full employment, then the deflationary gap would be £10 billion. Investment, exports or government spending would need to rise by £10 billion to eliminate unemployment in the economy. This is shown in Fig. 12.6. The rise in injections of £10 billion, the deflationary gap, raises income by £30 billion to its full employment level of £70 billion.

An **inflationary gap** is said to exist if full employment income is below actual income. In fact, this situation cannot exist in reality. National income cannot be greater than full employment income since by definition full employment income represents the maximum level of output in the economy.

What must happen is that prices go up, raising the level of money full employment expenditure to equal actual income, but leaving real full employment income unchanged. The size of the inflationary gap is given by the amount that injections (I, X or G) would have to fall to make actual income and full employment income equal at current prices. In Fig 12.7, full employment income (Y_{FE}) is below actual

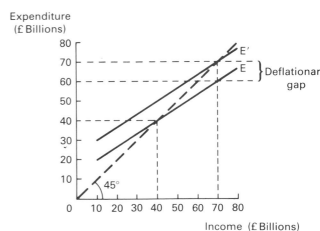

Fig 12.6

Data 12.4

Downturn threatens Birmingham revival

By Richard Tomkins

Recently Birmingham's economy has undergone a revival in response to the recovery of its manufacturing industry and rapid growth in business services such as banking, law and accountancy.

But forecasts produced for the council by the West Midlands Enterprise Board warn that the revival might prove short-lived against a background of high interest and exchange rates and a slowdown in economic growth.

That is because Birmingham's economy is still disproportionately dependent on manufacturing, not just in terms of direct employment but also through the services the manufacturing supports.

The report says the 6 per cent growth in Birmingham's manufacturing output over the past two years is likely to fall to 2.2 per cent this year and 1.5 per cent in the next two, with a consequent decline in manufacturing employment of between 2 per cent and 3 per cent over the period.

Meanwhile, growth in the city's service sector is forecast to slow markedly from between 6 per cent and 7 per cent in 1986–87 to a level below the national trend.

The report underlines the need to tackle the consequences for the city's inner-city areas, where male unemployment among former factory workers and large sections of the ethnic minority population is still at a disturbingly high 30 per cent.

The Financial Times. 4.5.89

1 *Explain why the West Midlands economy might suffer from a deflationary gap in the future.*

2 *Using a diagram, explain how this deflationary gap might be closed.*

income (Y_E). Consequently inflation will raise Y_{FE} to Y_E, although the real value of Y_{FE} will remain unchanged. A fall in injections (I, X or G) of AB would prevent this inflation. AB is therefore the size of the inflationary gap.

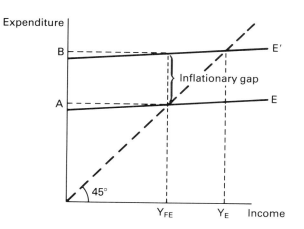

Fig 12.7

Crowding in and crowding out

In the simple Keynesian model, crowding in occurs. **Crowding in** is used to describe the situation where an increase in injection expenditure (I, X or G) actually increases other components of aggregate expenditure, in this case consumption. In Fig. 12.6, an extra £10 billion of injection expenditure crowded in £20 billion of consumption expenditure. **Crowding out** occurs if an increase in investment, exports or government spending does not lead to a multiple increase in aggregate expenditure or income, i.e. the value of the multiplier is less than 1. The simple Keynesian model concludes that crowding out cannot occur because:

1 I, X and G are exogenous and therefore cannot affect each other;

2 the MPC is less than 1 and therefore the multiplier must be greater than 1.

How might defence spending crowd-in consumer expenditure?

Limitations of the model

The simple Keynesian model of income determination described in this chapter worked well in the 1950s and early 1960s. It seemed to be able to explain how the economy had behaved in the past and what would happen in the future, particularly if the Government changed its level of taxation or spending. But this simple model could not explain the bouts of **stagflation** (increasing inflation at a time when unemployment too was increasing) which occurred during the 1970s and early 1980s.

The model did not work well because it assumed that a number of key variables were either constant or were relatively unimportant. These variables were:

1 the money supply.
2 the rate of interest.
3 the demand for money.
4 the demand and supply of labour.
5 aggregate supply in the economy.

In the next chapter a more sophisticated model of the economy will be developed. This model incorporates the variables listed above and will help to explain stagflation and the economic history of the 1970s.

Summary

The equilibrium level of national income is one where planned expenditure equals actual income. Expenditure (i.e. aggregate demand) comprises consumption, investment and government spending on domestic goods plus exports. I, G and X are exogenous variables in the simple Keynesian model. If I, G or X increase then income will increase too by the value of that increase times the multiplier. The formula for the multiplier is

$$\frac{1}{1 - \mathrm{MPC}}$$

Endogenous variables in the model (savings, taxes and imports) cannot change without a corresponding change in national income. If economic units change the value of their marginal propensities to save, tax or import, then the level of income will change; but the value of savings, taxes and imports will not change. In the simple Keynesian model, the economy may be in equilibrium at any point at or below full employment national income. This means that large scale unemployment could be a permanent feature. A deflationary gap can be corrected if investment, government spending or exports increase. An increase in such expenditure will crowd in consumer expenditure because the value of the multiplier is greater than 1. This simple Keynesian model does not help us to understand how stagflation occurs. A more sophisticated model, incorporating monetary variables and the concept of aggregate supply, is needed.

Terms for review

injections

withdrawals

real multiplier

aggregate expenditure or aggregate demand

equilibrium level of income

paradox of thrift

crowding-in

Essay questions

1 What is meant by the 'Keynesian multiplier'? Why might increases in public spending crowd in other expenditures?

2 How is the equilibrium level of national income determined? What effect would an increase in investment have on this equilibrium level?

3 Define 'aggregate demand'. What effect would a fall in public expenditure have on (a) the level of aggregate demand and (b) the level of national income?

13

Aggregate demand and aggregate supply

Introduction

Classical or monetarist economists believe that money plays a crucial role in the economy. In this chapter, we will introduce money into the simple Keynesian model of income determination, as well as considering the supply side of the economy. Although this will make the model of income determination more complex, it will enable us to understand a wider range of economic situations and it will be a more powerful tool for studying an economy facing problems of inflation.

The aggregate demand schedule

A number of important economic relationships have been explained so far.

1 In Chapter 4, it was shown that the demand for money is a function of both income and the rate of interest. If there is an increase in prices in the economy—i.e. there is inflation—there will be an increase in the demand for money. This is because households will need more money to pay for their ordinary shopping. Firms, too, will need more money to pay bigger bills, or perhaps larger pay packets for their workers. This increase in the transactions demand for money is shown in Fig. 13.1. A rise in prices will push the liquidity preference schedule (the demand for money curve) from LP_1 to LP_2.

2 In Chapter 5, it was explained that the rate of interest is determined by the demand and supply for money. If the demand for money increases, interest rates (the price of money) will rise. In Fig. 13.1, an increase in the demand for money will increase the rate of interest from r_1 to r_2.

3 In Chapters 6 and 8, it was argued that both con-

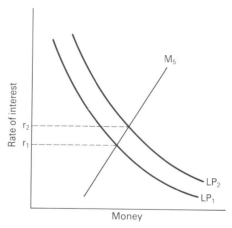

An increase in inflation will increase the demand for money from LP_1 to LP_2. This in turn will increase the rate of interest from r_1 to r_2.

Fig. 13.1

sumption and investment were functions of the rate of interest. A rise in interest rates will cut consumption, in particular of consumer durable goods. Equally, a rise in interest rates will lead to a fall in investment, according to the marginal efficiency of capital theory. So in Fig. 13.2, the $C+I$ line is downward sloping, showing that consumption and investment will increase as interest rates fall.

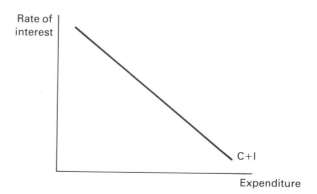

Fig 13.2

107

4 In Chapter 12 it was explained that a change in the marginal propensity to consume (caused for instance by a change in interest rates), or a change in the level of investment, would change the level of income in the economy. In Fig. 13.3, a rise in investment of △I would increase total planned expenditure from E₁ to E₂. This in turn would increase income from A to B.

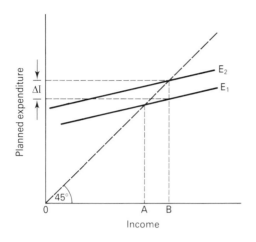

Fig. 13.3

5 Finally, we know from Chapter 10 that national income is also equal to national output. So, in Fig. 13.3, an increase in income of AB will mean that national output too will have increased by AB.

The logic of this argument can thus be summarised as follows: a rise in inflation leads to a rise in the demand for money; leading to a rise in interest rates; which in turn leads to a fall in consumption and investment, and therefore equilibrium income and output. Rises in inflation are thus associated, via changes in demand in the economy, with falls in national output. A curve can then be plotted, as in Fig. 13.4, showing the level of output that is associated with any given level of prices. The higher the level of prices, the lower will be the level of expenditure, income and output in the economy. Therefore this curve—which is called the **aggregate demand schedule** (or the **macro-economic demand schedule**)—is downward sloping.

The aggregate supply schedule

The aggregate supply schedule shows the quantity of output that producers wish to supply at any given price level. In micro-economics, it is argued that firms will increase supply if the price they receive increases—the micro-economic supply curve is upward sloping. However, economists disagree about the shape of the macro-economic aggregate supply curve.

The Keynesian aggregate supply schedule

No mention was made of an aggregate supply schedule in the simple Keynesian model explained in Chapter 12. This was because it was assumed that the aggregate supply schedule was shaped as shown in

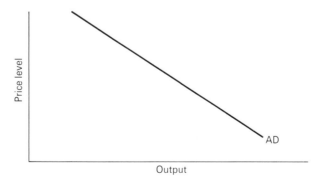

Prices in the economy increase
→ an increase in the demand for money → a rise in interest rates → a fall in consumption and investment → a fall in aggregate expenditure → a fall in national income → **a fall in output**.

Fig. 13.4

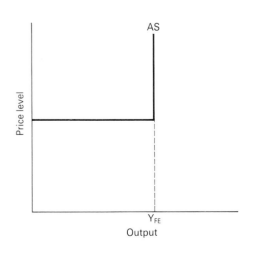

Fig. 13.5

Fig. 13.5. To the left of Y_{FE} (the full employment level of income), there is unemployment in the economy. An increase in aggregate demand at below full employment would lead to an increase in output without increasing prices. If the economy was already at full employment and aggregate demand increased, then that increased demand could not be matched by an increase in supply. After all, by definition the economy cannot produce more than full employment output. So firms would respond to any increase in spending by putting up their prices and not by increasing their output. The aggregate supply schedule is then vertical at full employment income.

Economists agree that this shape of aggregate supply curve is unlikely to be the correct one because it is based upon unrealistic assumptions. In particular, we know that inflationary pressures build up in the economy as it nears full employment. Some industries in the economy, for instance, will be working at full capacity when other industries might have spare capacity. The firms working at full capacity will be able to charge more for their products if demand increases because the supply of the product by the definition of full employment will be fixed. Equally, those firms may face increased costs. If the industry is working at the full employment level, then there is unlikely to be a large pool of skilled workers available to work to expand output. Firms will react by bidding up wage rates, trying to poach workers from other firms. But they will only do this if they know that they can pass on higher costs to consumers in the form of higher prices.

However, if there is mass unemployment in the economy, firms will be able to hire extra workers without needing to pay higher wage rates. Equally, individual firms will find it difficult to increase their prices to customers without seeing large reductions in the demand for their products. So at mass unemployment levels of income, the aggregate supply schedule is likely to be horizontal.

A more sophisticated aggregate supply schedule can now be drawn. In Fig. 13.6, the full employment level of income is Y_{FE}. The aggregate supply schedule is vertical at this level of output, showing that the economy cannot produce any more goods and services whatever the price level. Y_{MU} is the level of income below which mass unemployment is said to exist. To the left of Y_{MU} the aggregate supply schedule is horizontal. But between Y_{MU} and Y_{FE} the aggregate supply schedule is upward sloping, showing that increases in output will be associated with increases in prices. Between Y_{MU} and Y_{FE} there is a trade off between higher prices and lower unemployment.

The short run classical aggregate supply schedule

Classical or monetarist economists take a different view about the shape of the aggregate supply curve. They start by making two assumptions about production in the short run:

1 Resources are more or less fixed in supply in the short run—firms cannot build a new factory or double their workforce, for instance, overnight or even in a year.

2 The prices of the factors of production—wage rates, factory rents, the price of raw materials—are all constant.

So if a firm wishes to increase production it can do so, but only by utilising its existing resources. Workers can be put on overtime. The least efficient machines in a factory might be brought into operation after mothballing. Portacabins might be installed to provide extra office space. All of this is likely to raise the cost of production per unit. Workers will have to be paid at higher rates for overtime. Old machines cost more to operate than new machines. With higher costs, some firms will increase prices. However, the increase in prices will be relatively small because the underlying production costs are assumed to be constant.

If firms reduce their output, there will be some cost savings per unit of output. Expensive overtime will be

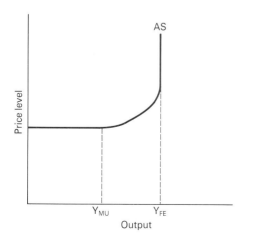

Fig. 13.6

reduced. The least efficient plant and machinery will be taken out of use. But firms will still have to pay the same for rent and rates, and many other costs will remain the same. So firms may reduce their prices in order to try to regain lost orders, but in the short run, firms will not be able to cut their costs—and therefore their prices—significantly.

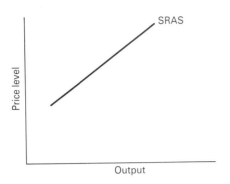

Fig. 13.7

The short run aggregate supply curve is therefore upward sloping, as in Fig. 13.7. Firms will supply more output but only at higher prices. However, the slope of the line is very shallow, indicating that prices will change little in response to changes in output.

What happens if the prices of resources do change? For instance, workers may obtain an increase in their wage rates. Or the price of oil or electricity may increase. Or the Government may increase the level of business rates. The short run aggregate supply schedule is drawn on the assumption that basic costs do not change. So a change in these costs will be shown by a

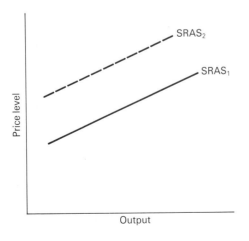

Fig. 13.8

shift in the aggregate supply schedule. For instance, the quadrupling of the world price of oil between 1973 and 1975 resulted in an upward shift in the short run aggregate supply schedule for nearly all producers in the UK at the time. In Fig. 13.8 the schedule will have shifted from $SRAS_1$ to $SRAS_2$.

The long run classical supply schedule

In the short run the prices of resources, particularly wage rates, are assumed to be fixed in classical theory. But in the long run all prices are assumed to be variable. Given that wages form 70% of national income in the UK, the most important determinant of aggregate supply is the price of labour—the wage rate.

In any normal free market, price is determined by the forces of demand and supply. If demand increases, there is a rise in prices. If supply increases, there is a fall in prices. If firms produce too much and cannot sell it all at the going price, they will be forced to reduce prices, for instance through having a sale. If, on the other hand, there is a shortage of goods on the market, firms and shops will tend to increase prices to obtain larger profits until demand and supply are again in equilibrium. In the long run, the market will always be in equilibrium where demand exactly equals supply.

The same will be true of the labour market if it too is a free market. If there is unemployment, it means that there is an excess supply of labour: too many workers want a job, in comparison with the number of jobs offered by employers. In a free market, prices will fall if this occurs. So if there is unemployment, wage rates will fall and will carry on falling until demand exactly equals supply. At this wage rate, there will be no unemployment, i.e. the economy will be at full employment.

If the economy is already at full employment, then an increase in the demand for labour from firms will drive wage rates up. Excess demand in the labour market results in higher wage rates and a return to equilibrium.

The conclusion that classical economists come to is that the economy will always be at full employment. There can be no unemployment in the economy in the long run if markets are free. This is true for the labour market. It is equally true for the markets for land and capital.

The long run aggregate supply schedule will then be vertical. Long run aggregate supply will be at the full employment level of output, whatever the price

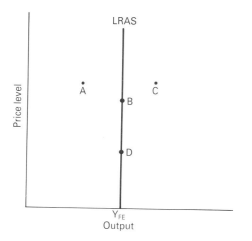

Fig. 13.9

Consider Fig. 13.10. The long run aggregate supply schedule is LRAS. The aggregate demand schedule is AD. In the long run, the equilibrium level of output is therefore OA and the equilibrium level of prices is OB. OA is not only the equilibrium level of output, it is also the full employment level of output. This is because the labour market too will be in equilibrium, with all workers wanting a job having one.

Assume that real growth takes place in the economy. This means that there is an increase in the quantity or quality of the factors of production available. The level of output associated with full employment output will be higher, i.e. the long run aggregate supply schedule will shift to the right. In Fig. 13.11,

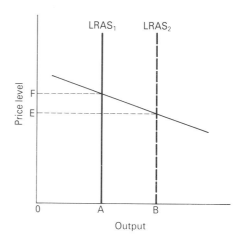

Fig. 13.11

level. This is shown in Fig. 13.9. The economy could be at B, or it could be at D or E. However, it cannot be at C because at C output is above full employment output—an impossibility by definition. Nor can it be at A because at A there is unemployment—an impossibility if all markets clear.

Equilibrium prices and income in the classical long run

It was explained in Chapter 2 that, in any individual market, the forces of demand and supply would establish an equilibrium price and quantity demanded. The same is true for the economy as a whole, but the analysis is a little more complicated.

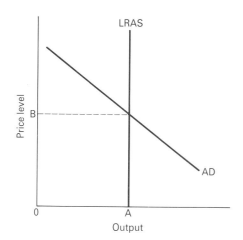

Fig. 13.10

economic growth is represented by the shift in the long run aggregate supply schedule from LRAS₁ to LRAS₂. Output will rise from OA to OB. Note also that the price level will fall from OE to OF. Increasing supply in the economy is one way of reducing inflationary pressures in the economy.

Now assume that aggregate demand increases without any increase in aggregate supply. For instance, the Government may increase spending on pensions, or provide better food in hospitals. Or foreigners may spend more on our exports. This is shown in Fig. 13.12. The aggregate demand schedule shifts from AD₁ to AD₂. Output however stays the same at OA. It must stay the same because OA is the full employment level of output—the economy cannot produce more than the full employment level. Prices however increase from OE to OF. So an increase in aggregate demand without any increase in aggregate supply will lead to inflation.

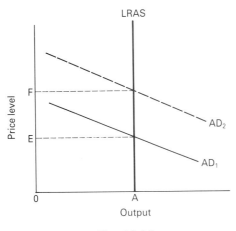

Fig. 13.12

Equilibrium prices and income in the classical model

The short run aggregate supply schedule is upward sloping. In Fig. 13.13, the economy is in equilibrium at its full employment level of output of OA. Here long run aggregate supply equals short run aggregate supply equals aggregate demand. Let us now discuss how changes in a number of economic variables will affect the economy. Assume that the economy starts from a state of full employment.

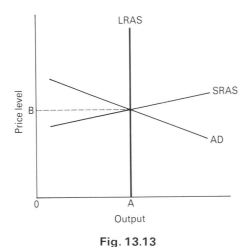

Fig. 13.13

1 The government increases state pensions This will increase the level of aggregate demand, from AD_1 to AD_2 in Fig. 13.14. Two things will now happen. Pensioners will spend the money but there will be few

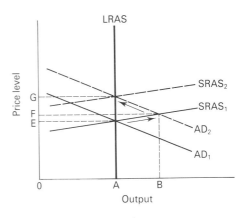

Fig. 13.14

extra goods in the shops, so inflation will take place. Prices will increase from OE to OF in Figure 13.14. There will also be an increase in aggregate supply. We have said before that in the long run the economy cannot be at more than full employment output. But in the short run it can be. Workers, for instance, are prepared to work a great deal of overtime to help their employers if they think it will only last a short period. A worker may be prepared to work 10 hours overtime this week but not be prepared to work 10 hours overtime every week of the year for the foreseeable future. The economy can therefore travel up the short run aggregate supply curve to OB. But now there is excess demand in the labour market. At an output level of OB, firms will want to recruit more workers, but there are no more workers in the market because OA was the full employment level of output. So if there is excess demand, firms will have to offer higher wage rates to their workers. This will increase their costs, and therefore the short run aggregate supply curve will shift upwards. (Remember the short run aggregate supply curve is drawn on the assumption that wage rates are constant.) SRAS will continue to shift upward until there is no more excess demand for workers, i.e. where there is just full employment. So it will shift upwards from $SRAS_1$ to $SRAS_2$ in Fig. 13.14. The price level will have increased but there will be no extra output in the long run.

2 Investment increases In micro-economics, a factor which causes a shift in the demand curve is most unlikely to shift the supply curve. In macro-economics, many changes in variables will affect **both** the aggregate demand and supply schedules. If there is an increase in investment, there will be a shift in the demand schedule, investment being a component of aggregate demand. In Fig. 13.15, the aggregate

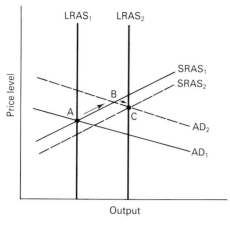

Fig. 13.15

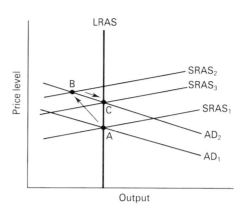

Fig. 13.16

demand schedule will shift from AD_1 to AD_2. In the short run, the economy will travel up to the short run aggregate supply schedule from A to B. However, eventually the extra investment spending will produce more factories, more offices and more machines. The long run aggregate supply schedule will therefore shift to the right, from $LRAS_1$ to $LRAS_2$. The short run aggregate supply schedule, too, is likely to shift downwards from $SRAS_1$ to $SRAS_2$. This is because the extra investment is likely to have reduced unit costs for producers, as new equipment is more efficient than old equipment. The economy will then move from the point B to the point C. Our model is not sophisticated enough to tell us whether prices will be higher or lower at C compared to A. That would depend largely on how efficient the new investment was.

3 Trade unions succeed in raising wage rates If trade unions succeed in increasing wage rates, two things will happen. Firstly, the short run aggregate supply curve will shift upwards, from $SRAS_1$ to $SRAS_2$ in Fig. 13.16. This is because the SRAS schedule is drawn on the assumption that wage rates are constant. Secondly, aggregate demand will increase because trade unionists will have increased incomes, and therefore will increase their consumption. This is shown by the shift in the demand curve from AD_1 to AD_2 in Fig. 13.16. The economy is now below full employment output. Firms will have laid off workers because they could not afford to pay the higher wages. Workers will have 'priced themselves out of jobs'. The forces of demand and supply will now act in the labour market, forcing wages down again to the situation where the demand for labour again equals its supply. This will push the short run aggregate supply sched-

ule downwards to $SRAS_3$. Here the economy returns to equilibrium at C. The actions of trade unions in pushing up wage rates in this model can be seen to be harmful. In the short term it creates unemployment. In the long term it is likely to increase prices.

4 The price of oil increases Between 1973 and 1975, the world price of oil quadrupled, sending shock waves through the world economy. In Fig. 13.17, this rise in the price of oil will have pushed up the short run aggregate supply schedule from $SRAS_1$ to $SRAS_2$. The UK economy, a major importer of oil at the time, will have moved from the point A to the point B. From this we can see that our model explains how the economy could experience both increased unemployment and increased inflation at the same time. But in

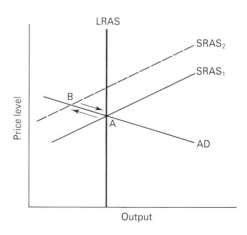

Fig. 13.17

the longer term, markets will slowly return to equilibrium. The price of oil, for instance, would come down as more oil was supplied and less demanded. Workers would have to accept lower wage rates because there is an excess supply of labour. The short run aggregate supply schedule would slowly return to SRAS₁, leaving both output and prices unchanged.

The classical—Keynesian debate

Aggregate demand and aggregate supply analysis is very important because it helps to explain some of the most important controversies today.

1 Can the economy be at less than full employment? Both classical and Keynesian economists agree that in the short run the economy can be at less than full employment. Classical economists argue that in the long run the economy will always return to full employment, but Keynesians disagree. They say that an economy can always have unemployment present. This is a disagreement about what is meant by the long run.

2 How long is the long run? In the long run, all markets will be in equilibrium. If there is unemployment in the short run, wage rates will fall until once again the demand and supply for labour are equal. Some classical economists—based upon a theory of rational expectations—argue that this will happen almost immediately. Most classical economists would

argue that this takes time—years, perhaps even a decade, for wage rates to fall far enough to eliminate unemployment. Keynesian economists argue that mass unemployement, such as we had in the 1930s and the early 1980s in the UK, took, or will take, decades to eliminate if left to free market forces. Wage rates only fall over very long periods of time. The long run is so long that it is hardly worth studying or considering.

3 Can a government spend its way out of unemployment? Classical economists would argue not. Look at Fig. 13.18. This shows two models of the economy, one a Keynesian model with an upward sloping supply curve, the other a classical model with a vertical long run aggregate supply schedule. An increase in government spending will increase aggregate demand, shifting the AD curve upwards and to the right. On classical assumptions, whilst this might increase employment in the short run, travelling up the SRAS, in the long run there will only be an increase in prices. Extra government spending is inflationary. For Keynesians, it depends on the level of unemployment in the economy. If the economy is at full employment with aggregate demand AD₃, an increase in spending will be inflationary, shifting the AD curve upwards. But if the economy is suffering mass unemployment, as with AD₁, then extra government spending can only be a good thing. It will shift the AD curve to the right, increasing output and reducing unemployment without any impact on prices. If the economy is somewhere between these two positions, then there will be a trade off—lower

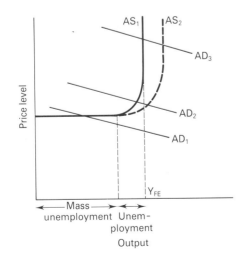

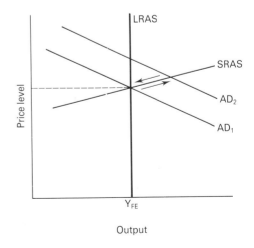

Fig. 13.18

unemployment can be achieved but only at the expense of higher prices in the economy. Keynesians would point out that the mass unemployment in the UK of the 1930s was finally brought to an end by big increases in government spending on defence in the early 1940s.

4 Are supply-side measures the only way to reduce unemployment? Supply-side measures are government policies designed to increase aggregate supply in the economy, pushing the long run aggregate supply schedule to the right. Since 1979, the UK Government has argued that extra government spending will not create jobs, and that the only solution to unemployment is supply-side measures. On classical assumptions, the Government is right. Pushing the LRAS to the right will create job opportunities. But on Keynesian grounds, it depends on the level of unemployment in the economy. If the economy is suffering from mass unemployment, then pushing the Keynesian aggregate supply schedule to the right from AS_1 to AS_2 (Fig. 13.18) won't have any effect on equilibrium output. It will help reduce unemployment a little if there is some unemployment. But Keynesians would agree with classical economists that supply side measures are the only way to create new job opportunities and expand the economy if the economy is at full employment.

Summary

The aggregate demand schedule for the economy is downward sloping. Economists disagree about the shape of the aggregate supply curve. Keynesian economists argue that it is upward sloping, whilst classical economists argue that in the long run it is vertical. The shape of the aggregate supply schedule has crucial implications for government policy. Classical economists argue that in the long run the economy will always be at full employment. They also argue that governments cannot use public spending to reduce unemployment whilst supply-side measures are very powerful.

Terms for review

aggregate demand schedule

aggregate supply schedule

Essay questions

1 Explain the concept of 'aggregate supply'. How might supply-side measures benefit an economy?

2 Outline a classical model of income and price determination. How does this model help explain (a) the stagflation which followed the two oil crises of the 1970s and (b) the impact of investment on employment and inflation in the economy?

Inflation

From the end of the Second World War until the mid 1960s, inflation was not considered a particularly important problem for the UK economy. This was because inflation during that period was very low and showed no signs of accelerating. At the time a low rate of inflation, as opposed to no inflation at all, was believed to be good for the economy. Low inflation made the real cost of borrowing lower, thus encouraging investment, and allowed workers to gain money increases in wages without the real cost being too high. Low inflation encouraged everybody to think that the economy was doing better than it was and consequently encouraged harder work, higher investment and higher growth than might otherwise have been the case. Inflation became a problem in the late 1960s, both in the UK and throughout the western world. As its seriousness became more and more apparent, so too the measures taken to combat it grew in importance. In this chapter we will consider the possible causes of inflation, and in Chapter 19 we will consider the policies designed to cure it.

The costs of inflation

High inflation is considered to be undesirable from an economic viewpoint for two main reasons, which are examined in detail below. Firstly, economic units incur expense in adjusting to new levels of prices. Secondly, inflation is likely to redistribute income in a possibly undesirable way.

Effects on costs and prices There is a wide variety of administrative costs involved at times of high inflation. For instance, firms will often be increasing the prices of their products. This means extra printing costs for packaging and promotional material, and extra manpower costs as firms have to decide on what their new prices should be. Consumers will be uncertain as to what is the 'right' price for a product and some will end up paying too high a

price as a result. Others will take more time to find out the best price than they would have done if prices have not been constantly changing. Psychologically, consumers feel that their real incomes are declining at times of high inflation and therefore they feel worse off. Workers will need to be prepared to confront their employers in order to obtain wage rises at least in line with increases in the cost of living. This may necessitate industrial action, which is another cost to society. It may also lead to worsening industrial relations in general and consequent loss of output.

Effects on redistribution The redistribution effects of inflation are many and varied, including the following:

1 Redistribution of income from persons on fixed incomes to persons on flexible incomes. One important group of fixed income earners are those on fixed occupational pensions. When they retire, the money value of their pension will remain the same from that point onwards. At an inflation rate of 10% a year, it only takes seven years to reduce the real value of that pension by approximately half. At 20% inflation, it takes only four years. Fewer resources available to persons on fixed incomes is likely to mean that those on non-fixed incomes, e.g. ordinary wage earners, can increase their share of national income.

2 Redistribution of income from lenders to borrowers. If the rate of inflation is above the level of interest rates, then real interest rates are negative. That means in effect that lenders of money are paying borrowers to borrow their money! Whilst real interest rates are negative there will be a redistribution of income from lenders to borrowers.

3 Redistribution of income from workers who are non-unionised, and those belonging to weak unions, to those who belong to strong unions. Workers who belong to unions with plenty of industrial muscle

Data 14.1

Lure of inflation

A symptom of how far the economy has been allowed to wander into inflationary territory is the revived debate on whether it is necessary to lower inflation at all. Such arguments are classic phenomena of the later stages of the economic cycle, when the bill for excessive earlier expansion falls due. They reflect a perfectly correct understanding that inflation can be lowered only by curbing demand, the scale of the required recession depending both on the extent of prior excess demand and the credibility of the Government's commitment to lower inflation. The interesting question is not how to lower inflation; it is whether the costs are justified.

It is simple to argue that the value of something that cannot itself be consumed should not be put above so much as a pound's worth of real output. Some even argue that a mild inflation, far from doing harm, is positively helpful, because it transfers income from rentiers to entrepreneurs.

On the first point, an advanced monetary economy like the British is not just a somewhat more developed barter economy. It is an entirely different creature. If the yardstick by which relative price changes are to be judged is highly uncertain in value, all decisions about the use of resources will be impaired.

Cheating people

More fundamentally, if inflation is to have significant real effects it is because it depreciates the real value of money or anything else relatively sticky in nominal value to a greater extent than generally expected. Inflation works by cheating people and will continue to work its expansionary magic only as long as the cheating goes on.

In an economy as attuned to inflation as that of the UK that will not be for very long. After the disinflation of the early 1980s and a few years of reasonably stable inflation, the Government had gained enough credibility for rapid expansion of demand to have sizeable real effects. But expectations are now adjusting upwards, as shown daily by events in the labour market.

Divided society

The main consequence of uncertainty about the prospects for inflation is that society becomes divided into organised groups whose main aim is to protect their members from its ravages. Not knowing where the rise in inflation may end, they naturally assume the worst. If the expansionary consequences of inflation are to continue, inflation must rise faster than expectations. Once

expectations catch up, a slowdown will ensue.

The question for the Government is whether the coming slowdown should be a relatively mild one, aimed at stabilising inflation at its new underlying rate (perhaps 6–7 per cent), or a relatively severe one, aimed at lowering inflation to where it was before it started its latest rise (about 4–5 per cent). If it chooses the former, the Government will lose much of the credibility it won so painfully in the early 1980s. When it has cheated once, what trust will be placed in promises not to cheat again? Inflation will again be seen as having only two directions: sidewards and upwards, with another severe disinflationary shock likely in the 1990s.

This then is the price of past mistakes. Either the Government acquiesces in higher inflation, so storing up problems for its successors, or it makes a serious effort to regain credibility now, inflicting significant economic damage in the process. It is too soon to tell which it will choose, since the going remains relatively smooth, so far. There is no simple way out of the dilemma, but it is amazing that the Government persists in rejecting the only available route to enhanced credibility right now: full membership of the European Monetary System.

The Financial Times. 15.6.89

---

1 What, according to the article, are the costs of inflation to an economy?

2 Explain why there might be costs to the economy in reducing the rate of inflation.

will find it easy to gain pay increases at least in line with inflation. Other workers will find it far more difficult and the result will be that pay differentials between these two groups will widen, in favour of the strongly unionised.

4 Redistribution of income from the private sector to the Government. Milton Friedman has called inflation an 'immoral tax' because only the government has the power to spend more than it earns and to finance it by effectively 'printing' the money. Printing money means that the government does not have to raise unpopular taxes. The results of more taxation or extra inflation are, however, the same: the government is able to secure a larger slice of the national cake at the expense of the private sector.

Ultimately, 'hyper-inflation' (very high rates of inflation) can cause such tensions in society that the economy breaks down. It may break down simply because people refuse to accept money for goods and services. Alternatively, it may break down because particular interest groups in society refuse to accept the consequences of future inflation and become locked in conflict with other groups in society.

Indexation—the linking of wages, interest rates, etc., to the rate of inflation—can only be a partial solution to the problem of inflation, although it is better than none at all. Indexation should prevent problems of redistribution of income. It should also reduce some of the administrative costs of inflation. Critics argue that governments which adopt indexation have accepted that inflation will be a long term problem which they are not going to be able to solve. This may well reduce their willingness to carry out painful anti-inflationary policies. Critics further argue that indexation also leads automatically to further bouts of inflation as one period's price rises are carried forward to the next period's wage increases. This is likely to be caused by workers attempting to obtain wage rises at least equal to the rate of inflation.

The causes of inflation

Two main schools of thought, monetarist and Keynesian, dominate the field. Keynes himself never fully developed a theory of inflation—he was far more preoccupied with unemployment in the 1920s and 1930s. He had, however, a very important influence on the policies designed to prevent inflation in the UK during the Second World War, by advocating the use of rationing rather than the price system to discourage consumption, thus releasing resources for the war effort.

Two basic ideas are put forward by Keynesian economists to explain inflation. Some believe it is caused by excess demand within the economy. Others believe that rises in costs explain the phenomenon of inflation.

Demand-pull inflation

In an individual market, if the quantity demanded exceeds supply at a given price, then prices will rise. Equilibrium will be restored when prices have risen, quantity demanded has fallen and quantity supplied has risen. The theory of demand-pull inflation argues that what is true of an individual market is equally true of the economy as a whole. Prices in general will rise (i.e. inflation will occur) if total or aggregate demand in the economy is greater than total supply.

At any point in time, the maximum level of supply in an economy is given by the value of full employment income. Full employment income is defined as that level of income where all factors of production are fully utilised, and therefore nothing more can be produced in the economy. So, if equilibrium income threatens to exceed full employment income, there will be excess demand in the economy. Prices will rise until that excess demand is eliminated. In other words, the money value of equilibrium income will rise until the money values of equilibrium income and full employment income are equal. Of course, no more goods and services are being produced than before.

The theory can be made more sophisticated if we assume that aggregate supply in the economy can be treated as fixed at levels of supply less than full employment national income. For instance, it could be the case that an economy is at considerably less than full employment but that the labour unemployed is 'unemployable' without considerable and time-consuming retraining, and that much capital is obsolete whilst still being in reasonable working order. Steel workers and shipyards have been in this position in the 1980s. An expansion of demand then sparks off demand-pull inflation because aggregate supply is unable to expand due to these **supply-side rigidities**. It then becomes perfectly feasible to experience inflation with high levels of unemployment.

Stagflation or **slumpflation**—the phenomenon of high inflation and high unemployment—is also possible within a demand-pull model if it is assumed that increases in the price of imports can lead to upward shifts in the domestic price level. The stagflation of the 1970s can be explained in these terms. High increases in the price of commodities, particularly oil, both in 1973/4 (after the Arab-Israeli War) and in 1978/9 (after the Iranian Revolution), led to high temporary domestic inflation

Data 14.2

Inflation: Retail price index, percentage change

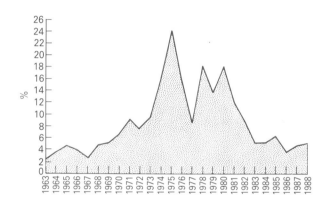

Unemployment UK, per cent

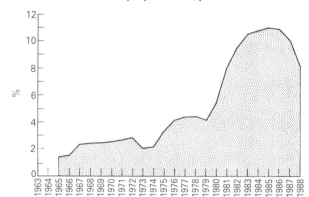

Vacancies notified to Jobcentres

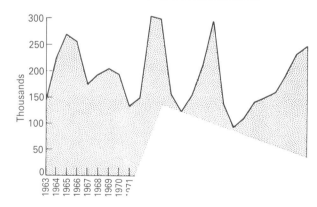

Source: CSO, Econom

To what extent was there excess demand in the UK economy over the period shown in the data?

2 Does the data s
mainly by der

rates. It also resulted in high unemployment as aggregate demand was cut to cope with the high inflation. However in the longer term, between 1975–7 and 1980–2, inflation fell, leaving the more normal situation of high unemployment and low inflation to prevail.

Demand-pull inflation can be illustrated diagrammatically. Aggregate demand or aggregate expenditure (E) in the economy is equal to consumption, investment and government spending on domestically produced goods, together with the value of domestic production which is exported. This is equivalent to the total value of expenditure on goods in the economy less the value of what is imported. This can be expressed by the equation:

$$E = C + I + G + X - M$$

Plotting E on an income–expenditure diagram with Keynesian assumptions about the consumption function, we arrive at Fig. 14.1. Equilibrium expenditure is at N, where expenditure equals income. At equilibrium income OP, consumption is PQ and QR represents the autonomous or exogenous expenditures in national income (I, G and X). Now assume that OS is full employment national income or a level of income beyond which supply-side rigidities are great. Then LN would represent excess demand in the economy. Prices will rise until such time as OS in real terms becomes OP in money terms. For instance, if OS were £200 billion and OP were £240 billion, then 20% inflation would occur. LM is termed an 'inflationary gap'. This gap can be eliminated either by a rise in prices or by a fall in expenditure of LM.

Cost-push inflation

The second strand of Keynesian thought has been the proposition that inflation is caused by the interaction between costs and final prices in the shops. In a normal market, as in Fig. 14.2, an increase in costs will result in an upward shift in the supply curve from S to S'. Firms are willing to supply the same amount as before, but only at a higher price, so equilibrium price paid will rise from P_1 to P_2. However, if this is a once and for all increase, then the process is hardly inflationary. Inflation is not just any increase in prices, but is a general rise in all prices over a period of time. This initial price rise from P_1 to P_2 must be followed by other movements in the economy.

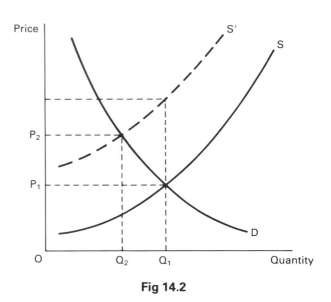

Fig 14.2

The cost-push theory argues that the increase in prices will lead to further increases in costs of home produced inputs to firms. For instance prices are likely to increase if producers experience:

1 rises in the cost of labour stemming from pay awards over and above increases in labour productivity;

2 rises in the cost of material inputs to the production process, such as fuel costs or local authority rates;

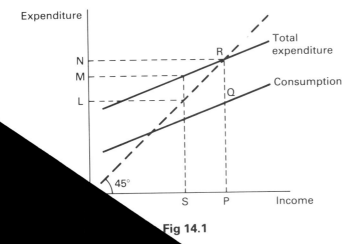

Fig 14.1

3 falls in the percentage profit that a firm is making on each item sold.

If a firm making steel puts up its price, it will push up the costs of motor cars. The motor manufacturer is likely to increase the price of cars, leading to an increase in the inflation rate. Trade unions will demand wage increases at least as large as the inflation rate in order to maintain their real standard of living. If firms grant such increases, then they will again have to increase their prices, pushing their supply curve even further to the left. Increased prices will lead to a loss of international competitiveness if other countries have lower inflation rates. Exports will become relatively more expensive and imports relatively cheaper. The resulting deterioration in the balance of payments could lead to a devaluation of the exchange rate.

Data 14.3

Inflation: Retail price index, percentage change

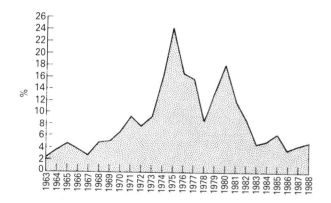

Change in average earnings

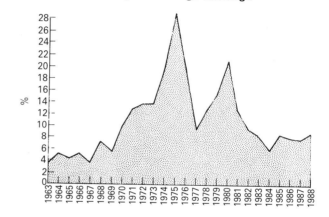

Change in import prices

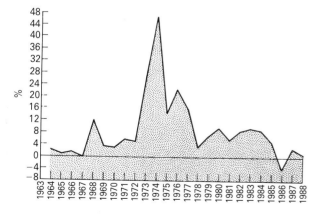

Change in gross trading profits of companies and financial institutions

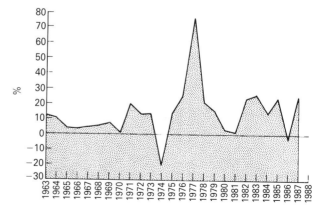

Source: CSO, Economic Trends, Annual Abstract of Statistics

1 What is meant by 'cost-push' inflation?
2 To what extent does the data support the hypothesis that inflation is mainly cost-push in nature?

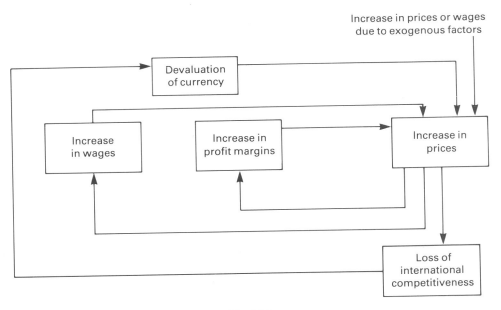

Fig 14.3

This will push up import prices and therefore increase costs to firms. Firms will be unwilling to see profit margins cut, so in money terms they will push up their prices as other costs increase. Figure 14.3 shows this in diagrammatic form.

A cost/price inflation cycle is thus in motion. The cycle may be explosive: that is, inflation increases at ever-accelerating rates. Or the cycle may be damped, so that the effects of the initial cost rise are slowly dissipated over time. Or the cycle may continue producing a constant rate of inflation over each time period.

For a cost-push spiral to be operating, firms and workers must be reacting to increases in prices and increases in costs. However, economists disagree about which group or which type of cost is most important in maintaining or starting off cost-push cycles.

Left wing economists see capitalist firms as continually pushing up profit margins in excess of the rate of inflation. Those on the political right are certain that it is trade union power which is at the root of cost inflation. The unions demand, and are able to get, wage increases well in excess of inflation by holding firms to ransom with the threat of strikes. Firms are then left with no option but to put up prices and restore profit margins in order to stave off bankruptcy. Other economists view cost-push inflation as being fuelled mainly by exogenous shocks to the economy. The Korean War led to massive increases in the price of raw materials and

hence to the price of imports for many countries. This generated an inflationary spiral in the early 1950s. The massive inflation of 1974/75 can be seen as the result of imported inflation, due again to massive increases in the prices of raw materials—particularly oil.

Monetarist theory

The traditional quantity theory approach to inflation was simple and direct. Using the transactions form of the quantity theory of money,

$$M V \equiv P T$$

if V and T are constants, then an increase in M, the money supply, will be transmitted to a resulting increase in P, the price level. V, the velocity of circulation of money, was determined by institutional constants, such as the sophistication of the banking system. T was dependent upon the level of national income. Therefore the money supply could grow without producing inflation if it were matched by any real growth in national income. Indeed if the money supply were not allowed to grow by the rate of real growth in income, then a decline in the price level could be expected. However, the traditional quantity theory fails to provide an adequate explanation as to why an increase in M should lead to inflation.

Data 14.4

Profit margins 'causing a third of rise in prices'

By Simon Holberton, Economics Staff

MANUFACTURERS' profit margins have been responsible for up to a third of the rise in factory-gate prices since 1980, the Bank of England says in its latest Quarterly Bulletin.

Manufacturers' profits have made a significant contribution to the growth in inflation over the period, but less so over the past two years than the Bank at first thought.

Recent data suggest that "the ten-dency of prices to outstrip costs has diminished somewhat as margins approach levels last seen in the early 1970s".

Looking back over the 1980s, the Bank says that while growth in margins has been an economy-wide feature, in the retail sector margins have actually fallen, although the rate of decline has moderated, probably reflecting excess retailing capacity in the UK.

The subdued level of margins has helped "retailed prices" – a measure developed by the Bank to disaggregate the retail prices index to arrive at a measure of retail inflation – to grow slowly from 1985 until the beginning of 1988.

Since then, however, other factors bearing down on price rises, such as a slow growth in costs, weak commodity and energy prices and high productivity growth have reversed somewhat.

The Financial Times. 11.5.89

1 *How does the data suggest that inflation is cost-push in nature?*

New monetarism is far more sophisticated in its explanation of inflation than was traditional monetarism. Its basic proposition, however, remains the same—that an increase in the supply of money over and above the rate of real growth in the economy will result in inflation. In the short run, the main effect of an increase in the money supply will be felt upon the money markets and the rate of interest. Real variables, such as the rate of growth of national income and unemployment, will change for the better through the operation of the transmission mechanism. In the long term these real variables will revert to their 'natural' levels and all of the effect of the increased money supply will come through in the form of increased inflation. The only way to reduce inflation is to reduce the rate of growth of the money supply.

The actions of firms, banks, trade unions, or any other group within the economy, might alter the path which the economy takes but the ultimate destination with regard to inflation is fixed. Milton Friedman would stress very strongly that governments cannot 'blame' anyone but themselves for allowing inflation to take place, as governments alone have the power to control the only determining variable—which is the rate of growth of the money supply.

The monetarist explanation as to why the money supply and the rate of inflation are linked was put forward in Chapter 13. However, traditionally the new monetarists have mainly defended their position on the empirical evidence available. They claim that it can be shown for any country at any time, that increases in the money supply have always been followed by increases in the price level.

Keynesians have counter-attacked by challenging much of the statistical basis on which this conclusion is reached. They also argue that there is a link between increases in prices and increases in the supply of money. Keynesians on the whole do not believe that the government can fully control the money supply. For instance, if the level of prices rises, more money will be demanded for the purpose of transactions. Price rises should increase the flow of money through the banking system, thus allow-ing the money supply to rise. Hence the pattern i not increases in the supply of money leading t increases in the rate of inflation, but precisely th reverse. Keynesians would argue that in numerou important instances, such as the economic situatio from 1929 to 1933, price falls preceded the fall in th money supply.

Data 14.5

Explaining broad money

From Mr Tim Congdon.

Sir, Mr Glenn Hoggarth (Letters, January 20) wonders how broad money can explain recent inflation trends, when the growth rate has been so much above the inflation rate. There are, in fact, several reasons for not expecting a precise relationship between broad money growth and the inflation rate.

The first is that extra money is needed to match more output as well as higher prices. If the trend annual rate of output growth in the UK in the mid-1980s is put at about $3\frac{1}{2}$ per cent, and the growth rate of broad money had been exactly equal to that of output and inflation combined (that is, of nominal GDP), an inflation rate of about 5 per cent would have been associated with broad money growth of about 8 per cent or 9 per cent a year.

The second is that the amount of money people and companies wish to hold may increase more quickly or slowly than nominal GDP because of institutional developments in the financial system and changes in the attractiveness of money compared to other things. During most of the 1980s such considerations seem to have been increasing the desired ratio of broad money to nominal GDP by about 3 per cent or 4 per cent a year. With inflation

of about 5 per cent, people and companies were therefore satisfied with their own money holdings while broad money was growing at about 11 per cent to 13 per cent a year. This was, indeed, the growth rate of M3 for roughly four years from mid-1981 to mid-1985.

But it is possible for actual money holdings to be higher than desired, with a sudden jump in the growth rate of bank deposits reflecting a surge in bank credit. The economy then has "excess liquidity". Companies, people and financial institutions find that they have more money than they expected, and they change their behaviour.

Most obviously, they spend a higher proportion of their income (that is, the savings ratio falls) and are more eager to purchase assets such as houses, shares and property. As a result, the prices of these assets are bid up, strengthening the incentive to invest. In due course the excess liquidity leads to a boom.

There is no way of telling exactly how much excess liquidity the economy can stand before the boom runs out of control. In the Barber boom of the early 1970s the ratio of broad money to GDP rose by almost 30 per cent in two years before the Government realised that there was "too much money chasing too few goods".

At any rate, by late 1986 it seemed to me that there had been a well-defined acceleration in broad money growth from that seen in the stable 1981–1985 period. The economy was about to enter a phase of excess liquidity, which would initially be accompanied by buoyant asset prices and above-trend growth, and would later be followed by rising inflation and/or deteriorating external payments.

The forecasts were not mechanical extrapolations from recent M3 figures. They involved considerable judgement and analysis, as well as much attention to non-monetary variables. It is nevertheless strange that we were virtually the only forecasters to believe that the rise in M3 growth from the 11 per cent to 13 per cent level of the 1981–1985 period to the more recent 15 per cent to 22 per cent range would have powerful effects on economic activity and intensify inflation pressures. There seems to be something fundamental here, as the consensus forecasters – who tend to neglect monetary variables – were even more badly wrong in the forecasts they made during and after the Barber boom.

Tim Congdon

The Financial Times. 24.1.89

---

1 Outline a simple theory of the relationship between 'money growth and the inflation rate'.

2 What arguments does the writer give to explain why this simple theory failed to predict the changes in inflation during the 1980s?

Data 14.6

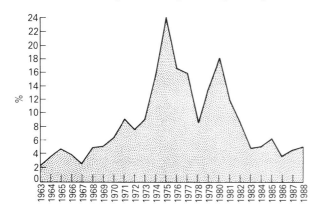

Inflation: Retail price index, percentage change

Change in money stock sterling: M_0, M_1, M_4

Source: CSO, Economic Trends

1 Can the causes of inflation be said to be solely a monetary phenomenon? Support your answer with evidence from the data.

The Phillips curve

One piece of empirical research must be cited at this point. In 1958, A. W. Phillips published a paper claiming that there was a stable relationship between the rate of change of wages and the level of unemployment in the UK economy. He plotted figures for the UK economy between 1862 and 1958, and the result was a downward sloping curve as in Fig. 14.4. The higher the level of unemployment, the lower the level of wage increases. Indeed, when unemployment was high enough (as in the early 1930s), wages actually fell. Over a long period of time, wage rises and inflation tend to move together. Hence economists concluded that there was some sort of trade-off possible between unemployment and inflation.

Phillips' empirical findings were almost universally accepted but can be interpreted in a variety of ways. Proponents of demand-pull inflation argue that the level of unemployment in the economy is a good measure of the level of excess demand. High levels of unemployment show that there is little or no excess demand, and hence inflationary pressures are minimal. However, as unemployment declines, the economy moves nearer and nearer to full employment. Certain industries will reach a state of excess demand more rapidly than others. These industries will see the price of their output start to rise. Gradually inflationary pressures will really start to mount, as all industries reach full capacity.

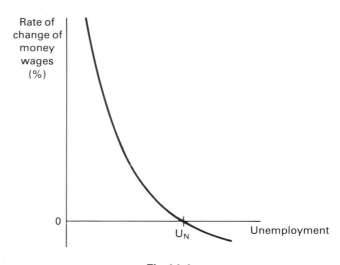

Fig 14.4

Inflation

Hence the Phillips curve can be used to modify the rather crude inflationary gap theory of demand-pull Keynesians. Instead of assuming that inflation only takes hold once full employment has been reached, this modified inflationary gap hypothesis argues that the nearer one gets to full employment, the more inflation there will be in the economy.

In Fig. 14.5, inflation is plotted against the level of income. The nearer the economy gets to being at full employment, Y_{FE}, the higher will be the demand-pull pressures and the higher will be the inflation rate. Any attempt to push the economy beyond full employment will only result in rocketing inflation rates. Notice that the diagram shows that 0% inflation can only be maintained at less than full employment.

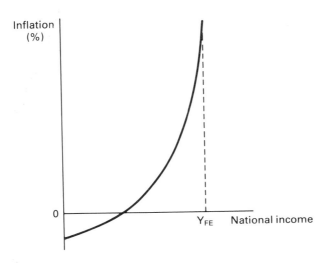

Fig 14.5

Proponents of cost-push theories of inflation can equally claim that the Phillips curve vindicates their hypothesis. The level of unemployment is a major factor in determining the militancy of trade unions, the ability of importers to raise prices and the desire of firms to push up prices to improve profit margins. If unemployment is low, trade unions will not be worried about the threat of redundancies if wage claims are too high for a company to bear. Their members will feel in a strong position to bargain for large pay increases. When unemployment is high, however, workers are often prepared to accept relatively low wage increases for fear of losing their jobs or because other groups of workers are getting lower settlements as well. Hence, low

levels of unemployment are associated with large increases in costs, including labour costs, whereas the reverse is true for high levels of unemployment. This is of course the prediction of the Phillips curve.

Monetarists point out that the point U_N in Fig 14.4 represents the level of unemployment at which price increases are zero. This level is called the natural rate of unemployment. When the money supply is increased over and above the rate of real growth in the economy, there are two consequences. Firstly, existing workers are able to secure higher money wages. Secondly, the rate of growth of real output will increase, thus lowering unemployment. Hence the economy will move to a point diagonally upwards and to the left on Fig. 14.4, as predicted by the Phillips curve.

However, this is only a short term move. The government will then have to decide on whether to increase the rate of growth of the money supply or to decrease it. If it is increased, unemployment will drop still further but wage inflation will further increase. If it is allowed to fall, recession will follow and the economy will travel back down the Phillips curve. Note that if the government decided to keep the money supply increase constant, then eventually the economy would return to equilibrium. This state of equilibrium would be one with unemployment at its natural rate and inflation at a rate determined by the rate of increase of the money supply minus the rate of real growth in the economy. This equilibrium level of inflation could be at any level. Hence, in the long term, the Phillips curve is vertical as in Fig. 14.6. There is no long term trade-off between unemployment and inflation.

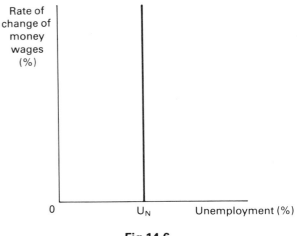

Fig 14.6

What the short term Phillips curve shows is the cyclical pattern of the UK economy, and in particular the never-ending pattern of different rates of growth of the money supply compared with increases in real national income over the period 1861–1958.

All schools of thought, then, can draw comfort from the Phillips curve! However, complications have arisen since the publication of Phillips' original article in 1958. The Phillips curve relationship predicted the UK economy with remarkable accuracy up to 1966. But after that date yearly readings were entirely unpredictable, as large wage increases started to become associated with historically high levels of unemployment. It quickly became apparent that the Phillips curve was shifting to the right as in Fig. 14.7.

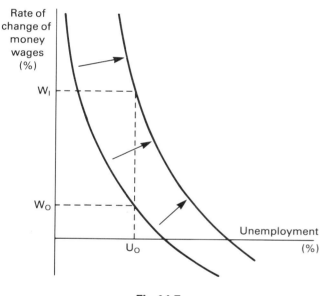

Fig 14.7

The most widely accepted argument explaining this was put forward by two monetarist economists, Phelps and Friedman. They argued that the Phillips curve was a good predictor over the chosen time period because economic units (workers, firms, consumers, etc.) had no expectations that prices would rise—that is, they suffered from money illusion. However, in the late 1960s inflation started to become a part of everyday consciousness in the UK. 1966 saw the first statutory prices and incomes policy, with all the publicity that that entailed. Economic units therefore revised their expectations.

At a given level of unemployment, workers sought and obtained wages equal to the amount implied by the original Phillips curve plus the expected rate of inflation. Firms were willing to pay these increases because they believed that they could pass on the wage increases in the form of higher prices. In Fig. 14.7, if unemployment is at U_0, the original Phillips curve would predict that the increase in wage rates would be W_0. However, if economic units expect inflation of W_0W_1, the final wage increase will not be W_0 but W_1. Hence, there will be a family of Phillips curves extending outwards from the origin, depending upon the level of expected inflation.

However, the Phelps-Friedman hypothesis, known as the 'expectations-augmented Phillips curve hypothesis', has not been the only one put forward. Other economists have argued that the shift to the right of the Phillips curve can be attributed to other causes. For instance, if trade unions have become more militant, they might obtain higher wage increases at any given level of unemployment. Higher unemployment benefits might encourage workers to be more selective in their choice of new job. This will result in workers staying longer on average in the dole queues. Statistically this results in higher measured unemployment. Hence unemployment will be higher at any given rate of inflation. Equally, higher redundancy settlements will encourage redundant workers to spend more time searching for new jobs. Note that these explanations can in fact be consistent with the Phelps-Friedman hypothesis. Friedman would argue that more trade union power results in a shift to the right in the natural rate of unemployment, dragging the short term Phillips curve with it. However, inflationary expectations can then push the Phillips curve even further to the right.

Summary

Since the mid 1960s, inflation has been an intractable problem facing western economies. Inflation distorts the workings of an economy and is disliked by producers, consumers and income earners. Three major hypotheses concerning the cause of inflation exist: the demand-pull theory, which argues that inflation is a result of excess demand in the economy; cost-push theory, which argues that inflation is caused by increases in costs of production; and monetarism, which argues that excessive increases in the money supply are the sole cause of inflation. The Phillips curve showed that for nearly a century there was a strong correlation in the UK between unemployment and the rate of increase in money wages. Since 1966, however, the Phillips curve has ceased to hold. One possible explanation of this is that rises in expectations have caused the Phillips curve to move to the right.

Essay questions

1 *What is meant by 'inflation'? Why is inflation considered to be a problem?*

2 *Do budget deficits cause inflation?*

3 *Can the oil price rises of the 1973/4 and 1978/9 be said to have been inflationary?*

Terms for review

inflation

indexation

demand-pull inflation

cost-push inflation

slumpflation

Phillips curve

expectations-augmented Phillips curve

15

Unemployment

Introduction

Any economy facing mass unemployment has a major economic and social problem on its hands. The economic problem lies in the fact that scarce factors of production are lying underutilised and wasted. Consumers want goods and services; workers want to provide them; factories and work-places are probably lying idle. Yet the economic system is unable to match up this desire for work with this desire for goods and services. The social problem lies in the poverty that unemployment brings with it, and this involves not merely a deprivation of material goods and services. It involves also the feelings of degradation and rejection that the unemployed feel, living in a society where a job gives status and satisfaction whilst unemployment is considered a failure of the individual. Poverty, both material and psychological, is the fate of the unemployed.

At its simplest, an analysis of unemployment rests on demand and supply analysis. In Fig. 15.1, demand and supply curves for labour are shown, and in equilibrium the wage rate OF will prevail. OB of labour will then be employed. One reason for the demand curve for labour being downward sloping is that producers can always substitute machines and other materials for labour. There will be some wage rate at which it pays the producer to get a machine to do the man's work. With micro-technology, one of the main trade union fears is that machinery will become so cheap in relation to labour that very few people will be employed. The supply curve is upward sloping for a number of reasons. For the individual, higher pay might induce him to work more overtime or take a second job. For the market as a whole, higher wage rates will lead to more women entering the labour force instead of remaining as unpaid housewives. Others outside the workforce will find it worthwhile to get a job, and fewer might leave the labour force as working becomes relatively attractive compared to having a child, undertaking further training or retiring.

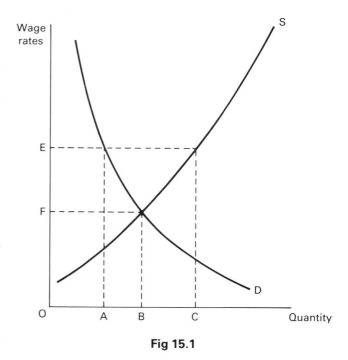

Fig 15.1

Unemployment will occur if more people are seeking a job than are employed at the current wage rate. In Fig. 15.1, if OC people want a job but only OA people have got jobs, then AC represents the amount of unemployment in the economy at a wage rate of OE. Full employment in the labour market exists where everyone who wants a job at the current wage rate has got one.

Of course it is unrealistic to consider that there is only one labour market. Each industry and each profession has its own set of demand and supply curves. There could well be unemployment in, say, the market for plumbers, but excess demand at the going wage rate for brain surgeons. Regional markets exist too, and whilst one region might be suffering from a shortage of workers, other regions might be suffering high unemployment.

Types of unemployment

Six main types of unemployment can be distinguished.

1 Frictional unemployment This occurs when workers leave or are forced to leave a job, and spend some time out of work looking for or waiting to take up fresh employment. Frictional unemployment is inevitable in any economic system, but its size depends very much on a number of factors. Firstly, the efficiency of systems designed to link employer with job seeker has an important bearing on the problem. This will include how well newspapers and other media can communicate, and how well private and public employment agencies link the two sides together. Knocking a couple of weeks off the time that the average job seeker takes to find a job could well reduce the unemployment rate by around 1% in many western economies. Also important is the ratio between benefits, current wage rates and average expenditure. Many western economies now run redundancy schemes whereby those workers dismissed through no fault of their own receive redundancy payments. Whilst unemployed, the state or private insurance schemes continue to pay benefits to the unemployed person. It is widely recognised by economists that the longer an unemployed person can stay unemployed and still maintain a reasonable standard of living, the higher will be the frictional unemployment figure. On the other hand, a reduction in the ratio of benefits to wages will make unemployment less attractive and obtaining work more attractive. For a small minority of the unemployed, increases in the benefits/wage ratio will mean that they effectively cease to look for work and prefer to live permanently on 'welfare'. For the majority, it will mean that they are a little more choosy about the job they take up. This increase in 'choosiness' will lead to an increase in the average length of time spent unemployed by job seekers.

2 Seasonal unemployment Many industries lay off workers at periods of low demand. Obvious examples are the building industry and the tourist industry. The unemployment caused by these regular fluctuations at different times of the year is called seasonal unemployment. It usually reaches a peak in mid winter and is at its lowest in mid summer. Much of the variation can be attributed to the weather, although not all seasonal unemployment is linked with poor weather conditions.

3 Structural unemployment Structural unemployment exists where the number of workers looking for jobs in a particular labour market far exceeds the number of jobs available and as a result those workers remain unemployed. Two main types of structural unemployment are commonplace. Firstly regional unemployment exists where unemployment rates in some regions of a country are consistently higher than in other regions. Much of the cause of regional unemployment can be attributed to the immobility of labour. Many workers may be unwilling or unable to leave an area familiar to them and where they have housing, to go and seek work in another area. Equally important is sectoral unemployment. Some sectors of industry decline whilst others emerge. Much regional unemployment is caused by the fact that the regions concerned are often dependent upon declining industries. However, sectoral unemployment will affect every region to some extent. In these industries, there are far too many workers with specific skills for that industry compared to the number of jobs available. Hence structural unemployment is present here too.

4 Cyclical, Keynesian or demand-deficient unemployment This occurs when there is too little spending in the economy to keep all the workers in jobs. Aggregate demand is not high enough and therefore a deflationary gap exists. Keynes argued that the main cause of mass unemployment in the UK economy in the 1930s was a lack of demand, and so this type of unemployment is sometimes called Keynesian unemployment. It is also called cyclical unemployment because it occurs during the period in the trade cycle when the economy is in recession or in a slump. During the trade cycle there are regular fluctuations in the level of economic activity. Sometimes the economy is in boom and there is full employment. At other times the economy suffers from unemployment and it is said to be in recession or in slump.

5 Hidden Unemployment Published unemployment statistics are notoriously unreliable as an accurate picture of the level of unemployment in an economy. Much depends on the definition of unemployment which is taken. Some countries define 'unemployed' as those collecting welfare payments for being unemployed. But this will not include a large number of others, particularly women, who are not able to draw benefit because they have not made necessary payments previously, but who are actively seeking a job. Other countries use returns from state employment agencies where the unem

130

Data 15.1

Unemployment by duration UK[1]

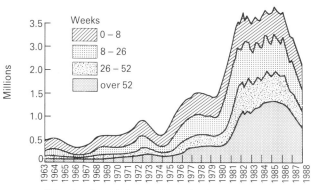

Weeks
- 0 – 8
- 8 – 26
- 26 – 52
- over 52

Millions

[1] There is a discontinuity in the data at October 1982.

Source; Department of Employment:

Unemployment UK, per cent

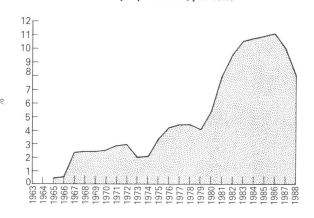

%

Change in gross domestic product at factor cost (at 1985 prices)

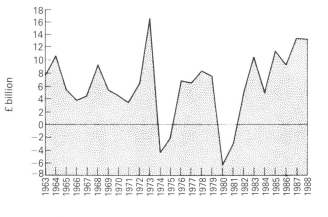

£ billion

Vacancies at Jobcentres

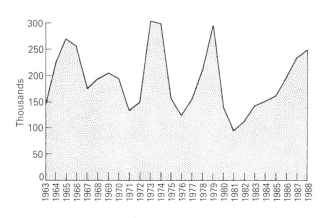

Thousands

Source: CSO, Economic Trends, Annual Abstract of Statistics

1 *To what extent have frictional, structural and cyclical unemployment increased over the period shown in the data?*

2 *How would you account for the relationship shown in the data between unemployment and unfilled vacancies?*

ployed go to find help in looking for a new job. This too will miss those who cannot be bothered to use state agencies, or who consider them inappropriate to their needs. Other countries use sample surveys, asking people whether or not they are employed and, if not, whether they are seeking work. This might include too many people, because a minority of respondents may say that they would take a job if offered, but are not prepared actively to seek a job. Doubts are expressed about those considered unemployed under any method of calculation who are 'unemployable'—for instance the severely handicapped and those who find it difficult to settle down in regular employment. Some economists argue that an unemployable person cannot be considered unemployed. Administration, too, can cause unemployment. Various categories of persons might have to declare themselves unemployed in order to receive rights and benefits from the state and other organisations, but have no intention of taking up employment. These can range from workers on private early retirement schemes to the so-called 'scrounger'. Hidden unemployment also occurs if workers are underemployed. A person might be underemployed if for instance he is in part-time work, but would like full-time employment. Again, a firm might keep a worker despite the fact that his output does not warrant the cost of employing him. This may occur either if the state is subsidising the work-place or if the cost of making the worker redundant, and subsequently taking on a new worker, is greater than keeping the worker whilst demand improves. Many women must also be included amongst the hidden unemployed as they are often prepared to work if jobs are easy to get but do not actively seek work if job vacancies are few. Equally school leavers on government work schemes form part of the hidden unemployed. The current UK official unemployment statistics, based upon a count of those receiving benefits for being unemployed, tell us little about how many people are unemployed in the UK. The way in which the figures were calculated was changed 19 times between 1979 and 1988, almost every change reducing the official number of people counted as unemployed. However, what the official statistics *can* tell us about is the trend in unemployment over time. Unemployment in the UK did rise dramatically between 1973 and 1977, and again between 1979 and 1984.

6 Classical or real wage unemployment In recent years, the theory of unemployment which Keynes attacked in the 1930s has returned to popularity as an explanation of the high levels of unemployment experienced by Western economies in the late 1970s and 1980s. This theory of unemployment is called the classical or neo-classical theory of unemployment. Neo-classical economists firmly rooted their analysis of unemployment on an analysis of the labour market. They argued that long term unemployment could not exist. In the short run, large scale unemployment might develop but this would quickly disappear as the real wage rate was forced down in the cut and thrust of the competitive labour market. Of course, certain types of unemployment were unavoidable. Frictional and seasonal unemployment would continue. Structural unemployment might also develop if workers were immobile, refusing to move around the country for new jobs, or refusing to change industries.

In Fig. 15.2, assume that the wage rate is W_U. Then OQ_S of labour will be supplied but only OQ_D demanded. Hence unemployment of Q_DQ_S would exist. Neo-classical economists argued that workers would be prepared to accept lower wage rates in

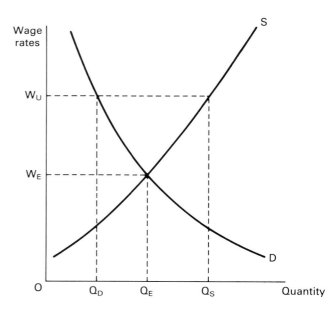

Fig 15.2

rder to keep a job or get a job. If wage rates are educed to W_E, then Q_EQ_S of labour would no longer wish to work (they are discussed below). On the emand side firms would wish to employ an extra $_DQ_E$ of labour. The result of the reduction in wages is equilibrium in the labour market. At a wage rate f W_E there is no unemployment in the labour market—Q_E is the full employment level of the economy. This is because at the given wage rate W_E veryone who wants a job has got one.

What has happened to those workers who have eft the workforce as a result of the fall in wages— $_EQ_S$ in Fig. 15.2? Some of them may consider memselves unemployed. Indeed they may appear in overnment statistics as unemployed. To neo-classical economists, they were 'voluntarily' unemployed. The **voluntary unemployed** were the orkers who were not prepared to work at existing age rates. In a modern economy, voluntary unemployment is likely to exist where state benefits eceived by an unemployed person, together with osts associated with work (e.g. bus fares, protective othing), are just below, equal to, or just above the ake-home pay of jobs which a worker is able to obtain. One way to reduce voluntary unemployment to cut state benefits. This would encourage workers who were only prepared to accept a wage above $_E$ to find a job at wage rate W_E or below. Put nother way, cutting unemployment benefits reuces measured unemployment.

Another cause of large-scale unemployment was rgued to be the trade union movement. If trade nions refused to allow real wages to fall, then this would allow mass unemployment to continue. Many eo-classical economists thought that trade unions layed an important role in preventing the economy rom recovering automatically in the Great Depression of the 1930s. The effect of trade unions can be llustrated diagrammatically in Fig. 15.3. In quilibrium, wages are W_E and the number employed is Q_E. If S and D represent the supply and emand curves for labour respectively, then Q_E ust be the level of full employment according to ne argument put forward above. Assume now that ne work force becomes unionised and wage cuts are uccessfully opposed. Furthermore, the economy oes into depression, shifting the demand curve for abour to the left, from D to D'. Firms now want ewer workers at the wage rate of W_E. At this wage te only Q_T workers will be demanded. Q_TQ_E orkers have been made redundant and there is nemployment in the economy. In this case, full mployment could be restored if the trade unions

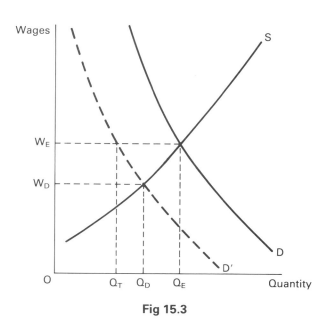

Fig 15.3

To what extent might trade unions cause unemployment?

133

Data 15.2

Job vacancies 'exaggerated'

By John Gapper

MOST JOB vacancies are being taken by people who are already in work and the idea that there is a large stock of unfilled vacancies which unemployed people are failing to take is false, according to a study of vacancies in Derbyshire.

The census of jobs on offer in Chesterfield during one week in July also found that the Government's method of calculating the number of vacancies available across the country produced an exaggerated count for the town.

The Department of Employment yesterday strongly criticised the study, carried out for the BBC programme Brass Tacks. It said a report of the findings was biased and drew unfair conclusions from limited evidence.

The census was intended to find all the jobs available in the town – selected as an average jobs market – and identify their characteristics. It concentrated particularly on the vacancies which became available that week.

It found that 55 per cent of the vacancies were notified in the local Jobcentre. The Government estimates vacancies at about three times those in Jobcentres. The census also found that 230 of the 845 vacancies became available in the week studied. A report of the findings says: "The flow of jobs is rapid: they disappeared pretty quickly and 89 per cent had gone in under three months."

There were around six unemployed people for every vacancy. However, a follow-up survey found that, of the jobs filled, only 23 per cent of those becoming available in the week went to unemployed people.

Fifty two per cent of vacancies paid between £2.01 and £2.50 an hour. The report says that many jobs were offering pay which was less than benefit entitlement.

The Department said the programme was based on "selective and subjective information" and the report, written by Ms Catherine Marsh, a Manchester University research fellow, had made a series of unsubstantiated assertions.

The Financial Times. 7.11.88

Warning on creation of 'underclass'

By Our Labour Staff

THE GOVERNMENT must encourage employers to recruit the long-term unemployed if a permanent underclass of so-called disaffected, alienated onlookers is not to be created, says a study published today.

The study suggests young long-term unemployed are willing to undertake poorly-paid and unattractive jobs to escape their predicament.

The report, by Dr Susan McRae, suggests long-term unemployed do not choose to become so but are the victims of a restructuring of the labour market that has cut the availability of jobs they can perform.

Dr McRae interviewed 119 people between the ages of 20 and 27 years picked at random.

Nearly three-quarters of the young men interviewed and half the young women had experienced five or more years of unemployment, in spells of varying durations, since leaving school.

In spite of the cost of job-searching, only six of the 119 had given it up altogether. Most sought work through Jobcentres because this avoided the feelings of inadequacy which came from asking friends about jobs.

The Financial Times. 14.12.87

---

1 To what extent does the data support the view that unemployment in the UK is mainly voluntary in nature?

2 Can unemployment be substantially reduced by cutting wage rates?

allowed a reduction in wages from W_E to W_D. At wage rate W_D, everyone who wanted a job could get one. However, if the trade unions continued to fight and maintain a wage rate of W_E, then unemployment was the inevitable result. Trade unions could thus be blamed for causing high unemployment in the face of recession.

Much importance, then, was paid by neo-classical economists to the reduction of wages in order to cure unemployment. They were particularly interested in analysing those forces which prevented the labour market from correcting itself and 'sticking' at a point which did not represent full employment equilibrium. This sort of thinking was predominant during the period from the turn of the century to the beginning of the Second World War. Hence the attempts by most governments to cure the great depression of the 1930's by wage cuts can be understood from this theoretical viewpoint.

Keynes' contribution

When Keynes wrote *The General Theory of Employment, Interest and Money*, in 1936, he was faced with a world in the grip of high persistent unemployment. The depth and severity of the great depression had scarred the thinking of politicians and economists alike and unemployment was considered the single most important economic issue of the time. Mass unemployment in nearly all western economies had started in 1929/30 and was to persist until the outbreak of the Second World War. Neo-classical economists had suggested that this was caused by rigidities in the labour market. Keynes was to put forward a very different idea.

Keynes pointed out that it was not unnatural for workers to resist cuts in their money wages, even if prices were falling at the same time. Money wages, he argued, were 'sticky' downwards. Hence the labour market would take a long time to return to equilibrium if mass unemployment resulted from supply exceeding demand. Whilst returning to equilibrium, the economy and, very importantly, individuals would suffer much hardship, as witness the terrible scenes of the 1930s. He also argued that the easiest way to cut real wages was not to reduce money wages, but to keep money wages constant and raise the general level of prices, i.e. inflation could help to reduce unemployment. But this would only work if workers did not try to get money wage increases to compensate for the increase in prices.

One reason why they might not do so would be if they suffered from 'money illusion'. Money illusion happens when economic units fail to take changes in prices into account in their decision-making. If prices go up, but their money wages remain the same, they fail to realise that they are in fact worse off. They do not try to restore their real wages by demanding higher money wages.

However, Keynes did not argue (as many of his critics and his followers have suggested) that this stickiness was enough to ensure that an economy could stay for ever in a situation of mass unemployment. Real wages could come down in the long run. But the long run might well be a period of 10–15 years, and in that time millions would have suffered the effects of unemployment.

If wage reductions were not the answer, what was? Keynes and his followers have argued that the only solution to mass unemployment, or indeed any degree of cyclical unemployment, is to increase aggregate demand. By increasing aggregate demand, governments can push the demand curve for labour to the right. This is because labour is a 'derived' demand. More labour is demanded when more goods and services are demanded.

This is shown in Fig. 15.4. If unemployment of $E_1 E_2$ exists, the solution is not to attempt to reduce wages from W_1 to W but to push the demand curve for labour from D to D'. One way of increasing aggregate demand, according to Keynes, is to increase government spending. Via the multiplier process, this will increase income by a larger amount and will therefore increase the demand for labour.

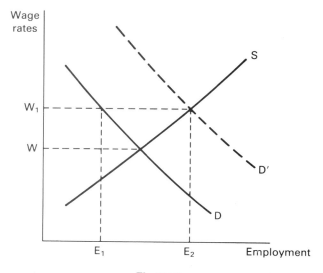

Fig 15.4

Unemployment

*The Jarrow March, 1936, and the March for Jobs, 1981.
Both marches asked Parliament to solve the
unemployment problem. Have governments the power
to do this?*

Data 15.3

An anniversary to forget

Ralph Atkins

Celebrations are unlikely as Britain this month marks the 13th anniversary of an unemployment figure over the million mark. Joblessness remains an unwelcome scar on the UK's economic performance.

Not since September 1975 have official figures measured unemployment simply in hundreds of thousands.

Since its peak of 3.2m in July 1986, seasonally adjusted unemployment (excluding school leavers) has dropped steadily.

Recent falls have coincided with two years when the UK economy has grown by about 4 per cent a year. If growth slows down in the 1990s, as is widely expected, the declining trend may peter out.

The high level of unemployment suggests that its causes in the early part of the decade are proving irreversible. In

the first years of Mrs Thatcher's premiership, strict monetary controls against a background of oil price rises and world-wide recession are widely blamed for the big shake-out in industry. Unemployment rose from a low point of 1.1m in September 1979 to more than 3m by 1986.

The economic outlook is now much rosier, although the rise in unemployment between 1979 and 1986 has been only slightly mitigated.

On the other hand, the Government can fairly argue that further improvement in the labour market may have been disguised for two reasons.

First, the effect of time lags: not surprisingly, the economic upswing appears to have been demand-led. Factories have responded to increased demand from consumers by increasing output, rather than the other way

round. This year the UK is enjoying a massive investment surge, which might increase future employment.

Second, demographic trends were unfavourable in the early 1980s. There was a significant increase in the size of the working population, especially in the group under 25, where unemployment rates tend to be higher.

When, then, will unemployment fall below 1m again? It is unwise to be too optimistic. On the optimistic assumption of 3 per cent growth a year, unemployment might fall to 2.2m next year and to 1.4m in 1992.

However, to expect 3 per cent annual growth may be unrealistic. Fast growth is already leading to a big trade deficit, which would get much worse if it were to continue. The Government would almost certainly be forced to take action to slow activity.

The Financial Times. 15.9.88

1 Explain how the author of the article accounts for the high unemployment of the 1980s.

2 To what extent might Keynesian policies of increasing aggregate demand be effective in reducing unemployment in the 1990s?

The classical view—the natural rate of unemployment

Monetarist views on unemployment are neo-classical in origin. Modern monetarists believe that unemployment is essentially caused by an imbalance of demand and supply. Unemployment could easily be solved if only workers were to price themselves back into jobs, i.e. accept real wage cuts.

Milton Friedman made a significant contribution to the debate on the labour market in the late 1960s by proposing that a 'natural rate of unemployment'

existed for an economy. He argued that the amount of labour employed in the economy was fixed by demand and supply conditions in the market. Factors affecting demand and supply would include the degree of trade union power, the mobility of labour, the availability and cost of information about job vacancies, the ratio between working pay and unemployment benefits, etc. All these factors change only very slowly. Trade unions, for instance, are not enormously powerful one year and very weak the next. The changeover in the UK from old-fashioned employment exchanges to newer and arguably more effective Jobcentres took well over ten years.

Unemployment

Workers do not suddenly become more prepared to move from region to region in order to find a job. Hence, whilst in the long term unemployment might increase or decrease due to changes in these structural characteristics of the labour market, in the short run this 'natural' level of unemployment will be constant.

Classical economists argue that unemployment can fall below the natural rate of unemployment if governments pursue appropriate policies. But a price must be paid for this, and that price is an increased rate of inflation. The natural rate of unemployment is defined as the rate of unemployment at which the price level will be constant over time.

In Fig. 15.5, the short run Phillips curve assuming 0% inflation is given by the line P_2. The level of unemployment where the demand for labour will exactly match the supply for labour is U_N.

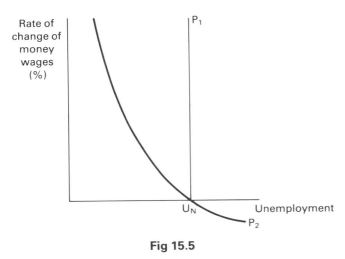

Fig 15.5

This is because at U_N, wages are neither increasing nor decreasing and hence there must be equilibrium in the labour market. The vertical line P_1, passing through U_N, is the long term natural rate of unemployment. Unemployment will always revert to that level due to the forces of demand and supply in the labour market.

Governments may attempt to reduce unemployment below the natural rate from U_N to U_1 in Fig. 15.6. They will travel up the P_1 Phillips curve. The result will be a new level of change in money wage rates (i.e. a new level of percentage wage inflation), W_1, and therefore almost certainly a similar new level of change in prices. In the long term, unemployment will tend to revert to U_N. Workers, however, will now be expecting inflation rates

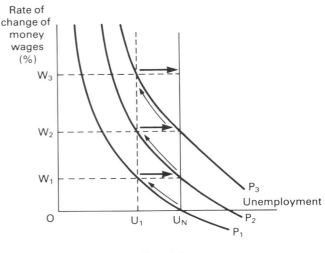

Fig 15.6

corresponding to wage increases of W_1. Therefore the new equilibrium will not be at 0% change in money wages, but at W_1 rate of change in money wages. This is the expectations—augmented Phillips curve hypothesis, which we looked at in Chapter 14. The economy will now be on a higher Phillips curve, P_2.

If the government attempts to reduce unemployment again, in the short term it can be reduced back to U_1 but at a cost of W_2 increase in money wages. In the long term, unemployment will go back up to U_N but the economy will move on to a higher Phillips curve, P_3. Unemployment can only be held at U_1 at the cost of ever-increasing inflation.

In the short term governments attempting to reduce inflation will face major unemployment problems. As shown in Fig. 15.7, the only path back down to a lower inflation rate and a lower Phillips curve lies via increased unemployment. A reduction

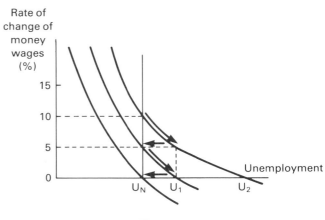

Fig 15.7

Data 15.4

Three telling questions about inflation

By Frank Blackaby

A good deal of the current analysis of Britain's economic predicament is flawed. In the 1980s a number of old, sensible economic truths have got lost, and a number of dubious propositions have crept in.

The dominant doctrine of economic management in recent years has been that the economy is self-regulating, with a simple rule: the job of the Treasury is to keep the public sector borrowing requirement low, and that is all. So long as the borrowing requirement is kept down, there can be no excessive monetary creation, and so no inflation.

The Chancellor has done exactly what the doctrine told him to do. Indeed he has overfulfilled the plan, and has been repaying the national debt. Yet here we have inflation moving up towards 7 per cent. Something has gone wrong. What is wrong is the doctrine.

The best thing to do is to start again, and to ask three questions about inflation.

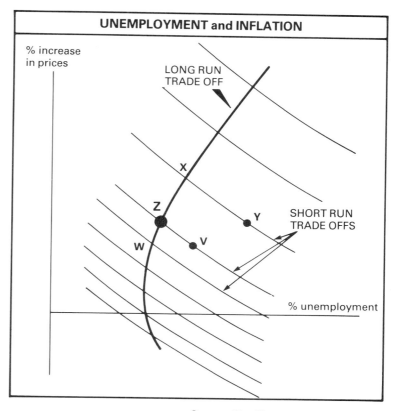

Source: The Financial Times. 12.5.83

● Why is it moving up? The central figure in the answer is not any of the myriad measures of the money supply. It is the rate of increase in average earnings. So long as average earnings are rising at around 9 per cent a year, there is no way that inflation can be brought down below 5–6 per cent a year for any length of time. For the economy as a whole, labour costs are by far the largest component of price changes.

● Why has the rise in earnings accelerated? It has gone up because unemployment has come down. One long-standing problem of the British economy has been to find ways of reconciling full employment with reasonable price stability. This Government has not attempted that reconciliation. It dealt with inflation by reducing the demand for labour, so that unemployment rose to 3m. Now it finds that even with unemployment (on somewhat manipulated figures) still around 2m, the rise in labour costs is excessive because the demand for labour is regionally maldistributed, and because so little has been done to meet the changing pattern of demands for skill.

● What can the Government do? There is only one thing it can do, since it can hardly talk to the unions. It will have to stop the fall in unemployment, and start it rising again. The growth rate will have to be brought down and kept down for a long time – employment is slow to react to growth-rate changes. Inflation will not just go away.

The Financial Times. 11.1.89

1 *What is the relationship between inflation and unemployment implied by (a) the chart and (b) the author of the article?*

2 *To what extent do the data suggest the existence of a natural rate of unemployment?*

in inflation from 10% to 5% in Fig. 15.7 would necessitate an increase in unemployment in the short term from U_N to U_1. A reduction from 10% to 0% would be even more painful—an increase in short term unemployment of $U_N U_2$.

The main monetarist conclusion is that it is futile for governments to attempt to reduce unemployment below U_N, given that the economy will always tend towards the natural rate of unemployment. If the attempt to reduce unemployment is made, the only result will be increased wage inflation. Attempting to get rid of that inflation will then necessitate short term rates of unemployment above the natural rate.

Summary

Unemployment represents a waste of scarce resources in any economy. Unemployment occurs because the supply of labour at a given wage rate is greater than its demand. Economists distinguish between various types of unemployment, including frictional, seasonal, structural, cyclical, hidden and classical unemployment. Classical economists argue that unemployment is a temporary phenomenon whilst wages are reduced in the labour market. Trade unions are one factor in the labour market failing to correct itself. By maintaining wage rates which are too high, they price workers out of jobs. Keynesians argue that long term unemployment such as experienced in the 1930s could not be solved easily by reductions in wages. The solution is to increase aggregate demand, thus increasing the demand for labour. Monetarists have developed the neo-classical argument and have put forward the concept of the natural rate of unemployment. Attempts by governments to reduce unemployment below its natural rate will only lead to increased inflation.

Terms for review

unemployment

frictional unemployment

seasonal unemployment

structural unemployment

classical unemployment

hidden unemployment

cyclical unemployment

voluntary unemployment

money illusion

natural rate of unemployment

Essay questions

1 What is the cost of unemployment to the economy? Is a zero unemployment rate ever likely to be attainable?

2 To what extent is unemployment created by wage increases?

3 What is meant by the 'natural rate' of unemployment? Can governments maintain levels of unemployment below this natural rate?

16

The trade cycle

Introduction

The trade cycle, or business cycle as it is sometimes known, has been a phenomenon of capitalist economies for at least as long as accurate economic records have been kept. The trade cycle is a regular fluctuation of economic variables around a trend line. The most important symptom of the cycle is changes in the level of economic activity, measured by national income or unemployment.

A typical trade cycle

No cycle is exactly the same as another cycle. However, cycles do have typical features, and it is these features that will be looked at here.

A cycle has four phases—(i) depression or slump, (ii) recovery or expansion, (iii) boom, and (iv) recession or deflation. These four phases are shown in Fig. 16.1. Consider how each variable behaves in the cycle.

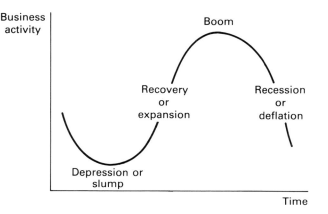

Fig 16.1

1 The level of output In the nineteenth and early twentieth centuries, the business cycle was characterised by changes in the level of output. During the recession phase, output fell, whilst during the recovery phase, output rose. Between 1950 and 1973, the business cycle was characterised by changes in the levels of growth of output. In the recession phase, output still rose but the rate of growth of output fell. In the recovery phase, not only did output rise but its rate of growth also rose. So depressions were periods of low economic growth, whilst booms were periods of high economic growth.

2 Unemployment Unemployment rises and falls with the cycle. In times of depression, unemployment is high, whilst at boom times it is low. Unemployment tends to lag behind the output cycle. Businesses are still taking on workers after the boom has passed in the mistaken belief that orders will be maintained at previous levels or previous growth rates. At the bottom of the cycle, even following the start of recovery, firms in financial difficulty will still be laying off workers. Extra output will be met by using the existing workforce more productively. In a five year cycle, it may take 12–18 months for unemployment to improve, following the bottom of the cycle.

3 Consumption Consumption follows the cycle. In a boom, consumption is high, whilst in a depression it is low. Fluctuations in expenditure on consumer durables, such as cars and televisions, are far more marked than fluctuations in expenditure of non-durables such as food.

4 Investment The investment cycle tends to precede the business cycle. During the depression, investment starts to increase, and continues to increase during the recovery phase. It then starts to go into decline before the top of the boom.

5 Stocks or inventories Firms keep stocks or inventories of raw materials or other inputs in order

Data 16.1

Three booms compared

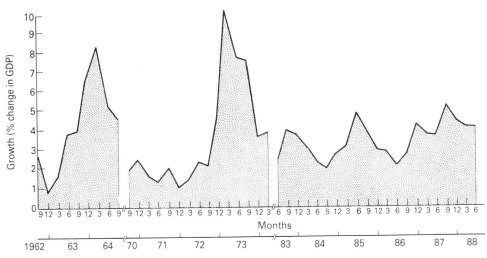

Source: CSO, Economic Trends Annual Supplement.

Tory Chancellors have a habit of engineering booms in the economy. Reginald Maudling did it in 1963–4. Anthony Barber can be blamed for the boom of 1973–4. Now it is the turn of Nigel Lawson.

The purpose of each boom has been to increase growth and lower unemployment. All were very successful in these respects. Maudling oversaw growth in GDP of 11% over two years. Barber did even better with 10% growth in a single 12-month period. Lawson has come in tamely with a maximum 5% in a year to the 3rd quarter of 1987.

On the negative side, each has coincided with a deterioration in the balance of payments situation and a rise in inflation. Lawson holds the booby prize on the former, with a deficit currently running at 2.5% of GDP.

With regard to inflation, Barber was unlucky. His boom coincided with the world commodity and oil price explosions of 1973–4, which sent inflationary shock waves throughout the world. Inflation under Maudling rose from just 2% in 1963 to 4.5% in 1964. Lawson has seen inflation change from just under 4% in 1987 to over 8% in 1989, albeit driven in part by higher mortgage costs.

The causes of each boom differ. Both Maudling and Barber increased the government budget deficit to stimulate demand. The 1963 budget raised the PSBR to $2\frac{1}{2}$% of GDP, whilst under Barber it went to 6%. Lawson steadily reduced the PSBR as the economy took off, creating today's budget surplus.

On the monetary side, the growth in money stock was modest under Maudling, but both Barber and Lawson presided over double-digit increases, Barber of a peak of 30% and Lawson of over 20%. Both Barber and Lawson could put down some of this increase to a restructuring of the financial system which led to a fall in the velocity of circulation of money. But monetarists blame the lack of monetary control in both periods for the surge in inflation in both booms.

With data from The Sunday Times. 9.10.88

1 *What, according to the article, have been the main features of recent booms in the UK economy?*

2 *To what extent are booms caused by changes in monetary policy rather than changes in government borrowing?*

to ensure the efficient production of goods and services. Equally, they may keep stocks of finished goods in order to satisfy consumer orders quickly. In a boom, stocks tend to be high. Firms produce at high levels, so they tend to keep high stocks of raw materials. Stocks of finished goods will be relatively high because firms know they will be able to sell their stocks quickly. In a depression, stocks tend to be low, because firms are producing at low levels and cannot afford to keep much stock.

6 The current balance (i.e. exports minus imports) During the recovery period, the current balance tends to deteriorate. This is because as business activity and incomes increase, imports tend to increase also. Equally during a recession, the current balance tends to improve as imports are squeezed out of the economy.

7 Profits Profitability declines in a recession, as companies face declining order books and greater price competition from their competitors anxious to maintain sales. In the recovery phase, profits start to increase again as output rises and firms can charge higher prices for their products without losing orders.

8 Interest rates Interest rates tend to be low during depressions and high during booms.

9 The money supply Like investment, the money supply or the rate of growth of the money supply, tends to anticipate the main business cycle. The level or rate of growth of money supply starts to go down about twelve months before the downturn in business activity, and increases about twelve months before the upturn in output.

10 Inflation Inflation increases during the recovery phase of the cycle, and declines during the recession. Boom years are years of high inflation, depression years are years of low inflation or even of declining prices.

Types of cycle

Four main types of cycle have been distinguished in the nineteenth century:
(a) A long wave innovation cycle of about 50 years;
(b) a building cycle of about 15–20 years length;
(c) a main trade cycle of between 7 and 11 years;
(d) an inventory cycle of about 3 to 4 years duration.

Since the Second World War, trade cycles have been of about five years in duration, although some economists feel that the fifty-year innovation cycle has not disappeared.

There are many theories about the causes of trade cycles. They can be classed into two types.

1 Exogenous theories stress that cycles are caused by random factors outside the socio-economic system and which are therefore not explicable within an economic model. Mass movements in population, wars, gold discoveries, changes in governments, revolutions, all have major impacts on the economy, and cause the phenomenon that we know as the trade cycle.

2 Endogenous theories stress that the trade cycle is too regular to be caused by random shocks. Major wars and the like do have important effects on the economy. However, they represent a disturbance to the cyclical pattern of business activity rather than its principal cause. The cause of the cycle needs to be found within the socio-economic system, not outside it.

Here, only endogenous theories will be considered. The exogenous/endogenous debate can only be settled by a careful consideration of the empirical evidence.

The transmission mechanism

Monetarists believe that the trade cycle is essentially a monetary phenomenon. In *A Monetary History of the United States, 1867–1960*, Friedman and Schwartz argued that changes in the level of business activity in the USA were preceded by changes in the money supply. They concluded that changes in the money supply must be the cause of cyclical fluctuations in the economy.

Monetarists argue that changes in the money supply not only affect inflation in the long run but also have a powerful effect upon employment and output in the short run. An increase in the money supply will temporarily increase output in the short run but only increase prices in the long run. The link between changes in monetary variables such as the money supply, and real variables such as unemployment and output, is known as the **transmission mechanism**. The theory of the demand for money is

The trade cycle

crucial to the adjustment process. Consider Fig. 16.2. The stages in the transmission mechanism are as follows:

1 There is a once and for all increase in the money supply. We assume it is a once and for all increase in order to keep the argument as simple as possible.

2 The money supply is now greater than the demand for money, so economic units have to adjust their portfolio of assets.

3 They do this by spending that excess money on physical assets and financial assets. The purchase of financial assets lowers the rate of interest.

4 A lower rate of interest and the purchase of physical assets leads to greater consumption and investment. Prices are already beginning to creep up due to the increased demand for factors of production and for goods and services.

The economy is now in boom

5 Greater consumption and investment increases national income. This increase in income, together with the increase in prices, leads economic units to increase their demand for money. This now means that the demand for money is greater than the supply of money. They adjust their portfolio of assets to obtain this money by:

6 reducing their expenditure on physical assets and financial assets. The sale of financial assets raises interest rates.

The economy is now in recession

7 A higher rate of interest and reduced expenditure on physical assets leads to lower consumption and investment. Prices start to fall.

The economy passes into depression

8 Lower consumption and investment reduces national income. This fall in income, together with the fall in prices, leads economic units to reduce their demand for money. But this now means that the demand for money is less than the supply of money. Portfolios are adjusted.

The economy now passes into the recovery phase

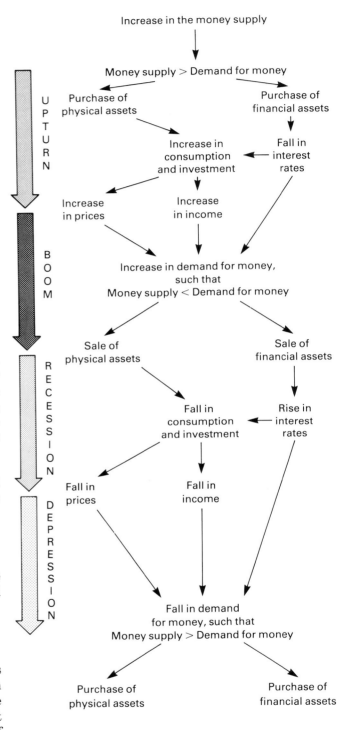

Fig 16.2

And so the cycle continues, potentially, for ever.

Milton Friedman believes that these cycles have a damped oscillation—that is, the cycles become less and less pronounced as time goes on. Eventually, the cycle would disappear. In Fig. 16.3, the monetarist view is represented graphically. Note that income is real income and not money income. In the long run real income cannot be affected by changes in the money supply. Note also the increase in the price level following an increase in the money supply. Interest rates remain unchanged in the long term.

Since the Second World War, all industrialised economies have seen year by year increases in the money supply. The above argument can easily be amended to cope with this by putting 'growth' wherever 'level' appears. So in the long term, an increase in the rate of growth of the money supply will increase the growth of prices, i.e. increase the inflation rate. In the short term, an increase in the rate of growth of the money supply will increase the rate of growth of real national income.

The depression of the 1930s was caused by the severe contraction in the money supply, which the US Government allowed to happen after 1929. Between 1929 and 1933, the US money supply declined by about 35%!

A Keynesian hypothesis—the multiplier-accelerator model

Monetarists argue that the trade cycle is essentially a monetary phenomenon. Keynesians on the other hand, stress the importance of real variables. One Keynesian theory of the cycle uses the concepts of the real multiplier (explained in Chapter 12) and the accelerator theory of investment (explained in Chapter 8).

Multiplier theory argues that if there is a change in an exogenous injection into the circular flow of income (the injections being investment, exports and government spending) then income will change by the change in value of that injection times the value of the multiplier. So if the multiplier were 3 and investment rose by £300 million, income would rise eventually by £900 million.

The accelerator theory of investment states that levels of investment are determined by past changes in income. At its simplest it is given by the equation:

$$I_t = a(Y_t - Y_{t-1})$$

This states that current investment (I_t) is determined by the change in income over the last period $(Y_t - Y_{t-1})$. However, statistically complicated formulae involving several time periods can easily be constructed.

Linking these two theories together can produce a model of the trade cycle. Assume that there is an increase in investment, exports or government spending. This by means of the multiplier process raises national income. Then investment will rise in the next time period because of the rise in income. If investment rises, income will rise too via the multiplier process. So investment rises in the next time period, and so on.

Income, therefore, rises steadily from time period to time period. There are two ways in which the multiplier-accelerator model can produce trade cycles. Firstly, the accelerator model itself can be formulated mathematically so that a peak in income is reached and income then starts to fall again. Eventually, the model predicts that income will start to rise.

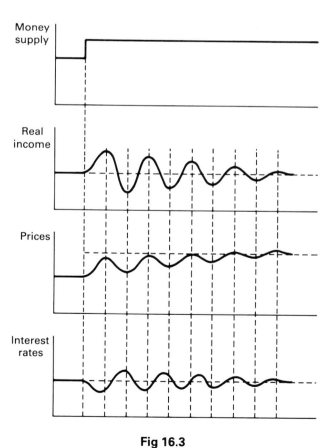

Fig 16.3

The second approach is to argue that there are limits to levels of income and investment. There must be an upper limit—a 'ceiling'—beyond which the economy cannot expand. There comes a point when there is no more labour to be hired, and when additional investment is not sufficiently labour-saving for this problem to be overcome. Once firms realise that extra investment will not raise income any further, they will cut back on that investment, producing a downturn in the economy.

At the bottom of the cycle, there comes a point when income can no longer fall. Consumers will still be demanding essentials (such as food) and firms producing these essentials will have to replace worn-out machinery in order to carry on producing. Any small increase in investment will set the multiplier-accelerator mechanism off again on an upward trend.

On this Keynesian model, then, it is changes in investment which produce trade cycles.

Another Keynesian hypothesis—the inventory cycle

Inventories are stocks of goods held by firms either ready for processing or ready for sale to customers. The inventory model of the trade cycle argues that fluctuations in inventories can cause fluctuations in the level of business activity.

Assume that export orders sharply increase, and that this increase is met by running down inventories of finished goods. Firms will then need to produce more, not only to continue meeting the higher export demand but also to rebuild their stock of goods. This increased activity will be felt throughout the economy via the multiplier process. Eventually, exporting firms will have produced enough to rebuild their inventories to their desired level. At this point they will start to cut back on production. The boom in the economy is now giving way to the

Data 16.2

Expanding economy

This is the first Budget the Chancellor has introduced against the background of an expanding economy. The expansion so far has been pretty modest, but at least it is in the right direction. The output measure of gross domestic product (considered the best indicator of the whole economy) increased fractionally in the last two quarters and is now almost $1\frac{1}{2}$ per cent above the trough of the recession in the second quarter of 1981.

The economy, which has contracted by over $3\frac{1}{2}$ per cent since the Government came to office in May 1979 now looks better simply because the much delayed end of the recession is now in sight. But the extent of the recovery will depend critically on growth in stockbuilding. Movements in stocks are so large within the business cycle that fluctuations account for almost three quarters of all recessions since the war. The mystery of 1982 was that there was a sharp rise in consumer spending (which has continued into the New Year), but no increase in industrial production.

The answer was that UK industry was feeding the extra demand (or that part of it not satisfied by imports) from its stock of unfinished goods. This had the added attraction of enabling companies to run down their large overdrafts since stocks have to be financed from somewhere.

Once de-stocking ends, or even slows down, factories will have to step up their own output to satisfy demand. This could happen at any time now. There is one possible catch. There is still a suspicion that most of the recent surge in consumer spending has gone on imports of foreign goods. Either things which are not made here (like videos) or products which UK companies have found it difficult to compete with because of the strong pound.

The January trade figures were not encouraging since they showed a three per cent increase in the volume of consumer goods imports in the most recent quarter.

The Guardian. 15.3.83

1 How far does the data support the view that trade cycles are caused by fluctuations in inventory levels?

recession period. Via the real multiplier process, this fall in spending by exporting firms will be felt throughout the economy. Other firms will cut back their levels of stock to meet the reduced spending. At some point, however, inventories will reach such a low level that firms will have to start reordering. The economy now passes into recovery. And so it goes on. The initial disequilibrium in inventories may be caused by a wide variety of factors, such as increased exports or more public spending.

Building, innovation and Kondratiev

The short trade cycle, lasting a matter of only a few years, is only one type of trade cycle which economists have claimed exists. There is some evidence that two other types of cycle exist. One is the 15–20-year cycle. Kuznetts, the economist who put forward the hypothesis in the interwar period, argued that the cycle was caused by fluctuations in the level of building and construction.

Of more interest today is the 50-year Kondratiev cycle. Kondratiev was a Russian economist working in the 1920s. He argued that capitalist economies have been moving in 50-year cycles at least since the first industrial revolution at the end of the eighteenth century. He charted three long waves between 1790 and 1920. These are shown in Table 16.1, along with an extrapolation of the long wave trends into the 1990s.

He correctly predicted that the world economy was moving into another severe depression during the 1920s. Fifty years on, his theory would expect the 1970s and 1980s to see another severe recession with recovery only starting in the mid 1980s or early 1990s.

Apart from the 50-year timing of the long cycle, Kondratiev saw two other important facets of his cycle.

1 During the recession of the long waves, an especially large number of important discoveries and inventions in the techniques of production and communication are made. These are usually applied on a large scale only at the beginning of the next long upswing.

2 It is during the period of the rise of the long waves, that the most disastrous and extensive wars and revolutions occur.

Kondratiev saw technological change as a facet of the trade cycle. Economic forces create an environment in which scientific knowledge can be translated into practical applications. The scientific knowledge may pre-date the application by ten, one hundred or a thousand years. Technological change is then an endogenous variable in Kondratiev's model.

An Austrian economist, Schumpeter, argued in the late 1930s that innovation was the main cause of the Kondratiev cycle. He identified the main elements of that technological change, as shown in Table 16.1. Technological change becomes an exogenous variable on this theory. The principal technological change which will cause the upturn of the 1990s is the microchip and its applications, together with developments in biotechnology, such as genetic engineering.

Innovation is important, it is argued, because of its impact on production and consumption. Innovations result in two important changes:

1 The new technology allows production processes to become more efficient. In the very nature of the competitive process, the individuals, firms or economies which innovate the most vigorously are likely to reap the greatest rewards in terms of lower cost, more sales and more output, and higher incomes.

2 The new technology creates new products which consumers want to buy.

Table 16.1

Long wave	Recovery	Decline	Innovation
1	1790 to 1810–17	1810–17 to 1844–51	Steam power
2	1844–51 to 1870–75	1870–75 to 1890–96	Railways
3	1890–96 to 1914–20	1914–20 to 1934–40	Electricity and the motor car
4	1934–40 to 1964–70	1964–70 to 1984–90	Nuclear power, chemicals/plastics, electrical consumer goods
5	1984–90 to ?		Microchips and biotechnology

Data 16.3

Economies in the quicksand of depression

The obstacles to growth posed by institutional rigidities and failure to adapt concern Professor Christopher Freeman and his colleagues at the Science Policy Research Unit at Sussex University.

In a new book, *Unemployment and Technical Innovation*, they argue that the world has entered the depression phase of "the fourth long wave" – economic cycles of roughly 50 years' duration often known as Kondratiev waves. It is, of course, 50 years since the last great depression of the 1930s.

The authors warn of growing technological unemployment as technical progress enables jobs to be shed in industries where there is little scope to expand demand. They argue that the depression will last until enough capital is scrapped or redirected to the expanding sectors of the economy.

Professor Freeman and his colleagues place little faith in the efficacy of demand expansion on its own to produce expansion, though they do not support the use of contractionary policies to fight inflation. What is needed, they believe, is a specific technology policy designed to "tilt" the economy out of long term structural

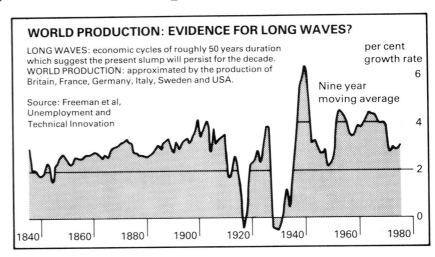

WORLD PRODUCTION: EVIDENCE FOR LONG WAVES?

LONG WAVES: economic cycles of roughly 50 years duration which suggest the present slump will persist for the decade.
WORLD PRODUCTION: approximated by the production of Britain, France, Germany, Italy, Sweden and USA.

Source: Freeman et al, Unemployment and Technical Innovation

per cent growth rate

Nine year moving average

recession on to a higher path of economic growth, with government playing a major role.

This would involve encouraging firms to embrace new technologies, stimulate their spread (the proposal to "wire" Britain for cable is an example) and import the best of foreign technology.

"A depression should not be necessary to generate a revival of growth,

and the task of intelligent economic and social policy is to find the way to stimulate a new flow of desirable combinations to technical innovations and social changes to prevent prolonged depression" the authors conclude.

The notion of long waves is however the subject of much scepticism in economic circles and the evidence for them is indicative rather than compelling.

The Times. 2.12.82

1 *What, in the view of Professor Freeman, is the cause of the recession of the early 1980s?*
2 *Does the data support the long wave hypothesis?*

3 *What are the policy implications if indeed the recession is primarily technological?*

New technology initially destroys jobs because output per man increases with the new machinery. But when the recovery advances, jobs are created as consumers demand more and more of the new products. Their extra incomes come from the increased investment which firms are making in the new technology. The peak of the cycle is reached when the previous technology has been completely superseded by the new. In the downswing of the cycle, the

new technology is being refined but no dramatically new products or techniques are developed. More and more investment is directed towards replacing existing worn-out capital rather than expanding the capital stock. Industry does not feel under pressure to scrap existing working machinery to replace it with new improved machinery. Profits are falling too, as firms find it more difficult to expand output rapidly or charge high prices for new products

THE KEY TO A GREAT FUTURE!

IS 3½ MILLION UNEMPLOYED ECONOMIC SUCCESS?

WE DEMAND THE RIGHT TO WORK

WE WANT JOBS

CHANCELLOR OF THE EXCHEQUER

MICROCHIPS

P.M.

*Can new technology cause unemployment
(a) in the short term? (b) in the long term?*

Summary

The trade cycle is a regular fluctuation of economic variables around a trend line. In a boom, inflation and economic growth are likely to be high, whilst unemployment is likely to be low. In a depression, growth and inflation are low, whilst unemployment is high. Monetarists argue that the cause of cycles lies in disturbances to the money supply. Keynesians argue that investment via the multiplier-accelerator mechanism, or changes in stocks, cause cycles. The Kondratiev 50-year cycle hypothesis argues that the early 1980s should see a major depression. Schumpeter argued that the main cause of the cycle was changes in technology.

Terms for review

trade or business cycle

depression or slump

recession

deflation

boom

transmission mechanism

multiplier-accelerator model

ceilings and floors

inventory cycle

Kondratiev cycle

Depression is reached when demand for consumer and investment goods of the existing technology is mainly replacement demand. However, the depression is also an exciting time in that the next generation technology is starting to appear in the market place. It is the demand for this new technology which eventually drags the economy out of recession and into recovery.

Many economists have dismissed the Kondratiev/Schumpeter theory on the grounds that 50-year cycles are little different from any other sort of cycle. They also argue that technology does not have discrete advances, but rather advances are continually being made such that it is impossible to pick out periods when advance was more rapid than in another. Nevertheless, economists agree that the 1960s was a period of higher growth than the 1970s and that the troubles of the 1980s seem to be far worse than those of the 1970s. Even the present major breakthrough in technology—the microchip—is easily discernible. In short, today's evidence appears to fit the Kondratiev theory.

Essay questions

1 What is meant by 'cyclical unemployment'? What part, if any, does investment play in causing cyclical unemployment?

2 Can technical innovation cause mass unemployment (a) in the short term and (b) in the long term?

Data 16.4

Change in gross domestic product at factor cost
(at 1985 prices)

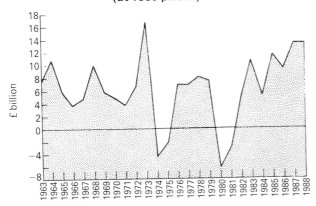

Unemployment UK, per cent

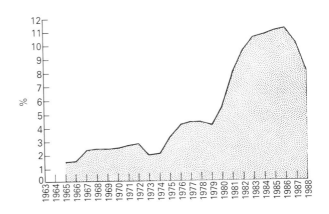

Change in gross domestic fixed capital formation
(at 1985 prices)

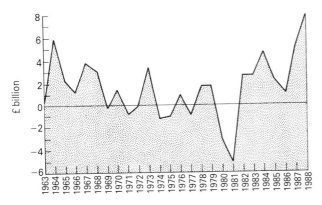

Change in money stock sterling: M_0, M_3

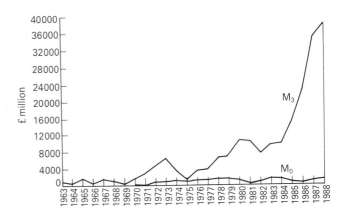

Stock changes: change in the value of physical
increase (at 1985 prices)

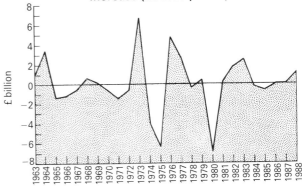

1 What is meant by the 'trade cycle'? Illustrate your
answer from the data.
2 What light does the data shed upon the possible
causes of the trade cycle?

Source: CSO, Economic Trends, Annual Abstract of Statistic

17

The balance of payments and exchange rates

Countries trade in order to obtain products which they do not produce domestically or which can be obtained more cheaply abroad. Countries also borrow and lend money abroad, or undertake international investment. All these transactions bring about flows of money across national boundaries. These flows of money are recorded on the balance of payments account. Flows of money can be divided into two basic categories:

1 Money which is used to pay for goods and services traded internationally—i.e. exports and imports. These flows are recorded on the **current account**.

2 Money which is used for purposes of international saving and investment. These flows are recorded on the **capital account**.

Flows of money across the exchanges must balance each other out. Imagine an economy which finds over a time period that it has spent more on imports than it has earned from exports. It will need to find foreign currency in order to pay for these extra imports. It can do this in one of three ways. It can sell assets it owns abroad (the equivalent of a household drawing on its savings in a building society account or bank deposit account, because it has spent more than it earned over the year). It can borrow the foreign exchange from foreigners (the equivalent of a household borrowing the money it needs to cover its overspending). Or the central bank of the economy can use its gold and foreign currency reserves to pay for the overspending of the rest of the economy (the equivalent of a household using money put by in previous years in tea jars and piggy banks and under mattresses, in order to finance this year's overspending). Whichever course of action is chosen, the result is the same. A deficit on the current account (i.e. imports are greater than exports) must be matched exactly by a surplus on the capital account (i.e. the country is running down its savings

abroad, is borrowing abroad, or is running down its foreign exchange savings domestically).

The same is true if the current account is in surplus (i.e. exports are greater than imports). If exports are greater than imports, the economy will have earned more foreign exchange than it needs to pay for its imports. So it needs to do something with that foreign exchange. Again it has three options: (i) The money may be saved abroad; (ii) it may be used to pay back previous loans taken out with foreigners; or (iii) it may be kept by the central bank and added to its reserves.

Hence the balance of payments must always balance. The sum of the current and capital accounts must always be zero. However, parts of the account can be in surplus or deficit. It is these surpluses or deficits which can have important economic consequences.

The composition of the balance of payments

1 **The current account** Trade in goods and services is recorded on the current account. **Visible trade** is trade in goods—raw materials, food, semi-manufactured goods and manufactured goods. **Invisible trade** is trade in services, such as financial services, tourism, earnings of workers sent abroad, and interest, profits and dividends from investments abroad. Of particular significance is the difference between a country's earnings (its visible and invisible exports), and its spending (its visible and invisible imports). Visible exports minus visible imports is known as the **balance of trade**. Invisible exports (or invisible credits) minus invisible imports (or invisible debits) is known as the **invisible balance**. Total exports minus total imports is known as the **current balance**.

2 The capital account Savings and investment made abroad or made by foreigners in the UK are recorded on the capital account. Savings are made in a wide range of paper securities from deposits in banks to purchases of government stock and shares in firms. Savings can be of a short or long term nature. Short term savings are often termed either 'speculative flows' because such money is placed in foreign currency in order to make gains, or 'hot money' because the money flows from one financial centre to another, seeking the highest reward. Possible future changes in exchange rates or interest rates can result in large movements of money into or out of any particular currency. As will be seen later, this can have important effects upon the exchange rate. Investments can also be made abroad. Japanese firms setting up manufacturing plants abroad are examples of such investment. On the UK account, savings and investment are recorded as **transactions in external assets and liabilities**.

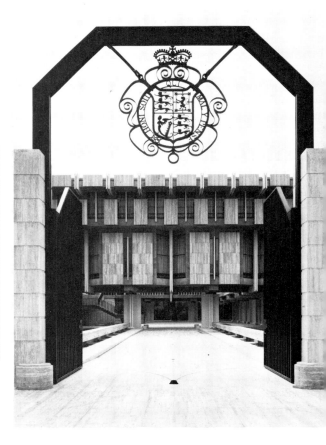

The above illustrate a holiday villa in Spain, French cheese, and a British embassy abroad. If each of these were purchased or paid for by British residents or the British Government, where would the resulting financial flow appear on the balance of payment account?

Toyota invests £700m in UK assembly plant

By Kevin Done

TOYOTA, the leading Japanese car maker, is to invest £700m in an assembly plant building 200,000 cars a year at Burnaston, near Derby, the biggest single Japanese investment made in Europe.

Last year, the UK produced 1.23m cars, but imports still accounted for 56.4 per cent of the UK new car market. The motor industry alone was responsible for 30 per cent of last year's total UK visible trade deficit of £20.34bn.

The Government is now confident that the build-up of production by Toyota and Nissan together with other expansion projects – including Honda of Japan which has a production agreement with the Rover Group – could push UK car production towards 2m a year by the late 1990s.

Lord Young said the Toyota plant would help redress the deficit in the UK trade balance.

The investment will be made in two phases and with the first a rate of 100,000 cars a year is to be reached in late 1995. Toyota is hoping to reach production of 200,000 cars a year by 1997/98. The first stage will involve an investment of around £400m and will create 1,700 jobs.

The Financial Times. 19.4.89

1 *What impact is Toyota's decision to invest in the UK likely to have on the different components of the UK balance of payments?*

One part of the capital account deals with government **reserves of gold and foreign currency**. For a variety of reasons, the Government may decide to allow a surplus or deficit on the combined total of current account and capital account transactions by the private sector and by government authorities and agencies. If a deficit occurs, it must mean that the Government has run down the gold and current reserves of the country. If there is a surplus the reserves must have increased.

The determination of exchange rates

An exchange rate is the price of one currency in terms of another currency. Like all prices, it is determined by the interaction of the forces of demand and supply. On the foreign exchange markets of the world, large sums of currency are demanded and supplied daily. Foreign exchange dealers are linked by telephone and telex, and their transactions affect each other. If in one financial centre for example the demand for pounds sterling exceeds the supply of pounds sterling, then the price of pounds sterling will increase. Similarly, if supply exceeds demand, then the price will fall.

The demand for pounds arises either out of the export of UK goods and services, or from owners of foreign currencies wanting to save or invest in the UK. The demand comes from abroad and so money is said to flow **into** the UK. The supply of pounds comes either from UK residents who have purchased imported goods and services, or from owners of pounds sterling who wish to save or invest abroad using foreign currencies. The supply, therefore, comes from owners of domestic currency who wish to send their money **out** of the UK. If the total flows of money out of the UK exceed total inflows (i.e. the balance for official financing is negative) then the supply of pounds on to the market will exceed the demand for pounds. A surplus or deficit on the balance for official financing means that the demand and supply of the currency are not equal.

Several factors can result in deficits or surpluses in the balance for official financing. Firstly, if a country is running a large current account deficit, it is likely that there will be an overall excess supply of currency on to the market. Thus, countries running current account deficits are likely to see a fall in their exchange rates.

Secondly, the level of interest rates in an economy

has a large influence on the investment and other capital flows account. Rises in domestic interest rate are likely to result in large inflows of speculative or 'hot' money. This results in greater demand for the currency and hence upward pressure on the exchange rate.

Thirdly, expectations are a major determinant of exchange rates. If foreign currency speculators expect the exchange rate to fall in the future, they will sell currency now in order to avoid future losses. This will have the effect of bringing about an immediate fall in the exchange rate. A country likely to incur a current account deficit or experience a fall in interest rates, is likely to see future falls in its exchange rate. These are discounted in advance by speculators so that exchange rates fall immediately.

Disequilibrium in the foreign exchange markets cannot persist for long. One of two things will happen to restore the market to equilibrium. Either the price of the currency will change to return demand and supply to equilibrium; or the Government will step in to supply or buy up the currency so that the exchange rate can remain stable.

Data 17.2

Central banks check dollar's rise

By Peter Norman in London, **Janet Bush** in New York and **Peter Riddell** in Washington

THE US Federal Reserve backed by several European central banks checked the dollar's rise in European currency trading yesterday, after a Bundesbank decision not to increase its key interest rates at one point pushed the US currency above DM1.98.

The news that the central council of the Bundesbank, the West German central bank, was keeping the country's discount and Lombard rates unchanged at 4.5 per cent and 6.5 per cent respectively caused the dollar to surge in hectic trading.

The dollar's strength was countered, however, by $1bn-worth of concerted central bank sales in European trading hours – despite Bank of Japan dollar sales overnight. This pushed it down by the end of trading in London.

The Financial Times. 19.5.89

1 *Explain what factors were influencing the change in the value of the dollar described in the article.*

Economic consequences of surpluses or deficits on the constituent parts of the balance of payments

A deficit on the current account is the equivalent of a household spending more than it earns. Running a persistent deficit results in a gain in welfare for the economy. This is because the country can consume more goods and services than it need sell goods to pay for them. However, a persistent current account deficit is unlikely to be tolerated by foreigners, for they will need to lend continually to the deficit country. Just as the ordinary bank manager is unlikely to allow a client to get deeper and deeper in debt, so international bankers will not allow a deficit country to borrow for ever. At some stage they will want to see their money repaid. To do this, the country concerned must run a current account surplus in order to finance the necessary deficit on the investment and other capital transactions account. Current account deficits, then, can only be tolerated in the short run. In the long run, a persistent deficit must be dealt with.

It is more difficult to evaluate the welfare implications of a surplus or deficit on transactions in external assets and liabilities. A deficit means that a country is a net exporter of capital—it is saving and investing more abroad than foreigners are doing in its domestic economy. This means that the country is adding to its stock of wealth. In the future, it will be able to draw on that stock of wealth if necessary. Moreover, it will be able to earn interest, profit and dividends on the capital.

However, a deficit on transactions in external assets and liabilities has its opportunity cost. The money saved and invested abroad could have been invested in the domestic economy. If the account were in surplus (i.e. more money was being saved and invested in the domestic economy than abroad) then that money could be used to build up the industrial base of the economy. It is often more profitable for a company to borrow money in order to finance an investment project than to stay out of debt but not undertake investment. So it is with a country. The importation of foreign financial capital allows extra resources to be devoted to investment.

The proceeds of a surplus may, however, be used for different purposes. A surplus of capital inflows may, for example, be used to finance excessive consumption in the economy. If an economy finds its current account is in deficit due to an imbalance of trade on consumer items, then one way to pay for that deficit is to borrow abroad—i.e. run a surplus on transactions in external assets and liabilities.

The Government creates the surplus or deficit on **private sector transactions** by its dealings with foreigners. If it decides to create a deficit, then it has to pick up the resulting bill either by borrowing or by running down its reserves. There is a limit to either option. Reserves are finite and lenders will want to see economic policies which will allow loans to be repaid. Large deficits can only be short term affairs.

If an economy borrows too much or allows its reserves to fall to very low levels, it will find that agencies which have lent it money, such as the IMF, will impose conditions for future borrowing. This means that the Government loses its ability to run its economy in the way it sees fit. Moreover, the money borrowed will be repayable at some time in the future with interest. Persistent surpluses on the balance for official financing, however, are not necessarily desirable either. Monies added to the reserves do nothing to increase the welfare of the economy. An individual who saves continually but never spends his savings may well acquire a small fortune, but he will get no benefit from it. Similarly for a country, welfare is created only in consumption, not in forever adding to a country's stock of savings.

Measures to deal with balance of payments disequilibria

Persistent deficits on the current account must be dealt with eventually. Moreover, large short term outflows on transactions in external assets and liabilities can precipitate crises on the foreign exchange market. In dealing with this problem, governments possess a number of options: devaluation, deflation, interest rate policy, exchange controls and import controls. The first four will be considered here and import controls will be discussed in the next chapter.

Changing the value of the currency

Devaluing the currency will make imported goods more expensive and exports cheaper for foreigners. Consider a **devaluation** of the pound sterling from £1 = $2 to £1 = $1.50. A £3 bottle of Scotch whisky which before cost $6 in the USA now only costs $4.50. Conversely a $6 bottle of American bourbon whisky cost £3 in the UK before devaluation but £4 after devaluation. There are two ways of looking at the results of devaluation: through looking at the price effects of devaluation, known as the **elasticities approach**, and through the income effects, known as the **absorption approach**.

Devaluation will make imports dearer in terms of the domestic currency. As a result, domestic consumers will buy fewer imports and switch to home produced products. On the export front, goods and services will become cheaper for foreigners and so they will buy more exports. The price in terms of the UK domestic currency will of course remain the same—a £5000 car costs £5000 before and after a UK devaluation, although the price will change in terms of foreign currency. Thus the revenue to be gained from exports is bound to go up since more will be sold at the same domestic price. Exporters may choose to put up their prices following devaluation. Although there will be less volume increase in sales, revenue is bound to increase so long as the percentage increase in price is less than the percentage devaluation of the currency.

The amount by which the current account will improve depends upon the relative price elasticities of exports and imports. The formula for price elasticity of demand is:

$$E_D = \frac{\text{Percentage change in quantity demanded}}{\text{Percentage change in price}}$$

The total value of exports or imports is given by multiplying the price of each item by the number bought, i.e. price times quantity. Hence the smaller the value of the elasticity of demand for exports, the smaller will be the improvement on the current account resulting from devaluation. For example, if a currency is devalued by 15% an elasticity of −4

Data 17.3

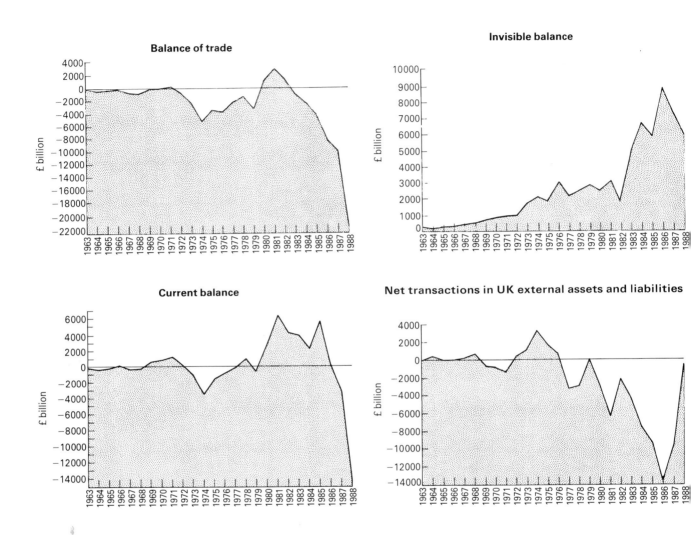

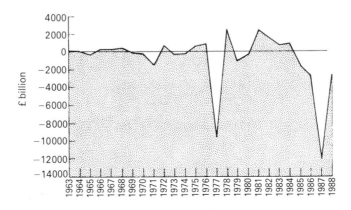

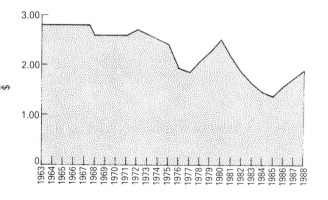

Sterling exchange rate: US dollars

Sterling effective exchange rate: 1985=100

Source: CSO, Economic Trends

Outline the constituant parts of the balance of payments, illustrating your answer from the data. Explain the relationship between the balance of payments and the exchange rate. Illustrate your answer from the data.

ill bring about a 60% rise in volume and domestic currency value whereas an elasticity of only $-\frac{2}{3}$ will ring about just a 10% increase in volume and omestic currency value.

On the other hand, the larger the elasticity of emand for imports the greater the improvement on he current account resulting from devaluation. A 5% devaluation will result in a 15% rise in price in nports; with an import elasticity of -3, this will ive a 45% fall in volume and therefore, in domestic urrency terms, a 30% fall in value of total imports. Vith an import elasticity of $-\frac{2}{3}$, a 15% devaluation ill give rise to a 15% increase in price but only a 0% fall in volume, and therefore import values will ise by some 5%. In general, with devaluation, nport elasticities of greater than 1 result in a fall in nport values, and import elasticities of less than 1 esult in a rise in import values. (These values are easured in domestic currency).

Thus the success of a devaluation depends upon oth the elasticities of exports and imports. It has een shown that, given certain assumptions, devaluation will improve the current balance if the ombined elasticities of exports and imports are reater than 1:

$$e_X + e_M > 1$$

This is known as the 'Marshall-Lerner condition' after the two economists who originally produced the result.

For an economy such as the UK, the medium term price elasticity of imports is probably less than 1. Devaluation will actually increase the total value of imports. However, the price elasticity of exports is greater than 1. The result is that the increase in the value of exports following devaluation is greater than the increase in the value of imports, thus bringing about an improvement in the current balance. An economy where the sum of elasticities is less than 1 would see a deterioration in its current balance following devaluation. It would need to revalue its currency to bring about an improvement in its current balance.

So far we have considered the medium term effects of devaluation. In the short term, devaluation is almost certain to result in a deterioration of the current balance. This is because devaluation results in an immediate rise in the price of imports. Most international trade is done by contract. Imports ordered cannot be cancelled immediately. Similarly, it takes one to two years for export volumes to rise to their new levels. Hence the value of total imports rises very quickly whereas the value of total exports rises only slowly. The result is an initial deterioration of the current balance. This is known as the

'J curve effect' since, as can be seen from Fig. 17.1, the dynamic path taken by the current balance following devaluation resembles a J.

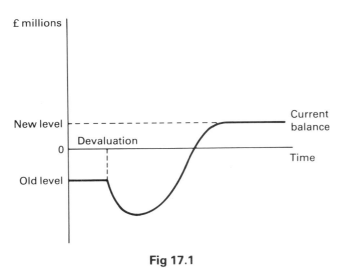

Fig 17.1

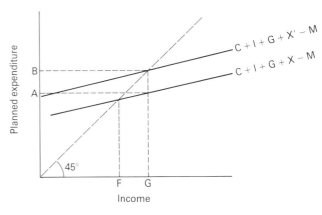

Fig. 17.2

income. Exports in the long run will remain the same but inflation will have taken place.

This can be illustrated using the aggregate demand and supply model explained in Chapter 13. In Fig. 17.3

The elasticities approach shows how changes in the price of imports and exports can affect the current account. However, devaluation will also have an impact on income, and in particular aggregate demand. Looking at devaluation from this perspective is called the **absorption approach**.

We know that for an economy to be in equilibrium planned expenditure must equal national income:

$$Y = C + I + G + X - M$$

If devaluation is successful, it will raise the level of exports and reduce imports. So $X - M$ will have a larger value after devaluation than before. Income, Y, will therefore increase.

If the economy is at less than full employment, an increase in income is possible. In Fig. 17.2, a simple Keynesian model of the economy is assumed. An increase in exports of AB will lead to an increase in income from F to G, where G is assumed to be a level of income at or below full employment.

But what if the economy is already at full employment when devaluation takes place? Then, devaluing the currency and increasing the demand for exported goods will push planned expenditure beyond full employment income. An inflationary gap now exists and demand-pull inflation will set in. Domestic prices will rise until the equilibrium level of national income once again equals the full employment level of

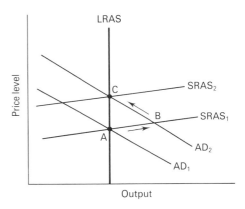

Fig. 17.3

the economy is in equilibrium at the point A, where the aggregate demand schedule and the long run aggregate supply schedule intersect. Devaluation has the effect of increasing the level of aggregate demand in the economy, pushing the schedule from AD_1 to AD_2. In the short run, the economy will move up its short run aggregate supply schedule, from A to B. The economy will be at over-full employment and domestic prices will already have started to rise. With the economy overheating, and with excess demand for workers, wage rates will rise. This will shift the short run aggregate supply schedule upwards, and it will carry on shifting upwards until the economy is back to long run equilibrium at the point C. The rise in rices from A to C will have wiped out any gains in competitiveness from a devaluation of the currency. Exports will have risen and then fallen again to their previous levels. On this analysis, devaluation cannot be successful in the long run.

Again this point can be explained using a cost-push theory of inflation. In a cost-push model, devaluation raises the costs of imports. This in turn can set off or fuel an inflationary wage-price spiral. In the long term the competitive benefits of devaluation will be entirely eroded by the domestic inflation which it has generated. In fact, it may lead to a deterioration of the balance of payments in the long run, if the cost-push spiral is explosive and there are not subsequent devaluations to keep exports competitive.

Another powerful argument which suggests that attempts to improve our trading position through devaluation are bound to be unsuccessful is that price is a relatively unimportant factor in determining world trade. Some goods traded internationally are homogeneous—that is, the goods are identical wherever they come from. Copper is essentially the same whether it comes from South America or from Zaire. Price is important for sellers of such homogeneous goods. However, exports of homogeneous goods are relatively unimportant for an economy such as the UK. At the same time, imports of homogenous goods are price inelastic. This is because many of these imports are the essential raw materials needed by British industry to produce its output.

If the UK is to solve a current account deficit, it is the trade of non-homogeneous goods that must alter. Non-homogeneous goods range from cars to video sets, and from machine tools to missiles. Price is far less important to the customer than the quality of the good, reliability, date of delivery and quality of after-sales service. Foreign cars, for instance, have taken a major share of the UK market despite being generally more expensive to buy and maintain than equivalent UK cars. On the other hand, our exports of cars have been particularly poor. The only conclusion to be drawn is that consumers of cars look for more than just the cheapest car on the market. On this hypothesis the current account problems of the UK are a direct reflection of the industrial decline of the UK economy over the past 100 years. Countries which experience fast rates of economic growth, such as Germany and Japan, are unlikely to develop long term balance of payments problems because their products are obviously selling well domestically and internationally. Economies such as the UK which seem unable to produce and sell the right goods, are likely to go on encountering balance of payments problems. It is only when the long term decline of the whole industrial base of the economy is checked that we can hope to see a solution to our external problem.

Deflation

A second important way of reversing a current account deficit is to deflate the economy. A reduction in income will lead to a reduction in aggregate demand. This in turn will lead to a reduction in imports. To put it more simply, if people's incomes are reduced they will buy fewer goods generally, and so they will necessarily buy fewer imported goods.

Deflation is a highly successful way of dealing with balance of payments problems. There are no associated inflationary effects as there are with devaluation. On the contrary, deflationary measures should help reduce inflation either on Keynesian demand pull grounds, or on monetarist grounds because governments are less likely to print money to pay for large budget deficits. But deflation does have a very heavy cost in terms of higher unemployment and lower growth. A country with reduced economic growth may experience long term problems. Reduced economic growth may make domestic industries less competitive than foreign industries, which are able to devote large sums of money to research and investment due to high levels of growth in their own economies. Despite these heavy economic costs, deflation is the commonest method used by governments to combat a current account deficit.

Interest rate policy

Changing domestic interest rates has an effect on both the current and capital accounts. Raising interest rates will result in an inflow of money on transactions in external assets and liabilities. International investors will switch money from a foreign to a domestic currency for two reasons. Firstly, they will be attracted by the higher interest rates available in comparison with other international interest rates. Secondly, speculators know that raising interest rates will produce an inflow of money, increasing the demand for the domestic currency and thus raising the price of the currency. Hence they will be encouraged to buy the currency.

Higher interest rates will also reduce aggregate demand. Monetarists believe that this reduction will be much greater than do Keynesians. Higher interest rates will reduce consumption, particularly of consumer durables, and will reduce investment. This will lead to a direct reduction in imports and an improvement on the current balance.

Exchange controls

Governments may take direct action to reduce outward flows on transactions in external assets and liabilities. The central bank normally operates the scheme. All persons wanting foreign exchange make an application to the central bank. The central bank then grants or refuses their request. In refusing requests for foreign currency, the central bank effectively reduces the supply of domestic currency on to the market, thus raising the price of the currency.

Exchange rate systems

The price of a currency is determined on a day to day basis by the demand and supply of the currency. Governments may choose to allow free market forces to determine the value of the currency entirely: that is, the government adopts a flexible exchange rate system. Alternatively, governments may choose to determine the rate of exchange for their currencies: that is, the government adopts a fixed exchange rate system. Or governments may choose a combination of these two.

Exchange rate systems are judged on a number of criteria:

1 The system should not discourage international trade. Discouragement is likely to take place if the currency fluctuates so much that traders cannot predict at what price they will be able to buy or sell currency.

2 The system should not have major consequences for the domestic economy when the constituent parts of the balance of payments fall into deficit.

3 The system should not run into difficulty because there is insufficient money to finance the volume of world trade.

A variety of exchange rate systems has been used in the past. None has been found to be efficient enough to establish itself as an obvious sole choice for a world-wide exchange rate system.

Flexible exchange rate system

Under a pure flexible or floating exchange rate system, governments do not intervene in the foreign exchange markets. The price of the currency is determined purely by market forces. The main advantages of such a mechanism are twofold.

1 Governments need hold no reserves of foreign currency to intervene in the market.

2 The balance of payments automatically balances and therefore it ceases to be a policy problem for the Government. This leaves the Government free to concentrate on pursuing other policy objectives.

However, there are a number of problems associated with the system.

1 If an economy had combined export and import elasticities of less than 1 (the Marshall-Lerner condition) then a balance of payments disequilibrium would not result in an automatic adjustment. On the contrary, a current account deficit would get worse following devaluation. Short term difficulties might be present too. It has been argued that following devaluation, the current account is likely to deteriorate before it improves in the J curve effect. But a deterioration will produce a further devaluation. Hence the current account will always be on the downward part of the J curve, whilst the currency is constantly being devalued.

2 Speculation may increase currency fluctuations. If speculators expect a currency to devalue, they will sell currency, thus further increasing the supply of the currency on to the market. This will produce a larger fall in price than would otherwise have been the case.

3 The constant fluctuations in exchange rates may discourage international trade. If exporters and importers are unable to say what price they will receive or pay for their goods next week, in three months or in three years, then they will be reluctant to trade. In practice, fairly sophisticated financial markets exist for exporters and importers to be able to buy currency now to be paid for and delivered at a later date. Speculators provide this service, known as the 'forward currency markets'. However, it is

Data 17.4

A play with no script

Peter Norman

Central bankers and politicians who attempt to manipulate exchange rates on the world currency markets were given a salutary lesson earlier this month.

The dollar's rise through the DM1.90 barrier on May 8 was a reminder that foreign exchange markets nowadays pay scant regard to the consensus views of economics and politicians.

For years, conventional wisdom has been that the dollar is vulnerable to weakness because of the huge and persistent US current account deficit, amounting this year to $135bn. The Japanese yen and the German Deutschmark, on the other hand, should be strong currencies because of their large current account surpluses.

However, with few controls left on the movement of money between countries, flows of capital funds can be a far more potent force in determining currency values than any concern about economic fundamentals.

The dollar has benefited recently from strong demand for high-yielding dollar assets from fund managers in Europe and the Far East. The Japanese yen, on the other hand, has weakened because of the resignation of the Prime Minister, Noboru Takeshita, following the wide ranging corruption Recruit* scandal which has rocked the government.

The weakness of the German D-Mark is in part due to the 10 per cent withholding tax on D-Mark assets imposed in October 1987. This has led to a massive capital outflow as speculators seek higher returns elsewhere. West Germany's DM85bn current account surplus last year was more than offset by a DM121bn outflow of long and short term capital.

The sheer unpredictability of exchange rates will ensure full employment for foreign exchange dealers, analysts and central bankers as long as there is more than one currency in the world. And the recent tussle between the dollar bulls and the central bankers brought back memories of the noise and panic that have marked currency crises since fixed exchange rates were abandoned in the early 1970s.

The Financial Times. 25.5.89

*Recruit was a Japanese Company which gave subsidised shares to Japanese cabinet ministers, allegedly to secure favours.

1 Explain what, according to the article, should have been happening to the value of the world's three major currencies in 1989 according to 'economic fundamentals'.

2 Discuss the importance of capital flows upon the value of a currency under today's floating exchange system.

3 What influences the size and direction of capital flows across foreign exchanges?

4 Why have exchange rates proved to be so unstable since the early 1970s?

provided at a price—speculators after all need to make more money than they lose in order to make a living. They are also unwilling to provide currency forward for many years in the future. Then governments may step in to guarantee export prices. All this adds costs to the exporter, importer or taxpayer, and reduces the advantages to be gained from international trade.

Fixed exchange rate systems

A fixed exchange rate system requires that all currencies be fixed in relation to each other. No change in the value of currencies is allowed. The only example of such a system in operation was the gold standard system which operated from about 1880 to 1914, and then again in a somewhat less perfect form between 1918 and 1931 (in the case of the UK, from 1925 to 1931). The essence of the system was that every country pegged its currency against gold. In doing so each currency became pegged itself against every other currency. If a country had a deficit, the central bank of that economy paid off the deficit with gold from its reserves. Equally, countries with a surplus received gold.

In order to bring about an adjustment in the balance of payments, the total money supply was linked to the stock of gold in the central bank. If the central bank lost gold due to a balance of payments deficit, then the central bank would reduce the money supply. This in turn, via the monetarist transmission mechanism, would result in a fall in the price level. This would lead to a rise in competitiveness of domestic goods and the elimination of the deficit.

However, whilst the system produced certainty

amongst traders, it also produced two major problems. Firstly, countries such as the UK were unable to maintain convertibility of gold for their currency. Their currencies became overvalued and they were unable to adjust. The system was so rigid that a major crisis, such as the Great Depression, broke the system in 1930/1. Secondly, the adjustment mechanism imposed heavy costs on the economy. Deficit countries were subject to high interest rates, unemployment and falling wages in the transitional phase to a lower price level. On the other hand surplus countries experienced inflation.

Intermediate systems

A number of systems exist which are partly fixed and partly flexible. The exchange rate system which existed between the end of the Second World War and 1971 was known as the **Bretton Woods System**. In 1944, the Allies met at Bretton Woods in the USA to discuss the future world economic system. Amongst the proposals was the setting up of a bank, the International Monetary Fund (IMF) which would police a new exchange rate system. Each country had to fix its exchange rate against either gold or the dollar. They then had to keep the value of their currency within 1% of that fixed value.

If the value of the currency threatened to fall below the 1% margin, the central bank would step in to buy currency. In doing this they created extra demand for the currency, and thus raised its free market price. If the value of the currency threatened to go above the margin, the central bank would step in and sell currency.

This process can be shown diagrammatically. In Fig. 17.2, the fixed value of the currency is P_E. It is allowed to fluctuate between limits P_1 and P_2. Assume that the currency is threatening to rise to price P_3 due to a rightward shift in the demand curve. Then the central bank will step in to supply AB of currency onto the market. This will reduce the price to its maximum permitted value of P_1.

The system required that each central bank keep gold and foreign currency reserves. These were not limitless, and one problem was that reserves could become exhausted at times when supply of a currency consistently exceeded its demand. In this situation, under the Bretton Woods System, a country should have devalued in order to restore equilibrium.

The great advantage of the system was that it produced certainty for traders. However, it had two disadvantages. Firstly, the failure of the system to maintain sufficient reserves (i.e. sufficient international liquidity) meant that when the system encountered large problems it collapsed. Secondly, individual countries failed to devalue in time. Devaluation came to be seen as a sign of economic disaster for an economy. Instead, deficit countries tended to deflate to correct current account disequilibria, creating a high cost in terms of increased unemployment and lower growth. This reluctance on the part of deficit countries to devalue, and the refusal of surplus countries to revalue, again contributed to the downfall of the system.

At the present time, most countries are on a **managed float** or a **dirty float**. This means that currencies are free to change value according to market forces. However, central banks intervene in the market if their currencies reach undesirable levels. It is the central bank that has to decide what exactly is an 'undesirable level'. The system has not provided as much stability as was once hoped. Currencies such as the pound sterling have fluctuated by over 50% in value in a period of just a few years. The system also requires the holding of reserves by central banks. The advantage of the system is that domestic economic policies are not so heavily tied by balance of payments constraints as under a more rigid system such as Bretton Woods.

A **wide band system** is similar to the Bretton Woods System. However, instead of the currency being only allowed to fluctuate by 1% around the mean it would be allowed to fluctuate by say 5%. The alleged advantage of such a system is that it would not produce the pressure on the reserves that the Bretton Woods System produced, whilst giving a greater amount of certainty for traders than a

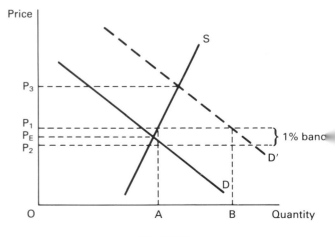

Fig. 17.4

managed float system. However, since 1971 some currencies have appreciated or depreciated rapidly by quite large amounts. It is doubtful whether the 5% limit would provide sufficient flexibility to avoid the same sort of crises encountered with the Bretton Woods System.

Data 17.5

Reserves edge higher to record $51.7bn

Britain's gold and foreign currency reserves edged higher last month to a record level of $51.7bn (£29.5bn), highlighting the funds available to the Government to defend sterling if necessary.

Treasury figures yesterday showed that UK official reserves rose by an underlying $330m in January. This compares with a rise of $461m in December.

Changes in the reserves reflect a variety of transactions but give a rough guide to the scale of intervention by the Bank of England in foreign exchange markets. The modest size of the latest rise suggests that action was limited.

The pound remained strong in January, particularly against European currencies. However the Bank is thought to have sold pounds and bought D-Marks to curb rises. Sterling has benefited recently from high UK interest rates relative to other countries, although the Bank has often checked some of its strength.

Mr Nigel Richardson, economist at Warburg Securities, said: "There is no doubt that there has been intervention to prevent the pound from rising, but it has not been on the scale that we saw back in 1987."

The Financial Times. 3.2.89

? How did the Bank of England intervene in the foreign exchange markets in December 1988 and January 1989?
? Using a diagram, explain what effect the intervention of the Bank of England had on the value of the pound.

A **crawling peg system** is again a more flexible version of the Bretton Woods System. A par value for the currency is fixed and the currency allowed to fluctuate by say 1% around that. However, every so often, say every 3 months, the currency is revalued. The new par value is fixed at the average value of the currency over the past 3 months. If the currency has tended to fall in value, then the currency will be devalued and vice versa. The system obviously needs central bank reserves. Whilst providing more certainty for traders than under a pure floating system, it is still unlikely to provide sufficient flexibility for currencies which need to devalue or revalue by large amounts in a short time.

A group of countries, if they so wish, can arrange a fixed exchange rate system between themselves whilst floating against all other currencies. An example of this is the European Monetary System, which has operated in one form or another since 1972. A group of West European countries have joined together and have agreed to keep their currencies within a $2\frac{1}{4}\%$ band of each other. The whole group of currencies is then free to float against all other currencies. When currencies threaten to break out of the system, the central banks of the system support the currencies involved. The major problem has been that certain currencies, such as the German Deutschmark, have always threatened to rise out of the 'band' whilst others, such as the French franc, have tended to fall out of the bottom of the system. This places the system under much strain.

Summary

The balance of payments comprises the current account and the capital account. The current account records trade in goods and services. The capital account records flows for investment and saving purposes. The exchange rate is determined by the demand and supply for the currency. Demand and supply are affected by the international competitiveness of an economy, by international interest rates and by expectations. There are several methods of dealing with balance of payments disequilibria including devaluation, deflation, exchange control and import controls. Exchange rates systems include fixed exchange rate (e.g. the gold standard), variable exchange rate (i.e. floating exchange rates) or a combination of both fixed and variable, e.g. the Bretton Woods System.

Data 17.6

Floating exchange rates 'failed'

BY SIMON HOLBERTON

THE 1990s international monetary system had to be based on explicit commitments by the Group of Seven industrial countries to pegged but adjustable exchange rates, Professor Peter Kenan said yesterday.

Prof Kenan, an international economist at Princeton University, was speaking at a meeting organised by the Centre for Economic Policy Research.

He said the post-Bretton Woods floating exchange rates system failed the international economy.

The 1985 Plaza Agreement on the dollar represented the first recognition of need for change in exchange-rate arrangements since leading economies ratified floating rates in Jamaica in 1976. The Louvre Accord last year was a further step towards exchange-rate stabilisation.

A system of pegged but adjustable rates with explicit margins that had to be defended would be a preferable extension of the trend, he said. The bands around the margins, within which exchange rates could move, would be wide to accommodate exchange-rate realignments.

Such a system would require:
● Scope for small but frequent realignments of currencies.
● Closer collective surveillance over national policies, especially fiscal policies.
● A change to the character of currency market intervention that would allow funds to be made available for intervention in the short term but with constraints.

He said his research showed that a floating exchange-rate regime might require more, not less, international coordination of economic policies and that economic performance might be less satisfactory under floating than under pegged rates.

The Financial Times. 10.5.88

1 What is meant by 'pegged but adjustable exchange rates'?
2 What would be needed to make such a system work in practice?

3 Why might a pegged system be preferable to a floating exchange rate system?

Terms for review

balance of payments	devaluation
current account on the balance of payments	deflation
capital account on the balance of payments	exchange controls
visibles and invisibles	flexible and fixed exchange rate systems
transactions in external assets and liabilities	Bretton Woods System
private sector transactions	managed or dirty float
exchange rates	crawling peg

Essay questions

1 How effective is devaluation as a way of curing a balance of payments deficit?

2 Define the 'effective' exchange rate of the pound. How might the effective exchange rate change if domestic inflation doubled?

3 Distinguish between a fixed and a variable exchange rate system. Do variable exchange rate systems discourage world trade?

4 What is meant by a 'balance of payments deficit'? What are the consequences for an economy running a persistent balance of payments deficit?

18

International trade

Introduction

The balance of payments and exchange rates were considered in the previous chapter. In this chapter, the advantages and disadvantages of foreign trade will be looked at more closely. We shall see why it is advantageous for a particular country to engage in foreign trade. Then we shall discuss why national economies might find it to their advantage to distort the pattern of free trade deliberately by imposing trade restrictions.

The theory of comparative advantage

Adam Smith, in his book *The Wealth of Nations*, explained why trade might be mutually advantageous to two parties. Table 18.1 shows two countries, A and B, which trade only two goods, cars and wheat. Country A is more efficient at producing cars than country B, because it can produce them more cheaply. Country A is said to have an **absolute** advantage in the production of cars. Similarly, country B produces wheat more cheaply than country A, and therefore country B has an absolute advantage in the production of wheat. If the two countries trade freely with each other, country A will specialise in the production and export of cars, whilst country B will specialise in the production of wheat and export it. It is assumed that transport costs are negligible and that the cars and wheat produced in each country are identical.

What Adam Smith did not see was that trade would be mutually advantageous even if a country did not have an absolute advantage in any commodity. Consider Table 18.2. Country A has an absolute advantage in the production of both cars and wheat.

Table 18.1

| | Cost per unit | |
	Cars	Wheat
Country A	5 000	100
Country B	6 000	80

However, country A has a **comparative** advantage only in the production of wheat. A unit of wheat in country A costs 1/50th of a car. In country B a unit of wheat costs 1/30th of a car. So wheat is relatively or comparatively cheaper in country A than in country B. Country B, on the other hand, has a comparative advantage in the production of cars. In Country A, a car costs 50 units of wheat. In country B, it only costs 30 units. So cars are comparatively cheaper in B.

Table 18.2

| | Cost per unit | |
	Cars	Wheat
Country A	5 000	100
Country B	6 000	200

It will be to both countries' advantage if they can trade wheat for cars. How much each country will benefit depends upon how much each country consumes domestically of each traded good, and upon the terms of trade. For instance, assume that country A consumes only cars and country B consumes only wheat. Each economy has a productive potential equivalent to 30 000 units of costs. The gains from trade are illustrated in Table 18.3. Before trade, country A produced and consumed 6 cars, and country B produced and consumed 150 units of

Data 18.1

Belgium's flexible methods lure international motor giants

Tim Dickson on the surprising size of the country's car industry

A SENIOR Ford executive who worked at the company's Genk plant in its early days recalls the social and political instability in France and Belgium in the early 1960s when the original choice of location was made. "Henry Ford arrived in Genk and found to his surprise a quiet, conservative, and highly Catholic people who, by contrast with the unrest elsewhere, were just getting on with their lives."

Ford's decision, announced on Monday, to switch most of its UK Sierra production at Dagenham to Genk provides a boost for the struggling, formerly coal-dependent Flemish town. It also highlights the surprising size and strength of the Belgian motor industry.

A total of 1.1m cars, roughly 10 per cent of total European production last year, were assembled in Belgium. Between 90 and 95 per cent of them were sold abroad for export, representing 15 per cent of the country's trade. And more than 30,000 people were directly engaged in their manufacture, with thousands more indirectly reliant.

Belgium's motor industry tradition – the technology as well as the skills – undoubtedly played a significant part in attracting the likes of Ford and General Motors, though other factors were at work. The location of the port of Antwerp (where GM had set up in the mid-1920s), generous tax incentives provided by the Belgian Government, the country's geographical situation at the crossroads of Europe and its marked neutrality and openness also played a part.

Belgium's wide and well built motorways – now backed up by one of the most advanced electronic systems for linking plants with customers – are still seen as key competitive advantages in the grim fight for European market share.

Above all, however, manufacturers in Belgium stress the attitudes and skills of the workforce in the Flemish half of the country, which so influenced Henry Ford.

at the plant, will be a test for Belgian flexibility.

The experience of General Motors at Antwerp should at least provide encouragement for the local Ford management. Last August GM successfully amalgamated its two production centres in the town, introducing six-days-a-week, 20-hour production through a new 11-day working cycle of longer shifts but fewer hours. Assembly workers do a cycle of two four-day weeks, followed by one three-day week.

Belgium's legislation on flexible working – allowing companies the possibility of night and weekend shifts, as well as seasonal patterns of production – is among the most attractive of its kind in Europe.

But while GM's spokesman concedes that the laws have been a help, he believes that the largely co-operative

HOW BELGIUM'S BIG FIVE COMPARE (1987)

	Vehicles assembled	Employees
General Motors	383,724	10,529
Ford	334,388	11,044
Volkswagen	210,562	5422
Renault	155,650	3828
Volvo	102,000	4600
Source: Fabiac		

The adaptation of the many ex-coal miners in the region brought its ups and downs to a plant which pioneered the electrocoating process in Europe in the mid-1960s and which has grown to provide jobs today for more than a third of the 30,000 working people in the town.

This week's announcement by Ford Werke, Genk's West German parent subsidiary, that it will now be seeking far-reaching changes in labour practices

attitude of the unions and work-force has been a key factor.

"Belgium has a lot going for it but there are also disadvantages with the small home market and the traditionally high labour costs. I think there is an awareness here as 1992 approaches that we have to compensate for these with things like flexibility, good delivery times, and an atmosphere of social and labour stability."

The Financial Times. 19.1.89

1 Why might Belgium have a comparative advantage in the production of cars?

wheat. After trade, Country B produces 5 cars to export to A. Country A produces two cars to consume domestically and devotes the rest of its resources (20 000 units) to producing 200 units of wheat for export to B. Here, country A is one car better off after trade, and B is 50 units of wheat better off. The exchange rate has been fixed at 5 cars for 200 units of wheat, i.e. 1 car for 40 units of wheat.

The theory of comparative advantage states that trade will be mutually advantageous to the two

Table 18.3

| | Before trade | | After trade | | | |
| | Production | Consumption | Production | | Consumption | |
	Cars	Wheat	Cars	Wheat	Cars	Wheat
Country A	6	–	2	200	7	–
Country B	–	150	5	–	–	200

Data 18.2

South Africa counts the high cost of self-sufficiency

By Bernard Simon in Johannesburg

South Africa's import replacement drive, for a long time an almost sacred part of the Government's economic strategy, is coming under increasingly heavy criticism.

The most spirited attack has come from the National Maize Producers Organisation (Nampo), a vociferous and politically powerful group of maize farmers who are fed up with paying hefty premiums for locally produced truck and tractor engines, fertiliser raw materials and other farm requisites. They want to be allowed to buy supplies from the cheapest source, whether in South Africa or abroad.

The motor industry also is worried by a recent spate of cost-raising import replacement projects, notably diesel engines, axles and gearboxes.

Moves towards self-sufficiency were spawned by fears that the South African national defence force would be cut off by sanctions from foreign supplies. This had a bearing on civilian needs when it became clear that plants needed longer production runs to make them reasonably viable.

The motor companies would prefer to buy components from the source of their choice. But if they are to be forced to support local suppliers, they at least want firm guidelines on the government's future import substitution plans.

The Government is caught between two stools.

On the one hand, it has actively encouraged import replacement in the past. The threat of trade sanctions and other "strategic" considerations have given birth to important sectors of industrial output, including the Sasol oil-from-coal plants, armaments factories, plastics, stainless steel and synthetic rubber.

On the other hand, Pretoria is being made increasingly aware of the costs of this policy. As Dr Brand said: "Any drive towards self-sufficiency tends to raise costs, and to harm the competitiveness of our (non-mining and non-farming) export industries."

The difference between prices of South African and imported items is sometimes large, especially now that international markets are depressed.

For instance, the local price of poly-vinyl-chloride (PVC) is R1,590 a ton, compared with around R600 currently on world markets.

But some key South African industries would not survive if they were not almost totally insulated from outside competition.

Mr Denys Marvin, managing director of AECI, South Africa's largest chemicals producer, noted recently that tight import controls have been a key factor in the expansion of the local chemical industry.

He said that if adequate steps were not taken to keep out cheap imports from the U.S., Europe and the Far East, "then at the very least, the question of building further high capital cost chemical plants in the Republic will receive more than the usual scrutiny."

The Financial Times. 31.1.83

1 Why are there such big cost and price differentials for some products between South African and other world producers?

2 What are the costs and benefits to South Africa of self-sufficiency?

economies if comparative costs of production of tradeable goods differ. Comparative costs are, of course, the same as opportunity costs. If comparative or opportunity costs between goods are identical, then trade will not be advantageous. A situation such as this is shown in Table 18.4. The opportunity cost of one car is 50 units of wheat in country A. It is identical in country B. Therefore neither country will benefit from trade.

Table 18.4

| | Cost per unit | |
	Cars	Wheat
Country A	5 000	100
Country B	10 000	200

The theory of comparative advantage was first propounded by David Ricardo. Ricardo's theory of international trade is one example of a general theory which applies to all forms of specialisation. If an electrician and a plumber work together it is obviously more efficient if each specialises in his craft rather than sharing plumbing and electrical work equally. What the theory of comparative advantage shows is that this true even if the electrician is a more efficient plumber than the plumber himself. In Table 18.5 the opportunity cost of 1 unit of electrical work is 3 units of plumbing work for the plumber but 0.8 units of plumbing work for the electrician. So the plumber should specialise in plumbing and the electrician in electrical work.

Table 18.5

| | Daily output in units | | |
	Plumbing		Electrical work
Plumber	60	or	20
Electrician	80	or	100

The exact rate of exchange of goods is not determinable within Ricardo's theory. Returning to the situation described by Table 18.2, country A will want at least 1 car for every 50 units of wheat it exports. If it received less, it would be more advantageous to produce cars domestically. Country B on the other hand would want at least 30 units of wheat for every car it exports. So the rate of exchange will have to be one car for between 30 and 50 units of wheat.

The reasons for international trade

Ricardo's theory argues that international trade takes place because comparative costs differ. He argued that the cause of the differences lay in varying labour costs. Countries with comparatively high labour costs for a good would import that good from a comparatively low labour cost country. So today, Far Eastern countries export textiles to the Western world because their workers are paid so much less. The Western world in turn exports high technology products back to them because they do not have the high quality labour needed to produce such goods. That is to say, the price of high quality labour in developing Far Eastern countries is infinitely high.

However, labour is only one component of costs. Land and capital also are needed to make goods and services. In the 1930's two Swedish economists, Hecksher and Ohlin, argued that different costs resulted from different factor endowments. Countries with abundant labour would produce labour–intensive goods. Countries with abundant supplies of raw materials would export these. And countries with abundant supplies of capital would supply capital–intensive goods to world markets.

Neither the Ricardian theory based upon labour costs, nor the Heckscher-Ohlin model based upon different factor endowments, provides a clear explanation of current patterns of trade. Both theories can help explain why trade takes place in homogeneous goods—that is, goods which are highly similar in content, e.g. copper or steel.

However, most world trade is in non-homogeneous goods and takes place between developed countries. Non-homogeneous goods include items such as cars, washing machines, and medical equipment, no two models of which are identical. There is a difference between a Ford Sierra and an Austin Maestro. Non-homogeneous goods are not bought on cost grounds alone. A customer is prepared to pay more for a particular model if he believes that quality and reliability are better, or if servicing will be more efficient, or simply because he has been misled about the superiority of a particular model through advertising.

If a country is to trade in non-homogeneous goods, it needs to be at a similar level of economic development to its main trading partners. It will tend to export goods which are particularly successful in its home market. This is because a successful home market will provide sufficient sales revenue to keep down costs per item sold, and to provide funds for research and development in the product. It will also tend to export in areas where companies have very much geared themselves to supplying the needs of their overseas customers. One of the reasons for the success of the post-war Japanese economy has been its painstaking efforts to fulfil the needs of their customers in Europe and America. A country will import in sectors where domestic firms are weak.

Two theories which have been developed to explain this are the **preference similarity theory** and the **technological gap theory**. The preference similarity theory argues that trade in non-homogeneous goods has developed because consumers desire more choice of goods. The goods must be geared to the needs of a particular domestic market, but must be different enough to draw customers away from other competing goods in the market.

The technological gap theory argues that trade occurs because of differences in technology between economies. Advanced Western economies tend to export goods in which they have a technological superiority, either in the production process or in the good itself being produced. Less developed countries tend to export low technology products. The western world is engaged in a vicious technology battle. Countries such as Japan, which have been particularly adept at implementing technological change, have performed particularly well in the international trade stakes. Countries such as the UK which have failed to develop its technology to its maximum have run into difficulties because they have been unable to expand their export markets sufficiently to keep pace with their growing appetite for imports.

The terms of trade

There is a variety of ways to measure the competitiveness of an economy in relation to other economies. One of these is the **terms of trade**. The terms of trade is the ratio of export prices to import prices

Can the success of Japanese exports over the past twenty years be explained by the technological gap theory?

170

Its formula is:

Index of the terms of trade =

$$\frac{\text{Index of export prices}}{\text{Index of import prices}}$$

All other things being equal, if export prices go up or import prices fall, then the index of the terms of trade increases in numerical value and is said to improve. Conversely, a deterioration of the terms of trade comes about due to a fall in export prices relative to import prices.

Movements in the terms of trade are not easy to interpret. In general, an improvement in the terms of trade will increase the economic welfare of the economy in the short run. This is because imports become cheaper in relation to exports. So the prices of goods and services bought goes down relative to the price of the goods and services that are sold to foreign customers. It is analogous to a worker's income increasing by a bigger percentage than the increase in the cost of living.

The welfare implications are more difficult to predict in the long run. A relative rise in export prices could make exports less competitive on world markets. Export volumes will drop, resulting in less production, less export-generated income and fewer jobs. A relative fall in import prices could make imports more competitive domestically, resulting again in a fall in domestic production and in lower incomes. Thus, a rise in the terms of trade tends to make an economy less competitive in the long run. The long run effects of lower output and lower income may or may not outweigh the short term gain of being able to exchange goods internationally at an improved price ratio.

However, if the rise in the terms of trade resulted from a fall in the price of imported raw materials not produced in the domestic economy, there is unlikely to be any fall in the country's competitiveness. In this case, the long run effect is likely to be beneficial as the economy's real income has increased.

Protectionism

Free trade—the ability of customers to buy goods and services anywhere in the world without government interference—confers important economic advantages. Ricardo's theory of comparative advantage showed that a country could consume more

Data 18.3

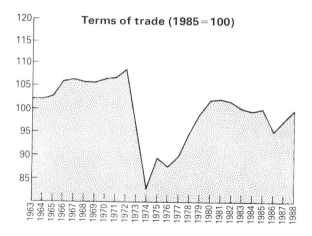

Terms of trade (1985=100)

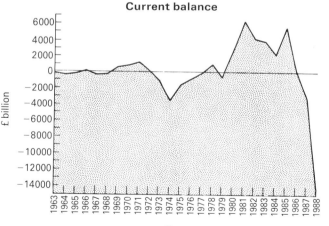

Current balance

Source: CSO, Economic Trends

1 Explain the changes in the terms of trade shown in the data.

2 What impact would you expect changes in the terms of trade to have on the balance of payments over the period shown in the data?

goods and services by specialisation and trading than by attempting to be self-sufficient. Even if foreign goods are little cheaper than domestic goods, consumers do gain greater choice of goods and services, which can add to their economic welfare.

Although the benefits of trade are well known, no developed economy permits complete free trade across its national boundaries. All economies follow protectionist policies to a greater or lesser extent. The effect of protection is to limit the extent of trade. Examples of protectionist policies which can be pursued are:

1 **Tariffs**—taxes on imported goods which increase their final price and therefore reduce domestic demand.

2 **Quotas**—limits on the number of goods which can be imported into an economy.

3 **Exchange controls**—imposing a variety of restrictions on acquiring foreign exchange to pay for foreign goods and services, or to undertake investment abroad.

Data 18.4

French don't play cricket

by Anne-Elisabeth Moutet, Paris

By now the Japanese should have learned. The French don't play cricket, haven't heard of the Marquess of Queensberry and hit below the belt. And they certainly have not forgotten what the Japanese did to the Renault 5.

"When we first unloaded the Renault 5 in Yokohama," says one senior French trade official, "we were told that the cars had to clear customs 200 kilometres away. There were no parking facilities so we had to buy our own ground. While we went through some extremely complicated and costly legal procedures, the cars had to wait for weeks in bad weather. It took us two years to get the building permit, six months to get it linked to the water mains and another eight months to get electricity."

By the time the French were in position to start selling, the Japanese had decided that no foreign company was to be allowed more than eight dealerships in the whole of Japan.

That cost the Japanese dear. A discreet word in the ear of the Japanese ambassador let it be known that the authorities would find it "unreasonable" if Japanese cars took more than 3% of the French market.

France's outspoken, diminutive minister for foreign trade, Michel Jobert, doesn't think that the Japanese have yet hoisted the message on board – which is why he intends that their video manufacturers should strike up a close relationship with Jean Grapillard, local customs director of Poitiers, population 100,000, location somewhere in western France.

Until last Wednesday, the testing pace of rural France saw Grapillard and his six staff processing local wheat and beef exports and a few steel tube imports for the factories around Poitiers. Now, with the help of two extra staff rushed down from Paris, Grapillard's team of eight has the job of processing all France's imports of VCRs.

If last year's rate is sustained, that means at least half a million, which won't be easy. First they will have to make their way to Poitiers from Le Havre, Holland or Germany. They will probably be wise to come by truck even though the roads aren't wonderful because the SNCF station there cannot handle containers and the railway authorities have made it clear that no one is going to clog up their tracks with stationary trainloads of VCRs. And by the way, there is no parking space for trucks, either.

Jobert's stance is that since everybody plays at protectionism, they should admit it and regulate it according to a "reasonable" framework. French officials quote the Franco-German car trade as an example of "neutral moderation." Four years ago, say the French, the Germans were clearly trying it on. They insisted that imported cars should have their door handles fitted with a device to stop them opening in a crash and they followed this up with new anti-pollution laws. When the French announced that the VW Golf's shock absorbers were unsound by their norms, the confrontation ended abruptly.

The French have no compunction about guarding their interests. "The ability to lie through your teeth for as long as possible and then gracefully accept sanctions is essential," says one French diplomat.

The Sunday Times. 31.10.82

1 *What protectionist measures are mentioned in the article?*

2 *What possible advantages would there be for France to restrict the imports of Japanese VCRs?*

4 Other physical controls—bureaucratic regulations, such as import licences which are difficult to get, or minimum environmental, safety or health standards, can be highly effective in preventing imports.

Although protectionist policies lead initially to a loss of economic welfare, the long term effects may be beneficial. The arguments in favour of protectionism will be considered more carefully in Chapter 19. However, the benefits revolve around the possibility of creating extra jobs in the economy which stimulates extra economic growth. Higher domestic incomes in the long term will outweigh any loss in real income in the short term resulting from protectionist policies. Protectionism is only successful if other countries do not in retaliation increase their own trade barriers. If they do retaliate, the dynamic gains from increased growth are unlikely to appear, leaving the domestic consumer with higher prices and less choice.

Why is this an example of trade diversion for the UK since entry to the European Community?

Economic integration

Groups of countries can join together to encourage greater economic integration. There are two main types of integration.

1 A **free trade area**, in which countries agree to allow free trade in certain goods and services between member countries. Each member country is free to decide upon protectionist policies with regard to non-member countries.

2 A **customs union**, in which member countries not only agree to free trade in goods and services between themselves, but also agree to common protectionist policies. In a free trade area, each member country can fix its own tariffs against other countries. In a common market, each member country has the same tariff on third country goods.

Joining a free trade area or a customs union may or may not increase the economic welfare of an economy. In the short term a country's pattern of trade is likely to change. It will now obtain some goods and services from cheaper sources than before. This is because tariffs or other protectionist measures lead to the same good being produced more expensively at home, or being bought from a more expensive source overseas. This is known as **trade**

creation. However, **trade diversion** will also occur. This is where a country was buying from a cheap source of supply before, but now because of tariff barriers buys from a more expensive source.

When the UK joined the European Community in 1973, trade diversion certainly took place as regards food. Before entry, the UK bought cheap West Indian sugar cane. After entry, protectionist barriers meant that higher-priced European sugar beet became far more competitive than before. So the UK increased its consumption of beet relative to cane. Similarly, with butter, sources of supply shifted from cheap New Zealand butter to more expensive continental butter.

A country will gain economic welfare if, following entry, trade creation outw[...] will lose e[...] weighs tra[...]

In the lon[...] be more im[...] tion. Follow[...] a larger 'hon[...] export to oth[...] policies. Gre[...] ment, a high[...] rates. Equall[...] as the firms[...] their market [...]

1 To what exte[...] in a shift in her[...]

173

International trade

The extent to which a country will benefit dynamically depends to a great extent upon the balance between the exports and imports created as a direct result of entry. Most of those exports and imports created will represent trade between member countries. If one country is particularly competitive and improves its balance of trade with other member countries, this could well be at the expense of other member countries. Countries which are particularly uncompetitive are likely to see their markets filled with foreign goods and their industries destroyed, only to be recreated in the economies of the more competitive countries of the customs union.

All countries may benefit if, following entry, firms are able to compete more effectively with non-member countries. Following membership, there is likely to be a rationalisation of industries. Each member country will tend to specialise to a greater degree in those goods and services in which it has a comparative advantage. Output per firm will tend to rise, meaning that costs per item sold will tend to fall. Thus, firms will now be able to export at cheaper prices to non-member countries, expanding their exports and creating extra economic growth.

The dynamic impact of membership of a union is a specialised case of more general theory applying to any type of economic integration. Neo-classical economics suggest that different regions in an economic union will benefit equally in the long run. To illustrate this, assume that there are only two regions,

Data 18.5

Visible exports: By trade area (£ millions)

1966

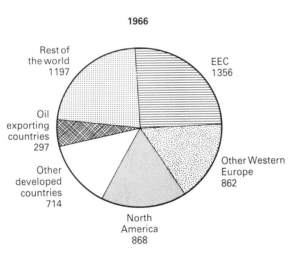

Rest of the world 1197 | EEC 1356 | Oil exporting countries 297 | Other developed countries 714 | North America 868 | Other Western Europe 862

Total 5276

1987

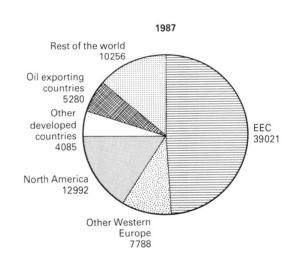

Rest of the world 10256 | Oil exporting countries 5280 | Other developed countries 4085 | North America 12992 | EEC 39021 | Other Western Europe 7788

Total 79422

Source: CSO, United Kingdom Balance of Payments

...t has Britain's entry to the EEC resulted
...pattern of visible trade?

2 How would economic theory explain this change?

say Britain and Europe, in the union. There is perfect mobility of goods, services, financial capital and factors of production. One region, Britain, has higher unemployment, lower growth and lower income than the other region. All other factors are the same in both regions. As a result, wages, factory rents and the cost of living should be lower in Britain. Then multinational firms wanting to expand will tend to expand in Britain rather than in Europe, because of the lower costs of production. Job places and financial capital will move to Britain at the expense of Europe. Unemployment will decline and growth rates will increase. This will continue until unemployment rates and growth rates are equalised between Britain and Europe, and Britain has lost its cost advantages.

Critics argue that this chain of events is reversed in practice. Empirical evidence tends to suggest that the gap between rich and poor regions does not narrow but may in fact increase. This is because many jobs are tied down to local markets. Firms need to be near their market in order to sell and respond to it. Economically successful regions are usually centres of high population. This population also has above average spending power. Therefore, not surprisingly, there is above average investment in those regions.

When firms do establish themselves in poorer regions, it is often large scale manufacturing plants which are attracted by large government grants. These plants are highly capital intensive, e.g. nuclear power plants and petro-chemical complexes. The result is that few jobs are actually created. Another unfortunate feature of these plants is that they tend to be subsidiary plants. At times of difficulty for the firm, it is these plants that suffer redundancies or actual closure. Plants near head office in the rich regions tend to remain unscathed.

Financial capital, then, remains in the rich regions or, even worse, tends to move from the poor regions to the rich as firms take advantage of the growing markets in the rich regions. Labour, too, trickles from the poor region to the rich region. The labour that is mobile tends to be skilled, young and enterprising, i.e. amongst the best in the poor regions. Not surprisingly, firms needing skilled, specialised labour are attracted to the rich regions where it is available, even if wages in general are high.

Economic integration, then, may well lead to a further impoverishment of already backward regions. It may retard their economic development rather than help it. A strong regional policy would be necessary to offset these damaging effects.

Summary

The theory of comparative advantage argues that countries will find it mutually profitable to trade if their opportunity costs of production differ. Ricardo argued that opportunity costs differed because of differences in labour costs. Heckscher-Ohlin saw differing factor endowments as the cause. The technological gap theory sees foreign trade being directed according to the differing degree of technological development between countries. The preference similarity theory argues that foreign trade is demand orientated, domestic consumers buying foreign goods in order to gain greater choice. The terms of trade are the ratio of export to import prices. A range of protectionist policies is used by countries to inhibit trade. They include tariffs, quotas, and exchange controls. Economic integration may benefit member countries. This is most likely to be true if trade creation effects outweigh trade diversion effects, and if increased economic growth follows integration.

Terms for review

comparative and absolute advantage

protectionism

terms of trade

free trade areas

tariffs

customs unions

quotas

trade creation and trade diversion

Essay questions

1 Why do countries trade? How would you expect a doubling in the price of primary products to affect the pattern of world trade?

2 Can the theory of comparative advantage explain the change in the UK's pattern of trade since it joined the European Community?

3 Define the 'terms of trade'. What effect would a deterioration in the terms of trade have on (a) the current account and (b) the level of employment in an economy?

19

Government macro-economic policy

The macro-economic goals of governments

Traditionally, four major macro-economic concerns of Government have been distinguished. These are:

1 unemployment;
2 inflation;
3 the balance of payments; and
4 economic growth.

There is wide agreement about what constitutes an ideal economy. It is one where unemployment is very low; e.g. where only frictional unemployment and a little seasonal unemployment exist. There is no inflation, i.e. prices are stable. The balance of payments is in long term equilibrium. This might mean that all parts of the balance of payments are in equilibrium. Or it might mean that because of that economy's state of development there is a long term current account surplus or deficit, with an offsetting deficit or surplus on the capital account. Economic growth should be at a rate which maximises the increase in living standards of an economy. The measurement of living standards should include not only national income but also other variables such as political freedom, pollution levels, income distribution and stress; factors which go to make up the quality of life of a citizen.

It has come to be argued that it might not be possible to attain all of the four goals simultaneously. For instance it might be that a trade-off exists between unemployment and inflation. Low unemployment might only be secured if high inflation exists and vice versa. The combination of goals to be pursued is ultimately a political decision. Economists can help in this political decision by attempting to cost out the different alternatives. For instance, keeping inflation at 5% per annum instead of 10% might cost the economy 1% growth per year and add an extra 1 million to the unemployment registers.

Thus, over a 25 year period, the cost of halving the inflation rate would be about 30% of national income, and would bring economic hardship for 1 million people. On the other hand, there are many economists who believe that in the long term trade-offs do not exist. In that case, difficult political choices can be avoided.

The instruments of government policy

Governments have a range of instruments through which they can effect their policies. Broadly speaking, these are:

1 **Fiscal policy**—affecting the economy through changes in the levels and direction of government spending, and through changes in the structure of taxes and their rates.

2 **Monetary or credit policy**—affecting the economy through changes in the money supply, in rates of interest, or the volume of funds available for borrowing.

3 **Prices and incomes policy**—affecting the economy by controlling either the prices of goods and services or the level of incomes received by labour or the owners of capital, or both.

4 **Trade policy**—affecting the domestic economy through the manipulation of exchange rates or by introducing more direct controls such as tariffs and quotas on foreign trade.

It is important to realise that for goal that a government sets itself instrument to implement th designed to reduce un might in turn increase inflation. A second policy instrument would be needed to tackle the inflation rate. It would be an extraordinary coincidence if one policy instrument were to achieve the desired policy effect on two goals. Governments therefore need a package of instruments if they seek to pursue several policy goals.

The need for government intervention

Economists disagree about how stable the economy is. If the economy is stable, and tends towards full employment, low inflation, high growth, and a problem-free balance of payments, then little or no government intervention is needed. If on the other hand the economy is unstable, producing large fluctuations in the level of economic activity and resulting in unacceptable levels of unemployment, inflation, etc., then government intervention to help improve the situation is highly desirable.

Monetarists argue that the economy is stable, and that government intervention in the economy is not only unnecessary but is likely to be damaging. Attempts to control the economy are futile in the long run. Keynesians, on the other hand, argue that the economy is unstable. To prevent tragic situations such as the depression of the 1930s, governments need to intervene in the economy to remedy the built-in defects of the free enterprise economy. It might be very difficult to implement policy successfully. Indeed, post-war economic history is littered with well-intentioned policies failing to secure their goals. But it is surely better to have some control, albeit crude, than to have none at all.

Demand management versus supply side economics

licy have effects
aggregate supply.
er whether it is
bout a desired
s designed to

manipulat-
ssible for
aggregate

demand in the economy. The supply side of the economy will adjust to accommodate the new level of demand.

Monetarists favour supply side economics. They argue that it is impossible for governments to manipulate aggregate demand in the long run, and very dangerous in the short run. Rather, the government's role should be to ensure a steady increase in the productive capabilities of the economy. By increasing supply, aggregate demand will grow too. The best way for the Government to support the supply side of the economy is for it to encourage the private sector to be as innovative, enterprising and competitive as possible. Hence supply side economics has come to be associated with anti-trade union policies, anti-monopoly legislation and the relaxing of laws relating to workers' rights, pollution, discrimination and health and safety at work.

Some Keynesians, however, could also be described as supply side economists. They argue that the private sector has consistently failed to innovate and be enterprising. It is then the Government's role to become the risk taker. Through its spending, it needs to invest in the industries of the future. More government control over the economy, not less, is called for.

In the rest of this chapter, the various instruments of government policy will be considered and their effectiveness appraised.

Fiscal policy

It is argued that fiscal policy can have an impact on the economy in two main ways:

1 The relative size of the public sector and the way it is financed can affect the level of aggregate demand in the economy.

2 The composition of public sector spending and taxation can have important micro-economic implications. These will be considered in turn.

The level of government spending, and the level of taxation need not be the same. If government spending is greater than taxation, a budget deficit is said to exist. That deficit is called the **public sector borrowing requirement** (PSBR). It can be financed either by genuine borrowing (i.e. from the non-bank sector), or by the creation of money, or both. If government spending and taxation are equal, a balanced budget is said to exist. If taxation is greater than government spending, then a budget surplus, or **public sector debt repayment** (PSDR), exists. The PSDR can be used to reduce the total value of past borrowing, called the **National Debt**.

Keynesians believe that changing the size of the budget surpluses or the budget deficits is a powerful method of affecting the economy. Increasing government spending and/or reducing taxation will increase the level of aggregate demand. If the economy is at less than full employment, this will reduce unemployment and raise the rate of growth. The increase in income is greater than the initial change in government spending or taxation, because of the real multiplier process. However, expansionary fiscal policy will also increase imports as consumers spend part of their extra income on foreign goods. This results in a worsening of the current balance. Expansionary fiscal policy will increase inflationary pressures too. The Phillips curve hypothesis states that the lower the rate of unemployment, the higher the rate of increase of money wages. The nearer the economy gets to full employment, the greater will be wage increases and therefore the greater will be the inflation rate. Of course, if the economy is already at full employment, the expansionary fiscal policy cannot reduce unemployment or increase growth. The total impact will be upon the price level.

This chain of argument is illustrated in Fig. 19.1. An increase of ΔG in government spending (on real goods and services) leads to an increase in income of Y_1Y_E, where Y_E happens to be full employment income. In Keynesian terms, a deflationary gap has been closed. Whilst this is good news for the unemployed and whilst growth figures have risen, imports rise by ΔM, and inflation increases by AB.

For Keynesians, then, governments have to make choices when using fiscal policy. Expansionary budgets are good for growth and unemployment, but bad for inflation and the balance of payments. Deflationary budgets are good for reducing inflation and helping to solve a balance of payments problem, but this is at the cost of reducing growth and increasing unemployment.

Expansionary and deflationary budgets need not mean greater or lower budget deficits or surpluses. According to the principle of the **balanced budget multiplier**, if government spending and taxation are changed by the same amounts, then the level of aggregate demand will change too.

Raising spending and taxes will raise national income. For instance, assume that government spending and taxation are both raised by £10 000

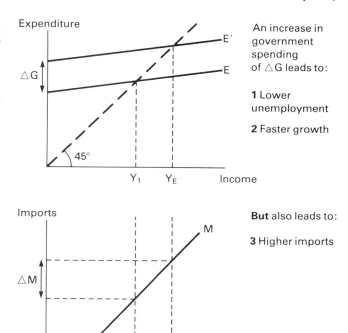

An increase in government spending of ΔG leads to:

1 Lower unemployment

2 Faster growth

But also leads to:

3 Higher imports

And

4 Higher inflation

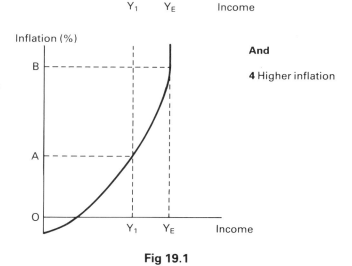

Fig 19.1

million. The marginal propensity to consume is 0.6. Therefore the value of the multiplier

$$\frac{1}{(1 - MPC)} \quad \text{is} \quad \frac{1}{(1 - 0.6)}$$

or 2.5. National income rises by £25 000 million. If the marginal propensity to tax is 0.4, taxation will rise by £10 000 million.

So, in this example, rises in government spending and taxation of £10 000 million have raised income by £25 000 million. This is a highly simplified example. For instance, the marginal propensity to save and to import are both 0 (since in this case $MPC + MPT = 1$). In general, the rise in taxation will lead to a dampening effect on income, but not by as much as the reflationary effect given by increased government spending. This is because the marginal propensity to tax will have to rise. In our example, it remained constant. In general, the bigger the value of the multiplier and the smaller the value of the marginal propensity to tax, the bigger will be the value of the balanced budget multiplier. If the multiplier is very small and the marginal propensity to tax is high, then the value of the balanced budget multiplier will approach zero.

The balanced budget multiplier has its effect on the economy because governments spend much of their revenues on domestically produced goods. If consumers and firms had kept those taxes only a part would have been spent domestically, the rest being saved or spent on imports. Equally, Keynesian economists have argued that fiscal policy will be more effective in changing aggregate demand if spending is concentrated on domestically produced goods, or if transfer payments are increased to consumers with very high marginal propensities to consume. For instance, government spending on an American nuclear missile system will not boost income. Building a nationwide system of nuclear shelters will. Raising child benefit, which goes to all families with children whatever their income, is likely to have less impact on aggregate demand than giving equivalent grants to sixth formers. This is because parents are likely to have a lower marginal propensity to consume than their children, as their incomes are much higher. Hence the multiplier effect of sixth form grants may be higher than the multiplier effect of child benefit. On the taxation side, to maximise demand impact, the Government needs to vary the rate of tax on those who would most likely have spent that tax on domestically produced goods. On Keynesian grounds, such people are the poor with high MPCs. The interests of demand management could well conflict here with the interests of equity and justice.

The government sector provides an important stabiliser within the economic system. If income rises, tax revenues will also rise. Since taxation is a leakage from the circular flow of income, the higher the marginal propensity to tax, the smaller will be the overall rise in income resulting from an increase

in an injection (I, X or G) or a fall in the marginal propensities to save or import. Equally, a rise in income at less than full employment is likely to cut government spending. The rise in incomes raises aggregate demand, the unemployed get jobs, and those in jobs see real increases in their incomes. Therefore the Government has to pay less unemployment benefit, and less social security benefit.

Equally, if the Government attempts to cut government spending, it may find that its attempts are frustrated. Falls in public spending result in lower income. This throws workers on to the dole and puts more people below the poverty line. Instead of spending money on roads and hospitals, the Government finds itself spending its money on keeping workers unemployed. The only way out of this vicious circle is for Government to cut away at the benefit system. Yet making the poor poorer by cutting their benefits is still only a partial solution. Government spending cuts will in turn have a multiplier effect on income, throwing even more people out of work, and on to the books of the government welfare service. Thus, taxation and government spending act as **automatic stabilisers** of the economic system, reducing the magnitude of changes in income that would otherwise have taken place.

Crowding out

Monetarist and classical economists argue that macro-economic fiscal policy is largely ineffective in affecting the level of real output and employment in the economy. Consider a situation where there is unemployment in the economy and the Government decides to close the deflationary gap by increasing its spending. In a simple Keynesian model, a deflationary gap of, for instance £10 000 million, could be closed by extra government spending of £5 000 million, assuming that the value of the multiplier were 2. But monetarists point out that the Government must find the money needed to pay for the extra government spending. It has three options:

1 It can borrow the money. But if it borrows the money, it borrows money which the private sector would otherwise have borrowed. Firms might have borrowed that money to invest. Consumers might have borrowed the money to spend. On this argument

an extra pound of public borrowing **crowds out** one pound of private spending. The net effect is no increase in aggregate demand.

2 It can raise taxes. But if it raises taxes, it will reduce the spending of households and firms. Again there will be no effect on aggregate demand.

3 It can print the money. The link between changes in the money supply and changes in aggregate expenditure is known as the **monetary transmission mechanism** and was explained in Chapter 16. Summarising the argument: printing extra money will increase the money supply. Initially, interest rates will fall and aggregate demand will increase. But as spending increases, so too will the transactions demand for money. With higher incomes, consumers and firms will need to hold more money to make day to day purchases. What is more, extra spending will have led to some demand-pull inflation. Higher prices will also lead to an increase in the transactions demand for money. The increase in the demand for money will lead to a rise in interest rates and this will then lead to a fall in spending. The monetarist position is that this fall in spending will roughly cancel out any increase in government spending. Again, extra government spending will have crowded out private sector spending and prices will have risen. Not only will unemployment have stayed the same, but the Government will have created inflation.

Governments, therefore, cannot spend their way out of recession. The key to reducing unemployment, according to classical economists, lies in supply-side measures.

Supply-side policies

Fig. 19.2 shows an aggregate demand and supply schedule for the economy on classical assumptions. In the long term, an increase in government spending which pushes the aggregate demand curve from AD to AD′ will have no effect on the equilibrium level of output in the economy, OA. Higher government spending will crowd out private sector spending. But the higher spending will be inflationary, raising prices from OE to OF. Contrast this with an increase in aggregate supply from AS to AS′. Output will increase from OA to OB, and there may even be a fall in prices if the aggregate demand schedule shifts less than the aggregate supply schedule as a result.

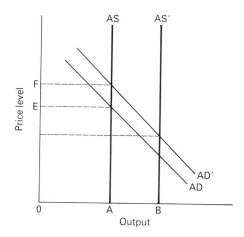

Fig. 19.2

Supply-side measures, then, are a powerful way of influencing both output and the level of employment whilst demand measures, according to classical economists, are positively harmful.

In general, aggregate supply will increase if there is an increase in the number of workers' willing to work at the going wage rate (many of whom may be counted officially as unemployed, but in theoretical terms form part of the voluntary unemployed); an increase in the stock of land or capital for production; more entrepreneurship; or an improvement in the efficiency of production in the economy. Classical economists argue that there are a number of ways in which the Government can increase aggregate supply in the economy:

1 Reduce marginal tax rates Classical economists argue that the higher the marginal rate of tax, particulary taxes on income and wealth, the less incentive there is to work. Reducing margin tax rates will increase workers willingness to work.

2 Reduce welfare payments for the unemployed Workers are less likely to be willing to take jobs if unemployment benefits are high in relation to average earnings than if they are low. Cutting unemployment benefits will encourage the unemployed to take jobs. They will spend less time looking for jobs and will be more prepared to take low paid jobs. On this argument, the workings of the welfare state create unemployment.

3 Encourage entrepreneurship Entrepreneurs are vital to any free market system. By taking risks they create new jobs, and today's small entrepreneur is tomorrow's large successful company. Cutting marginal tax rates, cutting government red tape (like health and safety regulations for employees, and planning permission for premises), and providing a reliable source of cheap labour will all help entrepreneurs to make the profits necessary for survival in a competitive environment.

4 Reform labour legislation Over the years, workers have gained rights in law. For instance, workers are protected against unfair dismissal. They can strike or take other industrial action. In some industries there are maximum hours of work per day or per week. Health and safety regulations protect workers. These all impose costs upon employers. Reducing the rights of workers will encourage firms to employ more people.

5 Privatisation There is no incentive for public sector enterprises and bodies to be efficient. The private sector, on the other hand, is subject to competition. If firms are inefficient they will be driven out of business. Privatising the public sector provision of goods and services will automatically increase efficiency in the economy as a whole.

6 Competition policy The forces of competition keep industries efficient. Therefore, competition should be increased wherever possible. In the 1980s, for instance, the UK Government increased competition in the provision of financial services by giving building societies wider powers to compete with banks, and through 'Big Bang'—the deregulation of the Stock Exchange and other money markets. The Government also has a responsibility to encourage free trade. Competition from foreign firms is essential if British industry is to remain efficient.

Keynesians dismiss many of the above arguments as being far too simplistic. They argue that the disincentive effect of taxation is not borne out by any empirical evidence. The large cuts in marginal rates of income tax in the 1980s, for instance, have had no effect on incentives to work. The existence of state unemployment benefits does increase unemployment but not to any great extent. In the 1950s and 1960s UK unemployment rates were between 100 000 and 250 000 despite the existence of unemployment benefits—so it is most unlikely that the millions of people unemployed in the 1980s all preferred to be on the dole than working. Entrepreneurs are important in an economy but it is important to remember that small firms only account for a fraction of national output, national employment and national investment. Reducing workers' rights may well lead, not to extra employment, but to greater profits and greater earnings for the owners of capital. Shareholders gain from the losses of workers. As for the public sector being inefficient, it is of course easy to find examples of corrupt civil servants or of bureaucratic nonsense. On the other hand, the private sector—with its management expense accounts, company cars with every conceivable gadget, and Christmas gifts of crates of whisky—can hardly be said to be always striving for maximum efficiency. Neither the public sector nor the private sector is inherently inefficient. Their efficiency depends to a great extent upon the quality of the management of the organisation—and in the public sector that ultimately means the Government itself.

Many Keynesians favour the use of the public sector to stimulate long term growth. Unlike monetarists, they view the private sector as often incapable of taking the correct policy decisions necessary for the well-being of the nation as a whole. In particular, they argue that the private sector may not undertake sufficient investment, that the investment that is taking place is not in the right industries, and that it is not in the right geographical localities. They favour direct government intervention to remedy these defects. Either firms can be given tax incentives or the state can give grants. A more radical solution to the problem is for the state to invest on its own behalf, building up a series of state-owned firms.

Monetarists argue that the state is incapable of managing investment wisely. Only the private sector can direct investment resources efficiently. If governments insist on pumping state aid into dying industries or industries in regions that are bound to decline economically, then yet more scarce resources are going to go down the public sector drain.

Data 19.1

CBI calls for £3bn boost to economy in the Budget

By John Elliott, Industrial Editor

Leaders of the Confederation of British Industry have urged the Chancellor of the Exchequer to stimulate the economy by about £3bn in a full year, when he produces his spring Budget.

During a meeting at the Treasury which coincided with the announcement of the increase in interest rates, the CBI leaders stressed that industry needs urgent help to improve its liquidity and to stimulate manufacturing activity.

Responding to the interest rates increase, Sir Terence Beckett, CBI director general, said: "This latest rise makes it even more important that the Chancellor should concentrate in his forthcoming Budget on measures to reduce industry's costs in every possible way."

Proposals now being prepared by the CBI are thought to call for net increases in public borrowing of about £2.2bn in 1983–84 or approaching £3bn in a full year. This is higher than the £1.8bn net figure called for last year but the CBI believes it is not inflationary because of the £2bn shortfall in the PSBR last year.

The figures are also slightly higher than Sir Geoffrey is thought to favour.

The CBI's main demand is total abolition of the National Insurance Surcharge which will have dropped to 1½ per cent by April. This would cost £1.2bn in a full year.

The CBI shopping list includes a sharp increase in public sector capital projects as well as other measures, such as relief on electricity tariffs, de-rating for business premises, and cuts in tax on derv.

For small businesses it wants tax concessions for a new category of small firms investment companies and the reintroduction of a scheme to stimulate engineering investment in small machine tools.

The Financial Times. January, 1983

1 Using diagrams, explain what effect the CBI proposals, if implemented, would have on the level of aggregate demand.

2 To what extent would the CBI proposals, if implemented, encourage expansion of supply in the economy?

3 Why does the CBI feel that the rise in interest rates makes it even more important for the Chancellor to implement their proposals?

Monetary and credit policy

Monetary policy can affect unemployment, inflation, growth and the balance of payments in one of three ways:

1 through the total money supply;

2 through the rate of interest (the price of money);

3 through the volume of money available for borrowing by certain sectors of the economy, such as the personal sector or the export sector.

It has been argued in Chapter 5 that Keynesians are sceptical about government's ability to control the money supply. In its extreme version this view argues that the money supply is potentially infinite.

The financial sector will create money for customers if the price is right. Attempts to control the economy through manipulating the money supply are obviously useless if the money supply itself cannot be fixed by the Government. However, for the sake of argument, we will assume here that the Government does have the power to control the money supply.

The monetarist transmission mechanism has been considered in Chapter 16. To recap, monetarists believe that an increase in the money supply over and above the rate of real growth in the economy will have the following effects:

1 It will increase aggregate demand in the short term, as asset holders readjust their portfolios to reduce their holdings of money and buy financial and physical assets, and take advantage of lower interest rates.

2 It will leave aggregate demand unchanged but increase prices in the long term as the economy moves back to some sort of equilibrium position.

3 It will cause further cyclical fluctuations.

Monetarists argue that monetary policy is powerful, and that many post-war governments have used expansionary monetary policy to solve short term problems. For the most part, these governments believed that they were using fiscal policy. In fact, fiscal policy was only having the desired effect because governments were printing the money to finance the increased budget deficit. In the longer term, those economies have had to pay the price of both increased inflation and rising unemployment. Therefore, the only sensible course of action for governments is to control the money supply and allow it to grow only at the rate of growth of the real economy. Inflation will be eliminated, the economy will return to full employment equilibrium and long term growth can be resumed.

Keynesians, on the other hand, are sceptical about the power of monetary policy. They argue that increases in the money supply will have the following results:

1 Increased holding of financial assets by asset holders. Few physical assets will be bought, as cars and factories are not good portfolio substitutes for the extra money now in the economic system.

2 A small fall in interest rates because the demand for money is relatively elastic.

3 A small rise in aggregate demand because consumption and investment are relatively interest-inelastic.

4 A small rise in inflation, if there is indeed some small rise in aggregate demand and the economy is near full employment.

The extreme Keynesian position is that monetary policy can have no effect on the real economy.

Interest rate policy and money supply policy are interlinked. If the level of the money supply is fixed, the Government cannot control interest rates, and vice versa. Keynesians have argued that interest rate policy could be important in two ways. Firstly, low rates of interest might stimulate investment to the extent that investment is not determined by income. Secondly, high rates of interest can help boost the value of the currency on the international exchanges. A sure way to halt the decline of a currency is to raise interest rates. For monetarists, if interest rate policy results in changes in money growth rates over and above the growth of the real economy, then the economy moves as described in their transmission mechanism. Interest rate policy is not a substitute for monetary policy.

Credit policy is associated with Keynesian thinking. For monetarists the effects of the change in the money supply will eventually filter through the whole economy. Initially it will be the financial sector which absorbs the change, but after a period of 6–18 months, the rest of the economy will start to change too. The granting of new credits is an integral part of this mechanism. Keynesians believe that the effects of a change in the money supply will be largely confined to the financial sector through increased holdings of money and other financial assets. Increases in credit and increases in the money supply are not one and the same thing.

Credit is a crucial link between the financial and real sectors of the economy. The financial sector grants credit to the real sector of the economy. If the volume of that credit could be manipulated or its direction could be altered, then Keynesians believe that the Government would have a powerful tool at its disposal. By manipulating the volume of credit (for instance by imposing lending ceilings on banks, or manipulating the terms of credit), the Government can affect the demand for goods commonly bought on credit. These tend to be investment goods or consumer durables. Imposing a credit squeeze will reduce aggregate demand—and therefore in Keynesian terms will raise unemployment and lower growth, but will reduce inflation and improve the current balance.

Ordering banks to give credit preference to firms wishing to invest or to firms in the export business, at the expense of consumers, is effectively rationing credit. It is a way of holding down interest rates for certain sectors of the economy deemed to be important. As with all subsidies, there is a subsidiser—in this instance it is the economic unit which would have taken the loan if free market forces had operated. Introducing a queueing system for loans on cars or foreign holidays might be a cheap price to pay for increased growth resulting from higher investment or a better balance of payments resulting from a more viable export sector.

Monetarists argue that backdoor subsidies to certain sectors of the economy are rarely justified. Sound monetary policy with the operation of free

Data 19.2

Stumbling back to stop-go

by Brian Reading

STOP-GO is back – and the Treasury is to blame. Whatever the Tory structural reforms may have done to improve the supply side of Britain's economy, mismanagement has made a muck-up of the demand side.

The phenomenon of stop-go was familiar to all in the 1950s and 1960s. Successive governments see-sawed between austerity and profligacy, depending upon whether curbing inflation or cutting unemployment was the No 1 priority of the day.

During the stop phase, unemployment rose while inflation abated. The government then over-stimulated demand, usually by higher public spending. The economy quickly recovered. Output and productivity rose rapidly and, with a lag, unemployment started to come down.

But within a year or two, capacity bottlenecks and labour shortages would appear, causing growth to falter, imports to surge and inflation to accelerate.

In those old Bretton Woods fixed-exchange-rate days, the go phase regularly ended in sterling crisis. Prompted by a run on the pound, the government would slam on the brakes, raising interest rates, tightening credit controls and raising taxes.

The stop-go cycle involved the alternating evils of inflation and unemployment. The government was constantly exchanging more of one for less of the other, which did nothing to improve the trade-off between them. Indeed it got worse.

Incomes policies were tried on several occasions. Harold Wilson's first Labour government gave economic planning a whirl. But they all failed. Whether by accident or design, Mrs Thatcher's was the first government to abandon the struggle.

Hard-line monetarists in the Tory party simply believed that inflation could not be cured without higher unemployment. Seen thus, the history of the 1980s can be regarded as another round in the old stop-go cycle.

In 1980–1 Britain suffered its worst recession this century. Industrial production fell further and faster than it did in the interwar years. Unemployment rose to a recorded 3m. The long slow-burn recovery that has followed is merely a consequence of the depths to which the economy plunged.

With unemployment down to 7%, inflation is making a comeback, the balance of payments is in a mess and a run on the pound a clear probability. On this gloomy view nothing has changed. But it has. There has been a distinct improvement in the trade-off between rival evils.

The jump in unemployment in the early 1980s was largely the result of a labour shake-out. Output fell less than employment. Exceptionally, productivity rose during a recession. British industry, or what was left of it, was considerably more efficient by the end of it.

Subsequently, the record fall of 1m in unemployment since mid-1986 has been accompanied by a remarkably modest rise in inflation. Average earnings growth has accelerated one percentage point to 8.75% since 1986, despite the fall of nearly four points in the jobless rate.

Manufacturing unit-wage costs rose only 1% last year, down from 2.2% in 1987 and 7.3% in 1985. While excluding mortgage interest payments, retail prices last year rose only 5.1%, up from 3.7% in 1987.

Britain's problem is excess demand. Rising inflation and a widening trade deficit are simply the symptoms. When British industry cannot make all that it could sell, it rightly puts up prices faster than its costs are rising, widening profit margins in the process.

This is benign inflation. It shifts income from consumers to producers, who consequently invest in expanded capacity. The boom in capital spending is wholly good, regardless of whether the new plant and equipment British industry is buying is homemade or imported.

There is nothing wrong with the performance of the supply side of the economy. The policy issue is therefore how to restrain consumers without clobbering producers.

In this respect, the Treasury's present policies are still mistaken. Penal interest rates cripple capital spending as much as consumption. The hard pound makes British industry uncompetitive. Falling domestic demand then cuts output instead of imports.

Present policies will undoubtedly curb total demand growth. They will probably produce a crash landing. But if, as seems likely, manufacturing gets mangled once more in the process, less inflation today will simply mean more inflation tomorrow.

The next time demand is allowed to expand, there will be even less British industrial capacity to meet it. Faced with the dilemma between raising interest rates to defend the pound, or lowering them to avoid a crash landing, the chancellor must opt for the latter. If he does not, stop-go will be back with a vengeance.

The Sunday Times. 5.3.89

---

1 What is meant by the stop-go cycle?
2 What part have fiscal policy and monetary policy played in causing the stop-go cycle?

3 Do high interest rates damage the future performance of the economy?

market forces in the financial sector is likely to result in a sounder economy than one in which market distortions arise through inefficient methods of monetary control.

Prices and incomes policies

Prices and incomes policies are designed to control the level of prices and incomes in an economy. Their main purpose is to control inflation.

There are two main theoretical arguments put forward in favour of such policies. Firstly, Keynesian economists have argued that they can push the Phillips curve to the left, allowing lower unemployment at any given rate of inflation. The Phillips curve, it will be remembered, shows that there is a relationship between unemployment and the rate of growth of money wages. In Fig. 19.2, the unemployment rate of OA is associated with zero wage inflation. If unemployment falls to OB, the rate of change of money wages will rise by OC. A prices and incomes policy, it is argued, can allow an unemployment rate of OB and zero wage inflation. In effect, the policy has shifted the Phillips curve back towards the origin.

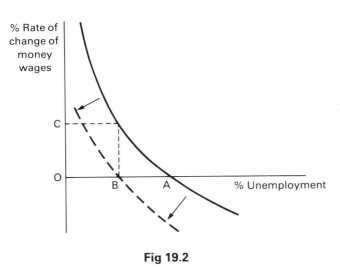

Fig 19.2

The second Keynesian argument develops from the cost-push view of inflation. A prices and incomes policy allows the Government to break into a wage-price spiral. Wage increases cause firms to increase prices of their products. In turn, workers put in for pay increases in excess of the inflation rate. By preventing workers from gaining this rise, firms can

reduce their price increases. Once inflation has been controlled, the prices and incomes policy can be removed.

Critics of prices and incomes policies come from all schools of thought. Monetarists dismiss them because they argue that the growth of the money supply is the sole cause of inflation. Experience has shown that prices and incomes policies have always failed to control inflation produced by too much money in the economy. Both monetarists and Keynesians are sceptical of any analysis involving the Phillips curve, given the fact that no one can be certain where a possible Phillips curve might be located today. They also argue that the demand-pull or cost-push forces causing inflation are too strong to be controlled by a prices and incomes policy, and there are loopholes and escape hatches for the determined firm or worker.

To understand why prices and incomes policies are difficult to implement, we need to know something about how they work in detail. Features of policies are as follows:

1 A policy can either be statutory or voluntary. A **statutory policy** is one enforceable in law. Workers or firms who break the policy can be prosecuted in the courts. In practice, the law is virtually unenforceable. The Government is not able to take 50 000 men to court or order a firm crippled by a strike not to end it by paying its workers above the maximum allowed. Statutory policies are also easy to evade. A **voluntary policy** is one where firms, workers and government together establish a policy and agree to abide by it. Workers are represented by their unions, and employers by their associations. The major problem with voluntary policies is enforcement. All will go well as long as workers and firms support the policy. But it only needs a small percentage of workers and firms flouting the policy for other workers and firms also to feel cheated and to break the policy.

2 The policy can cover prices, wages and dividend payments, or just some of these. Price control is normally applied only to goods and services produced by larger firms in the economy. It would be difficult to dictate prices of goods such as fresh vegetables which can fluctuate daily. It would also be impossible to control the price of many services such as painting and decorating, where no standard service is marketed. Wage control is often the centrepiece of the policy, the argument being that wages can be controlled, so can prices. However,

Data 19.3

Inflation and unemployment

By Richard Layard

With inflation low and unemployment relatively high it is important that economic strategies today concentrate on reducing unemployment. But how can the economy be reflated without a return to ever rising inflation? In my book, *How to Beat Unemployment*, I have tried to set out a strategy which would achieve this.

The strategy has many elements. Jobs must be targeted towards the long-term unemployed, through a job guarantee for which the Charter for Jobs will be seeking to promote a Private Members' Bill. There must be a huge expansion of training. There must be cuts in employers' national insurance contributions on disadvantaged workers. But above all, there must be a permanent incomes policy—to restrain the permanent inflationary pressure that will otherwise persist.

The aim of this incomes policy should be to lock in inflation at its present level. To be permanent, it must be consistent with free collective bargaining. Since collective bargaining mostly occurs at the level of the firm or plant, this rules out any policy in which specific rates of

pay are dictated from the centre. The broad frame of policy must of course come from the centre and be agreed if possible by the TUC and CBI. But the policy itself should consist simply of a mechanism which exerts a general downward pressure on wages, leaving actual wage rates to be determined through collective bargaining or by simple management initiative.

The best mechanism would be a counter-inflation tax. There are a number of misconceptions about this proposal. Let me clear them up.
1—There would be a nationally agreed norm (or other less offensive term). This would apply to the average level of earnings in a firm. It would not apply to the earnings of any particular individual or grade of workers.
2—If a firm paid more than the norm, the policy would not collapse. Instead the firm would pay a tax penalty equal to its excess wage bill.
3—The aim of the policy is to stop inflation rising, not to reduce real wages. Thus one could imagine a policy in which the norm was set typically at say 1 per cent below last year's price inflation. Some firms that wanted to

attract labour or reward extra productivity growth would find it worthwhile to pay more than the norm.
4—The scheme would be very simple to administer. Earnings would be defined as for Paye, and each firm would calculate its own tax liability and send off a cheque at the same time as its cheque for Paye.
5—It need not discourage productivity-improving deals between management and workers. These could be achieved if the limit on earnings growth did not apply to any growth in profit-related pay arising from genuine increases in profits.

Many firms dislike the idea of the counter-inflation tax. But they also want more business. Present government policy is not going to provide that. But other policies which do provide business will also provide inflation, unless we can devise some form of viable incomes policy.

The Financial Times. 10.9.86

What are the similarities and differences between Layard's proposed incomes policy and the types of incomes policies which operated in the 1960s and 1970s in the UK?

2 To what extent do you think Layard's proposals would be successful in allowing unemployment to fall without increasing inflation?

he reward to labour is to be fixed, there is a strong rgument that the reward to capital should also be ontrolled. It would be impossible for firms to make fixed level of profit—the free market economy is ar too uncertain for that. But a policy can attempt o prevent a firm from handing out increases in rofits to shareholders, through controls on dividend ayments.

3 The policy can fix a wide variety of targets for its components. A 'freeze' on increases can be imposed (i.e. no increases are allowed at all). Rises can be fixed in money terms (e.g. £6 a week), or in percentage terms (e.g. 4% a year), or some combination of the two. Alternatively, rises can be 'index linked' (i.e. rises are granted at the current inflation rate). Maximum rises may apply to every worker or to

INCOMES POLICY

INFLATIONARY SEA

Can an incomes policy stem an inflationary tide?

with strong industrial policy resent being fettered by pay policies. Equally, policies accumulate a series of distortions. Income differentials become eroded. Firms are unable to attract sufficient workers because they cannot increase their rates of pay. Firms are prevented from increasing their profit margins on a successful product. Such distortions become explosive at the end of two or three years. To be successful, prices and incomes policies must genuinely act as a constraint on inflation and have the support of both sides of industry.

Exchange rate policy

Fixing an exchange rate can rarely be achieved in the long run. Chapter 17 showed that governments can fix exchange rates in the short run by buying or selling currency. If a government wishes to maintain an artificially high exchange rate, it can only do this by buying its own currency with gold and foreign currency reserves. These sooner or later will become exhausted. So in the long term, a government cannot maintain an artificially high rate. It may maintain an artificially low rate by selling its currency. However, the extra money created is likely to increase the money supply, with all the problems which that brings.

Governments do not have a great deal of room for manoeuvre in the long run. However, they can incorporate exchange rates into a total policy package rather than simply allowing exchange rates to move up and down in response to changing trade conditions.

Many Keynesians believe that devaluation can help restore competitiveness to a domestic economy. Although devaluation will bring with it some imported inflation, the long run effect is to improve that economy's competitive position permanently. If a government wishes to use expansionary fiscal policy when the current balance is in balance, devaluation can help offset the resulting increase in imports. However, many other economists, including monetarists, believe that devaluation is inflationary and raises prices to such an extent that any short term competitive advantages are lost in the long run.

Exchange controls, which artificially increase the value of a currency, can be used to increase domestic investment. Exchange controls prevent firms and individuals from exporting capital freely. Advocates of exchange controls argue that money not invested

every product. On the other hand, rises may be averaged out for a labour force or for a product range. For instance, a company may not be allowed to increase its wage bill by more than 6%, but it can give some of its workers 9% if other workers get less than 6%. Rises may also be permissible for other reasons, such as productivity deals for workers. The more complicated the arrangements, the more opportunity there is for workers and firms to evade the policy if they so wish. The simpler the arrangement, the less opportunity there is for genuine grievances and injustices to be righted. The policy also becomes more inflexible and therefore more likely to shatter completely with one important test case. Prices and incomes policies have had a very mixed record since they were first implemented in the 1960s. In Britain, for instance, the three periods of incomes policy between 1966 and 1979 all ended with runaway inflation. The success or failure of a pay policy ultimately depends upon the good will of all the participants. If one party to the policy withdraws its support the policy will ultimately collapse. It is self interest which causes participants to withdraw. Some firms and some workers would be better off outside the policy than in it. For instance, unions

Data 19.4

Patchy outlook for clothing manufacturers

Alice Rawsthorn

THROUGHOUT 1988 the clothing industry watched the rise of the pound and the fall of the US dollar on the foreign exchange markets with ill-disguised alarm.

A strong pound makes it more difficult for the UK's clothing companies to compete overseas. A weak dollar makes it easier for producers in the Far East, where currencies are dollar-linked, to sell to the UK.

Last year the industry faced a rapid rise in imports and slow down in exports. But, thanks to buoyant consumer spending, it emerged unscathed. The outlook for 1989 is less reassuring.

An increase in imports affects every area of the industry. First, it threatens output by weakening the UK companies' hold on the home market. Second, it imposes pressure on prices and on profitability.

Last year the pressure on profits was intensified by the sudden surge of imports. It is instructive that one of the first sectors to suffer was children's wear: historically one of the less profitable parts of the clothing industry.

The labour content of a child's garment is only a little lower than that of an adult, yet the price of the finished product is far lower. Courtaulds closed two children's clothing plants on Merseyside in November with the loss of 540 jobs. Coats is also rationalising its children's wear interests.

This year the pressure on profits will intensify further. One factor will be the expected increase in imports. The pound is still higher than the $1.60 exchange rate with which the industry is comfortable. Even M and S, which still buys a quarter of UK clothing output, is increasing its imports.

Most of the large M and S suppliers bought or set up sourcing houses in the Far East last year. Some see these houses as a useful addition to their UK activities. Others are tussling with late deliveries, poor quality and other problems associated with importing.

The Financial Times. 31.1.89

Does the evidence presented in the data suggest that a high value of the pound or a low value of the pound is good for the UK economy?

broad will be invested domestically, creating wealth, incomes and jobs. Critics of exchange controls argue that money invested at lower rates of return domestically could have earned a higher rate of return internationally. The lost profits are worth far more than any beneficial effect caused by extra investment in second rate domestic industry.

Import controls

Another way of manipulating the balance of payments is through import controls. Since the Second World War, import controls have been discouraged in the international community. Most countries agree in theory that free trade is a better way forward than protectionism. However, despite the efforts of such organisations as GATT, import controls have remained a powerful weapon. All governments use open or concealed import controls to a greater or lesser extent.

The major disadvantage of the use of import controls is that it harms domestic consumer interests, at least in the short run. Import controls result in higher prices of imported goods and less choice for consumers, because some would-be importers are discouraged. In the long run, the effects on consumers are less clear. The loss in welfare due to higher prices and less choice will remain. Domestically produced goods may have gone up in price, too, and be poorer in quality due to lack of foreign competition. On the other hand, in the long run import controls may result in greater economic growth and more spending power for consumers. That increase in spending power could more than compensate for the loss in welfare due to higher prices and less choice.

The main danger in the use of import controls is that other countries will retaliate. It is argued below that import controls will only be of benefit if other countries do not follow suit. If they do impose import controls then exports will fall, offsetting any increased benefit from the original fall in imports.

Data 19.5

EC curb on Chinese knickers

By Alice Rawsthorn

In 1986 more than 12.5m pairs of Chinese briefs came into Britain. But last year the influx accelerated to an estimated 60m pairs, representing a fifth of the volume of the British market, according to the Knitting Industries Federation.

This surge posed a serious threat to the stability of the British knitting companies which have traditionally dominated the domestic underpants market. The Chinese briefs arrived in large quantities and were priced cheaply at an average 21p a pair.

The European Commission has now agreed on a formal quota. This will restrict imports to 30m pairs this year, half the estimated total for 1987.

Mr John Harrison, director of the federation, said that although this would enable Chinese manufacturers to capture a tenth of the British market in 1988, it should protect the British industry against the threat of further disruption.

The Financial Times. 6.1.88

1 What are the economic costs and benefits of the EC action described in the article?

The alleged benefits of import controls concern employment and growth. One powerful chain of reasoning has been put forward by a group of Keynesian Cambridge economists, the Cambridge Group. Consider the problems of an economy such as the UK, which has had a persistently poor growth record and is suffering a long term industrial decline relative to other more successful economies. The economy's lack of competitiveness means that it was constantly running into balance of payments problems at full employment. Keeping the economy at less than full employment to solve this problem merely exacerbates the growth problem. Indeed it is likely to make the economy even less competitive, as firms are discouraged from investing and workers constantly fighting for their slice of a barely growing national cake. Devaluation is unlikely to succeed because of the inflation it generates through rising import prices. It is also unlikely to lead to more jobs since many of our exports are bought not on price but on quality.

The solution according to the Cambridge Group is to follow reflationary policies combined with import controls. Reflationary policies will increase aggregate demand (on Keynesian grounds), thus raising growth in the short term and reducing unemployment. Import controls will help in two ways. Firstly, they will help prevent the otherwise large rise in imports, following the increase in aggregate demand. Thus there will be no balance of payments constraint on higher economic growth. Secondly, domestic firms will now be able to sell more goods in the home market. Faced with lack of competition they may choose to put up prices or to expand sales or to adopt some combination of both. Whatever happens, they are likely to increase profits. Increased profits and increased demand for goods will raise business confidence, and thus investment. Extra investment is the primary source of greater productivity and greater competitiveness. The result will be more exports. At this point, import controls can start to be dismantled. As British industry becomes more and more able to compete on world markets, so the prop of import controls can be taken away. The Cambridge Group argue that import controls are necessary as part of a medium term strategy lasting about ten years. This is the time necessary to turn round a declining economy (such as the UK's) into one of high growth and high productivity.

A second argument for import controls is the so-called **infant industry** argument. Assume that a country wants to develop a new industry but import

competition is so fierce that no domestic entrepreneur would be prepared to risk his capital.
Applying import controls would enable such a new
firm to make a good start. Eventually, import controls could be removed as the industry matures and
is able to compete successfully on world markets.

Critics of the infant industry argument say that if
an industry is going to be profitable in the long run,

then entrepreneurs will invest in it in the first place.
In the North Sea, for instance, time-lags of up to ten
years between initial exploration and the selling of
oil have not deterred oil companies from exploiting
this natural resource. If a government is genuinely
worried about the development of certain industries,
then it would be far more efficient for it to subsidise
the industry in its growth phase.

Data 19.6

Opening the gates of Europe's car market

Will Dawkins

THERE is one prize that Mr Martin Bangemann, the new European Commissioner for the Internal Market and Industry, wants more than anything in the world. It is to break down the protective quotas and technical and tax barriers that have traditionally insulated the EC's largest car industries from Japan and are possibly the biggest omission in the Community's single market plan.

The outspoken German liberal presented a paper for a free car market – in the Commission's name – to a stunned meeting of EC Industry Ministers in north Spain last month.

The paper's four main points are:
● To phase out by the end of 1992 the bilateral import quotas now restricting Japanese car sales in France, Italy, Britain, Spain and Portugal, which together produced 60 per cent of the 12.2m cars made in the EC last year. From early 1993, Japan would be asked to monitor its EC exports, 9.6 per cent of the Community's 13.2m car registrations in 1988, "for a clearly limited and fixed period", to be followed by complete market freedom.

While this clearly shows "Europe's will to be a partner rather than a fortress", the paper warns: "It should be

emphasised that the Community's willingness to be open must be clearly reciprocated by the conduct of international trade in fair conditions, as controlled by anti-dumping regulations."
● To make it possible for cars to obtain a single EC-wide technical approval for the first time. This process was started in 1970, with a plan for 44 voluntary technical directives covering all aspects of car design, of which 41 have been adopted by member states. But it was blocked by France 12 years ago because of fears that Japan would be the first to benefit.
● Reduce national disparities in value added tax and other kinds of car tax. This could mean pulling cars out of the Commission's indirect tax proposals, which are making slow headway in the Council of Ministers, suggests the paper. The Commision would take direct action to ban or cut additional purchase and registration taxes such as those charged in Greece and Denmark.
● A promise that there will be no specific local content rules to be observed by EC-assembled Japanese cars as a condition for investment or for access to the Community market. This has already annoyed France and Italy, following their abortive attempts to restrict the sale of British-made Nissans.

The paper adds that car industry investments must continue to be governed by strict controls on state aid, whatever the nationality of the company.

Mr Bangemann says the present strength in car demand provides an ideal moment for liberalisation.

EC car registrations rose by nearly 5 per cent in 1988, capping three years of strong growth, which many experts reckon will soon end. Annual growth of 1–2 per cent is the best European car-makers can hope for in the long term, estimates the Commission.

And despite this good fortune, they are still way behind in productivity, a reflection of the insulation of the market, economic liberals say. According to Mr Bangemann, European plants take on average 36 man-hours to make a car, as against 19 for their Japanese competitors or 26.5 for the US.

The French, Italian and Spanish car producers and their governments argue that a strong defensive industrial policy is needed for this strategically important sector, which directly provides 8 per cent of EC manufacturing jobs. France says it would be folly to open the Community car market until a clear quota system has brought trade with Japan much closer to balance than now. Japan sold 1.1m cars to the EC last year, 10 times more than the 110,000 EC vehicles sold in Japan, according to the Commission's own estimates.

The Financial Times. 19.5.89

Outline the arguments for and against the removal of European trade barriers against Japanese cars.

2 To what extent should this removal be conditional upon the 'conduct of international trade in fair conditions'?

Summary

Governments have four main macro-economic areas of concern: unemployment, inflation, the balance of payments and growth. Governments can affect the economy through fiscal policy, monetary and credit policy, prices and incomes policies and trade policy. Monetarists argue that the economy is self-correcting and that there is little need for government intervention, whilst Keynesians argue to the contrary. Similarly, there is a controversy over whether it is better to affect the supply side of the economy (the monetarist proposition) or the demand side (the Keynesian argument).

Keynesians argue that active fiscal policy has a direct and large effect on aggregate demand via the multiplier process. Monetarists claim that the real multiplier is negligible and that increased public sector spending crowds out private sector spending. On the other hand, they argue that monetary policy can have a powerful effect on the level of aggregate demand in the short term and on the price level in the long term. Inflation can only be cured for instance by tight control of the money supply. Keynesians argue that there is only a weak link between the money supply and real variables and inflation. Their favoured policy instrument to solve inflation is a prices and incomes policy. Exchange rate policy and import controls have many disadvantages as policy weapons. However, the Cambridge Group see import controls as the only way to stop Britain's slow economic decline, caused by the fundamental lack of competitiveness of British industry.

Terms for review

demand management

supply-side economics

fiscal policy

budget deficit

balanced budget multiplier

automatic stabiliser

monetary and credit policy

prices and incomes policy

exchange rate policy

import controls

infant industry argument

Essay questions

1 What is meant by 'supply side economics'? What effect might a cut in the basic rate of income tax of 5p in the pound have on aggregate supply?

2 Under what circumstances could governments achieve long term full employment through expansion of the public sector?

3 How would a fall in the rate of growth of the money supply affect (a) investment and (b) unemployment?

4 Can inflation be reduced through the implementation of a prices and incomes policy?

5 Under what circumstances could import controls lead to higher economic growth for the UK economy?

20

Development economics

Introduction

Development economics is an important branch of economics which considers the special problems of **third world countries**. These countries have been given a variety of different names including 'under-developed countries', 'less developed countries' (LDCs), and 'developing countries' (DCs). The poorest third world countries are sometimes called 'fourth world countries'. The most advanced third world countries are sometime called 'newly indus-trialised countries' (NICs). All these terms contrast third world countries with **first world countries** (the 'developed', 'industrialised' economies of West-ern Europe, North America and Japan) and **second world countries** (the communist block of the USSR and Eastern Europe).

It is important to realise that third world coun-tries are not in any sense uniform. The starving child outside a mud hut is about as typical of the third world as the slums of Glasgow are of the first world. It is all too easy to produce stereotyped images of the third world and to respond with stereotyped answers. Each country has its own set of circumstances, and therefore needs its own set of policies in order to progress.

However, developing countries of the world are likely to possess some of the following characteris-tics, which distinguish them from the more de-veloped nations:

1 lower average income per capita;
2 a large section of the population receiving very low incomes per capita;
3 low labour productivity;
4 low capital-output ratio;
5 low capital-labour ratio;
6 low level of human capital;
7 low level of social capital;
8 high mortality rate;
9 fast population growth;
0 low levels of literacy;
11 low housing standards;
12 low percentage of the population with access to piped water.

This list is in no sense exhaustive. Some develop-ing countries possess all of the above characteristics. Others possess surprisingly few.

The goals of economic development

The term 'developing country' implies that such countries are or ought to be developing towards certain goals. What should these goals be?

The most influential early development econo-mist, Sir Arthur Lewis, argued in the 1950s that **economic growth** was the most important indica-tor of development. He saw economic growth as benefiting all sections of society. His development model predicted that the benefits of growth would tend initially to benefit the better off in society. Later, as jobs in higher productivity industries in-creased, the newly created wealth of the economy would 'trickle down' to the mass of the population.

The growth of third world countries in the 1950s and 1960s was substantial in comparison with pre-vious periods. However, little 'trickling down' was experienced. 'Dual' economies tended to develop. One sector of the economy was a western-style industrially based economy in which participants could expect similar life styles to those in the West. The vast mass of the population lived in the other sector of the economy, in rural areas or in shanty towns springing up round the newly industrialised cities.

Economists then began to argue that the **creation of employment** should be the most important de-velopment goal. It was pointed out that few jobs were created in the new industrial sector of the economy. This was because firms often used world production techniques which were geared to minimising the use of labour, which was very expensive in the first world. It was further argued that many of the workforce were unemployed because they did not have jobs in the industrial sector of the economy. Creating jobs would help the mass of people because jobs result in incomes, which in turn mean the ability to secure a minimum standard of living.

This approach came under as strong an attack as the Lewis growth model. Economists found that unemployment was not as high as it first seemed. True, few people had jobs in the formal industrialised sector of the economy. But in the informal sector—the sector of the villages and the shanty towns—people generally worked very hard. They engaged in subsistence work, such as growing their own food and building their own houses. Many produced low technology goods and services—from blacksmith to shoeshine boy to the all-too-common prostitutes of the large city. The problem was not one of unemployment but of underemployment. People had jobs, but they were jobs with very low productivity. The disillusionment with the goal of creating employment was reinforced by the fact that approximately 20% of the population of the third world would not benefit from higher wages. These were people who did not belong to household units with a breadwinner. They included the old, the sick, the handicapped, and orphaned children.

The 1970s saw a growing concern with **equality** and **inequality**. The argument was that economic development should be concerned with providing improved standards of living for all the population. If this meant sacrificing some growth, it might be a small price to pay to increase the economic welfare of even the poorest in society. Unfortunately, inequality is difficult to measure. As a result, policies designed to reduce inequality are difficult to implement. For instance, nationalisation of foreign assets, redistribution of land in favour of the poor, expropriation of assets of the wealthy class in society should all theoretically result in greater economic equality. In practice their effects have proved uncertain. All too often the result has been the rise of a new monied and wealthy class, leaving inequalities barely reduced.

...most recent thinking on development goals is ...man needs approach, which argues ...licy should be directed at pro... ...dards of living for all of the ...of living' is precisely defined education, food, health, water,

transport, etc., as well as non-economic goals such as participation in society and maintenance of cultural traditions. This approach has a number of advantages:

1 It covers all the population, not just workers or households or capital owners.

2 It directly sets out what is to be achieved (whereas growth or income goals are indirect because they are the means to the ends of better education, better health, etc.). This has two important implications. Firstly, economic policies are relatively easy to design and apply. For instance, it is very much easier to succeed in "building 200 village schools this year" than to "raise income by 1% in 200 villages this year". Secondly, progress can be accurately monitored.

3 It is an easily understood and acceptable goal to governments, aid agencies and people in the third world.

4 The achievement of such goals does not rule out other economic choices—such as whether to lessen the degree of inequality in society, or whether basic human needs should be provided by the public or private sector.

Sri Lanka is an economy which has adopted a basic human needs approach since the 1960s. Despite very low income levels its population now enjoys levels of life expectancy, literacy and infant mortality which are on a par with western industrialised countries. Nutritional standards are high. This illustrates the fact that economic development can quickly benefit the whole population and not just a small section of it.

Important issues in development economics

If the 'basic human needs' approach has gained recent acceptance as a development goal, this does not mean that economic growth is not a useful, if crude, measure of the pace of development. Many of the most important issues in development economics are concerned with how growth rates can be increased.

Saving and investment

Increased investment (I) is often seen as necessary for faster economic growth. However, given an economy with no foreign trade, the only way to increase investment is either to raise savings (S) or to increase taxation (T). This is true because, in the circular flow of income model, injections (I and G) must equal withdrawals (S and T). The level of saving can then be seen as a barrier limiting economic growth. If savings could be increased, growth could be increased too.

A Keynesian analysis would suggest that one way of increasing saving is to increase income inequalities. Higher income earners have a higher marginal propensity to save than the poor. Redistributing income from low to high income earners could increase economic growth rates. Hence, Keynesian economics suggests that there is a conflict between growth and equality of income.

The monetarist permanent income hypothesis argues that there is no difference in the marginal propensity to save between differing income groups. Saving, therefore, cannot be increased by increasing income inequalities. Evidence from the third world tends to support this. During the **Green Revolution**—a time when new high–yielding varieties of wheat, rice and other crops were introduced into third world countries—very poor farmers were observed to save large proportions of their income in order to buy necessary seeds and fertilizers, i.e. to invest. This suggests that saving levels can be increased if savers gain a good return on their money. Increased investment opportunities and improved channels of saving such as rural banks are likely to help solve problems of low national propensities to save.

Marxist economists see the state as being the most important investor in the economy. The state, through taxes, has the power to 'force' the economy to save. Taxes, 'forced saving', can then be used to build factories, roads, etc.

Import substitution versus export-led growth

Import substitution, a policy of producing goods domestically which would otherwise have been imported, is as old an idea as economics itself. Proponents of import substitution policies argue that jobs and incomes are created domestically, domestic investment and innovation are encouraged and scarce foreign exchange is saved. In practice, import

---

Data 20.1

Gandhi says import substitution policy a mistake

By David Housego
in New Delhi

THIS WEEK has seen further action against the shibboleths that have long governed Indian economic and industrial policy.

Mr Rajiv Gandhi, the Prime Minister, told a gathering of scientists that it was time the mistake of import substitution was recognised. He said that by the time Indian scientists and technologists had developed third and fourth generation import substitution technology, other countries were way ahead with the next generation technology.

In similar vein, Dr Bimal Jalan, the outgoing chief economic adviser at the Ministry of Finance, who is moving to the IMF, said over the weekend that India's system of industrial licencing had "in several cases led to a mis-match of supply and demand, high costs and rigidity in industrial structure".

He said that import controls had "created shortages, led to the emergence of blackmarket premia and, in the end, had not saved much foreign exchange".

The Financial Times. 20.10.88

1 What is meant by a policy of 'import substitution'?
2 To what extent can such a policy improve the industrial performance of an economy?

---

substitution policies may be carried out simply by imposing tariffs and quotas. More sophisticated policies include ordering importing firms to increase gradually the domestically produced content of the import. For instance, a car importer may be told that 50% of the value of the car must be produced in domestic factories within five years if imports are to be allowed to continue.

Critics point to the fact that import substitution

often leads to inefficient domestic producers producing much higher cost and lower quality products than are available internationally. The resources that these inefficient firms use could be better employed in industries where costs of production are much more competitive internationally.

Proponents of **export-led growth** argue that countries which encourage exports are encouraging the growth of those industries which have a comparative advantage in production. Because they have to compete in world markets, they need to be efficient and profitable. By 'encouragement' of exports we do not mean crude subsidising of exports—that would simply result in third world countries paying their customers to buy their goods. What is meant is the easing of barriers to production in export industries. This would include the easing of import restrictions on essential products required for the production of exports, as well as the provision of a western style industrial environment for production (building roads, providing essential utilities and encouraging worker training). Exports result in new jobs, directly and indirectly: in the export industry itself, in supply component industries and in the rest of the economy where workers spend their new incomes. It also eases balance of payments problems. One criticism is that dual economies may be created, with the majority of the workers living in the rural underdeveloped sector, untouched by the export-orientated industrial sector.

Agricultural versus industrial development

Traditionally, economists argued that economic development was likely to pass through the stages of growth experienced by the developed nations. A predominantly rural economy would be transformed into an economy based on manufacturing industry. Finally, the service sector of the economy would develop. The conclusion was that the rural countries of the third world should concentrate their investment on manufacturing industry. Indeed, Marxist economists strongly advocated transferring resources from the agricultural sector to the industrial sector: that is, the surplus or profit produced in the agricultural sector should be used to finance investment in manufacturing industry. This view was supported by the belief that industrial projects would show a greater rate of return than low profit agricultural projects.

Over the last twenty years, economists have become disillusioned with this approach. Firstly, industrial projects have failed to create jobs on a sufficiently large scale. Population pressure together with lack of rural development, can explain in part the large scale migration to the cities in the third world. In the shanty towns bordering the cities, underemployment of scarce labour and squalid living conditions are all too common. Large scale job creation in the rural sector could have prevented this. Secondly, industrial projects have all too often shown very poor rates of return, whereas rural projects have earned high returns. It has come to be argued that growth is unlikely to be maximised by one-sided development of either the rural sector or the industrialised sector of the economy.

Foreign aid

One way of increasing investment is to receive **foreign aid**. Such aid will not only cover an inadequate level of savings (the **savings gap**); it will also enable a country to increase investment in foreign capital goods without reducing imports, imports which may be essential for the running of existing industries in the economy (the **trade gap**). The case for foreign aid is obvious and persuasive. International agencies, reports and commissions since 1945 (including the recent Brandt Report) have advocated a much larger transfer of resources from first world to third world economies. A foreign aid target of 1% of GNP of the first world economies is typical of the recommendations.

The case against foreign aid does not argue that it is always bad. What it does argue is that in practice much foreign aid is damaging to the developing world. There are a number of possible reasons for this. Firstly, foreign aid may be inappropriately used. All too numerous are the stories of subsidised western food flooding a third world market, putting local farmers out of business and bringing about a long term shortage of domestic supply; or factories which create a few jobs but as a result destroy many more workplaces in local small enterprises. Often donor countries or agencies or even local governments have not seen the real needs of the economy.

Secondly, foreign aid may displace local investment. Foreign aid has often been given for large scale prestige projects such as dams or steel mills. These projects would have taken place anyway and have been financed by local government or local industry. Foreign aid then releases resources which the government or industry can use elsewhere. But these resources are more likely to be used on consumption goods—extra tanks, more cars, more imported food—than on extra investment. Put another

Data 20.2

World Bank Experience with Rural Development

Julian Blackwood

The rural development strategy pursued by the Bank over the past 15 years emerged out of a combination of changes in development thinking, based on experiences of the previous 25 years. The severe food shortages in South Asia in the mid-1960s had drawn attention to the fact that food production needed more concerted attention. It seemed clear that any long-term solutions to food shortages in countries with rapidly growing populations would require substantial increases in the productivity of smallholders, who controlled a large part of the arable land in most developing countries. It was also argued that to make development more equitable would require direct investments to increase the productivity of poorer groups in society.

At about this time the Green Revolution technology, based on high yielding varieties of grain, became available. This not only had the potential for increasing food production and farm incomes, but could also be used almost equally efficiently on small and large farms. Thus it became possible to envisage a production-led rural development strategy affecting millions of small farmers and serving the aims both of

economic growth and of equity.

Given the pervasiveness of poverty and hunger, it was widely advocated that health, nutrition, education, shelter, and related services should be provided for in development programs, both because beneficiaries had a right to them, and as a means of helping beneficiaries contribute to the productive economy and thus raise their incomes.

All of these factors caused the Bank, like other development agencies, to reconsider its policies. Selecting from and building on the experience of governments, bilateral aid agencies, and nongovernmental organizations in village development and rural reconstruction, the Bank formally adopted its "rural development strategy" in 1973.

The strategy had a major influence on the Bank's lending program and operational policies. Both in volume and in coverage the Bank became preeminent among development agencies seeking to improve rural living standards. Between FY1974 and FY1986 it lent $38.5 billion worldwide for 943 agricultural projects, with estimated total project costs of $104 billion. Half of the agricultural lending, channeled through 498 pro-

jects, was for rural development projects with estimated total project cost of $50 billion.

The strategy was successful in several important respects, especially in the wide-spread adoption, by the Bank and other agencies, of the focus on small farmers and in the amount of lending achieved. About two thirds of the rural development projects audited on completion by the Bank's Operations Evaluation Department were expected to achieve satisfactory economic rates of return. Millions of the rural poor benefited from project facilities to provide social services and investments to improve the quality of rural life, and especially from infrastructure to which the poorest have access.

The main production goal of the strategy – to increase smallholder productivity by 5 per cent a year, or double the historical growth rate – was more elusive. Of the rural development projects designed to raise food production that were audited on completion, only a third seemed likely to meet their production targets.

Furthermore, project failure rates were unacceptably high in some cases, even for such an innovative program, particularly in Sub-Saharan Africa, where area development projects were concentrated and where barely one in three were successful. This high failure rate partly reflects internal and external factors constraining African development in general.

Finance and Development. December 1988

1 *Why has the World Bank promoted rural development?*   **2** *To what extent has this strategy proved successful?*

way, foreign aid may well result in reduced local savings.

Thirdly, much foreign aid is **'tied'**—that is, the recipient country has to buy goods from the donor country. The donor country is often far more interested in its own needs—to boost exports, to create jobs, to defeat communism or capitalism—than in

the genuine needs of the recipient country. This results in a distorted third world economy—an economy trying to support and maintain 'gifts' of tanks, fighter planes, steel mills, tractors, etc., all of which contribute little or nothing to the welfare of that economy.

Fourthly, foreign aid may well have to be repaid

Data 20.3

Strategy for debt

From Mr Jonas Nycander.

Sir, The Third World debt crisis has been going on for years with no solution in sight. On the contrary: debt burden is increasing.

Two different strategies have been tried. Commonly, repayments are deferred after negotiations with the International Monetary Fund (IMF) and the banks, and the indebted country receives new loans to pay the interest. In return for these it agrees to liberalise the economy, reduce the budget deficit and various subsidies, and devalue the local currency.

These programmes have managed to increase growth in some countries (the social consequences have sometimes been severe). The main weakness, however, is that the indebted countries have still not been able to keep the new repayment plans; these have to be negotiated again and again. Actually, most people seem to agree that, in many cases, the debts are so big that it is completely out of the question that they can ever be paid back.

In the second strategy the indebted country takes the consequences of this fact and unilaterally stops paying (or pays only a small part). Because it is then denied new loans, a foreign account deficit will result in immediate payment crisis. Even the most necessary imports cannot be paid for, and the general state of the economy becomes chaotic. Finally the country is forced to negotiate with the banks again – but now its position is much worse. (This strategy was tried by Peru, but the consequences were discouraging.)

The lesson is that none of these strategies can succeed separately. The solution is to follow both simultaneously.

Jonas Nycander
Uppsala, Sweden

The Financial Times. 22.5.89

---

1 Outline the two strategies outlined in the article for dealing with the debt crisis in the Third World.

2 What arguments do you think the writer might have used to support his contention that the solution to the debt crisis would be to 'follow both (strategies) simultaneously'?

---

with interest at some future time. Many third world countries have found that investments made with first world loans have not been as profitable as anticipated. The result is that they are left with a crippling burden of debt, and have to finance repayment from existing low income.

The experience of foreign aid over the past thirty years has shown that giving or lending money to the third world can do as much damage as it can do good. However, that does not imply that first world countries should cease their aid programmes. What it does imply is that donor countries and donor agencies need to spend more time considering the real needs of the economies that are being aided and less time considering their own interests.

Multinational companies and foreign investment

Multinational companies are companies which produce goods or services in more than one country. First world multinationals have acquired an unenviable reputation for damaging the interests of third world countries in which they operate. They are alleged to do this, for instance, by paying low prices for domestic labour and raw materials, forcing local competitors out of business, polluting the environment, selling products irrelevant if not damaging to the welfare of the citizens of the country, and influencing local political elections.

Can chocolate bars confer any benefits on a third world country?

Whilst many of these accusations may be true, it is important to realise that the behaviour of multinationals is predictable. They are in business to further their own interests, not those of the countries in which they operate. A quick path to bankruptcy for the multinational would be to pay high wages to local workers, encourage local competition and pay money into funds of political parties committed to nationalise the assets of multinationals.

Multinationals can help a third world economy develop by providing scarce extra capital, new jobs and foreign exchange. But a local government needs to keep a tight rein on the activities of its multinationals lest the harmful effects of their presence outweigh the positive effects.

Population growth

Population growth in some developing economies has been alarming. Populations have grown at a faster pace than the rate of economic growth, leaving a lower per capita income than before. Population growth is not likely to be a long term problem. This is because rising living standards, particularly reductions in infant and child mortality rates, have historically been correlated with falls in birth rates. What is worrying is the time scale for this reduction in the birth rate to take place. A country which stabilises its population in twenty years' time will have far more problems than a country which can do it in five years.

Some of the problems of fast population growth include insufficient domestic food supplies, lack of jobs, overcrowding, insufficient educational provision and insufficient resources for the development of infrastructure. A basic human needs development approach could be a great help in this context, because population can be stabilised at lower levels of income than would otherwise be the case.

The third world debt crisis

During the late 1970s, western banks were awash with funds. As a result of the massive increases in the price of oil, oil producing countries were generating surpluses on their current accounts and lending those surpluses to western banks. Developed countries were trying to balance their current accounts and therefore did not want to borrow this money. The banks, anxious to make profits and lend this oil money, targetted third world countries as potential borrowers. During the late 1970s, many third world countries were persuaded to borrow huge sums of money, much of which was wasted on military spending, large scale infrastructure projects which failed to be completed, and on consumption spending, particularly for the ruling elites in those countries.

The early 1980s saw steep rises in interest rates, a sharp rise in the value of the dollar—the currency in which many loans were denominated—and falling commodity prices. The result was that the cost of paying back loans with interest soared for third world countries as their export earnings declined. First world banks reacted by refusing to lend third world countries any more money, but demanded repayment of existing loans.

Today many third world countries, particularly in South America and Africa, are basically bankrupt, unable to repay existing loans and with crushing external debt. Despite foreign aid, there is a huge net transfer of funds from the poorest countries of the world to the richest as some of the loans are repaid. Far from developed countries helping third world countries to develop, it is third world countries who are contributing to the high living standards of people in the West. (It is hardly any wonder that many of the poorest countries in the world, such as in Africa, have seen declines in their living standards over the past ten years, whilst those living in the West have been able to buy more and more as each year passes.)

Summary

Underdevelopment is a term used to describe an economy which has a relatively low per capita income, and low levels of human and non-human wealth, as well as other relative disadvantages. Development economics studies these disadvantages and considers goals and strategies for development. These goals have included growth, employment, income, equality and basic human needs. Some of the important issues in development economics include saving and investment, agricultural versus industrial development, import substitution versus export-led growth, foreign aid, the role of multinational companies and population growth.

Terms for review

economic development

underdeveloped or less developed or developing countries

dual economies

basic human needs

the Green Revolution

import substitution

export-led growth

foreign aid

multinational companies

third world debt crisis

Essay questions

1 What is meant by a 'developing country'? Would you expect a fall in the birth rate of such a country to benefit or hinder its economic development?

2 Can foreign aid substantially increase the growth rate of a developing country?

3 Explain the term 'economic development', illustrating your answer with examples from the Third World. To what extent is national income an accurate measure of the state of development of a Third World economy?

21

Prices and markets

Sufficient price theory was introduced at the start of this book to allow the reader to understand important macro-economic issues. In this chapter we will consider the topic in more depth.

Individual and market demand and supply curves

So far it has been assumed that demand and supply curves were market demand and supply curves. These curves represented the quantity a population would demand and the quantity an industry would supply. But we can also look at an individual demand or supply curve: that is, the quantity one consumer would demand of a product or one firm would supply of a product.

It is possible to derive market demand and supply curves from individual demand and supply curves. Table 21.1 shows the individual demand curves for a product of Mr A and Mr B. Their combined demand

is found by adding up their individual demand at any price. This is known as 'horizontal summing', because if the two individual demand curves are plotted on a graph, the combined demand curve is found by adding the amounts on the horizontal (quantity) axis but not on the vertical (price) axis. In Fig. 21.1 the three demand curves from Table 21.1 are plotted. So, for instance at price 8, the total demand is the horizontal sum of 3 and 4. At price 4, the total demand is the horizontal sum of 8 and 16. The same principle of horizontal summing applies to individual and market supply curves.

Table 21.1

| Price | Quantity demanded | | |
	Mr A	Mr B	Total demand
10	2	1	3
8	3	4	7
6	5	8	13
4	8	16	24
2	12	32	44

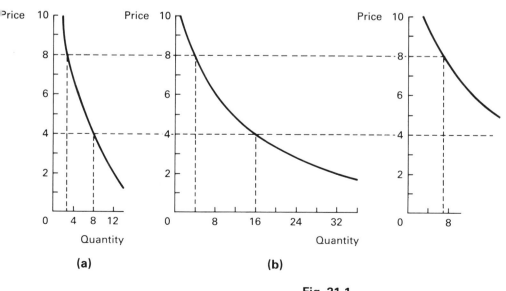

(a)   **(b)**

Fig. 21.1

In practice, economists do not often want to calculate total demand from individual demand data. However, they may wish, for instance, to calculate the total supply of the detergent industry by summing the output of each detergent manufacturer. Or they may wish to calculate the demand for sophisticated military hardware by summing the demand of each purchaser. It would be difficult, however, for economists to calculate the demand curve for a product if there were millions of individual consumers.

The market—a definition

So far the word 'market' has been used rather loosely. A simple definition is that a market exists where goods or services are bought and sold. There has to be a buyer and a seller, a price has to be agreed upon, and a quantity exchanged.

Markets can vary in size. For instance, in any town there is a local market for petrol, so a driver in, say, Manchester will not drive to Birmingham to buy her petrol. Petrol stations in a local area are therefore in competition with each other, and together they provide the market supply. Equally, there is a national market for petrol. The suppliers are the oil companies, rather than petrol stations. There is also an international market for petrol. The market for petrol is interlinked with the market for all petroleum products.

Economic theory suggests that all markets function according to the same laws. Whatever the size or location of the market, the interaction between the wants of consumers and the products available will determine price and quantity exchanged.

The path to equilibrium in a market

An equilibrium situation is one where there is no tendency to change. We have tended to assume that if a market is disturbed it will return to equilibrium automatically. This requires further explanation.

[...] 21.2 reflects a market in which there is [...]ium. Price is P_A and Q_D is demanded. [...]re an excess supply of $Q_D Q_S$ at price [...]ists believe that equilibrium is

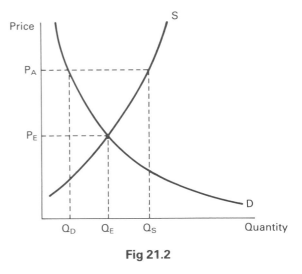

Fig 21.2

restored by suppliers dropping their price. Consequently more is demanded and new supplies will fall. Other economists believe that equilibrium is restored by suppliers cutting back on their production, and then charging a lower price per unit on their remaining output. Yet other economists believe that it is a mixture of both factors which causes the initial move to equilibrium. It is important to note that in reality goods and services are often sold at **disequilibrium prices**—that is, at prices which do not represent the equilibrium price in the market.

All our analysis so far has been of a **static** nature. This means that there is no time element in the model. However, economists are interested in how long markets take to return to equilibrium. They are also interested in the path that the market takes to return to equilibrium. It is simplistic to assume that a market in disequilibrium will tend towards equilibrium anyway.

A **dynamic** model is one which has a time element built into it. A dynamic model of this readjustment process is called the **cobweb theorem**. An important assumption is made—that producers base their output on the price they received in the last time period. The effects of this are best seen diagrammatically. In Fig. 21.3, the price in the first period is P_1. On the basis of this price, producers supply Q_2 on the market in the second time period. But they cannot sell Q_2 at price P_1. In order to sell Q_2, they have to accept price P_2. In the next period producers assume they will only get price P_2. Hence they will only produce Q_3. But if they produce Q_3

Data 21.1

Why producers are bullish about the pig market

By David Richardson

LAST WEEK IN the intensive livestock producing areas of Britain there was cause for modest celebration. Pig farmers had just seen the UK Average All Pigs Price rise above 100p a kilogram for the first time in more than two years.

The AAPP is calculated weekly using a complicated formula which includes prices paid for pig meat at a variety of outlets and forms the basis of most contracts between farmers and abattoirs. It is also a reliable barometer of the health of the pig industry.

Back in the autumn of 1984 the AAPP peaked at its highest ever level of 116p a kilogram, dead weight. Profits from efficient pig production at that time were good and, as so often before, farmers both in the UK and Europe, where similar prices applied, expanded their herds. It was the beginning of another wave in the notorious pig cycle. By December 1985 increased supplies had driven the AAPP down to 105p a kilogram; a year later it was 100p; and a year after that 96p.

The pre-Christmas period is traditionally one of maximum demand for pig meat, however, as housewives stock up with joints and hams on which to feed their families over the holiday. Almost invariably there is a so-called seasonal fall in pig prices in the new year which often continues until the spring. Last February the AAPP fell to 86p a kilogram and only rose above 90p at the beginning of the summer holiday period in June. The sharp rise to present levels began in October, in anticipation of this year's Christmas trade.

Financial losses were so severe earlier this year that many pig farmers were forced out of business. We sold out of our own herd on this farm in May, after months of losing big money on every pig marketed.

By August the European breeding herd had fallen by 5.2 per cent from the level a year earlier. The British herd had disposed of 3.5 per cent of its breeding sows and as losses continued through the summer it is almost certain that numbers continued to fall. This month's UK census of pig numbers, not yet published, is expected to show a further significant decline.

European production and consumption of pig meat are now close to equilibrium, however; hence the rise in prices. But to make pig farming worthwhile returns need to rise substantially. According to Mr Bob Ridgeon, who runs the Cambridge University Land Economy Department's pig management scheme, most pig farmers are probably still barely breaking even.

The Meat and Livestock Commission is forecasting a steady rise in price to an AAPP of 102p to 104p a kilogram next autumn. But Mr Ridgeon believes the shortage of pig meat will be more severe than the MLC's predictions imply and that the AAPP will be 106p to 108p by the spring and 110p and 115p by the late autumn.

All in all therefore British pig farmers can perhaps afford to be bullish about pigs – at least I sincerely hope so. Having sold out during the worst of the crisis, we have now restocked our farm buildings and expect to have pigs for sale within two to three months.

The Financial Times. 21.12.88

1 Summarise the movement of pig prices described in the data.

2 To what extent can these movements be explained by a dynamic model of the market?

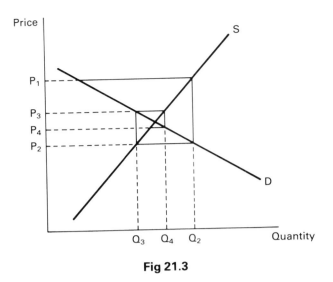

Fig 21.3

of an industry where this is often **not** possible is agriculture, in which food deteriorates quickly and must be sold before the next crop is due. Secondly, producers are unlikely to base their production for ever on past prices. They will base their current production on the price they expect to sell it at. Of course this will partly be based on past prices, but producers would quickly learn that they were getting the wrong answer everytime by using the cobweb assumption. They would therefore adjust to a better way of predicting price.

However, the main point of the cobweb theorem is to introduce a simple time element into an otherwise static model. Economists can then start building more complicated and more realistic models based upon the hypothesis that current output is determined by previous price levels.

consumers will pay a price of P_3 for it. So next period, producers will produce Q_4 but will only receive P_4 for it. As can be seen from the diagram, this market is getting closer and closer to equilibrium.

If the slope of the demand curve is steeper than the slope of the supply curve, as in Fig. 21.4, the market moves further and further away from equilibrium. There is no reason to assume that the stable cobweb is more likely to occur than the unstable cobweb.

The simple cobweb theorem is unrealistic. Firstly, in many markets producers need not sell all of their produce in a time period. If the price were not good enough, they might well prefer to put their goods into stock and sell them at a later date. An example

Inter-relationships between markets

The demand and supply of one good may be affected by the demand and supply of other goods. One such case is where two goods are **substitutes** for each other. This means that the buyer is easily persuaded to switch from one good to the other because they are very similar. Examples of good substitutes are butter and margarine, pork and mutton, one brand of chocolate bar and another. The more perfect the substitute for a good, the higher will be the price elasticity for that good (that is, a small percentage change in price will bring about a large percentage change in quantity demanded). A small rise in price will drive many consumers into buying the substitute product. A small fall in price will result in many consumers switching away from the substitute and a large percentage increase in sales of the product.

Complementary goods are goods which need to be consumed together. Hence sand and cement, tyres and headlamps, electricity and electric cookers are all complements. If the price of one of them changes, there will be a change in demand for the other. For instance if the price of electricity goes up some consumers will be put off buying electric cookers because of the extra running costs, and will prefer to buy gas or solid fuel cookers. If there is a fall in the price of tyres, this will reduce the price of cars and hence more cars will be demanded. This in turn will increase the demand for headlamps.

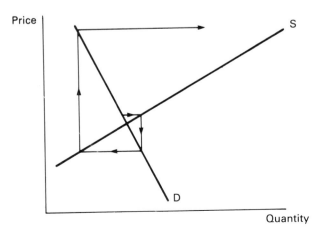

Fig 21.4

What complementary goods can be seen here?

Stabilisation

A major problem facing some industries is the large fluctuation in price of their product over a short time period. This is particularly true of primary industries. In agriculture, for instance, the amount produced in a season can depend as much upon luck—the weather factor—as upon the decisions or competence of farmers. Governments or agencies have the ability to intervene in the market place in order to alter either prices or incomes of producers. Two examples of this are OPEC (The Organization of Petroleum Exporting Countries), which attempts to maintain high prices for crude oil, and the Common Agricultural Policy, which attempts to raise the incomes of farmers in the European Community (EC).

A minimum price can be guaranteed for a product, either if demand is increased or supply is reduced. In

the case of the Common Agricultural Policy, the EC will buy produce at a guaranteed minimum price. If the farmer cannot sell his produce in the market at this minimum price, he sells it to the EC. This is illustrated diagrammatically in Fig. 21.5. I equilibrium, Q_E of a product will be bought and s in the market at price P_E. But assume that th sets a minimum price for the product of P_M tively this distorts the ordinary demand c puts a kink in it. The new demand curve i follows the ordinary market demand c is horizontal showing that the EC is any amount of this produce at pr consumers are prepared to buy The EC buys the rest of that p

What to do with the surplu difficult problem. In theor set so that when harve above the minimum surplus produce. This

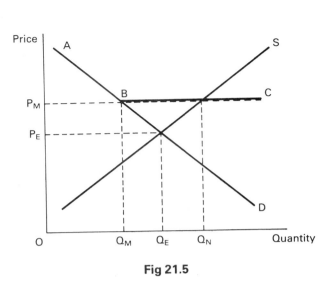

Fig 21.5

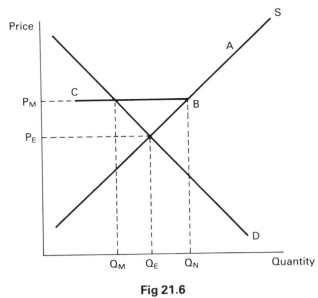

Fig 21.6

The consumer should neither gain nor lose because he pays higher than market prices when market supply is high and lower than market prices when market supply is low. In practice, the minimum price is often set too high. The EC can rarely get rid of its surplus in the way just described. Hence it has to be disposed of in other ways at knock-down prices: for instance to the Russians, or fed to pigs, or distributed cheaply to selected groups such as old age pensioners, hospitals, or to a specially selected EC nation. This type of price stabilisation scheme depends upon manipulating the demand curve for the product.

A cartel such as OPEC influences price by mani-
~~nlv. Price is pushed up by cutting back
~ $_{\scriptstyle G}$ the market price of oil is P_E,
~lied in equilibrium.
~~~ They can

stabilise incomes rather than prices. Whatever the price, the income received will be roughly the same. This only occurs if the demand curve is of unitary elasticity. If the demand curve has a price elasticity of 1, a change in price will result in an exact and opposite change in quantity demanded. Hence

How does OPEC try to maintain an artificially high price for world oil? Why is Saudi Arabia especially important in this respect?

206

Data 21.2

Oil prices fall

By Steven Butler

OIL PRICES fell yesterday as markets reacted with concern to manoeuvring by key members of the Organisation of Petroleum Exporting Countries in advance of the Opec ministerial conference in Vienna, on June 5.

Saudi Arabia plans to reintroduce proposals to set a $15 a barrel floor price on oil produced by members of the Organisation of Petroleum Exporting Countries.

Meanwhile, Petroleum Intelligence Weekly, the oil industry newsletter, said yesterday that Kuwait was ready to flood the market with oil unless the

Opec ministers agreed to increase its share of Opec production. Sheikh Ali Khalifa Al-Sabah, the Kuwait minister, suggested in March that both the United Arab Emirates and Kuwait should receive a higher allocation, although he later said this was merely an idea to be considered.

The Saudis evidently believe their proposal would help to prevent a collapse of prices, while allowing the market to determine prices according to supply and demand conditions above this level. This would involve scrapping the $18 reference price for Opec oil and

allowing prices to rise possibly higher than $18.

King Fahd recently said that oil prices would rise to $26 a barrel by next year if Opec members stuck to their quotas. Many analysts saw the King's statement as a rebuff to Kuwait demands for a higher production ceiling and a greater quota allocation, as well as a criticism of overproduction by Opec members, who are believed to be producing at roughly 2.5m b/d over the Opec ceiling of 18.5m b/d.

The Financial Times. 23.5.89

1 Using a diagram, explain why 'oil prices fell yesterday'.

2 Explain why cartels, such as Opec, find it difficult to maintain a stable price for their products.

revenue, which is price times quantity, remains exactly the same. For instance a 10% rise in price will result in a 10% fall in quantity demanded if elasticity is unitary. Thus the amount of money spent does not change.

Governments or agencies can alter the demand curve to one of unitary elasticity by the same methods used to stabilise price. The same problems arise with income stabilisation schemes as with price stabilisation schemes. Incomes are set too high, with the result that large amounts of produce are bought from the market and stored. The scheme becomes excessively expensive. Obviously it is in the producers' interests to keep prices and incomes high. The consumer loses out because he has to pay higher prices for the product. The taxpayer loses out because he has to foot the bill for the produce taken into store and either destroyed or sold at knock down

prices. A successful scheme, however, will be advantageous to all. It will have low administrative costs. Consumers and producers alike will benefit from more stable market conditions.

Taxes and subsidies

An indirect tax or subsidy on a product will alter the price of that product in most cases. The **incidence** of tax describes the direction of the burden of tax. The incidence of income tax falls on inc The incidence of property taxes falls property. However, economic ther the incidence of indirect taxes entirely on consumers.

In Fig. 21.7, supply is orig

S. Thus at this stage, equilibrium price is P_E, and equilibrium quantity demanded and supplied is Q_E. A tax is then put on the product. It is a fixed tax remaining the same in money terms whatever the price of the product. For instance, if a supplier is willing to sell goods at £10 each and the tax is £1, the final price will be £11. If the supplier wishes to sell his goods at £20, the tax is still £1 and the final price is £21. In terms of Fig. 21.7 this means that the supply curve shifts vertically upwards. Suppliers are willing to supply the same amount as before but at a higher price—the original price plus the value of the tax. The vertical distance between the new supply curves S' and S represents the unit value of the tax. Because the tax is the same in money terms whatever the original price, S' and S are parallel.

Originally the price was at P_E. As can be seen, the new price is P_T and not P_R as might be expected. This is because a rise in the price of the good has caused a fall in the demand for the product, so that only Q_T is now bought. This means that suppliers are willing to supply at a price of P_F instead of P_E. Thus the final price is P_F plus the value of the tax $P_F P_T$, that is P_T. The price to the consumer has risen from P_E to P_T. The rest of the tax, $P_E P_F$, is paid for by the industry itself. Thus economic theory suggests that part of the incidence of an indirect tax falls on the consumer, and part on the producer. The government receives in revenue the tax per unit ($P_F P_T$) times the quantity sold ($O Q_T$). Hence it receives an amount represented by the rectangle $A B P_T P_F$.

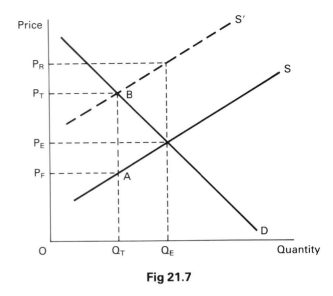

Fig 21.7

A subsidy will have the opposite effect. It will push the supply curve downwards and to the right because producers can now offer a lower final price to the consumer at every level of output. But only part of the subsidy will be passed on to the consumer in lower prices. Part of it will be used by producers to increase production.

The elasticities of demand and supply affect the balance of incidence on consumer and producer. If, as in Fig. 21.8a, either the demand curve is perfectly elastic, or the supply curve completely inelastic as in Fig. 21.8b, price will not change at all after the

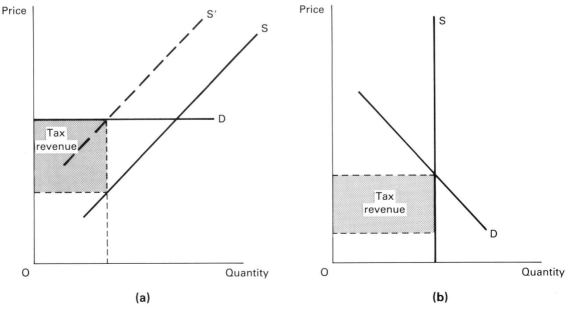

(a)   (b)

Fig 21.8

Data 21.3

Cheaper wine but dearer beer likely after court ruling

By Patricia Clough and Ian Murray

A bottle of wine may become cheaper and a pint of beer dearer after a ruling yesterday by the European Court of Justice that Britain's rate of taxation on wine is illegal.

The Luxembourg court found that the ratio of tax on wine to that on beer—currently just over 4:1—is discriminatory. It violates the EEC treaty which forbids member countries to tax imported goods indirectly to protect their own.

The British system of excise duty "has the effect of subjecting wine to an additional tax burden so as to afford protection to domestic beer production", the 11 judges declared.

The effect was "to stamp wine with the hallmarks of a luxury product which, in view of the tax burden which it bears, can scarcely constitute in the eyes of the consumer a genuine alternative to the typical domestic beverage".

The Chancellor now has to decide whether to reduce the tax on wine or increase that on beer or – as appears most likely – to do both. A spokesmen for the Treasury said only that the matter was being studied.

The court did not set any time limit for the Government to comply with its

20p Wine

27p Bottling and shipping

48p Distribution, retail promotion, costs and profits (variable according to import systems, firms etc)

26p VAT

79p Excise duty

VIN ORDINAIRE £2

ruling and government officials indicated that the most likely moment would be in next year's Budget.

The wine trade greeted the news with delight and the beer producers with gloom and warnings against hitting the beer drinkers too hard. Mr Arnold Tasker, deputy chairman of the Wine and Spirits Association, said the wine trade had long been urging

successive Chancellors to lower tax on wine. "If the ruling leads to an early reduction of wine taxes the Wine and Spirits Association will be overjoyed", he said.

"British beer drinkers are already among the highest taxed in the world at 23p in VAT and duty on the average pint", a spokesman for the Brewers Society said. Beer drinkers were going to be handing over £2,600m to the Chancellor in the coming financial year.

"It would be wrong and very unpopular with 30 million beer drinkers if beer taxes were substantially increased", he said. It would also lead to a drop in consumption and therefore in the Treasury's takings.

The judgment ended a five-year court case brought by the European Commission against the Government. The Commission was supported by the Italian Government, which was obviously upset at the fact that Britain had successfully argued before the court that whisky was unfairly taxed in Italy compared with grappa. The court agreed with the Italian argument that beer competes with the "lightest and cheapest wines". The court did not specify what a fair tax ratio would be.

The Times. 13.7.83

1 Explain, using diagrams, the likely effect of the European Court of Justice decision on the price and quantity demanded of both beer and wine.

2 Under what circumstances would a rise in beer taxes lead to a 'drop in the Treasury's takings'?

imposition of a tax. In this case the incidence falls entirely on the producer, and the consumer pays no tax. At the opposite extreme, if the demand curve is perfectly inelastic or the supply curve perfectly elastic, the price will go up by the full amount of the tax, i.e. the tax incidence falls entirely on the consumer. In general, the more inelastic the demand curve, or the more elastic the supply curve, the greater will be the incidence of tax on the consumer.

Summary

Price and quantity sold are determined in a market by the forces of demand and supply. Individual demand and supply curves can be constructed to determine equilibrium in a market for an individual consumer or producer. Equally, total demand and supply for a group of consumers or producers can be constructed by horizontal summing of individual demand and supply curves. The cobweb theorem is an attempt to bring a dynamic element into the discussion of the path which a market takes when in disequilibrium. Markets are interrelated—markets for substitute and complementary goods are particularly so. Price and income stabilisation can be achieved either by altering the demand curve or the supply curve of a product. Such schemes tend to be costly and their success to date has been mixed. The incidence of an indirect tax is likely to fall partly on the consumer and partly on the producer.

Essay questions

1 Distinguish between a 'static' and a 'dynamic' model. Use models of price determination to illustrate your answer.

2 What do economists understand by a 'market'? How can governments intervene to stabilise prices in a market?

3 Define the 'incidence' of tax. What effect would you expect an increase in excise duty on tobacco to have on (a) the price of a packet of cigarettes and (b) government tax revenue from tobacco?

Terms for review

individual demand and supply curves

horizontal summing

markets

cobweb theorem

substitutes

complementary goods

price and income stabilisation

cartel

incidence of tax

22

Demand theory

Demand theory is an area of economic theory which has seen little fruitful development since it was first outlined by neo-classical economists in the second half of the nineteenth century. Three different neo-classical theories will be considered in this chapter —marginal utility theory, indifference theory, and revealed preference theory.

Two fundamental questions need to be answered by any theory:

1 Is the price of an economic commodity inversely related to the quantity demanded (i.e., is the demand curve downward sloping)?

2 What is the exact relationship between price and quantity demanded, apart from the fact that they are inversely related?

Marginal utility theory

Utility refers to the 'satisfaction' gained in consuming an economic good. This 'consumption' could refer to anything—a chocolate bar, a bed, an hour of one's time which has an opportunity cost, a donation to charity. **Marginal utility theory** does not attempt to explain why satisfaction is gained from a particular economic good. That question is the province of psychologists, biologists and sociologists. The economist simply assumes that everything that an individual experiences has some utility. It could be negative. The utility derived from a spell in prison, for instance, is likely to be negative—or as it is sometimes said, to have 'disutility'. A week spent on holiday, on the other hand, is likely to have positive utility.

Marginal utility theory makes the assumption that utility is measurable by the individual. The individual can not only say that he prefers one good to another, but he can also more precisely say that it gives twice as much satisfaction, or half as much satisfaction, or 3.76 times as much satisfaction. In order to make this explicit, **units of utility** will from now on be called UUs. They are to be seen as much a measure of a quantity as metres are of length or grams are of weight. Note that neo-classical economists have never been able to find an actual measure of satisfaction, and this is certainly a weakness of marginal utility theory.

Total utility refers to all the satisfaction gained from the consumption of a given quantity of economic goods. Average utility is the average satisfaction per unit gained from the consumption of those goods. It can be found by dividing total utility by the number of goods consumed. Marginal utility is the satisfaction gained from the last economic good consumed.

In Table 22.1, a set of utilities is displayed which illustrate the main ideas of marginal utility theory. Note the relationship between total, average and marginal utility. Marginal utility can be found by subtracting successive total utilities. For instance, the marginal utility of the fourth good consumed is the difference between the total utility of consuming four goods (68) less the total utility of consuming three goods (54), i.e. 14.

Table 22.1 Total, average and marginal utilities

Number consumed	Total utility (in UUs)	Average utility (in UUs)	Marginal utility (in UUs)
1	20	20	20
2	38	19	18
3	54	18	16
4	68	17	14
5	80	16	12
6	84	14	4
7	84	12	0
8	80	10	−4

Note also that marginal utility declines as the number of goods consumed increases. This is known as the **Law of diminishing marginal utility**. Neo-classical economists argue that it is always true that

Demand theory

as the number of units of a good consumed increases, the marginal utility declines. For instance, if Table 22.1 referred to a chocolate bar, the first bar would yield 20 UUs. The second would yield less. By the sixth bar, the marginal utility is down to 4 UUs. The seventh bar yields no utility at all. The eighth bar yields −4 UUs: the consumer is probably feeling rather sick at this stage. The defence for this law is that it is empirically true, and secondly that it is just common sense. The utility gained from a chocolate bar for a man who had nothing to eat for 40 days is likely to be greater than from someone who has eaten regularly over the same time period.

The law can be expressed diagrammatically. In Fig. 22.1, the marginal utility line is downward sloping. This shows that as quantity increases, marginal utility declines. Note that total utility can be measured by calculating the area under the marginal utility curve. In Table 22.1, the total utility can be found by adding up the marginal utilities. Hence, if

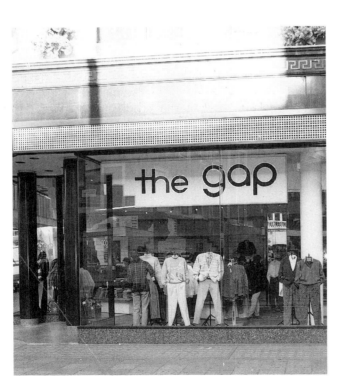

The above illustrate a hi-fi system, a second-hand motorcycle, clothes and books. If the consumption of £300 worth of new clothes gave you 1 unit of utility, what values of utility would you personally place on the consumption of these other items?

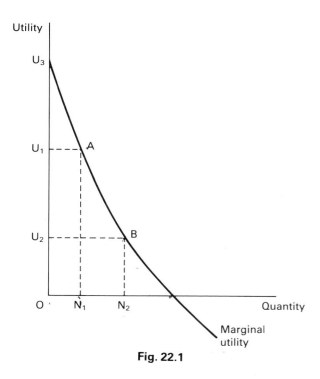

Fig. 22.1

the marginal utility of the first item is 20 and the second is 18, the total utility gained from the two items is 38. In Fig. 22.1, if N_1 units are consumed, the total utility of consuming N_1 can be found by adding up the marginal utility of each good consumed up to N_1. The marginal utility is given by the vertical distance between the y axis and the marginal utility curve. Adding up each strip under the marginal utility curve between U_3 and A will give an area, the area OU_3AN_1. If N_2 goods are consumed, then the total utility is given by OU_3BN_2.

Each economic good gives a utility through its consumption. This, however, does not tell us how much of each good will be consumed. For instance, one good might yield 1000 UUs. Another good might yield just 10 UUs. But if the first good is one million times more expensive than the second, it is unlikely that a consumer will choose to buy the first. It is also important to realise that marginal utility, rather than total utility, determines patterns of consumption.

In Table 22.2, good A has considerably more total utility than good B. By consuming three units of A the consumer can get 210 UUs, whereas he can only get 80 UUs by consuming 3 units of B. But it is obvious that the consumer would not want to consume 3 units of A as the last unit actually produced disutility. In fact, all other things being equal, if he had to choose between a second unit of A and a

second unit of B, he would prefer B which gives him 30 UUs, whereas A only gives him an extra 20 UUs.

Table 22.2

Number	Good A		Good B	
	Total utility (in UUs)	Marginal utility (in UUs)	Total utility (in UUs)	Marginal utility (in UUs)
1	200	200	40	40
2	220	20	70	30
3	210	−10	80	10

So a consumer determines his patterns of consumption by reference to the prices of goods and their relative marginal utilities. The consumer is assumed to maximise his welfare. Hence he wishes to maximise his total utility. He does this by comparing marginal utilities of goods and their costs. If he has just £1 left to spend, he will want to get as many UUs as possible with the £1. He may be able to get 2 UUs by consuming good A, but only 1 UU with good B. He will choose to buy A because he can get 2 UUs per pound spent, whereas with B he can only get 1 UU per pound spent.

Suppose that in consuming good C a consumer gets 20 UUs for £2, but in consuming good D he can get 15 UUs for £1. With good C he is getting 10 UUs per £1 compared with 15 UUs per £1 with good D. According to the law of diminishing marginal utility, if he consumes more of good D, he will get something less than 15 UUs per unit consumed. If he consumes less of good C, then his marginal utility on the last unit will rise. It is likely to pay him to consume more D, so that he gets perhaps 12 UUs per £1 spent at the margin, and less of C, so that he gets again say 12 UUs per £1 spent at the margin. It can be seen that he will find it better to redistribute his expenditure so that the marginal utility gained per £1 spent will be equal for all the goods he consumes. Expressed mathematically:

$$\frac{MU_X}{P_X} = \frac{MY_Y}{P_Y} = \ldots$$

where MU_X is the marginal utility of good X, P_X is the price of good X, and so on.

Hence an important prediction of marginal utility theory is that in order to maximise utility, the consumer will consume where his marginal utilities per amount of money spent are equal. This enables us to prove that the demand curve is downward sloping. If the price of a good increases whilst all

YES, MRS. BRAGG FOUND THAT SWITCHING TO GREASO MARGARINE INCREASED HER UTILITY. WHY DON'T YOU TRY IT TODAY?

GREASO MARGARINE

Can advertising affect the amount of utility gained from the consumption of a product?

others remain constant, the consumer will find that he is no longer in equilibrium. The good that has gone up in price will now give a lower marginal utility per amount spent than before. For instance, if he got 20 UUs from the last unit consumed at a cost of £4, he would get 5 UUs per pound. If the price now increases, to say £5 for the same amount, he would only get 4 UUs per pound spent. In this situation, he will cut back on his consumption of the good, and spend it on other items which will yield him more UUs per amount spent. So a rise in price has resulted in a fall in demand for the good. The opposite is also true. A fall in price will result in disequilibrium. He will spend more on the good and less on other goods in order to restore equilibrium.

However, marginal utility theory does not allow us to say how much of a good will be consumed at any given price. It can prove that the demand curve is downward sloping, but it can not say where the demand curve will lie. The theory also relies upon the law of diminishing marginal utility—the assumption that consumers maximise their utility and that utility can be measured. The first two assumptions are fairly uncontroversial, but many

economists would argue that utility can not be measured. If it can not be measured, the marginal utility theory is an unhelpful hypothesis.

Indifference theory

Indifference theory and marginal utility theory differ mainly over the measurement of utility. Marginal utility theory assumes that utility can be measured. **Indifference theory** only requires that consumers can put their preferences in rank order. For instance, in marginal utility theory it is assumed that a consumer can place a value on the differences in satisfaction gained from a chocolate bar and a packet of crisps. Indifference theory only requires that the consumer can tell whether he would prefer a packet of crisps or a chocolate bar. He does not have to put a value on the difference in satisfaction.

Assume that a consumer has 100 chocolate bars in his possession but no water. If he were offered 1 litre of water in exchange for 10 chocolate bars he might well accept. Assume that later he has 10 chocolate bars and 9 litres of water. If he were offered 1 litre of water for his last 10 chocolate bars it is unlikely that he would accept. His 10 chocolate bars are far more precious to him now than when he had 100 of them, yet he is being offered the same rate of exchange. He is likely to demand considerably more than 1 litre of water for his last 10 chocolate bars, i.e. he demands a better rate of exchange.

This can be represented diagrammatically. In Fig. 22.2, a graph is drawn with the quantity of chocolate bars on one axis, and the quantity of water on the other. The line II is drawn so that the consumer is indifferent between any point along that line. For instance, he does not mind whether he has OA of chocolate bars and OE of water; or OD of chocolate bars and OH of water.

The **indifference curve** is drawn convex to the origin because the more a consumer has of a commodity, the more he is assumed to be willing to give it up for a unit of another commodity. If a consumer had OA of chocolate bars, he would be willing to give up AB of them for just EF of water. In other words, he would give up a large number of chocolate bars for a small quantity of extra water. If however, he had only OC of chocolate bars, and he were asked to give up the same number, CD (where CD = AB), he would want considerably more water in exchange. He would want GH of water. It is important to remember that the points J, K, L, M, and N are

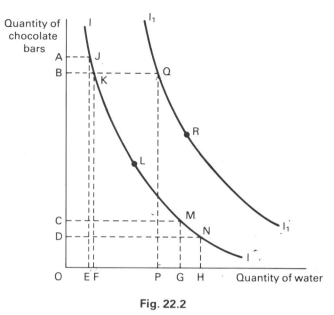

Fig. 22.2

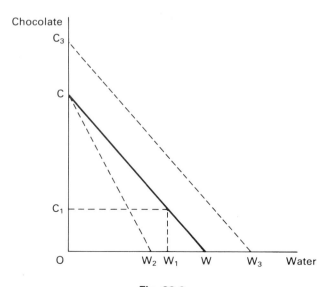

Fig. 22.3

points between which he is indifferent. If he were at point J, he is no better off in terms of utility than if he were at point N.

It is easy to prove that a consumer would always want to be on his highest indifference curve possible—highest meaning farthest out from the origin. Assume that in Fig. 22.2 a consumer can either be on indifference curve II or I_1I_1. If he were on II, he would be just as happy to be at the point K as anywhere else on the line. At K, he is able to consume OB of chocolate bars and OF of water. If he were on indifference curve I_1I_1, he would not mind whether he is at point Q or any other point. At point Q, he can consume OB chocolate bars and OP of water. Comparing II with I_1I_1, it can be seen that at point Q, the consumer is as well off as at K in chocolate bars but is better off than at K in terms of water. He can get an extra FP of water by being on indifference curve I_1I_1 rather than II. Consumers wish to maximise their utility, and FP water will result in extra utility being obtained. Hence, the consumer prefers to be at point Q rather than K. Hence, he would prefer to be anywhere on this indifference curve on which Q lies than any point on the indifference curve on which K lies.

Two indifference curves can not cross. Assume that in Fig. 22.2 an indifference curve I_2I_2 goes through the points K and R, i.e. cutting both indifference curves II and I_1I_1. We know that the consumer does not mind whether he is at K or R since both points are on his indifference curve I_2I_2. We also know that he does not mind being at Q or R since

these two points are on his indifference curve I_1I_1. If he does not mind being at K or R, or Q or R, it follows he does not mind whether he is at K or Q. But we have already proved that he would prefer to be at Q rather than K. Hence the initial assumption that I_2I_2 can cross other indifference curves must be wrong.

A **budget line** shows how much a consumer can buy with a fixed income. For instance in Fig. 22.3, if he spent all his income on chocolates, he could get OC chocolates but no water. If he spent all his income on water he could get OW water and no chocolates. He could spend so that he obtains a combination of goods such as OC_1 of chocolates and OW_1 of water. The budget line is straight on the assumption that he can not obtain either chocolates or water any more cheaply by buying in bulk, i.e. the price per unit is constant for each product.

The line CW and all lines parallel to it represent the relative prices of chocolate and water. If prices change, the price line too will change. A rise in price will mean that less can be bought of that commodity than before relative to the other good. So in Fig. 22.3 a rise in the price of water will mean that the budget line swings round to CW_2. The consumer can now only buy OW_2 of water (if he spends no money on cholocates), but he can still get OC of chocolates as before (if he spends no money on water). A rise in income will be shown by a parallel shift in the budget line, for instance up to C_3W_3. Relative prices have not changed but now the consumer can buy more of both goods.

With a budget line, the consumer's point of consumption can be found. In Fig. 22.4, a consumer's budget line is given by the line CB. He is indifferent between D and F on his indifference curve I_1I_1. But he could do better by consuming at E as this lies on a higher indifference curve. Point E lies on the highest indifference curve he could possibly be on, as it is where the indifference curve touches but does not cross his budget line. Mathematically speaking, it is the point where I_2I_2 is tangential to the line CB.

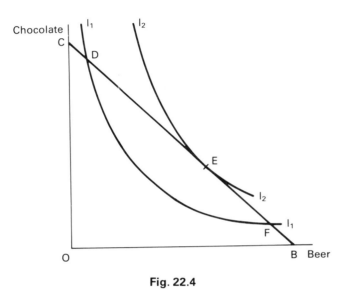

Fig. 22.4

Indifference curve analysis says that it is likely that the demand curve is downward sloping but that it is not necessarily so. The proof of this is complex. In Fig. 22.5, the price of beer increases so that the consumer's budget line moves from LM_1 to LM_2. Previously the consumer was consuming at the point P where the indifference curve I_1I_1 was tangential to LM_1, his budget line. After the price increase he consumes at the point R, where his new budget line LM_2 is tangential to the lower indifference curve I_2I_2. At P he consumed OB_1 of beer, whereas at R he consumes OB_2. So a rise in the price of beer has led to a drop in the consumption of beer. Part of this drop in consumption is due to the fact that his real income has dropped. He still has the same amount of money income of course, but he can now buy less with it. It is likely that he will buy less beer and indeed fewer chocolates as a result. This is known as the **income effect**. Part of the drop in consumption of beer is due to the fact that the price of beer has gone up relative to other goods, so

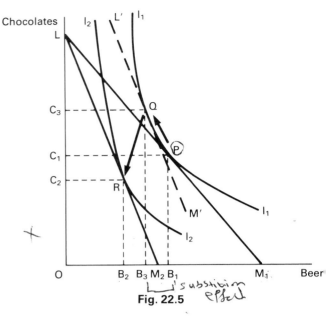

Fig. 22.5

making beer less attractive and chocolate for instance, more attractive. This is known as the **substitution effect**.

In Fig. 22.5, we can differentiate the two effects. Assume that the price of beer has risen, but that the consumer is as well off as before. So he must still consume on his indifference curve I_1I_1 if he is not to suffer a drop in real income. But price has changed and the new price ratio will be given by any line parallel to the budget line LM_2. Hence without a drop in living standards but at the new price he would prefer to consume at Q. The movement from P to Q is the substitution effect—the effect of a change in price without a change in income. As a result it can be seen that he buys less beer (B_1B_3 less) and more chocolate (C_1C_3 more). But his income does decline. The rest of the change from Q to R must be the income effect—the result of a fall in real income but without a change in price. As a result of this fall, his consumption of beer drops from OB_3 to OB_2, and his consumption of chocolates falls from OC_3 to OC_2. Overall, consumption of beer has dropped from OB_1 to OB_2.

In Fig. 22.5, both income and substitution effect were 'positive': a rise in price led to a fall in consumption due to the substitution effect **and** the income effect. But this is not always the case. In Fig. 22.6, a rise in the price of margarine leads to movement from point P to R and so to a fall in the consumption of margarine from B_1 to B_3. The substitution effect is normal. A rise in price leads to movement from P to Q and so to a fall in quantity

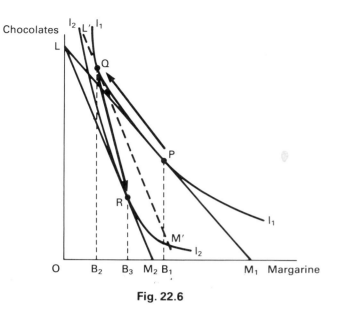

Fig. 22.6

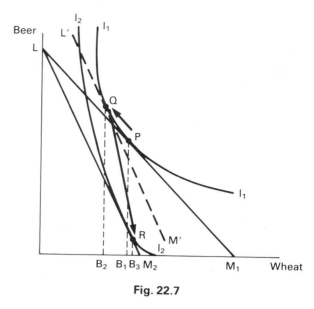

Fig. 22.7

demanded from B_1 to B_2. But the fall in real income as a result of the rise in price leads to movement from Q to R and to a rise in demand for margarine from B_2 to B_3. The income effect is said here to be 'negative'. Inferior goods, where a fall in income leads to a rise in consumption and vice versa, have already been discussed in Chapter 2. Figure 22.6 is a diagram treating margarine as such an inferior good. Still, a rise in price has led to an overall fall in consumption of margarine of B_1B_3.

But in Fig. 22.7, a rise in the price of bread leads to a rise in consumption! The substitution effect from P to Q is still positive. But the income effect from Q to R is negative, and is bigger than the substitution effect. Here we have a very special type of inferior good. It is called a **'Giffen good'**, after Sir Robert Giffen. He argued that the labouring classes in nineteenth century England bought more bread as the price increased and less as prices decreased. The income effect of a rise in price far outweighs any substitution effect. They would have bought less bread if price had gone up and their real income had remained the same. But the price rise did mean a fall in real income. As a result, they cut out the luxuries of life and concentrated on buying what they considered the necessities, that is bread. Hence their consumption of bread actually rose when prices rose. There has been much dispute since about Giffen's findings. But indifference curve analysis does allow for this possibility of an upward sloping demand curve due to a special type of inferior good.

Revealed preference theory

Both marginal utility theory and indifference theory use the concept of utility. Utility is a difficult concept to pin down and many economists are unhappy with it. An approach which does not use utility is **revealed preference theory**. In Fig. 22.8, C_1B_1 is a budget line before an increase in the price of beer, and C_1B_2 is the budget line after the increase. A consumer is observed to consume at point A before the beer price increase. Therefore assuming that he is rational, he prefers point A to all other points within the triangle OC_1B_1. Now assume that there is the rise in the price of beer. To distinguish between the income and substitution effects, assume that the new relative prices prevail but that the consumer's real income remains the same. This is shown by the line C_3B_3. The consumer will not consume on the line AB_3, since he previously preferred A to other points on the line AB_1. This is because any point on AB_1 gives him more beer than on the line AB_3, for a similar amount of chocolates. Therefore he must consume at A, which is unlikely since prices have now changed, or consume on the line AC_3. In other words, the substitution effect of a change in price is positive. A rise in price leads to a fall in quantity demanded. The income effect (the move from AC_3 to somewhere on C_1B_2) can either be positive or negative. It can also outweigh the substitution effect.

Note that the income compensation (rotating the price line round the point A) is not the same as under indifference curve analysis. Note also that the only conclusion of revealed preference theory is that the demand curve is likely to be downward sloping. It also assumes that the consumer is rational. The idea of consumer rationality has come under as much attack in the past as the idea of utility.

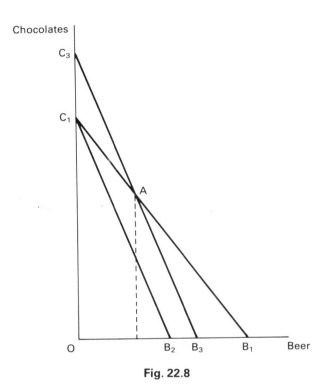

Fig. 22.8

Essay questions

1 Outline a theory of demand. Use that theory to explain what effect a rise in the price of food would have on a consumer's pattern of spending, all other things remaining equal.

2 Distinguish between the 'income' and 'substitution' effects of a price change. How does such a distinction enable us to differentiate between normal, inferior and Giffen goods?

3 Explain the law of diminishing marginal utility. What is its significance in determining the amount of a commodity a consumer will produce?

Summary

Marginal utility theory assumes that utility can be measured and that as consumption increases the corresponding marginal utility diminishes. A consumer will be in equilibrium where the marginal utility per unit of money spent is equal for all goods and services consumed. Indifference theory assumes that consumers can place their preferences in rank order. An indifference curve shows all combinations of goods between which a consumer is indifferent. A consumer will always prefer to be on his highest indifference curve. A budget line shows what combination of goods a consumer can buy with his income. The equilibrium point of consumption will be where his budget line is tangential to an indifference curve. A normal good is one where income and substitution effects are both positive. For an inferior good, the income effect is negative. For a Giffen good, the negative income effect is larger than the positive substitution effect. Revealed preference theory does not use the concept of utility. Like the other theories of demand discussed, it too concludes that the demand curve is downward sloping.

Terms for review

utility

marginal and total

law of diminishing marginal utility

indifference curve

budget line

income and substitution effects

Giffen good

revealed preference

218

23

The theory of costs

The economic meaning of cost

'Cost' has a precise definition in economics. Cost is defined as opportunity cost—that is, the value of alternatives foregone. This has a number of important implications. Firstly, many costs will be valued at their face value. For instance, if a firm buys £50 000 of gas during a year, the alternative foregone is £50 000 of other sources of energy or indeed anything else that £50 000 could have been spent on.

However, many costs are **imputed**. This is where a firm owns a factor of production and therefore does not have to 'pay' for its use. Nevertheless, it represents an economic cost. For instance, nearly all firms keep back part of their profits to reinvest in their company. From a simple accounting point of view, this money is costless. To an economist, however, it does have an opportunity cost. That money instead could be deposited in a bank, or used to buy other types of financial assets. These assets should then earn a return. Hence, the cost of that money is the amount that could be earned in its next best use.

Equally, many small firms undervalue the cost of their labour. A small corner shop might see a 'profit' of £7 000 a year. However, the owner who works the shop might not be drawing a salary. If his opportunity cost (the amount he could be earning if he were in his best paid alternative employment) were £6 000, then the true economic profit is only £1 000.

Depreciation is another example of an imputed cost. A firm may buy £100 000 of machinery. The machinery is highly specialised and no other firm would want to buy it at any price. The firm estimates that the machinery will last ten years. It may look as if the machinery depreciates by £10 000 each year. In fact the machinery depreciates by £100 000 the moment the firm signs a binding contract for the delivery of that machinery. This is because there is no alternative use for the machinery. It has no second-hand value and hence it is worthless the moment it is bought. Thus the true cost of the machinery is not £10 000 for ten years, but £100 000 in the first year, and £0 in the next nine years.

Risk is also a cost, and must have a value put on it. Risk is very difficult to measure. Take two investment projects. One involves risk and the other does not. The returns on the two projects are such that the businessman is indifferent about which one he undertakes—that is, from the profit point of view, the businessman sees the projects as equally desirable. Then the difference between the rates of return on these two projects is the risk premium. Assume the businessman could earn 10% a year on government stock maturing in 10 years' time. If he is indifferent between that project and a ten year project involving risk which brings in 15% a year, then the 'cost' of risk, or the 'risk premium' is 5%. The higher the risk, the greater will be the risk premium. So the rate of return earned by a stable, and in many countries nationalised, industry such as gas, should be considerably lower than in a high risk industry such as micro-technology.

All costs need to be calculated and included in a project for the true economic cost to be brought out. In the real world, what an accountant and the taxman would count as a cost is often very different from the economist's meaning of the word. Hence care needs to be taken when assessing costs as to which definition of the word is used.

Time Scales

Costs can be divided into two types—fixed and variable. **Fixed costs** do not vary with output. A machine, for instance, may need to be bought before even one unit of output is produced, but the cost of that machine does not vary with output. A factory building may need to be erected before production can start. Yet the wear and tear on the building will be the same however much is produced within it. **Variable costs** are costs that vary with output—

raw materials are a good example. The amount of wood used by a furniture manufacturer varies directly with output. It is often true that a cost may have a fixed and variable element in it. Labour, for instance, is often cited as a variable cost because extra production usually requires extra man-hours to produce it. On the other hand, it is often difficult and costly to shed or to take on labour. Many firms prefer to employ a fixed number of workers and work them more or less hard over their standard working week according to how much output is needed. In this case, labour is a fixed cost. Any overtime worked would be a variable cost for the firm. In

general, the distinction between fixed and variable costs is a useful one, even if in reality there are many borderline cases.

The **short run** is defined as a period of time when some costs are variable and at least one cost is fixed. For instance, in the short run a firm might have to decide how many men or what amount of raw materials to use with one machine. In this case labour and raw materials are the variable factors of production, but capital is fixed. In the **long run**, all factors of production are variable. In the long run firms can change machinery, build new factories and offices and make significant changes in their

Data 23.1

Just what Dr Martens ordered

Alice Rawsthorn

Griggs has been making Dr Martens boots since 1960. Its fortunes have waxed and waned over the years but since the mid 1980s – when Dr Martens suddenly became fashionable everywhere from Manhattan to Milan – it has prospered.

It began with boots. The first Dr Martens product to roll off its production line was a classic working boot.

The boots were sold to factory and farm workers. In the late 1960s they were adopted as regulation footwear by the skinheads, one of the youth cults of the era. By the mid 1970s Griggs was churning out 5,000 pairs of Dr Martens a week and even introduced shoes. It began to boost production by buying other local factories.

But by the end of the 1970s, Griggs, like the rest of the footwear industry, was in trouble. The economic recession had taken a devastating toll on manufacturing employment with inevitable consequences for a company that was largely reliant on selling shoes to factory workers.

Griggs was forced to cut costs. It laid

off workers and closed a few of its smaller factories. In 1984 its fortunes revived. The biggest boost came when Jean-Paul Gaultier, the enfant terrible of Paris fashion designers, used Dr Martens in one of his collections.

Griggs has at least benefited from the boom in demand. It now employs 1,100 people in 20 factories across the east Midlands. At its peak last autumn, the overall level of production reached 85,000 pairs a week. The group made record sales of £38m last year.

Sales have since slowed down. The level of weekly production has slipped to 75,000 pairs. It is too soon to tell

whether Griggs has simply fallen victim to the sluggish state of consumer sales or whether the fashion for Dr Martens has fizzled out.

The company has started to cut costs. So far it has managed to avoid redundancies, but has reduced its workforce by natural wastage and has put some of its factories on short-time working.

In the meantime, it is overhauling the Dr Martens range by introducing new colours and leathers. But the basic style will not change. Griggs depends on economies of scale for its profitability, so the Dr Martens shoes and boots will stay exactly the same.

The Financial Times. 20.5.89

1 Describe the costs which Griggs faces in its manufacture of Dr Martens boots.

2 What might be meant by the 'long run' for Griggs?

3 Explain which costs might be short run costs for Griggs.

workforce. In the very long run, the state of technology can change too. New inventions can alter the different ways of production open to a firm.

It is important to note that in these definitions no mention is made of a specific time scale, such as three years, or six months. The short run for one industry might be very different in time from the short run for another. Indeed the short run for one industry might be longer than the long run for another. This micro-economic definition of time is based upon the concepts of fixed and variable costs, and not upon a specific time period.

Taking another example, in Table 23.2, the total cost of producing 40 units is given as £80. The total cost of producing 50 units is £120. So the average cost of producing 40 units is £80 ÷ 40, or £2 per unit. The marginal cost of the last 10 units produced, between a total output of 40 and 50, is £120 less £80, or £40.

Table 23.2

Output	Total cost	Average cost	Marginal cost
40	£80	£2	
50	£120	£2.4	£40

Total, average and marginal costs

Total costs are defined as all the costs of producing a fixed quantity of output. In Table 23.1, the total cost of producing 100 units is £100. The total cost of producing 101 units is £121. The **average cost** is defined as the average cost per unit produced. Hence, the average cost of producing 100 units is £1 per unit. The average cost of producing 101 units at a total cost of £121 is approximately £1.20 per unit. The **marginal cost** is defined as the change in total costs resulting from a change in the level of production by one unit, i.e. the cost of producing an extra unit of production. So the marginal cost of the 101st unit is the difference between the total cost of 100 units and the total cost of the 101st unit: i.e. £121 less £100, or £21.

The analysis can be carried further by thinking about fixed and variable costs. Total cost must equal fixed costs plus variable costs. Hence the following relationships must apply:

Total fixed cost (TFC)
        + total variable cost (TVC)
        = Total cost (TC)

Average fixed cost (AFC)
        + average variable cost (AVC)
        = Average total cost (ATC)

These relationships are brought out in Table 23.3. Total fixed costs remain the same whether 100 or 101 units are produced. Only total variable cost changes with output. The average cost figures are calculated by dividing the relevant total cost figures by output. The marginal cost of producing the 101st unit is the total cost of producing the 101st unit (£121) less the total cost of the 100th unit (£100). However, because total fixed costs do not (by definition) vary with output, marginal cost can also be calculated by subtracting the total variable cost of the 100th unit (£50) from the total variable cost of the 101st unit (£71).

Table 23.1

Output	Total cost	Average cost	Marginal cost
100	£100	£1	
101	£121	£1.20 approx.	£21

Table 23.3

Output	Total fixed cost	Total variable cost	Total cost	Average fixed cost	Average variable cost	Average total cost	Marginal cost
100	£50	£50	£100	£0.5	£0.5	£1	
101	£50	£71	£121	£0.49	£0.71	£1.2	£21

Data 23.2

The cut price airline heads for a loss

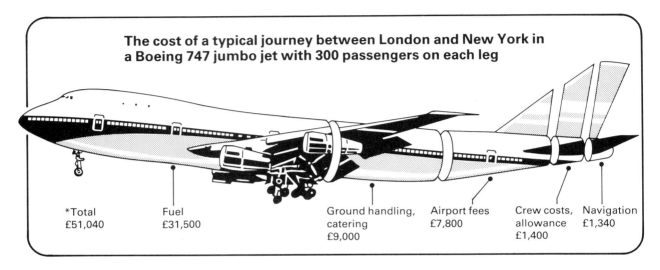

The cost of a typical journey between London and New York in a Boeing 747 jumbo jet with 300 passengers on each leg

*Total £51,040 | Fuel £31,500 | Ground handling, catering £9,000 | Airport fees £7,800 | Crew costs, allowance £1,400 | Navigation £1,340

Michael Smith

The American airline, People Express, will almost certainly lose money with every passenger flying between London and New York for the proposed cut price fare of £99.

This is how the costs break down on a typical daily schedule, flying a 747 jumbo jet from London to New York and from New York back to London.

In this case, the 747 is three-quarters full with 300 passengers spread around the first, business and tourist classes. The aircraft will weigh 374 tons on take-off and meet 200 mph headwinds on the west-bound leg to New York, which will eat up more gallons of fuel than on the homeward journey where the winds will help push the aircraft along.

The biggest single item of expense is fuel, which on this typical return journey of around 6,000 miles will cost the airline £31,500.

Next comes the cost of airport handling and supplies of food and drink for the two seven-hour flights, amounting to a total of £9,000.

After that comes the cost of parking, landing and taking off from the two airports. The cost for using London's expensive Heathrow and New York's Kennedy airports at the appropriate times would amount to £7,800.

The airline will also have to pay £1,340 to use the navigational facilities across the Atlantic and in Britain, which come under Euro-control.

A more variable but inescapable cost to the airline is the sum paid to flight crews and cabin staff for overnight hotel accommodation, meals, information packs and other small items. In this case the assumption is a total cost of £1,400.

Therefore, the total operating cost of this typical return transatlantic journey in a 747 is a shade over £50,000.

If People Express were to attract 600 fare-paying passengers on each return trip—300 per leg—the basic overheads would absorb £83.30 of each £99 ticket.

However, this calculation does not take into account salaries for the firm's 1,000 staff, administration costs, engineering and repair facilities, promotional fees and other items needed to keep any business going.

Another substantial money problem for People Express lies in the cost of renting the secondhand jumbo jet.

According to the airline, the 747 will cost about £33,000 a month to rent until September this year. The airline will be making five trips a week, which implies that the 747 effectively costs £1,650 every working day.

That pushes the essential costs of each return journey well over £50,000 and once again narrows the gap between every £99 ticket and the basic overheads. The profit margin is disappearing.

But any profit which People Express might make between now and September will surely be demolished when, from October 1, 1983, the monthly cost of leasing the 747 rises five-fold from £33,000 to £165,000.

From October, the daily cost of the jumbo jet soars from £1,650 to £8,250. Adding the daily cost of the 747 from October onwards to the basic operational overheads suggests that, if People Express carries 600 passengers on each return journey, the profit per passenger is £2. But this does not take into account other overheads like wages, engineering, etc.

The conclusion, therefore, must be that the £99 fare will be a loss-maker for People Express.

The unanswered question, however, is whether People Express can retain such a "loss leader" for very long and whether the £99 is a gimmicky launch price, to be raised at a later date.

The Guardian. 26.4.83

a) What fixed costs and
b) what variable costs do People Express face on their new transatlantic route?

What is the approximate average variable cost for People Express of a return transatlantic flight carrying (a) 300 passengers and (b) 400 passengers?

3 If a flight carries 300 passengers, what is the approximate marginal cost?

Economies and Diseconomies of Scale

The scale of production confers certain advantages and disadvantages upon the producer. Every industry will differ in what these are and at what point they start or stop having an effect. Assume that the shape of the long run average cost curve facing a firm will be U-shaped. This is shown in Fig. 23.1. The long run average cost curve (LRAC) declines to start with as output increases to a lowest long run average cost point output of OA. Between points O and A, **increasing returns to scale** or **economies of scale** are said to exist. Between A and B, long run average costs do not vary with output—**constant returns to scale** are said to exist. Output between OA and OB is sometimes described as the point of **optimal production** because long run average costs are at their lowest point. At output greater than OB, long run average cost starts to rise. Here, **diseconomies of scale** or **decreasing returns to scale** are said to exist.

The main sources of these **internal economies of scale** are as follows:

1 Technical Economies. Technical economies arise because the cost of plant and machinery does not go up in line with output. An example is an oil tanker, where doubling the length and breadth of the ship will quadruple the volume of the ship. Hence for roughly twice the cost, the ship can carry four times as much cargo.

2 Managerial Economies. Managerial economies arise due to the division of labour. A small businessman may have to be an accountant, a salesman, an engineer and a shop floor worker. Because he is unable to specialise in any one, he is likely to be less efficient at any task than a true specialist. A larger firm would be able to employ and occupy full time an accountant, a salesman, etc., each of whom would be more efficient.

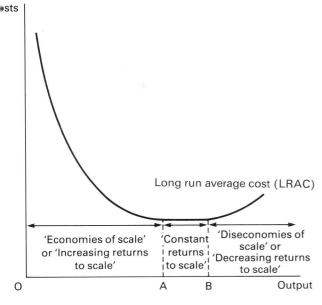

Fig. 23.1

3 Financial Economies. Large firms are able to take advantage of many economies in relation to the money they handle. The size of the business often means that they can borrow money at lower rates of interest compared to smaller, riskier businesses. They may also be able to gain insurance at a lower relative cost, more able to obtain government grants, etc.

4 Marketing Economies. Larger firms are often able to use their market powers to lower the price they pay for raw materials and obtain higher prices for the products they sell. These gains arise from two factors. Firstly, buying in large quantities often results in lower costs per unit. Transport may be cheaper, accounting procedures less in cost per

transaction, and so on. Secondly, gains can also aris from the sheer market muscle of the firm. A larg firm may be in a position virtually to dictate term to a smaller firm which supplies it, as the smalle firm may face bankruptcy if it loses the contract t supply.

5 Indivisibilities. Fixed costs will not rise as pr duction increases. A firm may have to buy a piece capital equipment but only be able to use it for pa of the time. A building firm, for instance, may buy lorry but only use it on three days out of five a wee A bigger firm which could use it every working da would have lower unit costs. This is an example an indivisibility—a cost which is incurred regard less of output. One important general example of a

What economies of scale might the supermarket enjoy which the smaller business would not?

indivisibility is research and development expend ture. This must be undertaken before even one un is produced. The bigger the firm, and the productio run, the lower the cost per unit of research an development.

However, diseconomies of scale can arise if pr duction is too great. Management may be unable cope with the size of the firm. Poor industrial rel tions, lower worker motivation and productivity, la financial and production controls can be the resul (These factors are known as 'X-inefficiency' and wi be considered in Chapter 27). This causes averag costs to start rising again. Moreover, large plant not always technically more efficient than sma plant.

There is much controversy in applied economi about the existence of diseconomies of scale. Mo research suggests that in practice, the average co

Data 23.3

Global production and local markets

Unilever, the largest consumer products company in the world, has been weighing up the advantages of economies of scale in a world market with the special needs of complex, fast-moving marketing-led businesses. On the one hand, centralising production can reduce costs substantially. On the other hand, Unilever sells into specialised markets. A personal toiletry which sells well in Palermo may be unappealing in Wigan.

Its speciality chemicals business is a clear case for scale economies. In common with other chemicals companies, its capital intensive nature and its production of components common to a wide range of industries makes it the ideal candidate. Accordingly, output of its oleochemicals, special starches, adhesives, fragrances and flavours has long been managed on a global basis.

Toilet soap output has also been rationalised. From 13 in 1973, the number of factories in Europe next year will be down to three with a finishing plant in Portugal. In the US, a factory at

Hammond, Indiana, will turn out 100,000 tonnes of bar soap a year when a current extension scheme is complete in 1990. Four US detergent plants make 1.1bn tonnes of powder and liquids a year and the number of work hours per tonne has been cut from 4.7 in 1983 to 3.1 last year; a further 10 per cent reduction is planned.

Similarly, oil refining for the core margarine business lends itself to focused operations. Four main plants crush 25 per cent of the European rape and sunflower seed crops. But although each group accounts for about 30 per cent of global margarine production and 50 per cent in Europe, each country or region has its own expensive manufacturing and packaging plants. In Europe, with 14 factories each trying to work at full capacity, there have been unsuccessful attempts at co-operation.

By its nature, batch processing (commonly used in personal products and especially in food), as opposed to continuous operations (in chemicals and detergents), offers reduced scale economies from focused manufacture. Costs

of distribution and stock holding also weigh heavily.

Distribution costs are relatively low with high-value, low-weight products like personal products, so the savings on focused manufacture are reduced accordingly. Production accounts for only 7 per cent of total costs in this sector, compared with marketing's 30 per cent.

As things stand, the group is making the most of its bulk-buying power for raw materials, food ingredients, packaging and equipment. There may also be strategic shufflings in the toothpaste business, which logically belongs in the detergents business. Proctor and Colgate have already centralised European output of dispenser dentifrice which demands costly equipment.

Reducing costs is essential for survival. But Unilever insists that long term success will go to the company which sticks closest to its customers. There are no prizes for producing at lowest cost if the products are not bought by customers in the many fragmented markets in the world today.

The Financial Times. 16.1.89

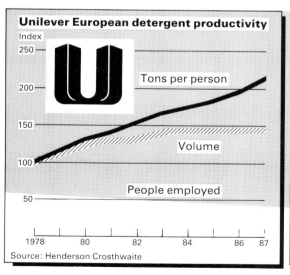

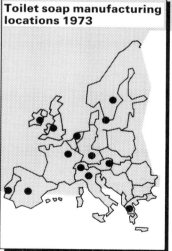

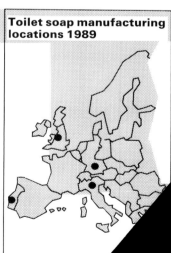

1 Outline the scope for achieving economies of scale in the different parts of Unilever's business.

2 To what extent should Unilever centra[lise] its global business?

curve of a firm is not U-shaped but L-shaped, as in Fig. 23.2. Large firms are able to maintain constant average costs at very large units of production. Firms which do suffer diseconomies of scale due to poor management are taken over by more efficient firms or go bankrupt. If they are taken over, and the takeover is successful, the firm's average cost curve will revert to its normal L–shape. However, this process may need time to take effect. Therefore, a U–shaped average cost curve may exist for a short period.

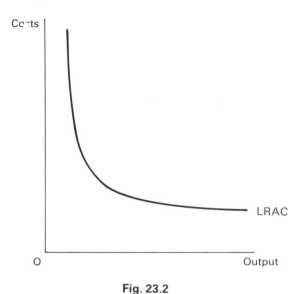

Fig. 23.2

External economies are experienced when economic growth in an area, or in an industry, results in a reduction in average costs for a firm. The building of a motorway near the site of the firm, or the growth of suppliers, are likely to result in ˡ economies of scale. External economies ˑ curve downwards since aver- ˡᵒᵛel of output.

worker. This is because some tasks need co-operation between workers. A third worker may add on even greater output than each of the first two. Eventually, a worker will be employed whose net addition to production is not as great as the previous worker. It is then likely that each additional worker will add less and less to production. Finally, if enough labour were taken on, production might start to decline as workers get in each others way. Note that we have assumed that we are changing one factor of production whilst keeping all others constant.

This is an example of the law of diminishing returns: the gradual addition of units of one factor of production to a fixed quantity of other factors of production will eventually lead to a decline in marginal, average and total product. In Table 23.4, the process just described is put into figures. Land and capital are kept constant. The amount that each man produces is known as the 'marginal product'. Remember here that 'marginal' means the addition to the total by the last unit of a factor. The first man employed produces 5 units. So the total product of the factory is 5 and production per man or 'average product' is 5 also. The second man employed produces an extra 13 units—his marginal product is 13. Total product is therefore 18, and average product is 9.

Table 23.4

Land and Capital	Labour Employed	Total Product	Marginal Product (i.e. addition to production by each unit of labour)	Average Product
Constant	1	5	5	5
	2	18	13	9
	3	30	12	10
	4	36	6	9
	5	35	−1	7

This is graphed in Fig. 23.3. Diminishing marginal returns set in at a total production level of 14 units. Diminishing average returns set in a little later at a total product of 30 units. Diminishing total product sets in at a production level of 37 where five units of the factor are employed. Two points should be noted here which are mathematically true. Firstly, the marginal product reached a peak before the average product. Secondly, the marginal product curve cuts the average product curve at its highest point.

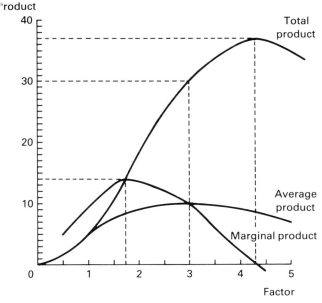

Fig. 23.3

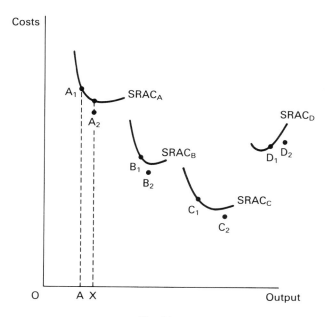

Fig. 23.4

Returning now to the relationship between short and long run costs, consider Fig. 23.4. Assume that a firm invests in plant and machinery. It decides beforehand that it wants to produce OA of output. Therefore it invests in such a manner that the costs of producing OA will be at a minimum. Having made the investment, orders increase to OX. In the short run, the firm can not change its fixed factors of production. Therefore it will have to increase the use of its variable factors of production if it is to meet the increased orders. The average cost of producing OX in the short run will be greater than if it could change all its factors of production. The fixed element represents inflexibility and therefore greater average costs than a totally free situation. So the short run average cost of producing OX is likely to be greater than XA_2, where XA_2 represents the cost of producing OX if all factors of production could be varied. This does not mean to say that the short run average cost of producing OX must be greater than that of producing OA. On the contrary, it is likely that the firm will experience reductions in cost. The short run average cost curve going through the point A_1 is likely to decline. But average cost could have been even lower if all factors of production could have been varied instead of only some. The short run average cost curve is bound to be U-shaped because eventually diminishing average returns will set in. This will cause the short run average cost curve to start to rise. In Fig. 23.4, points A_1, B_1, C_1, D_1 represent points where firms have certain fixed costs. In the

short run, they can increase or decrease production as shown along the associated short run average cost curves. But the long run cost of producing at anywhere except the original optimal point will be lower than the short run cost.

Thus for every point along the long run average cost curve, there is an associated short run average cost curve. But, the long run curve envelopes all of these as in Fig. 23.5.

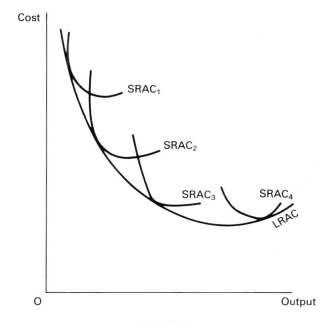

Fig. 23.5

227

The marginalist controversy

Factors of production, total and average costs, economies of scale, and the law of diminishing returns are all standard concepts in economics. Thus the theory of costs is a fairly non-controversial area. There is one exception to this, and that is the concept of marginal cost.

It is very important to realise at the start, that marginal cost can be derived from total and average costs. There is a precise mathematical relationship between them. So, where total costs exist, so do marginal costs. Marginal cost is simply a different way of looking at cost. Diagrammatically, a U–shaped average cost curve determines the shape of the total cost curves and the marginal cost curve. This family of curves, derived mathematically from the average total cost curve, is shown in Fig. 23.6. Note the presence of turning points, and the fact that the marginal cost curve cuts both the average variable cost curve and the average total cost curve at their lowest points.

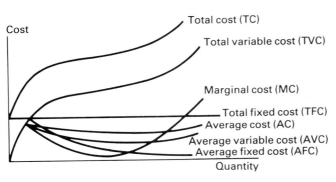

Fig. 23.6

Neo-classical economists use marginal concepts as the basis of their theory of the firm. They do **not** argue that businessmen necessarily use marginal concepts. What they **do** argue is that businessmen act in a way which supports the predictions of marginalist neo-classical theory.

Neo-Keynesians and managerial economists on the other hand argue that economic theory should mirror what really goes on in the boardrooms of companies. The concepts that businessmen use should be the concepts which appear in theory textbooks. Moreover, theories which use this 'artificial' concept of marginal cost fail to explain the workings of the firm in a modern economy. The marginalist controversy will be developed more fully in the following chapters.

Profit

Profit is the difference between the money a firm receives for selling its goods—its **revenue**—and the amount a firm has to pay out to produce—its **costs**. Profit is earned by the owners of capital who undertake risk.

Earlier in this chapter it was pointed out that economic cost includes an allowance for:

1 risk;
2 opportunity cost: in this case the money that could have been earned on the best riskless alternative investment, such as government stock.

These two components of costs are the **normal profit** earned on the capital employed by the firm. Another way of defining normal profit is that it is the minimum profit needed to prevent the owners of capital switching it to its next best use. **Abnormal profit** is any profit earned over and above normal profit.

Normal profit is included as an economic cost. If revenue is greater than cost, abnormal profit must be earned. Note that in the real world, cost does not include any allowance for normal profit, i.e. cost is accounting cost and not economic cost.

Summary

An economist defines cost as opportunity cost. Imputed costs, such as risk, must be included in costs of production. In the short run, some costs are fixed (i.e. they do not vary with output) and some are variable (i.e. do vary with output). In the long run all costs are variable. Economists distinguish between total cost, average cost and marginal cost. Economies of scale are said to exist where long run average costs are declining. Sources of internal economies include technical economies, managerial economies, financial economies, marketing economies and indivisibilities. The long run average cost curve envelops the corresponding short run average cost curves.

Terms for review

cost

short run and long run

total, average and marginal costs

economies and diseconomies of scale

increasing, constant and decreasing returns
to scale

internal and external economies

diminishing returns

marginal product

revenue

normal and abnormal profit

Essay questions

1 Distinguish between the 'short run' and the 'long run'
in the neo-classical theory of the firm. What is the
relationship between short run and long run average
cost curves?

2 What is meant by an external economy? How would
the building of a motorway affect the costs of production
of firms in its vicinity?

3 What do economists understand by the term 'cost'?
What costs of production would face the owner of a local
shop?

24

The goals of firms

Introduction

In order to understand how any organisation works, we must understand its goals. A firm is a complex organisation. At its simplest, one person owns it and works for it. However, it will interact with a great many other economic agents—consumers, other workers, other firms, and governments for instance. Some firms are so large and complex that they produce more than the entire output of many a developing country. In this chapter, we will consider competing theories of the goals of firms.

Short run profit maximisation

Neo-classical economists argue that firms aim to maximise their profits in the short run. Profit is the return on capital, just as wages are the return on labour. Neo-classical theory argues that the owners of capital want to gain the highest possible return from that capital. Just as a consumer would prefer to have more rather than less of a good, so a capitalist would prefer to have a greater rather than lesser income from the deployment of his capital.

The short run for a firm may vary considerably if measured in years. For a firm with very little fixed capital, the short run could be a period of just a few months. However, a large multinational corporation may see the short run extending into tens of years. A

large investment in plant and machinery running into hundreds or perhaps thousands of millions of pounds is unlikely to be scrapped except in the face of very bad trading conditions.

If a firm is short run profit maximising, by definition it will have some fixed costs and some variable costs. If its total costs are less than total revenue, then it will produce at a profit. However, neo-classical theory argues that even if the firm operates at a loss (i.e. total costs are greater than total revenue) it may still continue to produce. If the firm is to remain in existence it must pay its fixed costs whether it produces or not. Therefore if its total revenue is greater than its total variable cost, it will make some return to offset its fixed costs.

This is illustrated in Table 24.1.

In period 1, the firm makes a profit of £10 000. In period 2, it makes no profit at all. But if alternatively it did not produce in period 2 it would lose £10 000—the value of its fixed costs which it has to pay to stay solvent. In period 3, it loses £5 000 by producing. The alternative is a £10 000 loss if it produces nothing. Similarly, in period 4, a £2 000 production loss is better than the alternative £10 000 loss resulting from non-production.

Thus short run profit maximisation implies that firms will produce and sell even if the price they obtain does not cover the total cost of production. They will produce so long as total revenue is greater than variable costs (the costs which they incur directly as a result of their decision to produce rather than not produce in short run).

Table 24.1

Period	Total fixed cost	Total variable cost	Total cost	Total revenue	Profit or Loss — If it does produce	If it does not produce
1	10 000	20 000	30 000	40 000	+10 000	——
2	10 000	20 000	30 000	30 000	0	−10 000
3	10 000	20 000	30 000	25 000	− 5 000	−10 000
4	10 000	20 000	30 000	28 000	− 2 000	−10 000

Data 24.1

Paper makers recoil from a pasting

Britain's paper and board makers have been hanging on grimly since recession began to bite in 1980. The latest spate of redundancy announcements shows that the market remains weak, but there are signs of emerging strength.

At Bowater, UK demand recently has risen an estimated 5 to 10 per cent. But the group, which now has much larger U.S. interests, would like a bigger jump in demand.

With profits suffering from the weak U.S. newsprint market, Bowater has been badly affected by soft demand in the UK. Dr Ingram Lenton, managing director, believes that past rationalisation, including some machine closures in 1982, will help its UK operation this year. But he sees no solid improvements in the market this year "until very, very late."

At Hoare Govett, the London stock brokers, analyst Mr Peter Large estimates that Bowater lost as much as £10m on UK papermaking last year, though much of this reflected redundancy costs.

Thames Board has lost £8.7m over five years on its waste paper-based packing board operation at Warrington, Cheshire. Capacity is 145,000 tonnes a year, but falling demand meant output last year was little over 100,000 tonnes.

Wiggins Teape sweetened its move out of the packaging paper sector with sinking of £9m into fine papers. In the first half of last year it made a near £3m trading loss in the UK, against foreign profits of nearly £20m.

Mr Alex Halliday, chief executive of Wiggins Teape, does not think this year will be better than last. But UK losses are not worsening.

The Financial Times. January, 1983

1 *For what possible reasons have British paper and board makers continued to remain in operation despite making losses?*

Long run profit maximisation

Neo-Keynesian economists agree with the neo-classical hypothesis that firms aid to maximise profits. However, they argue that firms are long run profit maximisers rather than short run profit maximisers.

At the heart of their argument is the belief that firms fix prices by calculating cost and then adding a standard profit margin to it. For instance, assume that the standard profit margin in supermarkets on tinned food is 5%. In this case a large supermarket chain will calculate the price at which to sell tinned food by adding together all its costs and adding 5%. If it finds it difficult to sell a particular line of food, it will not immediately engage in price cutting. Rather it will sell the batch over a longer period of time than expected and not reorder stocks. Equally, it is unlikely that it will continue to stock that brand since it failed to return 5% over the correct period of time.

This example illustrates that firms using **cost plus pricing** techniques are far more likely to change output levels than price levels in the short run. If a firm is unable to cover both fixed and variable costs, it will prefer not to sell rather than indulge in price cutting exercises. An important argument in favour of this is that constant changes in price, resulting from responses to short term demand conditions, damage the market for the firm. It can make higher profits in the long term by keeping prices steady and adjusting output, than by constantly changing prices and introducing uncertainty into the market. This may mean that in the short term it incurs higher losses than if it were to produce and sell.

Managerial theories

Profit maximisation assumes that businesses are aiming to make the greatest profit possible. This may seem common sense if the people who run firms are also the people who stand to gain from higher profits, i.e. the owners. But industry does not correspond to this model. Although there are a very large

Data 24.2

Shareholders? Who needs them!

Clive Wolman

NEVER SINCE the rise of British managerial capitalism has so much deference – and power – been accorded to the ordinary shareholder. In the 1970s, militant trade unions and mediocre managers led to a slump in profitability and the value of his holdings. Both groups have now been routed, not least thanks to the boom in hostile takeover bids launched in the name of shareholder rights. The proportion of national income now going in profits to shareholders is one of the highest in the world.

It is mandatory for the 1980s-style company chief executive to sprinkle all his public pronouncements with phrases like "serving the interests of our shareholders" or "maximising shareholder wealth." But the biggest economic success story of the 1980s is to be found at the other end of the Eurasian land mass, in Japan. Yet there are few places in the world where shareholders count for less.

Japanese companies pay a tiny proportion of their cash generated in dividends. Independent non-executive directors representing outside shareholders are almost unheard-of. And any shareholder who becomes too large and aggressive will have his holding bought out or diluted away.

What drives the relentless search of these companies for defect-free production, product enhancement and market share? The most revealing answer was given recently by Hiroshi Okuda, Toyota's finance director, when asked why Toyota's cash could not be distributed to its shareholders: "Our members (i.e. employees) would go on strike."

As all the opinion polls show, the Japanese believe that enterprises belong primarily to their work force, that managers serve as their custodians, and that shareholders rank well behind. When top managers are dismissed, the responsibility more often lies with the employees than the shareholders. Few Japanese companies have employee share schemes because share ownership is superfluous.

These differences mean that Japanese companies put more emphasis on sales and market share than profits. But such pressures do not appear to have forced most Japanese companies to pursue profitless growth. Since 1950, shareholders in Japanese companies have achieved far higher returns than anywhere else in spite of their lowly status – or perhaps because of it.

What is clear is that the Japanese have been better off without elevating the anonymous shareholder to the status of ultimate beneficiary of all corporate endeavour.

The Financial Times. 8.4.89

1 To what extent (a) do and (b) should firms be controlled by their shareholders?

number of firms where owners and managers are the same people, they tend to be very small and produce a fairly small proportion of national output. In the United Kingdom, it is currently estimated that the top 100 manufacturing companies produce 40% of the total output in the manufacturing sector of the economy. Hence most markets in an industrial economy are dominated by large companies, called public limited companies (**plc**) in the UK and corporations in the USA.

In a plc, ownership and control are arguably divorced. A large number of shareholders, each having a small proportion of the shares, elect directors to look after their interests. However, directors leave the day-to-day running of the firm to salaried managers. It is most unusual for shareholders to elect directors critical of existing directors. Equally it is most unusual for directors to sack their managers. One conclusion that can be drawn is that shareholders (the owners of the firm) have little influence over managers (the people who run the firm). Therefore managers can sometimes safely pursue policies not necessarily in the best interests of the shareholders.

Economists who argue that managers' interests are paramount in explaining a firm's decision taking, differ over what those interests are. An early theory by William Baumol suggested that managers attempt to maximise the sales of a company. This is because firms with large sales are more likely to pay their managers high salaries than firms with small sales. Other economists have put forward more complicated models. Williamson suggested that managers have a utility function which they attempt to maximise. This would include salary, size of workforce directed by the manager, the amount of money under his or her control, and the number of perks, such as company cars, that the manager receives.

Most managerial models recognise that managers are subject to constraints. They will not for instance run their firms permanently at a loss as they would lose their jobs in the resulting bankruptcy. Indeed, they need to make a minimum level of profit because, even if shareholders accept low profits, other firms may intervene by attempting to take over the firm. Firms with poor profitability tend to have low share prices as well. By 'low', we mean that the market value of the firm is below the true value of all the assets of that firm. For instance, a firm may have a quoted share value of £30 million. However, the total value of the assets of that firm, such as buildings, machinery, stocks and customer 'goodwill' may be £40 million. Obviously anyone who takes over such a firm at its quoted share value is getting a bargain. The likely fate of some managers after take-over is the sack. Hence it is in the best interest of managers to make their company sufficiently profitable to avoid attracting the attention of other companies who are looking for existing firms to buy.

High profitability is likely to lead to increased expansion of the firm and therefore better promotion prospects and higher pay for its managers. However, making a profit which satisfies the interests of managers (**profit satisficing**) is unlikely to be the level of profits which maximises the reward to capital (profit maximising).

A shareholder's meeting. Can these shareholders exercise any control over the company which they own?

Behavioural theories

A large firm is a complex organisation embracing many interest groups. Typically, owners want to see their return to capital maximised. Managers seek to pursue policies in their own best interest. Other workers, probably through trade unions, want their reward for labour to be maximised. The firm's bankers prefer security to high risk investment. The Government may try to get the firm to export or invest more, or move to unemployment black spots. The local environmental group may be trying to get the firm to reduce the level of pollutants it releases into the atmosphere. Different groups have different powers within a firm. Managers might have most power, followed by workers and owners. However, no one group has a monopoly on decision-making. Decisions are the result of a bargaining process between all the interest groups concerned. Hence different decisions will be arrived at according to who can manipulate the decision-making process to best advantage.

Behavioural theory, then, argues that firms try to satisfy the interests of all groups both inside and outside the firm. Because only some groups are interested in maximising profits, it is unlikely that the firm will profit maximise. Rather it will profit satisfice—i.e. make a level of profits which will prove satisfactory to those concerned with profits.

Behavioural theory is relatively new. The strength of its challenge to existing theory can be judged by the fact that one of the economists who pioneered this approach, Professor Herbert Simon, won the Nobel Prize for Economics in 1978.

Summary

In order to understand how a firm operates, it is essential to understand its goals. Neo-classical economists argue that a firm attempts to maximise its short run profit. One result is that it will produce at a loss in the short run so long as its average revenue covers its average variable cost. Neo-Keynesians argue that the commonest method of pricing found in industry is cost plus pricing. This leads to long run profit maximising as a goal. Managerial theories emphasise the separation of control and ownership in firms. These theories argue that because managers run the large modern firm, they are able to operate the company in such a way as to maximise their own utility. This leads to profit satisficing rather than profit maximising. Behavioural models argue that decisions are taken within firms according to the bargaining power of competing interest groups, each out to maximise its own utility.

Terms for review

goals of firms

public limited companies

short run and long run profit maximisation

behavioural theories

managerial theories

profit satisficing

Essay questions

1 What is meant by 'profit maximisation'? Do large firms necessarily have the same goals as small firms?

2 In what circumstances would a firm continue to produce even if it were unable to cover its total costs?

25

The firm and its industry

Introduction

A firm works within an industry. What constitutes an industry is difficult to define precisely. For instance, the motor industry is obviously made up of car and commercial vehicle manufacturers. But should manufacturers of farm tractors, fork-lift trucks, gear boxes, tyres and glass windscreens also be included? Equally, is rail transport an industry on its own or is it part of a bigger transport industry, including road, sea and air transport? In order to make sense of our economy, economic statisticians eventually have to make decisions on these questions. All industries contain cases where the decision is open to dispute. But classification is necessary if we are to make sense of raw data.

In this chapter, we will consider ways in which a firm operates within its own industry.

The number of firms in an industry

The number of firms within an industry is important because the behaviour of these firms may well differ according to the degree of competition they face. An industry may consist of a large number of small producers. On the other hand, it may consist of a few large producers. A situation where most of the output of an industry is in the hands of a few firms is known as an **oligopoly**. A situation where one firm dominates the industry is known as a **monopoly**.

The number of firms in an industry gives little indication of power within that industry. An industry with 100 firms each producing 1% of the market is very different from a 100 firm industry where three firms account for 90% of the market. The latter, despite the fact that there are 100 firms in the industry, would be classified as oligopolistic because of the importance of the three major firms. In theory a monopoly exists where there is only one firm in an industry; however, in practice an industry of,

say, 100 firms, in which one firm produced 90% of the market output, would also be regarded as a monopoly by economists.

The behaviour of firms in an industry is likely to be conditioned not only by the number of firms and their relative size but also by the number of possible new entrants into the industry. A monopolist may react very differently if it thought other firms were considering entering the industry than if its monopoly were totally secure from outside predator firms.

Product characteristics of the industry

In some industries a firm is unable to make its goods distinctive from other firms' products. Take agriculture as an example: one farmer's beetroots are pretty much the same as another's. Certainly, consumers do not ask for Farmer Brown's beetroots rather than Farmer Smith's. In contrast, they do demand one type of tinned baked beans rather than another. Beetroots are an example of a homogeneous product—that is, one in which goods are effectively identical. Tinned baked beans are an example of a non-homogeneous product—that is, goods which are differentiated. Non-homogeneous products are branded goods. Sometimes, firms give names for their brands such as 'Omo', 'Persil', 'Daz', 'Ariel'. In other cases, the firm's name is a brand name—an IBM computer, or a Pan Am air flight, for instance.

In general, branded goods are an advantage to an individual firm. There is no consumer loyalty to Farmer Brown's beetroots. On the other hand, a consumer may well continue to fly Pan Am out of habit, despite the fact that a rival airline might provide an identical air service at a slightly cheaper price. For this reason, individual non-homogeneous products tend to have a lower price elasticity of demand than homogeneous goods. Customers are more likely to go on buying branded products, despite price rises, than unbranded products.

Firms can also be split into two categories—one-product firms and multi-product firms. A product here should not be defined too narrowly. For instance, a product may well be kitchen furniture, or cereal crops. Examples of multi-product firms might be farms which both grow crops and keep livestock, or firms which make kitchen furniture and washing machines.

Multi-product firms may behave differently from one-product firms for two reasons. Firstly, multi-product firms may find it impossible to allocate costs accurately between different products. For instance, how does a farmer allocate his telephone bill between his cereal crops and his beef cattle? Hence the prices of products may differ according to how costs have been allocated. Secondly, a multi-product firm may wish deliberately to distort prices. It may decide for a variety of reasons to cross-subsidise—that is, to charge a higher price for product A than it would if it were a one-product firm, in order to enable it to lower its price on product B. It may thus gain a greater share of a market, drive out potential rivals, or avoid taxes, and so on.

To what extent are oranges homogeneous?

From branches all over Israel
Jaffa Navels will be arriving soon by ship. So clear the decks. **Jaffa**

Data 25.1

Why Gateway believes it is leading a retail revolution

Maggie Urry

Gateway, the UK supermarket chain, is well known to be suffering from many problems. But in one area it is claiming a success – that of its "exclusive brands".

These brands sell under a variety of names and are available only in Gateway stores; they have been developed by Gateway together with its suppliers and are the company's alternative to the own-label ranges of other supermarkets.

"We believe we have initiated a marketing success story," Bob Willett, marketing director at Gateway, boasted at a recent conference held by Super Marketing, the trade journal.

Willet admits that the decision to go for exclusive brands was in part prompted by one of the chain's weaknesses. Since Gateway was the product of the merger of a number of chains – culminating in the acquisition of Fine Fare in 1986 – the Gateway name did not have a strong national image.

"Gateway was trading with an indistinct image," he says and since "own label is sold on the back of the retailer's name and its positioning in the high street," that was a distinct disadvantage.

So Gateway decided to turn "exclusives" to its advantage. Willett explains: "Starting from scratch with an indistinct image, we have had to move quickly to establish exclusive brands as a major marketing tool." Work began in the late summer of 1986.

By 1990 Gateway plans to have 2,500 lines covered by 80 brand names. They will, he expects, be generating turnover at an annual rate of £1bn – 30 per cent of Gateway's grocery takings – by the end of the 1989–90 financial year. By the end of this year there will be 1,000 exclusive lines in Gateway stores.

Each brand takes six to nine months to develop. So far it has mainly been a question of taking an existing product

and developing a brand. The next, and more exciting, stage is developing new products – a phase which Gateway is now entering.

Gateway's exclusive brands include Bella for its pasta range, Men for men's toiletries, You for women's toiletries, Good Morning for breakfast cereals, Kind and Gentle for baby products, and Supreme for fruit drinks and juices.

Typically the package carries a sentence saying that the product has been developed with a major manufacturer for Gateway, and Willet says customers do not find the idea confusing.

The group has supported its brands with press advertising. For example £250,000 was spent on the launch of both the Bella pasta and Kind and Gentle brands. Once launched, each brand has to "stand on its own two feet," Willett says, and to justify its shelf space in the same way as any other brand.

Willet says that the exclusive brands are of vital importance to the future growth of Gateway. He argues: "In every market segment where exclusives have been introduced, we have consistently increased our market share."

He also believes that exclusive brands offer much more flexibility than own-label. "With own-label we would be restricted by the ability to develop only at one level – that which reflects consumer perception of us as a retailing group. With exclusives we have the flexibility to attack the market on different levels."

Gateway can offer products through the vertical range – premium, mid-range and economy. The positions are backed up by the style of packaging – impossible with the old-style Fine Fare "yellow packs" where each product was wrapped in the same, bright colour.

Gateway cannot move to being an entirely exclusive brand store – customers want to find manufacturers' brands available as well. But Willett believes the exclusive brands are helping to build both an image for the chain and customer loyalty. And – if imitation is the sincerest form of flattery – Willet says he can detect retailers moving towards the exclusive brand approach. Own-label, he claims, is declining overall; with exclusives "we are well-placed at the start of a retail revolution."

The Financial Times. 3.11.88

1 *How is Gateway attempting to make the products it sells less homogenous?*

2 *Why is it adopting this retailing strategy?*

Barriers to entry and exit

Many people dream of owning a small store or pub rather than being tied down to a nine-to-five job. For some, their dreams come true and they enter the retailing industry. A surprisingly large number, a few years later, leave the retailing industry, having failed to make a success of their venture. Far fewer people dream of opening up a new firm to mass-produce family cars or to make engines for aircraft. Recent UK experience also shows that it is very difficult for mass-producers of cars (e.g. British Leyland) or jet engine manufacturers (e.g. Rolls Royce) to go bankrupt and leave their industries.

There are a number of reasons why it is far more difficult to set up in some industries than others. High **barriers to entry** to an industry exist in the following cases:

1 Where the cost of setting up in business is prohibitive. The average person may realistically dream of one day owning a small local shop. He would be unrealistic if he dreamt of owning a modern chemical complex costing several hundred millions of pounds to build. Because manufacturing industry is more highly capitalised than service industries, barriers to entry tend to be greater in manufacturing industry than in the service industries.

2 Legal barriers may prevent new entrants. Monopoly state-owned industries are often protected by laws which prevent private firms setting up in competition. Patents and copyright laws too can prevent other firms from selling products of an original nature.

3 The ownership of the means of production in an industry will obviously prevent new firms entering the industry. For instance, if the existing firms in a mining industry owned all existing mines and land on which potential mines could be sunk, then it would be impossible for a new firm to enter the industry. Equally, entry would be difficult if existing firms could always produce at a lower cost than the new entrant.

4 Existing firms in the industry may have greater marketing power over their industry. In the detergent industry in both the UK and the USA, the few large firms in the industry advertise so heavily that it is very difficult for other firms to break into the market with a new product. A national launch of a

What are the main barriers to entry to the detergent industry in the UK?

new soap bar in the UK will cost a main manufacturer millions of pounds. Equally existing firms in the industry may be prepared to use their marketing powers to drive out new entrants. It may well pay an existing producer to lower prices and make losses in the short term in order to bankrupt a new entrant who, if allowed to survive, would provide strong competition in the longer term.

Barriers to exit exist too. Firms, or parts of firms, may be prevented from leaving an industry for the following reasons:

1 Governments may consider that it would not be in the national interest. The firm may be producing vital defence equipment, or be a large exporter or a large employer.

2 Financial markets may malfunction. A firm's bankers or shareholders may mistakenly allow a firm to continue trading although it is unlikely to return to reasonable profitability. Equally, other firms which could be interested in taking over that firm may be less than fully efficient themselves and may ignore the opportunity.

Data 25.2

Black cabs win battle

Rachel Johnson

LONDON'S CABBIES are crowing with joy following the surprising about-turn by Mr Michael Portillo, the Minister of State for Transport, who this month dropped proposals to shake up the cab trade.

Mr Portillo had made speeches making clear his strong views on the cab trade. It was a restrictive practice that limited the number of cabs on the roads and kept fares unnecessarily steep.

In central London, minicab drivers are not licensed and cannot ply for hire. Outside London, local authorities distort competition and the free market by rationing the issue of licences to minicab drivers.

Taxi drivers became convinced that Mr Portillo intended to scrap the "knowledge" – a three-year entry test into the trade over 468 London routes. The cabbies were furious.

Why should Mr Portillo change the system, they asked? Black cabs are strictly regulated by the Public Carriage Office, a self-financing branch of the Metropolitan Police. The PCO issues licences and checks cabs every three months. It carries out the "knowledge" test – which two thirds of applicants fail – and can order cabbies off the road for such minor infringements as driving with a dirty windscreen. Self-employed cabbies are responsible for buying taxis and keeping them in mint condition.

The Financial Times. 23.5.89

To what extent are barriers to entry to the London taxi-cab business high?

---

3 Workers may refuse to allow the firm to leave the industry. Workers' co-operatives may be set up, or other owners found through the mediation of the workforce. Workers, of course, are interested in the survival of their firm, since their jobs are at stake.

4 Consumers may object. In the UK, consumer groups have been responsible for re-opening several railways lines up and down the country which British Rail had closed as uneconomic.

Relationships between firms in an industry

If there is more than one firm in the industry, two relationship possibilities exist:

1 Firms may be **independent** of each other. This means that the actions of one firm have no significant impact on any other single firm in the industry. In an industry such as agriculture, adjoining farms are not in direct competition with each other. Each farmer is competing with all the firms in the industry. The result is that local farmers are normally fairly open about their business affairs. The fact that the farmer next door knows how many acres are being planted with such and such a crop, or which wholesaler a farmer sells his crop to, is not going to result in lower prices or worse crop yields.

2 If firms are **interdependent** in an industry the actions of one firm will have a direct impact on other individual firms in the industry. If there are just a few firms in the industry a change in quantity produced, or a change in price by one firm, will have an impact on the other firms. Methods of production, marketing strategies, research projects are all closely guarded secrets. In interdependent industries, large firms may sometimes be prepared to spend millions of pounds on industrial espionage—i.e. for information on how their rivals are likely to behave in the future.

Knowledge

Firms may face different conditions of knowledge in the market place. If there is complete or **perfect knowledge**, then a firm will have access to all the information needed to make its business decisions. It will be able to obtain information about the size of the market, the shape of the demand curve it faces, the various technologies available for production, and so on. Agriculture is a market which is often cited as having perfect knowledge. At relatively low cost, individual farmers can find out about the best production techniques, where markets are, etc. Note that perfect knowledge does not imply that all firms will have all information. Poorly run firms are likely to only have part of the information available. The price they pay for their inefficiency is that they are eventually driven out of the market. The farmer who uses outdated machinery and production techniques is likely eventually to go bankrupt.

If there is less than perfect knowledge, firms have to guess at the information which is not available. They may be able to guess on the basis of evidence. If this is the case, then some measure of probability can be given to the likelihood of something occurring. Businessmen's 'hunches' are assessments of probabilities. On the other hand, a firm may be faced with total uncertainty on some issues. It may have no idea whether a rival firm is or is not developing a new product, for instance.

Summary

A firm works within an industry. It may be the sole producer, in which case it is a monopolist. Or an oligopoly might exist, where a few large firms dominate output in an industry. Or there may be a large number of relatively small firms in that industry.

Each firm may produce an homogeneous product or a branded non-homogeneous product. The firm may produce only one product, or it may be a multi-product firm. Barriers to entry or exit may exist for an industry. The decisions of one firm in an industry may have no effect upon any other single firm in the industry. Alternatively, firms may be interdependent. Firms may have varying degrees of knowledge, ranging from perfect knowledge to total uncertainty.

Terms for review

oligopoly

monopoly

homogeneous and branded goods

multi-product firms

barriers to entry and exit

interdependence

perfect knowledge

Essay questions

1 What barriers to entry exist in (a) the retailing industry and (b) the steel industry? Do barriers to exit exist in any UK industries?

2 What would an economist understand by 'perfect knowledge'? To what extent do UK firms possess perfect knowledge?

26

The neo-classical theory of the firm

Introduction

The neo-classical theory of the firm was first developed in the second half of the nineteenth century. This was a time when markets were made up of large numbers of small producers, producing unbranded goods. In response to the gradual concentration of industry, neo-classical economists in this century have developed models concerned with firms producing branded goods.

All neo-classical theories assume that firms:

1 are short run profit maximisers;
2 possess perfect knowledge.

In Chapter 24, it was argued that the neo-classical assumption of short run profit maximisation implied that firms would produce as long as their total revenue exceeded total variable cost. In the short run, firms incur fixed costs. Any revenue gained over and above variable cost will help offset these fixed costs. Marginal cost (the change in total costs resulting from a change in the level of production by one unit) is the variable cost of producing an additional unit of output.

The assumption of short run profit maximisation leads to a very important and simple rule. Short run profit maximisation (or loss minimisation) is achieved where:

Marginal Cost (MC) = Marginal Revenue (MR)

Consider Fig. 26.1. The marginal cost of the 100th unit of output is £10. The marginal revenue (the change in revenue resulting from a change in the level of production by one unit) of the 100th unit is £30. So, the 100th unit contributes £20 towards offsetting the fixed costs of production. It would pay the firm to expand production further. The 200th unit contributes £8 (£20–£12) to offsetting fixed costs. Indeed, it would pay the firm to go on expanding output so long as marginal revenue were greater than marginal cost. In Fig. 26.1, this would mean

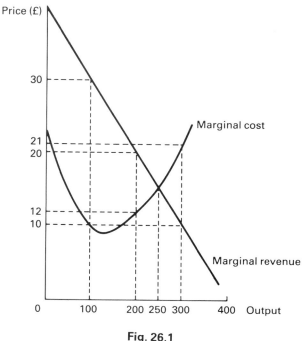

Fig. 26.1

expanding production to 250 units. If it expanded production to 300 units, it would not cover even its variable costs on the units between 251 and 300. On the 300th unit, for instance, the marginal cost is £21 whilst the marginal revenue is only £10.

Two important points must now be mentioned. Firstly, it will produce units up to **and including** the point where MC = MR. This is because cost includes an allowance for normal profit. So, although the last unit produced makes no contribution to offsetting fixed costs, it does contribute normal profit to the firm. Secondly, it is likely that marginal cost will exceed marginal revenue at low levels of output. This is shown in Fig. 26.2. At output levels below OA, the firm definitely makes a loss as MC is greater than MR and thus the firm does not even cover its variable costs. The firm will

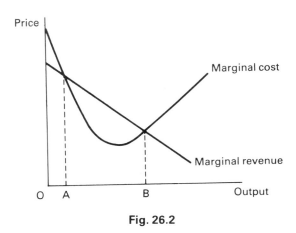

Fig. 26.2

not start to make abnormal profits until it has recouped in revenue both its fixed costs and the losses made on the units up to OA. This profit point must occur to the right of OA. Hence an output of OA (where MC = MR) is **not** a profit maximising point. A second condition to our MC = MR rule therefore needs to be made. A firm will maximise its profits where MC = MR and where MC is greater than MR for units of production over and above that level of output. In Fig. 26.2, this is true at OB, the profit maximising level of output, but not at OA, a loss-making level of output.

The theory of perfect competition

The theory assumes the following:

1 That there are sufficiently large numbers of firms in the industry for each to produce relatively small amounts.

2 That this ensures firms are independent, i.e. the actions of one firm do not have any impact on any other single firm in the industry.

3 That firms are producing homogeneous products.

4 That there are no barriers to entry into and exit from the industry.

Agriculture is an industry which could be argued to possess the characteristics of a perfectly competitive industry. In agriculture, a large number of firms each produce relatively small quantities of output, so that the actions of one farmer will have no impact on other firms in the industry. There are no real barriers to entry and exit, and the products produced such as beetroot or beef are arguably homogeneous. At relatively little cost farmers can obtain information about the best farming techniques, the best markets, etc., so that perfect knowledge could be said to prevail. Lastly, since most farmers farm their own land or rent it from landlords, there are relatively few firms where ownership and control can be said to be divorced. Hence, profit maximisation seems a reasonable goal of the firm. The question as to whether a farmer is a short run or long run profit maximiser is more difficult to settle.

The theory of perfect competition yields a number of very important conclusions.

(1) Firms are short run profit maximisers and therefore will produce where MC = MR. This has already been proved.

(2) In long-run equilibrium, no firm in the industry will make abnormal profits or make losses: that is, AC = AR. A firm can not go on making losses for ever, and so firms which are unprofitable will eventually leave the industry. If firms are making abnormal profits then, by definition, they are making a greater rate of return than on comparable investments in other assets. What will then happen is that new firms will enter the industry, attracted by the abnormal profits. This will result in more being supplied to the market at the same price: that is, the supply curve for the industry shifts downwards and to the right. If more is supplied to the market, prices will fall. New firms will continue to enter the industry and prices will continue to fall until such time as no abnormal profits can be made. If no abnormal profits are being made, this must mean that total revenue and total costs are equal for the firm. Equally this means that average revenue and average costs are identical

Hence, in equilibrium, AC = AR

(3) Each firm faces a perfectly elastic demand curve for its product and therefore is a 'price taker'. This is because there are a large number of firms in the industry, each producing very small amounts of homogeneous product. So if one individual firm decides to reduce or to increase its output, this will have virtually no effect on the total output supplied in the industry. Hence it will not affect the price received.

The vicious circle of the Britis

Alice Rawsthorn

Mr Turon Miah rents one of the tiny workshops on Brick Lane in the East End of London.

A year ago Mr Miah employed 15 machinists, all fellow Bangladeshi immigrants, to make leather jackets. But business is bad. The Pakistani wholesaler, with whom he deals, has started to import from India. Mr Miah has not been able to increase his prices for three years. Now he employs just eight people and the workshop is making a loss.

Mr Miah runs one of thousands of sweatshops that make up the "rag trade", or the squalid side of the fashion industry. During the 1980s, the rag trade has spread out of London into the back streets of the North and the Midlands. The British Clothing Industry Association estimates that the sweatshops provided a tenth of the industry's £4.5bn output last year.

The number of clothing companies in East London has increased from 10,000 to 30,000 since 1980, according to the National Union of Tailor and Garment Workers. The West Midlands industry has multiplied from 5,000 to 25,000. Many of these new companies conform to the sweatshop stereotype. And, although the sweatshops may have increased in number, there has been no corresponding improvement in profitability. Most, like Mr Miah's workshop, still struggle to scrape a living.

One of the principal problems is the fragmented structure of the rag trade. Since a workshop does not deal directly with the retailer, it is at the mercy of the wholesalers, which shop around for the cheapest merchandise. Many workshops accept some orders at a loss simply to stay in business.

Ken Shirt, who works for the Tower Hamlets Small Business Centre, describes the cost structure of a typical

tr
for
£23.

The
costing a
turer is exp
like zips and
on labour a
pocketing a pro

The rag trade is
be no new influx of
the place of the Asians
onwards and upwards
Lane. Plump pay packets
tages may chase the sweat
Mrs Thatcher's sunrise Sout
as long as there are depressed
Britain, the rag trade and wor
like Mr Miah's will survive.

The Financial Times. 19.11.8

1 To what extent can the 'rag trade' be said to be a perfectly competitive industry?

This is illustrated in Fig. 26.3, which shows the output for a) a single firm and b) for the market as a whole. The single firm initially produces 10 000 units for which it receives a price of 75p per unit. It decides to double its production to 20 000 units. This has the effect of shifting the supply curve to the right. But the shift is so small that the price remains unchanged at 75p. In our example, the increase in quantity supplied to the market represents 0.05% (10 000 on 20 million) on the original quantity. If all

firms in the industry doubled their production at the same time, there would be a large shift in supply, resulting in a fall in price. But the output decisions of any single firm will have no impact on the price it gets for its product.

To say that a firm is a 'price taker' means that it has no influence on the price it can charge for its product. This is due to the fact that it faces a perfectly elastic demand curve. It can of course charge a lower price than the market price, but

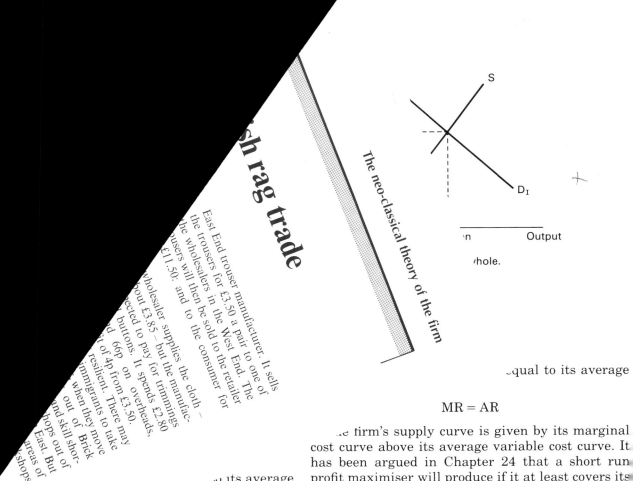

The neo-classical theory of the firm

East End trouser manufacturer. It sells
the trousers for £3.50 a pair to one of
the wholesalers in the West End. The
...users will then be sold to the retailer
£11.50: and to the consumer for

...holesaler supplies the cloth –
...bout £3.85 – but the manufac-
...ected to pay for trimmings
...buttons. It spends £2.80
...d 66p on overheads,
...t of 4p from £3.50.
...resilient. There may
...immigrants to take
...when they move
out of Brick
...and skill shor-
...hops out of
East. But
...areas of
...hops

...ɔ its average
... In Fig. 26.3, the
...n was perfectly elastic at a
...ce the average price or average
...ceived was 75p. If the firm sells an
...ional unit, it will receive the same price, 75p.

_qual to its average

$$MR = AR$$

..e firm's supply curve is given by its marginal
cost curve above its average variable cost curve. It
has been argued in Chapter 24 that a short run
profit maximiser will produce if it at least covers its
variable costs. When deciding at which price it is
willing to sell output, a firm will look at its marginal
cost data. It makes no sense for a firm to produce an
additional unit at a cost of say £1 when it will only
receive 50p for it. Hence marginal cost represents

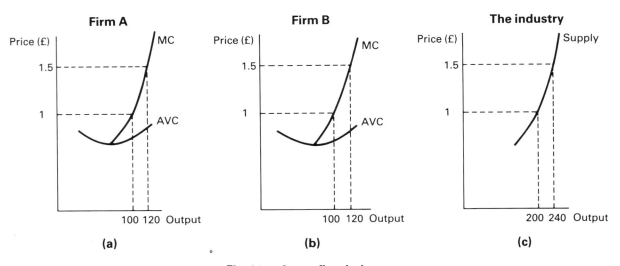

Fig. 26.4 A two firm industry

the minimum price a firm is willing to receive for an additional unit of product. In other words, marginal cost represents the supply curve for the firm. Putting these two arguments together, a firm's supply curve is its marginal cost curve above its average variable cost curve.

6 The supply curve for the industry can be found by summing horizontally the supply curve for each individual firm in the industry. If there are 100 firms in the industry, each prepared to produce 10 000 units at £1 each, then the industry as a whole will be prepared to sell 1 000 000 units at £1. Hence at any given price the market quantity supplied can be found by adding up the quantity supplied from each firm. It is called horizontal summing because one is adding quantity together, but not price.

Figure 26.4 illustrates horizontal summing for an industry of two firms. At a price of £1 each firm produces 100 units. So the supply of the industry at £1 is 200 units. At a price of £1.50 each firm is willing to supply 120 units. Therefore total supply for the industry is 240 units.

Many of the above points can be presented diagrammatically. In Figs. 26.5 and 26.6 short run disequilibrium exists in the market. The firm produces where $MC=MR$, and the short run equilibrium output is Q_E. At output Q_E in Fig. 26.5, AR is greater than AC. Hence in the short run the firm will earn abnormal profit; new firms will be attracted to the industry and prices will fall. At output Q_E in Fig. 26.6, AC is greater than AR. Hence the firm will be making a loss in the short run; firms will leave the industry as a result, allowing prices to rise. Figure 26.7 represents the long run equilibrium position as $AC=AR$ at the point of production. Note that this means that in the long run the firm produces at its optimum level, where optimum is defined as lowest average cost production.

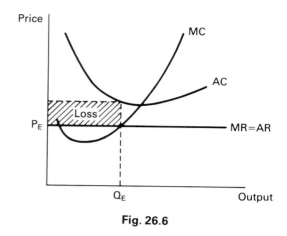

Fig. 26.6

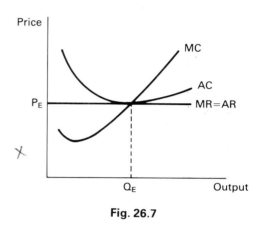

Fig. 26.7

Theories of imperfect competition

The theory of **monopolistic competition** was developed by E. H. Chamberlain in the 1930s. He argued that branded rather than homogeneous goods were produced in many industries. He then developed a model of the firm which used the assumptions of perfect competition, apart from this assumption of branded goods.

The implications of the theory are:

1 Output will be determined where $MC = MR$, due to profit maximisation.

2 In equilibrium $AC = AR$, i.e. no abnormal profits are being made. This is because there is freedom of entry to and exit from the industry.

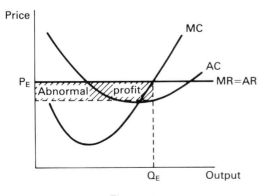

Fig. 26.5

The neo-classical theory of the firm

3 Firms face a downward sloping demand curve. This is because they produce branded goods. With branded goods, there is a certain amount of consumer loyalty to the product. Consumers will continue to buy the product even if it goes up in price relative to similar branded goods. However, they will buy less if there is such a price rise. The degree of consumer loyalty will also be fairly weak due to the large number of competitors in the industry. This means that the price elasticity of demand for the branded product will be relatively high.

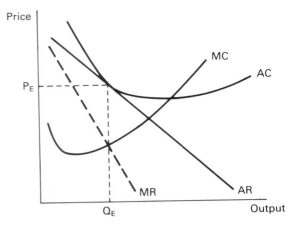

Fig. 26.8

Do these firms operate in a monopolistically competitive industry?

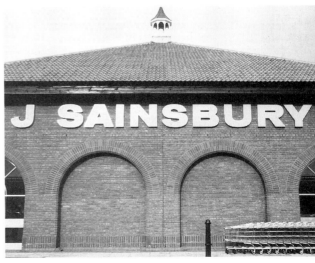

246

Diagrammatically, this is represented in Fig. 26.8. The firm will produce at its profit maximisation point Q_E, where MC = MR. It will price on the demand curve facing the firm, which is also its average revenue curve. Hence at output Q_E it will price at P_E. The diagram shows a position of equilibrium for the firm since AC = AR, i.e. no abnormal profits are being made. The AC curve must be tangential to the AR curve equilibrium or the firm would be making abnormal profits or losses.

It is important to mention the relationship between the AR curve and the MR curve. It is a purely mathematical relationship. It has already been shown that if the demand curve facing a firm is perfectly elastic, then the AR and MR curves are identical. However, if the demand curve or the AR curve is downward sloping, then the MR curve is downward sloping too, and falls with a steeper gradient than the AR curve.

Data 26.2

Opticians set sights on longer-term profits

Maggie Urry

OPTICIANS were working late into the night yesterday in advance of the ending of "free" sight tests on the National Health Service. From today, 60 per cent of people will no longer be eligible for free tests.

Most opticians are confident that the long term outlook is for further growth in the £400m-plus a year market. Over the last few years a series of changes have been made to the system for dispensing spectacles and contact lenses, and the way opticians can advertise themselves. The abolition of free tests could mark the end of the image of glasses as being ugly, state-provided necessities and allow the optical market to expand.

Mr Brian Keefe, managing director of Dollond & Aitchison's professional services, argues that the NHS system has prevented the market developing naturally. Under the old NHS system people were allowed only one pair of frames at a time, which were often unflattering. If an eye test showed no change in the prescription, people had to make do with the same glasses for longer.

As a result, most spectacle wearers in the UK have only one pair, whereas in

LEADING UK OPTICIANS

Company	Turnover	Pre-tax profit
Dollond & Aitchison group*	£94.5m	£8.7m
Boots Opticians	£39.8m	£3.0m
Miller & Santhouse	£13.0m	£1.5m
Rayne & Keeler	£10.0m	£2.2m
Batemans	£9.5m	£258,000
Melson Wingate	£7.9m	£394,000
Pearle Vision*	£7.6m	(£213,000)
Specialeyes	£6.5m	£528,000
For Eyes*	£5.7m	(£156,000)
First Sight*	£3.8m	(£370,000)

*part of Gallaher Ltd
Figures are for latest available financial year. Brackets indicates losses
Source: Retail Rankings 1989 (including some estimates by Corporate Intelligence Group)

continental Europe and in the US, people often have three or even more pairs.

Many opticians are now attacking the market in a more dynamic way. Dollond & Aitchison has split its branches into a number of differently-named chains, aiming at different segments of the market offering younger, fashionable styles, up-market spectacles, or more staid, value-for-money types.

Specialeyes, a smaller, but fast growing, chain of opticians has opened concessions inside BhS shops and Allders department stores. Miller & Santhouse,

a Liverpool-based group, has doubled in size over the last 15 months.

Increasingly, chains of opticians are likely to expand their market share at the expense of independents, a trend which has developed in virtually every other retail sector.

Competition between opticians has helped to keep prices of glasses low – the average pair of privately-bought spectacles has risen in price from £56.39p in 1983 to £58.14p in 1987, with prices practically static over the last two years, except for the imposition of VAT in September 1988.

The Financial Times. 1.4

1 To what extent could the market for glasses be described as monopolistically competitive?

The neo-classical theory of the firm

Table 26.1

Units sold	Average revenue (= Price)	Total revenue	Marginal revenue
1	60	60	60
2	50	100	40
3	40	120	20
4	30	120	0
5	20	100	−20
6	10	60	−40
7	0	0	−60

Consider the example in Table 26.1. Total revenue can be worked out by multiplying units sold by average revenue. Marginal revenue can then be worked out by calculating the addition to total revenue made by each successive unit of production. If this is plotted, we arrive at the position shown in Fig. 26.9. Note that MR curve falls twice as steeply as the AR curve. Hence at any single price AR is exactly twice MR. This is true of all linear average revenue curves.

An **oligopoly** exists where:

1 A few firms dominate production in the industry.
2 Barriers to entry exist to the industry.
3 Each oligopolistic firm sells branded products.
4 Each firm is interdependent with other firms, as the actions of one firm will directly affect the demand for another firm's product.

Evidence suggests that most manufacturing industry and much of service industry in the UK is dominated by oligopolistic firms. One particular characteristic of oligopolistic industries is that there is relative price stability. In a perfectly competitive

market, prices are usually unstable, often varying sharply over quite short time periods. The price of fresh tomatoes, for instance, varies according to season. But the price of canned tomatoes, arguably produced by an oligopolistic firm in the food processing industry, changes relatively infrequently. On the other hand, non-price competition is often fierce. Where competition is at its keenest in an oligopolistic industry, it is usually evident in advertising wars, special offers or competitions, but not in direct changes in price. The neo-classical **kinked demand curve** model attempts to explain this phenomenon.

Assume that an oligopolistic firm has an existing price for its product. If it attempts to raise that price, then it is argued that other firms will keep their prices constant. This allows them to take market share from the price-raising firm. The firm raising its price will suffer a significant fall in the demand for its product. Put another way, the price elasticity of demand for a rise in price will be relatively high. If the firm lowers its price, then its rivals will lower their prices too. This is because they do not wish to lose market share. The initial fall in price will result in a small gain in market share. In other words, the price elasticity of demand for a fall in price is relatively low.

This is illustrated in Fig. 26.10. Assume that the price set is P_E. At prices above P_E, the price elasticity of demand is higher than at prices below P_E. Hence there is a kink in the demand curve at price P_E. Given this kinked demand curve, a discontinuous marginal revenue curve results. This means that where the demand curve kinks, the marginal revenue curve jumps from P_1 to P_2. Because the firm

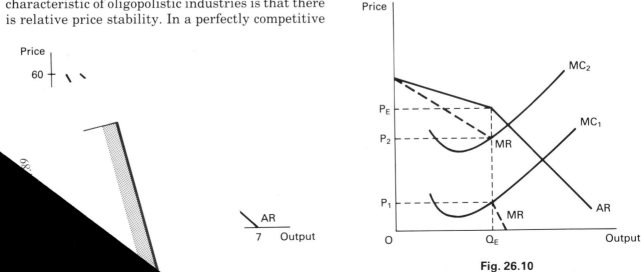

Fig. 26.10

Price

60

AR

7   Output

Data 26.3

How Premier Brands is stirring up the tea market

Philip Rawsthorne

The British drink 190m cups of tea a day – but since the introduction of the teabag 35 years ago, there has been little innovation in the £600m a year market.

Total market volume has been slowly declining. Twenty years ago, six cups of tea were drunk for every cup of coffee; today it is only two to one.

Now Premier Brands – makers of Typhoo, Ridgways, Glengettie and Melroses – is investing £15m in an attempt to revitalise the market and increase its share of it.

The main thrust of Premier's marketing initiative is redesigned packaging for Typhoo teabags and its sister brands. The flimsy carton with its Cellowrap covering, used by virtually all tea manufacturers, is to be abandoned. It will be replaced by a rigid carton with a tear-strip opening in which the tea bags will be sealed in foil pouches.

Premier began to review the options open to it for relaunching its brands two years ago.

It first considered possible improvements in the product itself. Could changes in the way tea is grown, produced and transported lead to better quality? Could the blend, taste or appearance be improved?

The standard of the products already on the market, it concluded, were excellent; and any change in blend would not necessarily appeal to customers.

Premier then reassessed its marketing support – advertising and sales promotion.

Advertising, it decided, could only be used to emphasise a point of difference.

Pricing policy was reviewed. But it soon became clear that there was little scope for change. Typhoo has a 21 per cent share of the UK tea market compared with Brooke Bond Oxo's 30 per cent and Lyons Tetley's 18 per cent – and could not, therefore, attempt to assume the role of price leader.

"Moving the price of tea down would merely solicit a mirrored response," says Derek Reid, director of Premier's tea division. "Moving it upwards would require justification to the trade and consumer."

Premier debated whether it could use design to give its brands a new image. But it concluded that to do no more than that would merely amount to "reclothing" the same product. It finally decided that a complete change of packaging offered the most promising prospects.

Packaging improvement and innovation, it noted, had already transformed other markets. Such moves had dramatically changed the image, quality and sales of coffee, single portion drinks, yoghurt, and microwave products.

Yet virtually all the leading brands of teabags were packaged in exactly the same way regardless of price or quality; and Premier's research showed signifi-

cant consumer dissatisfaction. A majority found the packs dated, unattractive, and difficult to open. Most transferred teabgs, 40–50 at a time, into caddies to keep them fresh. "Our research identified that housewives wanted a tea brand which embodied freshness, convenience and quality," says Reid.

Premier appointed a specialist company, Marketing Solutions, in mid-1987 to devise new packaging that met these demands and would set Premier's brands apart from their competitors.

More than 100 possible packs were considered before the choice was narrowed down to ten and shown to consumers in February last year. The one that won the overwhelming vote of approval was a rigid carton, with new graphics and logo, containing two sealed foil pouches of 40 teabags each.

Premier has spent £8m to buy, on an exclusive basis in the UK, packaging machinery which is being patented.

During the second half of the year it will put £6m in marketing support behind the relaunch of Typhoo, its flagship brand. For the first time in three years, the entire Typhoo range will be advertised on national television in a £4m campaign designed to reach 90 per cent of housewives 15 times each.

Premier has retained the advertising slogan "You only get an OO with Typhoo," adding a support line for the relaunch: "OO that's NOO."

The television campaign will be backed by extensive colour advertising in the press (including women's magazines), and by a national poster campaign. A programme of promotions aims to provide 10m potential sampling opportunities for Typhoo.

The Financial Times. 20.4.89

1 To what extent is the tea market in the UK oligopolistic?

2 Using examples from the data, explain how oligopolistic firms compete with each other.

is a short run profit maximiser, it produces at output Q_E because MC = MR at that output. It can be seen that there are a number of different MC curves which will give this result. They range from the lowest curve, MC_1, to the highest cost curve, MC_2. The firm can experience changes in costs without necessarily changing its level of output or its price. Any level of costs between MC_1 and MC_2 will give an equilibrium output of Q_E and a price of P_E. Hence there is relative price stability in the industry.

Two criticisms of the kinked demand curve approach are:

1 There is no explanation of how the original price and quantity were set.

2 It assumes that firms behave differently when their rivals raise rather than lower price. There is little evidence to suggest that oligolistic firms do tend to react in this way.

Monopoly

A monopolist is a firm which produces all the output of an industry. In other words, it is the sole producer in an industry. Neo-classical theory argues that monopolies exist because the monopolist is able to maintain the barriers to entry to an industry, as discussed in Chapter 25.

The demand curve for the monopolist is the demand curve which faces the whole industry—the monopolist, by definition, is the industry. The demand curve is also the firm's average revenue curve, because the price of the product is the average revenue received by the firm. The average revenue or demand curve is downward sloping, just as nearly all demand curves are downward sloping, and this is shown in Fig. 26.11. The marginal revenue curve falls beneath it, as explained on page 248.

In equilibrium the firm will produce Q_E where MC = MR, because this is the condition for profit maximisation. It will price at P_E because this is the highest price it can receive for production of Q_E. Remember that the average revenue curve is the demand curve for the firm and that the demand curve shows the price which consumers are prepared to pay for any given quantity of output.

Monopolists are usually in a position to make abnormal profit on their production. The price, or average revenue, that a monopolist receives is OP_E in Fig. 26.11. The average cost of production, however, is

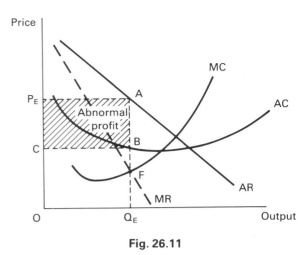

Fig. 26.11

only OC. Therefore the monopolist will make an abnormal profit per unit of CP_E. The abnormal profit on its total production will be CP_E times CB, i.e. the abnormal profit per unit times the total output of the firm. It is represented on the diagram by the area P_EABC.

Note that abnormal profit per unit is calculated by taking average cost away from average revenue, i.e. the vertical distance AB. A common mistake is to assume that abnormal profit per unit is AF, the difference between average revenue and marginal cost and that total abnormal profit is the area represented by the OQ_E times AF.

If the monopolist were to make a loss in the long run, the average cost curve would be above the average revenue curve. Neo-classical theory would predict that the monopolist would cease all production—what is the point of producing if a profit cannot be made even in the long run? If society wished to consume this product, the state would have to subsidise production.

It may well pay a monopolist to **price discriminate**: i.e. a monopolist can increase profits by charging different prices to different customers for the same product. Examples of price differentiation are different tariffs for electricity use by industrial and domestic users, and car manufacturers who sell cars at different prices in different countries.

Different markets may have different costs, and therefore to some extent price discrimination may be regarded as justifiable. For instance, the cost of producing electricity at peak times is higher than its off peak cost. This is because the electricity generating company needs to operate some power plant which only produce at peak times. However, often costs bear no relation to prices being charged

Producers of cars, for instance, may well charge higher prices in their domestic markets than in export markets despite the fact that the cost of export (transport, foreign specifications, etc.) may be higher.

Price discrimination will benefit a monopolist if:

1 There are distinct markets for the product and it is difficult for consumers to cross market boundaries. For instance, large numbers of consumers are unlikely to travel to foreign countries to buy goods more cheaply. Therefore domestic and export prices can be kept separate.

2 The price elasticity of demand for the product must be different in the two markets. If it is not, then the producer will not be able to make one section of the market pay any higher price than if all products were sold at a single price. There must exist a difference in the willingness to pay on the part of different consumers.

Summary

Short run profit maximisation is achieved at the output where MC = MR. The theory of perfect competition assumes many firms in an industry with freedom of entry and exit, producing homogeneous goods. Amongst its conclusions is that in equilibrium no abnormal profits will be made. The theory of monopolistic competition assumes that firms in the industry produce branded goods. Each firm faces a downward sloping demand curve. In oligopoly there are only a few firms in the industry producing branded products, with barriers to entry. The kinked demand curve model argues that price elasticity will be different for price rises compared to price falls. In monopoly a single firm supplies all output in the industry. As a result, the monopolist is able to obtain abnormal profits.

Terms for review

short run profit maximization conditions

perfect competition

price taker

monopolistic competition

kinked demand curve

price discrimination

Is she right?

Essay questions

1 Outline a theory of oligopoly. To what extent does it explain the behaviour of oligopolistic industries in the UK today?

2 Can perfectly competitive firms earn abnormal profits?

3 Distinguish between a monopolistic industry and a monopolistically competitive industry. Can firms in either type of industry price discriminate?

27

Other theories of the firm

The neo-Keynesian theory of the firm

Neo-Keynesian economists argue that two distinct sets of markets exist. In the one, called the 'market sector' by J. K. Galbraith, large numbers of small firms compete. Examples of these markets are agriculture, and many personal services such as hairdressing and retailing. On the other hand, a majority of production is concentrated in the 'planning sector'. Here, a small number of large firms dominate markets. Any industry where sizeable barriers to entry exist will form part of the planning sector.

The behaviour of firms in the market sector of the economy is relatively easy to predict. Firms are price takers because no single firm can charge a higher price than other firms without losing its market. Firms will continue in business if they can cover their average cost plus a modest profit mark-up. If firms in the industry are able to obtain a large profit mark-up (i.e. earn abnormal profit in neoclassical terms), new firms will be attracted into the industry, forcing existing firms to lower their prices and hence their mark-ups. If firms cannot cover their average cost, then some firms will leave the industry, allowing the remaining firms to raise their prices to profitable levels. Neo-Keynesian economists accept that neo-classical demand and supply theory gives a good explanation of how such markets behave.

In the planning sector of the economy, barriers to entry enable firms to earn larger mark-ups than in the market sector. Neo-Keynesian theory predicts that the mark-up for the industry will be high if the following occur:

1 Barriers to entry are high for that industry. High barriers to entry will discourage other firms entering the industry, thereby reducing competition and encouraging high prices and high profits.

2 The number of existing major producers in the industry is small. An industry with only two major producers (a **duopoly**) is likely to be less price competitive than an industry with six major producers. Thus, the duopolists are likely to be able to charge higher prices than the firms in the six-firm industry.

3 The industry sells its output to an industry with many firms. If for instance, the industry had to sell to a **monopsonist**—a firm which was the only buyer for the industry's product—then competition is likely to be fierce. The monopsonist will be able to play off one firm against another, forcing them to cut their profit margins to the bare minimum.

4 Firms in the industry **collude**, that is, they combine together to agree on what price is to be charged, how much is to be sold, etc. This eliminates the competitive element in the industry and effectively turns the industry into a monopoly.

Firms produce under conditions of uncertainty. Many firms have to produce before being able to sell their goods. Hence they have to estimate demand when deciding on their output levels. Firms are in a position to decide on the price to be charged. This is because each firm is producing a branded product and therefore consumers will continue to buy some of the product even if prices rise relatively to its main competitors. In other words, each firm is facing a downward sloping demand curve for its product.

Prices will be relatively stable. Firms in the planning sector take a long term view of the market. Frequent price changes to take account of changing market conditions are not in the best interests of the firm, because they will involve the firm in considerable administrative expense. Even then, there is no guarantee that the new price set will necessarily result in more profits, or increased sales, than the previous price. This is because the response to a

*Why is it that the price of frozen vegetables is far more
stable than the price of fresh vegetables?*

change in market conditions is likely to be lagged. For instance an increase in demand may have vanished by the time the firm can enforce an increase in prices. Moreover, customers may dislike frequent price changes. Hence firms will set prices at a given level for a certain period ahead.

Firms will respond to changes in demand by changing their output levels. In Fig. 27.1, the firm aims to produce where its average cost-plus-mark-up curve cuts its expected demand curve. At Q_E, price is equal to average cost-plus-mark-up: **cost-plus pricing** is a central premise of the neo-Keynesian model. Therefore in the short run the firm will be prepared to supply any amount at price P_E. In other words its short run supply curve is given by the horizontal line S. If actual demand turns out to be greater than expected demand (e.g. D' instead of D in Fig. 27.1), then the firm will attempt to expand output to Q_1. What it will not do is to raise its price as neo-classical theory would predict. If it can not expand output to Q_1, the firm will allow waiting lists to develop rather than allocate existing production to the highest bidder. If actual demand is below expected demand, it will cut back on production. If it has already produced the goods ready for sale, it will stockpile the unwanted goods and try to sell them in the next pricing season.

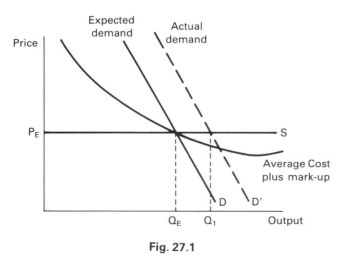

Fig. 27.1

The goal of the firm is long run profit maximisation. In order to achieve this, firms have to invest. Most funds for investment come from retained profits—i.e. profits which are not distributed to shareholders as dividends. Investment should ensure the long term growth of the firm. Competition forces firms to invest and to keep abreast of their main competitors. In a world of real economic growth, this means that firms need to get bigger in order to survive. The larger the firm, the more likely it is that it will be able to finance the necessary research and development expenditure needed to produce ever more sophisticated manufactured goods. Hence competition does not, as in the neo-classical model, have major effects on prices. What it does affect is the range of goods available to the consumer. Competition in the planning sector of the economy promotes investment and technological change, not price wars. In the long run, the mark-up needs to cover the required investment for the firm. If the firm cannot obtain a sufficiently high mark-up, then it will slowly decline.

The managerial and behavioural approaches

The **managerial theory of the firm** assumes that firms are run by managers rather than entrepreneurs. In other words, it takes as its starting point the idea that the ownership and control of a firm lie in different hands. Just as owners are interested in securing profit maximisation, so managers are interested in maximising their own rewards. The neo-classical theory of the firm assumes that owners can enforce their wishes on management. The managerial theory of the firm, on the other hand, takes the view that to some extent managers can be free from shareholders' control in order to pursue their own objectives. It is recognised that managers must produce sufficient profits to keep their shareholders from sacking them and to deter other companies from taking the company over. However, subject to a profit satisficing constraint, managers are free to maximise their own utility. In Williamson's model, their utility is measured amongst other things in terms of managers' salaries and other perks, as well as number and quality of staff at their disposal.

Managerial models tend to be mathematically complex. A number of conclusions tend to characterise these models.

1 Firms will produce at higher levels of output than in the neo-classical theory of the firm. This is because higher sales tend to benefit managers in terms of justifying higher salaries and increased expenditures on plant and staff.

2 Firms will have higher costs than in neo-classical theory. Managers are interested in maximising their returns. These will include unnecessary expenditure on salaries, company cars and houses, investment and research expenditure, and so on.

3 In recessions, managers may have to forego many of the benefits accruing to them in order to maintain a satisfactory level of profits. In boom times, at the top of the trade cycle, much of the benefit from improved trading conditions will go to managers rather than shareholders.

Obviously, managerial theories are directed at explaining how medium and large companies operate rather than small companies where the entrepreneur is still very much in existence. On the whole, medium and large companies operate in oligopolistic markets in the developed world.

Equally **behavioural theories of the firm** try to explain how large organisations function. H. A. Simmons argues that the firm is a complex organisation made up of different competing groups. Shareholders, managers, workers, government, consumer interests and so on all have a part to play in the decision-making process of a firm. Each group will have its particular interests and will aim to maximise its own utility. The policy outcome will depend on the nature of decision-making procedures and the strengths of each interest group in the firm. The firm is likely to pursue a profit satisficing rather than a profit maximising goal, since shareholders are only one interest group amongst many in the firm.

The process of bargaining will lead to a situation where **X-inefficiency** or **organisational slack** occurs. The American economist Leibenstein has argued that, in many firms, factors of production receive 'payments' (e.g. money, prestige, perks) in excess of that needed to keep them in the firm. Managers of one firm may be given company cars in an industry where company cars are not usually given. Workers may receive holidays in excess of the norm for their industry. The value of organisational slack is the difference between the minimum payment needed to keep a factor of production in employment and the actual payment made.

Data 27.1

Attracting the talent

THE WAYS in which companies allocate executive cars not only give an indication of the general health of UK corporations but also provide an idea about the difficulties – or otherwise – that companies are having in recruiting and holding senior people.

One indicator is the choice of vehicles that companies give executives. At the senior level the car is very rarely a tool of the trade or a necessity. It is simply a perk. In those circumstances it would be counter-productive for a company to impose a take-it-or-leave-it approach to the executive car.

Even clearer evidence that the car is a valuable recruitment and effective motivation tool, was provided by the Executive's Car Survey conducted by Hertz Leasing and HR&H Marketing Research. The survey showed that 26 per cent of executives agreed that "gaining a company car would be even more important than a salary increase when changing jobs."

The concept that a better car "is a strong incentive to work for promotion" was greeted with general agreement among the executives surveyed. But decision-makers at director level had a greater belief in its effectiveness than their juniors' attitudes warrant.

The directors, with 62 per cent agreeing with the statement, had a greater faith in its promotional appeal, whereas only 53 per cent of middle managers and salesmen agreed with the statement.

The Financial Times. 22.6.89

To what extent can a company car be seen as an example of X-inefficiency?

Organisational slack occurs because:

1 In practice it is difficult for decision makers to quantify exactly the minimum level of payments needed and so they tend to overshoot. Workers may be poorly paid in comparison with similar workers at other local firms and yet still be overpaid in the sense that they would be prepared to go on working at even lower rates of pay.

2 It is difficult for decision makers to calculate the actual level of payments: e.g. how does a firm put a value on the prestige associated with a certain job.

3 Organisations are conservative in outlook and tend to change only slowly.

Organisational slack increases when demand for the company's product is high. Competing interest groups in the firm find it easy to justify extra payments. If they fail to receive such payments they may resort to various forms of industrial action. Most obviously, shop floor workers can exert pressure for higher rewards through the threat of strike action. When the firm is doing badly, organisational slack lessens. A company faced with the threat of liquidation may see huge changes in work practices, value of perks and even wage levels, which can dramatically improve its financial performance.

The behavioural approach to the theory of the firm provides strong insights into how firms work. It does not, however, provide a powerful generalised model of the firm. It is useful only when detailed knowledge of the organisational structures of a firm is available. Indeed, many economists would argue that it is impossible to generalise as specifically as neo-classical theory attempts to do.

The model of The New Industrial State

In his book *The New Industrial State* Galbraith argues that the economy is split into two parts: the market sector where firms are small and are subject to strong market pressure, and the planning sector where firms are large and to a great extent can control their own destinies. In the modern developed economy, firms dominate production in the planning sector.

The large company is controlled and run by the **technostructure**. This consists of the high level personnel in the company who direct its main activities. These include production, marketing, research and finance. The technostructure is interested in the long term survival of the firm. This means that they have to take account of the wishes of all the interest groups in the company. These sources of 'countervailing power'—power centres which set up to combat the power of the technostructure—include shareholders, government, consumer organisations and trade unions. These interest groups are unlikely, however, to divert the technostructure from its aim of ensuring stability and long run growth.

A feature of firms in the planning sector is the large amount of capital needed to continue production. No firm in the planning sector can afford to put new products on to the market and see them fail. Yet if they do not launch new products, their rivals will do so and steadily erode their market share. Thus firms have to go to great lengths to ensure that products launched are a success—hence the phrase 'planning' sector.

Firms plan in two ways. Firstly, they attempt to discover through market research what the consumer wishes to buy. Secondly, once firms have made heavy investment in plant and machinery they attempt to ensure through advertising and other sales techniques that consumers buy their new products.

The neo-classical theory of the firm argues that **consumer sovereignty** exists in the market. Consumers vote for firms with their money. If firms do not provide the products which consumers want those firms will be unable to sell their goods. Sooner or later, firms with a poor record of responding to the wishes of the consumer will go bankrupt. Firms with a good track record will prosper and grow. In the market place, the consumer is king.

Galbraith argues that this sequence is broadly correct in the market sector of the economy. The sequence is 'revised' in the planning sector. Here firms first produce goods and then persuade the consumer to buy them. In this model, the firm is king and consumers are the servants. There is no doubt at all that advertising does change consumer spending patterns. Some consumers can be persuaded to buy a car, or a television set or a packet of soap powder, because that product has been heavily advertised. Advertising does change people's attitudes to products. In this sense, Galbraith's 'revised sequence' is undoubtedly correct.

However, critics have pointed out that it is nevertheless the consumer who is king because there are

Data 27.2

Jelly Baby falls for charms of chocolate soldier

Lisa Wood explains why Cadbury decided to bid for Bassett Foods

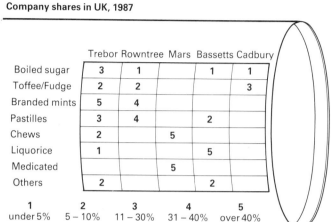

Company shares in UK, 1987

	Trebor	Rowntree	Mars	Bassetts	Cadbury
Boiled sugar	3	1		1	1
Toffee/Fudge	2	2			3
Branded mints	5	4			
Pastilles	3	4		2	
Chews	2		5		
Liquorice	1		5		
Medicated			5		
Others	2			2	

1	2	3	4	5
under 5%	5 – 10%	11 – 30%	31 – 40%	over 40%

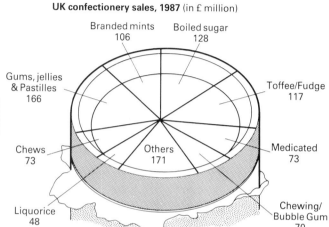

UK confectionery sales, 1987 (in £ million)

Branded mints 106
Boiled sugar 128
Gums, jellies & Pastilles 166
Toffee/Fudge 117
Chews 73
Others 171
Medicated 73
Liquorice 48
Chewing/Bubble Gum 70

While Cadbury, along with Rowntree, dominates the £2bn UK chocolate confectionery market, with brands such as Dairy Milk and Wispa, it has only got a 3 per cent share of the £1bn-a-year UK sugar confectionery market.

This is a fragmented market with Trebor, the market leader, taking an estimated 15 per cent stake by value, followed by Rowntree at 14 per cent and Bassett with 11 per cent.

Demand for sugar confectionery in the UK, the second-largest market in Europe after West Germany, dropped sharply in the early 1980s, from about 44 per cent of the total confectionery market to consolidate at around 37 per cent.

Within this market, however, there are niches – including gums, liquorice and medicated sweets – which are showing healthy growth.

Cadbury, which has a presence in several overseas markets with its sugar confectionery brands, believed it had to either get bigger in those growth areas or get out of the sector altogether.

Independent consultants last year conducted a three-month analysis for the company of opportunities and concluded there was potential for greater brand buildings and improving profit margins, which traditionally have been nearly half those of chocolate confectionery.

Basset, with sales of £81.6m in the year ended April 1988, was identified long ago by Cadbury as having brands which were complementary to its own and in growth sectors of the market, such as Liquorice Allsorts.

Today, Cadbury, with the full agreement of Bassett, plans to back its own small sugar confectionery business, with its Pascall-Murray and Lion Brands, into that of Bassett.

Considerable cost savings can be made, say Cadbury, which it claims fully justify the £91m price it is offering. Synergies, it says, will come in research and development, purchasing of raw materials, production rationalisation and distribution.

Bassett will also bring manufacturing plant in the Netherlands at a time when Cadbury, which bought Poulain, the French chocolate group two years ago, is seeking to improve its distribution on the Continent.

The Financial Times. 3.2.89

Describe the nature of competition in the confectionary market.

2 What are the advantages of the bid described in the data (a) for Cadbury Schweppes and (b) for the consumer?

Data 27.3

All steamed up in cool jeans

Alice Rawsthorn on Levi's latest promotional push

THE SCENE is a seedy hotel diner in the sweltering heat of the American Mid West in the late 1950s. A young man, clad only in a shirt and boxer shorts, smoulders at the owner's déshabillé daughter and retrieves his jeans from the refrigerator. He pulls on the jeans and roars off on a Harley-Davidson motorcycle: all to the tune of Muddy Waters' blues music.

The hotel diner, the young man and his refrigerated jeans are part of the new commercial for Levi 501s, the leading brand of jeans made by Levi Strauss, the US jeans giant. This commerical – which cost more than £300,000 to make – is the centrepiece of Levi's 1988 European advertising campaign. It will be unveiled across the continent in early July.

For the past three years the advertising produced by Levi – and Bartle Bogle Hegarty, its European agency – has achieved the double coup of winning awards by the bucketful and boosting sales. The only "problem" is the need to maintain momentum: by ensuring the new commercials are as successful as the old.

Three years ago when Levi relaunched 501s in Europe such a problem would have seemed improbable. The company had just emerged from a shattering year of restructuring, in which dozens of factories were closed worldwide and thousands of jobs lost.

Levi's difficulties had begun a few years earlier when the jeans market lurched into decline. The principal problem was that to the teenagers of the early 1980s the denim jean was a tired legacy of their parents' younger years, not an emblem of their own adolescent

revolt. The US jeans market was bolstered by sales of workwear to blue collar workers, but European sales slumped from 250m pairs in 1981 to 150m pairs in 1985.

Levi's response was to cut costs and to return to its roots as a traditional jeans manufacturer. The linchpin of this new strategy was the relaunch of 501s – the original fly button blue jean – to the US in 1984 and, in the following year, to Europe.

The first European 501s commerical starred a young man who stripped down to his boxer shorts to wash his 501s in a 1950s launderette. It launched the young man, Nick Kamen, in a new career as a pop star and revitalised the jeans market.

In the UK alone, where "Launderette" was first shown, the jeans market has risen from £550m to £800m between 1985 and 1987, while Levi's share has rocketed from 13 to 18 per cent.

Levi has achieved this by adopting a strategy of establishing 501s as its "classic jean", while introducing new styles in response to changes in fashion. The core product range – like its advertising – is uniform throughout Europe although each national division is able to choose its own "peripheral" merchandise.

This year's new product is a range of "chinos", the pleat-front, cotton twill trousers worn by the US armed forces. Chinos have caught on almost as quickly as 501s in the UK and US, and are now gathering momentum in the Benelux and Scandinavia.

The company is also introducing the Levi shops – established in Southern Europe and the Benelux – to other countries including France and the UK. The shops help to tackle the parallel problems of the diversity of its retail base and the lack of control over presentation by acting as showcases for its products.

In the meantime Levi is considering a change of theme for the next 501 campaign. So far the commercials have been set in the 1950s but, according to Andrew Knibbs, head of marketing for the UK, future campaigns could move to another era: "The first 501s were made in the mid-1800s, not in the 1950s. It may be time for a change."

The Financial Times. 25.5.88

---

1 Using evidence from the data, suggest why brands are valuable to producers.

2 To what extent does sovereignty exist in a market such as that for jeans?

mits to the power of advertising. The public is not gullible enough to buy large quantities of black soap, cars with five wheels, or green hair dye. At some point, consumers are beyond the influence of the marketing section of a firm. Galbraith freely admits this but would argue that firms are not in general so stupid as to try and sell products such as black soap. Firms take great pains to ensure that their new products are acceptable. Advertising can turn a mediocre product into a highly successful one.

Firms are only in part subject to market pressures, just as the technostructure of the firm is only in part subject to the control of its shareholders. Within limits, the technostructure can pursue its own goals. Galbraith goes on to argue that these goals may not be in the interests of society in general. For instance, firms may be relatively unconcerned about pollution, the safety of the products they sell, the needs of local communities, and the working conditions in their plants, offices and factories.

It is the role of Government to enforce minimum standards in these areas. Hence the Government needs to pass anti-pollution laws, adopt consumer protection measures, encourage firms to have a social conscience, and so on. If the Government does not do this, then the technostructure will be the dominant power group in the economy and this is likely to be detrimental to the interests of society.

Summary

The neo-Keynesian theory of the firm argues that firms in the planning sector of the economy are long run profit maximisers. They price at cost-plus-mark-up and produce in oligopolistic markets. Price stability is a feature of such markets, as firms dislike disrupting long term trading conditions for possible short turn gain. The response of firms to excess demand in the long term is investment. Managerial models of the firm take as their starting point the divorce between ownership and control of the modern firm. Because managers aim to maximise their utility, output and costs tend to be higher than neo-classical theories predict. The behavioural theory of the firm predicts that organisational slack will develop amongst the competing interest groups in a firm. Galbraith in his book *The New Industrial State* puts forward the hypothesis that large firms dominate the present day economy. Through skilful planning, advertising and marketing they can within reason sell all their products to the consumer, i.e. consumer sovereignty does not exist. Given the power of the technostructure, Galbraith argues for strong governmental control of the economy.

Terms for review

market and planning sectors	cost-plus pricing
duopoly	organisational slack or X-inefficiency
monopsonist	technostructure
collusion	consumer sovereignty

Essay questions

How would a firm in an oligopolistic industry set prices for its products? What effect would you expect the bankruptcy of an existing firm in the industry to have on industry prices?

To what extent does consumer sovereignty exist in (a) the agricultural market and (b) the volume car market in the UK?

3 Why do firms invest? Can investment ever be detrimental to the welfare of society?

28

Markets and efficiency

Introduction

All existing economies rely to some extent upon an allocation of resources through markets. In the Western world, the market system is the major mechanism by which goods and services are distributed. Economists are therefore interested in the extent to which a market can be said to be 'efficient'.

Economic efficiency and the market

There are generally considered to be two elements of economic efficiency:

1 **Productive efficiency:** this refers to whether or not the firm is minimising its costs at any given level of putput. Productive inefficiency is present if for instance a firm could produce 10 000 units at a total cost of £1 million but because of X-inefficiency, finds its total costs are £1.2 million. The consumer will have to pay higher prices because the firm is not cost efficient.

2 **Allocative efficiency:** this refers to whether or not firms supply the right goods, in the right quantity and at the right price, to consumers. Firms may, for instance, sell poor quality goods, or goods which are not as technologically advanced as they could be for the price. They may be supplying fewer goods on to the market than efficiency warrants. They may be charging a higher price than is necessary. All these are examples of allocative inefficiency and will be discussed in more detail below. Sometimes a third type of efficiency, distributive efficiency, is distinguished. This refers to the ability of the market to distribute goods and services to the consumers who desire them. For instance, distributive inefficiency is said to occur if through rationing some consumers receive goods which they do no want, whilst other consumers want the goods bu cannot get them.

Productive efficiency

The main concern here is the extent to which firm can minimise their costs of production. The 'opti mum size' of the firm is defined as that point wher average cost is at a minimum. In other words, th firm is at its optimum size when all economies o scale have been exploited.

In the neo-classical theory of perfect competition firms in equilibrium are producing at precisely thei optimum size. In Fig. 28.1, it can be seen that th average cost curve is at its lowest at output Q_E Hence perfect competition leads to productiv efficiency. Compare this with the neo-classica models of monopolistic competition, oligopoly o monopoly, in which it is most unlikely that firm will produce at optimum size. In Fig. 28.2, the mono polist shown produces at Q_E where there are stil unexploited economies of scale. The optimum siz

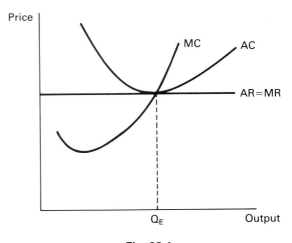

Fig. 28.1

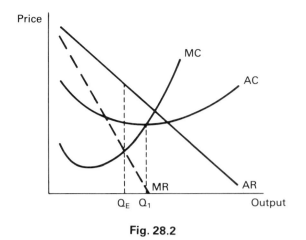

Fig. 28.2

for the firm is Q_1. Therefore, productive inefficiency exists here.

On the other hand, there are many arguments which suggest that oligopolists or monopolists may well be nearer the optimum size of the firm than firms in perfect competition. Two arguments in particular are important.

1 Economies of scale may be such that it is impossible for even the largest firm to exploit them fully. It is possible, for instance, for a monopolist to give away the goods or services it produces and yet still not exploit fully the economies of scale present. In Fig. 28.3, demand for the product of the monopolist is OA where price is zero, i.e. the product is given away free of charge. Yet cost per unit could be

reduced below OB if only consumers were to demand more. 'Natural' monopolies are said to exist where it is impossible for just one firm producing the whole output for an industry to exploit potential economies of scale fully.

2 If the average cost curve is L-shaped rather than U-shaped, firms may be virtually at their optimum size despite not being in a perfectly competitive industry. Consider an oligopolistic industry where a firm is operating, as in Fig. 28.4. Producing at output OA, the firm is faced with costs per unit of OC. Expanding output to OB will bring about a reduction in average costs, but the reduction will be negligible. In other words, the firm is operating at approximately optimum size at OA.

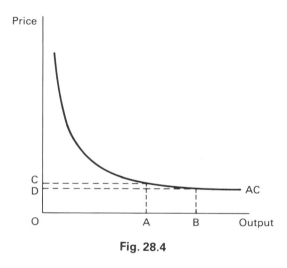

Fig. 28.4

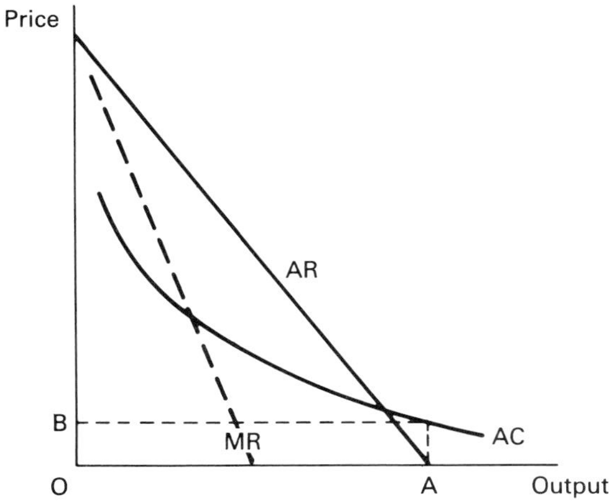

Allocative efficiency and barriers to entry

Allocative efficiency is indicated by price, quantity and quality of goods supplied to the market. Theory would suggest that barriers to entry (such as high capital costs or patent laws) allow firms in that industry to earn higher than average profits. In the neo-classical theory of the firm, the inability of new entrants to come into the industry allows firms to earn abnormal profit. It is argued in neo-Keynesian theory that firms with little potential competition are likely to charge a higher mark-up than firms in industries where competition is fierce.

Fig. 28.3

Thus, in oligopoly and monopoly, firms are able to exploit the consumer. Exploitation is here used to indicate that firms can charge a higher price for their product than would be the case if the industry were more competitive. In other words, an oligolist or monopolist is able to use its industrial power to appropriate resources at the expense of the consumer. If higher prices are charged, it follows that consumers buy less than they would under more competitive conditions.

All governments of industrialised economies recognise the potential power of oligopolists and monopolists and attempt to protect the consumer. There are three main ways of doing this.

1 By nationalising firms. In this way governments have potential or complete control over the market and can therefore influence the price and output decisions of the firms involved. The pricing policies of nationalised industries are considered later in this chapter.

2 By regulating industries. In the UK, gas, electricity and water have regulatory bodies which restrict the actions of these private monopolies. Legislation allows the Monopolies and Mergers Commission to investigate oligopolists and monopolists, and to recommend courses of action if they are found to be abusing their market power. The Commission also has the power to investigate proposed mergers which would create a monopoly as defined by law.

3 By breaking up firms which are either too large or which can be shown to have exploited their market power. In the USA, for instance, monopolies are illegal.

Data 28.1

War on free-sheet 'was unfair'

By David Churchill, Consumer affairs correspondent

The fierce marketing war between local newspapers and free-sheets was taken a stage further yesterday when the Office of Fair Trading declared that Scottish and Universal Newspapers, a subsidiary of the Lonrho group, was acting anti-competitively by trying to force a free-distribution newspaper out of business.

The decision, is an important test case in the conflict between paid-for and free papers. The OFT has received a number of allegations that the large newspaper groups have been acting in an unfair way to protect their interests.

Scottish and Universal Newspapers is a dominant publisher of newspapers in the Hamilton and Motherwell area near Glasgow.

The OFT was called in after complaints by a new free-sheet, the Hamilton and Motherwell People, that the paid-for newspaper group was unfairly trying to put it out of business.

After an investigation lasting several months, the OFT found the group had put pressure on the free-sheet's printer not to procede with the contract. It had also started its own free newspaper, the Lanarkshire World, and given away advertising or sold it below the marginal cost of producing the paper.

It had also told advertisers at first that they could have space only if they did not advertise in the rival free-sheet.

Sir Gordon Borrie, Director General of Fair Trading, said yesterday Scottish and Universal had "followed a course of conduct which constitutes an anti-competitive practice" and that the issue should be referred to the Monopolies Commission to determine whether the group was acting in the public interest.

The group has until March 8 to decide whether to stop the anti-competitive practice. If it does not, the commission's investigation, which would take about six months, will go ahead.

The OFT's investigation was made under the 1980 Competition Act which enables it to investigate any alleged anti-competitive practice by a single company.

The Financial Times. January, 1983

1 How and why were Scottish and Universal Newspapers attempting to 'force a free-distribution newspaper out of business'?

2 What effect would Scottish and Universal Newspapers' actions be likely to have on economic efficiency?

Thus market power can lead to allocative inefficiency and governments have responded to this by attempting to control market abuse. The extent of that power is indicated by the fact that no Western Government is entirely happy with control measures taken to date. Despite a vast amount of Government legislation, firms continue to abuse market power.

Allocative efficiency and restrictive trade practices

Restrictive trade practices are agreements between firms which result in gains to the firms involved at the expense of the consumer. Examples of restrictive trade practices are price-fixing agreements, output agreements and sharing of market information.

Consider an industry which is perfectly competitive under neo-classical assumptions. Firms in that industry are able to come to an agreement which has the effect of putting all the output of that industry

under the control of the cartel. The profit maximising cartel naturally want to raise prices. As a result demand will fall. Therefore they should raise prices to the point where their abnormal profit is maximised, i.e. where MC = MR, as shown in Fig. 28.5. The profit maximising cartel will produce at OA and

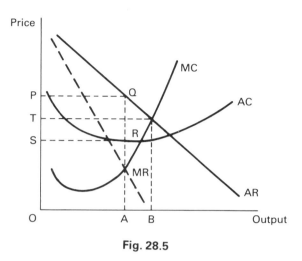

Fig. 28.5

How can restrictive trade practices harm the consumer?

price at OP. Abnormal profits of PQRS will be earned. These profits can be distributed to each of the participating firms. If the industry were operating under perfectly competitive conditions, they would produce where MC = price, i.e. at OB. This is because the MC curve represents the supply curve of the industry. The AR curve represents the demand curve for the industry. In equilibrium, demand must equal supply. Therefore the industry will produce and price where the MC curve cuts the AR curve. Price at OT is lower than the cartel agreement price of OP, and output of OB is higher than the cartel output of OA.

All cartels face common problems. Firstly, the cartel must be able to control the level of output in the industry. If output expands, prices will fall, defeating one of the main objectives of most cartels. An expansion of output can come from one of three sources. New firms may enter the industry; thus the cartel needs to maintain high barriers to entry. Existing producers outside the cartel may expand sales; thus the cartel needs to be able to control the activities of non-member firms. Lastly, there is every incentive for a firm in the cartel to expand output and charge slightly below the agreed price. In practice, they will do this through devious routes. They may have frequent 'sales' or 'bargain offers'. They may sell perfect goods as 'seconds'. They may attempt to persuade the cartel that their share of output is too low and needs to be raised, and increase their production whilst negotiations are taking place.

Secondly, no firm in the industry must be allowed the exclusive marketing of a new product which will destroy the demand for existing inferior products. Hence it is much easier to organise a cartel where the product is homogeneous (e.g. oil) or where the product technology is unlikely to be improved (e.g. cement) than in an industry such as electronics where technological change is rapid.

Restrictive trade practices increase the market power of producers and allow them to reallocate resources from consumers to themselves. This being the case, they allow allocative inefficiency to exist. Western Governments, recognising this, have legislated to counter the worst abuses. In the UK the Restrictive Trade Practices Court, a full court of law, is able to declare such practices illegal if they cannot be proved to be in the interests of the economy. Equally, anti-restrictive trade practice clauses are enshrined in the Treaty of Rome and firms are being prosecuted in the European Court more and more frequently.

Data 28.2

BR deal with Godfrey Davis ruled as anti-competitive

By Andrew Cornelius

The Office of Fair Trading has censured British Rail for granting exclusive self-drive car hire facilities at 73 main stations to Godfrey Davis Europcar.

Sir Gordon Borrie, director general of Fair Trading, said in a report yesterday that British Rail had pursued an "anti-competitive" course of conduct in making the agreement.

However, the rival car hire companies including Avis, Hertz and Swan National – which have criticized the Rail Drive scheme will find no comfort from the report's conclusion.

Sir Gordon says that since the total business diverted to Godfrey Davis by the agreement is insignificant in the context of the £200m-a-year self-drive car hire market, no further action will be taken by the OFT to refer the agreement to the Monopolies and Mergers Commission.

British Rail also headed off criticism of the arrangement whereby rival firms are allowed to advertise at any railway station by removing the advertising restriction at stations where Rail Drive facilities are not available. Sir Gordon sees no reason to dispute the view that a restriction of advertising is necessary at Rail Drive stations if the scheme is to operate successfully.

Last night, Mr Bill Dix, marketing director at Avis, one of the firms which is trying to change the arrangement, said that the company is consulting its lawyers over the OFT ruling.

The Times. 19.5.83

1 *Has the BR deal with Godfrey Davis impaired economic efficiency?*

Allocative efficiency and nationalised industries

Nationalised industries are industries owned by the State. At what level should they price their goods or services? The theoretical answer is they should set a level which will maximise the welfare gain to the community as a whole.

This may involve them in making a loss. Consider a railway line losing £20 million a year. If it were to be closed, the community at large would suffer. Subsidised buses would have to be provided, there would be extra congestion on the roads, new roads might have to be built or existing roads upgraded, there would be extra pollution, etc. If the resulting cost to the community is greater than £20 million, then the community should subsidise the railway.

Neo-classical economists argue that nationalised industries should price at marginal cost. Given certain assumptions it can be shown that marginal cost pricing will maximise welfare.

Consider Fig. 28.6. The demand curve shows how much consumers are prepared to pay for a given level of output. So if 20 units are supplied, consumers are prepared to pay at least £3 for each unit. If 40 units are supplied, the price must fall. In other words, not all consumers value the 40th unit of output as much as the 20th unit of output. The price consumers are prepared to pay, then, is a measure of the minimum value that they place on consumption.

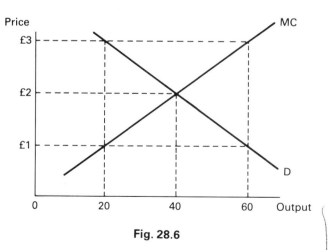

Fig. 28.6

The marginal cost curve shows the cost of producing an extra unit of output. So the cost of producing the 20th unit of output is £1. Extra output will increase marginal cost. Hence at an output of 40

units the cost of the last unit of output is £2. The cost of production not only represents the cost of production to the firms or the consumer. It represents the cost of production to society as a whole. If the firm were to decide to produce 39 units instead of 40 units, then £2 worth of resources would be liberated. These resources could be used elsewhere in the economy. In other words, the price of the product represents the opportunity cost of production to society.

It would then seem reasonable to suggest that, to maximise economic welfare, price should be set equal to marginal cost. If price is below marginal cost, consumers say that they do not value that production as much as it costs society to produce it. At an output of 60 units, for instance, some consumers say that the 60th unit is worth only £1 to them. Yet it costs society £3 to produce it. It would be better not to produce that 60th unit and allocate the resources to production which is valued at more than £1 per unit by the consumer. On the other hand, if price is above marginal cost, then some consumers say that they value that production more than the cost of producing it. At an output of 20 units some consumers value the 20th unit at £3, although it only costs society £1 to produce it. Therefore it would surely be better for society to expand output whilst price is still above marginal cost. In that way the welfare gain from production will be maximised.

It is therefore argued that total welfare is maximised where the cost of production to society (the marginal cost) is just equal to the value that consumers place on that good (its price). Hence nationalised industries, which should be interested in maximising the welfare of society, should price at marginal cost.

It is interesting to note that in the neo-classical theory of the firm, only firms in perfect competition price at marginal cost. In all other models—monopolistic competition, oligopoly and monopoly—equilibrium price is above marginal cost. In other words, only perfect competition results in true allocative efficiency.

There are some major problems in implementing the principle. For instance, it is difficult to define what is meant by marginal cost. In the case of railways, is marginal cost the cost of transporting one extra passenger (which would result in free fares), or of transporting an extra 10,000 passengers a day, or of transporting an extra 10 million passengers a year? Secondly, the cost to society of production may be very different from the cost to the producer. For instance, if the producer is receiving a subsidy from the state, or is a major polluter of the environment, then the marginal social cost will differ from the marginal private cost. Marginal cost pricing only works if all the costs of production borne by society are set against price. Obviously it is very difficult for a nationalised industry to calculate its social cost of production.

Moreover, marginal cost pricing only results in a maximisation of welfare if all firms in the economy price at marginal cost. In the mid-1950s Lipsey and Lancaster showed in an article entitled 'The General Theory of Second Best' that if just one firm were not marginal cost pricing then it would not necessarily maximise welfare if another firm were to price at marginal cost. In the real world, there is a sizeable number of firms which are not setting price equal to marginal cost. Therefore it is most unlikely that welfare will be maximised if nationalised industries do price at marginal cost.

It is also the case that splitting up a monopoly (where, in a neo-classical theory, price is above marginal cost) into firms which are in perfect competition (where price is set at marginal cost) will not necessarily even in theory result in better allocative efficiency if other firms in the economy are not marginal cost pricing. Indeed, it could well be that better allocative efficiency would be achieved by monopolising a perfectly competitive industry. Without knowledge of the particular industry and economy concerned, it is impossible to say in general what level of prices will maximise welfare.

Economic efficiency and privatisation

Since 1979 in the UK, the Government has energetically pursued a policy of privatisation. This has tended to mean either selling off state owned companies and organisations to the private sector or inviting private firms to tender for work previously done solely by public employees and departments. Electricity, gas, water, oil, telephones and banks have just been some of the companies sold off whilst private firms are now tendering for cleaning schools and hospitals, collecting rubbish and looking after old people. Arguments in favour of this policy include:

1 Productive efficiency would increase. It is argued that state-owned companies or government departments have little incentive to produce at lowest cost.

Private enterprise, on the other hand, has to produce at lowest cost in order to survive in the market place. If they are not cost efficient, their prices will be higher than their rivals. The result will be loss of market share and possible eventual bankruptcy. High costs may also lead to low profitability, a situation which private shareholders would quickly rectify.

2 Choice would increase. Some industries which could be privatised in the UK are in competitive markets already—choice hardly increased when British Leyland was privatised, for instance. However, in many industries, government has or had a monopoly—water, electricity, gas, health provision and education are examples. Privatisation of these monopolies would, it is argued, lead to a considerable widening in the choice of products available to the consumer. Instead of consumers being forced to go to one doctor or one hospital, for instance, they would have a free choice. Instead of having to buy gas from a gas board, there would again be choice.

3 The quality of goods and services provided would improve. Lack of competition in the public sector, it is argued, encourages the provision of second-rate services. Privatisation would increase this aspect of allocative efficiency because of competitive pressures.

4 Privatisation would improve the responsiveness of producers to the real wants of consumers. The public sector, it is argued, provides goods and services irrespective of consumer interests. It can do this because of the lack of competition it faces. The gas consumer, the parent or the patient are forced to put up with the service the State deems sufficient rather than that which the consumer wants. Privatisation, by introducing competitive pressures to the market, would force producers to supply products that consumers really want.

5 Privatisation would encourage technological change. Competitive pressures in the free market force companies to innovate. Companies which fail to do so are likely to see their market share decline. Lack of competition in the public sector means that state industries have little incentive to innovate.

Critics of privatisation make two major points. Firstly, privatisation may lead to an undesirable redistribution of income and wealth in the com-

Data 28.3

The deregulation of the buses

Kevin Brown

The 1985 Transport Act swept away more than 50 years of tight control through local authority route licensing, and provided for the privatisation of the state-owned National Bus Company

Yet objective evidence produced by the government-funded Transport and Road Research Laboratory makes it clear that deregulation has been, at best, a partial success, even when measured against the Government's targets.

NBC was split into 72 operating companies which eventually sold for more than £300m – up to three times initial City forecasts.

Local authority subsidies fell by around £40m in the first year after deregulation, and will have fallen further in the second year.

There has also been a rapid increase in the overall provision of services, measured by vehicle mileage, which is up by at least 16 per cent in rural areas, and 8 per cent in the metropolitan areas.

Essential services have been protected by councils which have found

their budgets underspent because of the increased level of commerical operations.

On the debit side, deregulation has failed to create the "explosion" of competition promised by Mr John Moore, the former Transport Secretary, and has brought higher fares and fewer passengers.

Only about 400 new operators have entered the market, compared with more than 5,700 before deregulation, and the private sector share of total vehicle mileage has increased by only 5 percentage points to 15 per cent.

Most of this is due to the transfer of NBC vehicles to the private sector, and to private operators' success in tendering for subsidised services.

Fares in rural areas have hardly changed since deregulation but there have been large increases in the metropolitan counties – including 238 per cent in South Yorkshire.

Passengers have been voting with their feet. Total usage is down 12 per

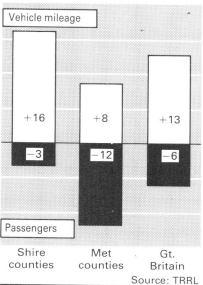

Bus industry

% Changes 1986/7 over 1985/6

Vehicle mileage

Shire counties: +16, −3
Met counties: +8, −12
Gt. Britain: +13, −6

Passengers

Source: TRRL

cent in the metropolitan counties, and 3 per cent in the rest of the country – after three years of relative stability.

The Financial Times. 26.10.88

---

1 To what extent has privatisation and deregulation in the bus industry increased economic efficiency?

---

munity. This is especially true where the State provides 'free' products to the consumer—as in health and education in the UK. For the poor who are no longer able to afford adequate health and education provision, more choice, improved quality or even lower cost of services would be irrelevant. Only the better-off would gain from privatisation. Secondly, critics cast considerable doubt over whether or not there would be improvements in productive or allocative efficiency. Privatised firms would enter oligopolistic market places. In other words, privatised firms would enter markets where there was little genuine competition, little accountability of firms to their shareholders, and where there was X-inefficiency, high prices and a lack of consumer sovereignty. The 'discipline of the market place' which proponents of privatisation talk of is not one where competitive pressures force firms to satisfy consumer wants, but one where producers discipline consumers to buy their products. Critics argue that the state sector is

not inherently less efficient than the private sector. The degree of efficiency to be found in any enterprise is dependent upon the extent to which economic efficiency is a goal of the enterprise, and upon the quality of the workforce (particularly that of management). On this argument, an inefficient public sector is caused by a government interested in goals other than economic efficiency (e.g. the maintenance of employment in a region of high unemployment) or a government which exercises too little control over its departments and industries. The solution to an inefficient public sector is not privatisation but more efficient control over their industries by those in government.

Allocative efficiency and externalities

An externality is defined as a cost or benefit which is not borne or not received by an economic agent which has produced it. Examples are pollution created, but not paid for, by a firm; beautiful buildings paid for by the owners but giving pleasure to the wider public; and traffic congestion caused by individual motorists who inflict time losses on other motorists.

It is easy to show why externalities can be important as regards allocative efficiency. Imagine an aluminium plant which is discharging cadmium waste into a local river. Local farmers grow crops which contain dangerous levels of cadmium, and the result is severe illness or death. The cost to society of that pollution is high: the cost to the firm is zero. The firm could at relatively small cost discharge its waste in more socially acceptable ways. It is obviously better for the firm to be forced to bear that cost and for aluminium prices perhaps to rise, than for the firm to continue producing such a large externality. There would be better allocative efficiency if the externality were eliminated.

Eliminating an externality is known as 'internalising' the externality. It involves forcing the producer of an externality to bear its cost (or to receive its benefit) rather than allowing others to bear that cost. The smaller the difference between social cost (the cost to society of production) and the private cost (the cost to an individual economic unit of production), the more likely it is that allocative efficiency will be high. Large externalities will result in over-production or under-production of the good concerned. As societies have become more

A nuclear power station. What externalities does this power station produce?

Data 28.4

Why Tasmania's wilderness row is assuming national importance

By Michael Thompson-Noel, recently in Tasmania

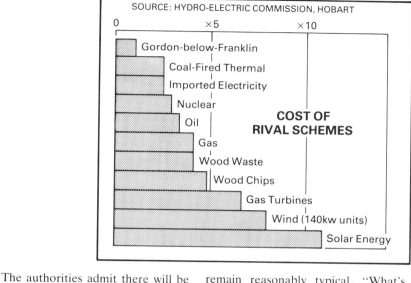

SOURCE: HYDRO-ELECTRIC COMMISSION, HOBART

0   ×5   ×10

Gordon-below-Franklin
Coal-Fired Thermal
Imported Electricity
Nuclear
Oil
Gas
Wood Waste
Wood Chips
Gas Turbines
Wind (140kw units)
Solar Energy

COST OF RIVAL SCHEMES

Tasmania is plugged into a bitter controversy over plans by the HEC and the Liberal State Government of Mr Robin Gray, the Prime Minister, to install a 180 Mw hydro scheme on the Gordon River in Tasmania's south-west wilderness.

In a recent mainland advertising campaign—"A watertight case for Tasmania's new dam"—costing A$75,000, the State Government and the HEC explained that water power was Tasmania's only major economical energy resource. The dam is due to be built at a point below the Gordon's confluence with the Franklin River—hence its description, the Gordon-below-Franklin.

Before recommending the Gordon-below-Franklin scheme, says the State Government, the HEC analysed all possible alternatives (see table) but found them to be too expensive. The cost of the Gordon-below-Franklin scheme is put at A$530, to be financed by HEC funds and public market borrowings. Physical construction of the dam is unlikely to start before 1987, with commissioning of the power station planned for 1990–91.

The HEC claims work on hydro schemes in Tasmania, creates 3,500 jobs. It says its biggest industrial customers, together with its own operations, have created 40,000 jobs, about one-in-four of every employed Tasmanian. All of which is fine—except that the site chosen for the dam is in one of the world's great wildernesses, in an area recently awarded a UNESCO World Heritage listing.

The authorities admit there will be some flooding but say that only the lower third of the 127 km Franklin will be affected and that the scheme will only flood "1 per cent of the area of south-west Tasmania."

However, according to the conservationists, the scheme would not only flood the lower Franklin, but reduce the south-west wilderness by an estimated 16 per cent; affect a rich collection of varied, obscure and often endemic species, from the orange-bellied ground parrot to the broad-toothed rat to numeous crustacea and a host of plants; destroy important ancient aboriginal cave networks; threaten temperate rainforests, 2,000 years old; and possibly help introduce weeds, pests and plant disease. In short, they say it would destroy the heart of a world-class wilderness for a mere 180 Mw of power for which there are alternatives to hand.

There is still widespread support for the Gordon River scheme among ordinary Tasmanians—who approved it in a referendum and in a state election. But support is now wavering under the impact of outside scrutiny.

Yet the remarks served up to me in Hobart (by a government employee)

remain reasonably typical. "What's the use of the river?" I was asked. "It's a dirty big gorge—bloody dangerous and with virtually no wildlife. There are heaps of other rivers on the west coast for people who want to float down them."

Michard Barnard, a writer for The Age, of Melbourne, added recently that the south-west wilderness was so vast, rugged and dense with trees that many people would not find the eventual dam if dropped within five kilometres of it.

Yet for Prof David Bellamy, the British botanist arrested recently for protesting at the dam site, the issue is one of preserving what is left of the wilderness in a world of expanding deserts, disintegrating soils, and an increasingly chemico-plastic lifestyle.

"I hope it is going to be a victory," said the professor, shortly before being clapped in Hobart lock-up. "But if it is a defeat, the world has got to know that Australia has done a pretty bloody shady thing."

The Financial Times. February, 1983

Footnote: The proposed development ultimately did not go ahead.

---

1 Distinguish between the private and social costs of the proposed Gordon–below–Franklin Scheme.

2 What evidence is there to show that the proposed scheme is economically efficient?

aware of externalities, so pressure has mounted to have them internalised. Some industries have been greatly affected as a result. The asbestos industry world wide has shrunk as the dangers to health of asbestos have been recognised. Nuclear electricity generation is another industry where much of the argument as to its desirability centres around externalities.

A whole branch of economics has grown up centred on analysing externalities. 'Cost-benefit analysis' attempts to lay bare all costs and all benefits, whether private or social, associated with a particular project. An important early cost-benefit study was done by Foster and Beesley on the proposal to build the Victoria Line on the London Underground. The study concluded that the line would make a private loss in the sense that the operators, London Transport, would lose money on the line. However, it would make a social profit because the benefits of less congestion, shorter journey times and less pollution would outweigh the private losses. Hence it recommended that the line should be built. Inevitably, the tax-payer would have to pay for the private losses.

Allocative efficiency and innovation

Allocative efficiency is not only a concept which covers the idea of the right price for a good. It also deals with whether firms are supplying the right goods to the market. A major factor affecting this is the rate of innovation. If the rate of technological change is fast, then this will allow new products to come on to the market and existing products to be improved. This is likely to increase the consumer's welfare.

It has been argued that market structures strongly affect the rate of innovation in an economy. These arguments include the following:

1 There is no incentive to be innovative in industries where there is perfect knowledge. In perfect competition, for instance, no single firm will undertake research, or develop and launch costly new products, if its numerous rivals can go out and copy the technique or product at a fraction of the cost. Hence in perfectly competitive industries, such as agriculture, it is often the case that research and development has to be undertaken by government-

sponsored agencies. The price mechanism then has no influence on the amount of research being undertaken and hence allocative inefficiency is likely to result.

2 Galbraith has argued that only large oligopolistic and monopolistic firms have the financial resources to undertake research and development. In the planning sector of the economy, firms need to innovate in order to ensure their long run survival. By making large profits they are able to finance the research that is so vital to their continued existence.

3 Schumpeter argued that monopoly power enabled firms to make large profits. Other firms attracted by these high profits would find difficulty in entering the industry. This would encourage them to innovate, either by introducing new processes of production for the same good or by inventing new goods which would diminish the market of the existing monopolists. He called this 'the process of creative destruction'. Any allocative loss due to higher prices under monopoly would be far outweighed by the allocative gain of rapid technological development afforded by large firms with strong market power.

Economic efficiency and advertising

Advertising can be divided into two main types:

1 'Informative' advertising attempts to improve consumers' knowledge of the product. For instance, 'small ads' in newspapers or a marketing campaign for a new product could be seen as informative.

2 'Persuasive' advertising attempts to alter consumers' tastes. Much advertising on television is persuasive in the sense that virtually no consumer watching needs to be informed that a particular product is on the market. Rather, the advertiser is trying to alter the consumer's opinion of his product.

No advertisement is purely informative or purely persuasive. However, the distinction is useful in that the degree to which an advertisement is informative or persuasive can affect its impact on economic efficiency.

Advertising affects the costs of firms. Higher advertising results in higher total costs. From a

Data 28.5

Tales of Big Mac could turn out to be Whoppers

People in Hampstead and people on Martha's vineyard won't need to read this because fast food restaurants are banned in both. But for the remaining four billion souls on this planet, the titanic burger battle between number 1, MacDonald's, and arch-enemy Burger King is a tale well worth the telling.

Starting last October, American TV viewers were greeted by Burger King advertisements implying that MacDonald's Big Macs caused heart attacks and killed. Burger King's stalwart Whoppers, the advertisements proclaimed, were made without any fat; but MacDonald's loathsome Big Macs, the advertisements showed in revolting detail were soaked in it.

American law allows competitors to denigrate each other publicly like this (it's called comparative publicity), and American manners allow the denigrations to take on particularly vivid form. The UK's paltry butter-versus-margarine campaign became a model of Old World gentility when Burger King ($2.3 billion annual turnover) and MacDonald's ($7.6 billion per annum) went at it in the buff.

Burger King followed its televised attack with a magazine advertising campaign explaining that their hamburgers were for real men because the competitor's patty was a sickly thing with only 80 per cent as much meat. They confirmed the taunt by showing that in blind trials before three unidentified hamburgers, Americans, real Americans, would infallibly go for the Whopper.

By implication then a MacDonald's eater was an unpatriotic homosexual coronary case. The charge did not stand uncontested for long. Indignant executives from MacDonald's headquarters of hamburgerology (honest, that's what they call it) in suburban Chicago were quick to take the Whopper makers to court. It was all lies, more lies, and damned lies, they insisted. And they wanted $25 million and an apology to make up for it.

The judge found in Burger King's favour; the men from MacDonald's decided they would have to fight dirty to win.

American network television received a second onslaught. Big Macs are made fresh in front of you, the prime time viewers were told, but Whoppers are kept soaking in steam for hours and only reheated just before being sold. And the reheating's done by microwave radiation! Which would you prefer, har har har, the ads mockingly dug in.

But Burger King wouldn't give. In scattered stores for several weeks thereafter, anyone coming in who would proudly say "Your Whopper is better than any Big Mac" was given two Whoppers for the price of one.

Laugh, but the battle has already crossed the Atlantic. Burger King has just opened the world's largest Whopper outlet on the Champs Elysées in Paris, and MacDonald's has forced its independent French franchisers to give up the MacDonald's name on a technicality, so clearing the way for a full-fledged Big Mac attack directed by the boys from Chicago.

David Bodanis

The Guardian. 18.5.83

1 Using diagrams, explain why each company is engaging in 'comparative publicity'.

2 Have the advertising campaigns of both companies affected economic efficiency?

productive efficiency viewpoint, advertising results in inefficiency if consumers do not benefit from it. They will benefit if their knowledge of products on the market is increased. Thus consumers will be able to allocate their scarce spending power in a more rational way. On the other hand, if advertising distorts their perceptions of products, consumers are worse off. They are less able to allocate their scarce spending power in a rational way. Hence informative advertising can be said to improve productive efficiency, whilst persuasive advertising lowers productive efficiency.

A similar conclusion is reached with regard to allocative efficiency. Informative advertising allows the market to function better by enabling firms to tell consumers about new products. It also has no distorting effect on the relationship between price and marginal cost. Persuasive advertising on the other hand is anti-competitive and can be a major barrier to entry to an industry. By shifting the demand curve to the right and by lowering the price elasticity of the product, it enables a firm to increase its abnormal profits or its mark-up. It enables a firm to increase the value of the difference between price and marginal cost. It may also discourage research and development by diverting scarce resources into marketing budgets rather than research budgets.

Thus persuasive advertising diminishes economic efficiency, whilst informative advertising increases it. The power of the advertising industry and its clients is reflected in the fact that advertising is largely uncontrolled in Western economies.

Economic efficiency and profits

According to neo-classical economists, profits are an indicator of how resources should be allocated. For instance, assume that firms in an industry are making abnormal profits. This indicates that consumers are paying a higher price than it is costing firms to produce. Hence, economic welfare will be increased if productive resources are increased in that industry, thus increasing output and lowering price.

In perfect competition abnormal profits lead to new firms entering the industry, increasing output and lowering price, until such time as only normal profits are being made. On the other hand, in industries where there are barriers to entry—i.e. oligopolistic and monopolistic industries—new firms cannot enter the industry to provide the extra goods and services that consumers indicate that they want. Neo-classical economists conclude that in industries where there is freedom of entry, fluctuations in profits lead to an efficient allocation of resources. In industries where there are barriers to entry, profitability is not used to allocate resources and output is most unlikely to be at a level which maximises consumers' welfare.

Critics point out that firms earning abnormal profits may bring long term benefits to consumers. If that profit is used for research and development then the short term losses of higher prices are likely to be outweighed by long term gains in the form of better quality products, possibly at lower prices.

Summary

A market can be considered efficient from two standpoints: productive efficiency and allocative efficiency. Perfectly competitive firms enjoy perfect productive efficiency in theory. In practice, since firms are unable fully to exploit economies of scale, oligopolists and monopolists may be nearer to achieving productive efficiency than perfectly competitive firms. Barriers to entry are likely to impair allocative efficiency, allowing firms to make abnormal profits. Restrictive trade practices are another way in which firms, for their own gain, can impair allocative efficiency. Nationalised industries may maximise welfare if they price at marginal cost, but this is only true if all other firms are marginal cost pricing. An externality is a cost or benefit not borne or received by the producer. Externalities can lead to a misallocation of resources. Cost-benefit analysis attempts to include all externalities. Many economists have argued that a perfectly competitive structure for an industry will lead to below optimal innovation. Only oligopolistic and monopolistic firms have the funds and the incentives to undertake research and development. Persuasive advertising in general results in a misallocation of resources, whilst informative advertising increases knowledge and therefore leads to greater economic efficiency.

Terms for review

economic efficiency

productive and allocative efficiency

optimum size of the firm

restrictive trade practices

nationalised industries

marginal cost pricing

externalities

cost-benefit analysis

technical innovation

advertising

privatisation

272

Essay questions

1 *What is meant by 'economic efficiency'? Could the privatisation of the National Health Service in the UK lead to greater economic efficiency?*

2 *What price should a nationalised industry charge for its product? Is profitability an indication of the economic efficiency of such an industry?*

3 *Do all restrictive trade practices impair economic efficiency? What measures have been taken in the UK to curb these practices?*

4 *To what extent does advertising impair or improve economic efficiency?*

29

Factors of production— the neo-classical approach

Introduction

A factor of production is an input to the production process which yields a consumable good or service. Traditionally, economists have distinguished three (sometimes four) factors of production. Land embraces not only agricultural land or urban land, but all natural resources. So a shoal of fish, a natural forest, or fresh air, are classified by the economist as land. Labour is the human input, from poet and peasant to Prime Minister and country parson. Capital is the stock of existing goods used to produce other goods. Machines and buildings are the main types of capital.

A fourth factor of production, entrepreneurship, is sometimes distinguished. An entrepreneur is a person who risks his own capital in producing goods or services for the market. Risk-taking and organising production are the two key elements of the entrepreneur's role. The true entrepreneur has to some extent become far less important in the production process over the past 100 years. The manager of the large company has come to fulfil the role of organising production. The institutional shareholder—the pension fund or the insurance company—has come to bear much of the risk. Hence the entrepreneur could be regarded as relatively unimportant. Moreover, many economists argue that the entrepreneur is only a specialised form of labour, and that therefore only three factors of production exist.

Each factor of production receives a payment or return: land receives rent, labour receives wages, capital receives interest, and entrepreneurship receives profit. In general it is difficult to distinguish between interest and profit when received by the owners of capital. Only some of the owners of capital are entrepreneurs. Therefore it is usual to assume that capital receives both interest and profit.

If rent, wages, interest and profit are added up,

they come to the total income of the economy—its national income. Hence economists can use these concepts to study the distribution of income in an economy. This distribution of national income is known as the **functional distribution of income**. It is to be distinguished from the **personal distribution of income** which considers how income is divided up between individual persons. The functional distribution of income is the distribution in the form of wages, rents, etc. The personal distribution of income considers how much income an individual receives in relation to national income, but is not concerned whether that income is rent or wages or interest.

The demand for a factor of production is necessarily a derived demand. This means that consumers do not demand the factor of production directly. What they want is the goods or services which the factor of production can give. So a hairdresser is not consumed, but the service he gives is; a factory machine is not consumed but the car it makes is; a beautiful stretch of coast line is not consumed but the enjoyment it can give to a rambler is.

In this chapter, we will consider how neo-classical economists explain the level of payments received by factors of production. They argue that one single theory can explain these payments.

Price theory

Neo-classical economists argue that factor markets are in no way different from ordinary markets. The price of a factor is determined by the interaction of demand and supply. So, if demand for labour goes up, the wage rate will rise. If the supply of capital increases, then the rate of profit will fall. We assume here that all other factors remain constant. It remains to develop a theory of demand and a theory of supply for factors.

Demand and marginal revenue product

The concepts of total, average and marginal products were introduced in Chapter 23. Product refers to actual output, e.g. 10 cars, 1 ship, 100 000 yogurt cartons. Hereafter, it will be referred to as 'physical product' to distinguish it from 'revenue product' which refers to the value of what is produced, e.g. £10 000 of car, £1 million of ship, £1 000 worth of yogurt cartons. Total physical product is the total volume of production of a given number of factors of production. Average physical product is the volume of production per unit of factors used. Marginal physical product is the volume of production produced by utilising one extra unit of a factor.

In Chapter 23, the law of diminishing returns was outlined. The law states that if the quantity of a factor of production is increased, all other factors being constant, then eventually the marginal physical product will decline, followed by a decline in average physical product. A standard example is the addition of units of labour to an acre of land with a fixed amount of machinery. To start with, each man will produce more than the last because of the possibility of co-operation, i.e. marginal physical product will rise. But at some stage, marginal physical product is bound to start declining as each worker adds less and less output to the total.

This is illustrated in Table 29.1. Diminishing marginal returns set in when two units of the factor are used. Marginal revenue product can then be calculated by multiplying the marginal physical product by the price per unit received for that output. It is assumed in Table 29.1 that the firm receives the same price per unit for its output whatever its size. Thus we are assuming that the firm is facing a perfectly elastic, horizontal demand curve for its product. In neo-classical theory, the firm must be perfectly competitive.

Given the law of diminishing returns, how much of a factor will a producer demand? It would not be sensible for a firm to hire or buy a factor at £150 when marginal revenue product was only £70, as it would lose £80 on that transaction. On the other hand, if the marginal revenue product were £200, the firm could make a gain of £50. By hiring further

---

Data 29.1

The rise and rise of top people's pay

The pay of Britain's top earners is increasingly tied to the performance of their companies.

A recent study by Korn/Ferry International, the executive search consultants, found that 81 per cent of companies had a performance-related cash bonus plan.

For instance, Sir Ralph Halpern, chairman of the Burton Group became the highest paid executive in Britain in 1986 with £1 million in salary and performance payments. His rewards were tied to exacting performance targets including a requirement that Burton's cumulative earnings per share growth put it in the top 25 companies making up the FT-SE 100-share index.

The pay of other top earners is also tied to performance, their defenders arugue. Mr Stanley Kalms, chairman of Dixons, has seen his pay fall as well as rise. Higher executive pay is, to a large extent, 'a response to a much more performance oriented society', says Mr Philip Burnford of Hay Management Consultants, the remunerations specialists.

The Financial Times. 17.7.89

1 Can economic theory explain (a) why some company executives receive such large salaries and (b) why pay is linked to performance?

Table 29.1

Units of a factor used	Marginal physical product	Marginal revenue product if price per unit of output = £10
1	21	£210
2	24	£240
3	20	£200
4	15	£150
5	7	£70

factors, a further gain could be made. The firm will make the greatest gain in fact where the extra cost of hiring or buying an additional factor is equal to that factor's marginal revenue product. If a factor were priced at £150, then the firm in Table 29.1 would hire 4 units. The firm's profit on hiring the factors would be £210–£150 or £60 from the first factor, £240–£150 or £90 on the second, and £50 on the third, i.e. a total of £200.

Figure 29.1 illustrates this in diagrammatic terms. OABC represents the total reward to the factor of production at output of 4 (e.g. wages or interest), BCD represents the profit to the firm arising from that use.

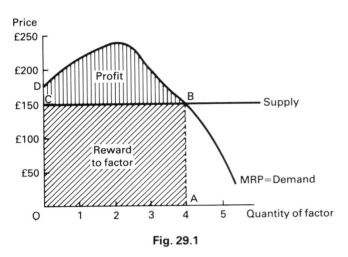

Fig. 29.1

The marginal revenue product (MRP) represents the demand curve for the factor. It shows how much an additional factor is worth to a firm. The firm will be willing to buy or hire that factor if its price is equal to or greater than the marginal revenue product. In other words, the MRP curve shows how much a firm will demand of a factor at any given price.

The supply of factors

Neo-classical theory has no simple theory of supply, as it has of demand. It argues that the supply curve for a factor in general is upward sloping, as for any normal good, although there are exceptions. Apart from this, neo-classical theory argues that each factor has its own set of supply determinants. These are now considered.

The supply of land

The total world supply of 'land' (in its economic sense) is more or less fixed. However, the total supply of land is not a particularly useful concept here. It is almost always the supply of a particular type of land which interests economists and laymen. The supply of agricultural land, or of crude oil or of forests need to be considered rather than the world's total natural resources.

The supply of types of land tends to be fairly inelastic in the short run. As the 1970s have shown, the supply of oil in the short run is highly inelastic. Very large increases in price have not been matched by large increases in supply. Equally, it is not possible to reclaim land quickly for agricultural purposes. In Western economies, the supply of building land is fixed in the short run because of laws requiring planning permission, etc. In the long run however, the supply of the factor, land, tends to be far more elastic. The world's proven reserves of oil increased dramatically in the 1970s as high prices encouraged further exploration. The supply of agricultural land in the UK would have seen a significant increase over the past 200 years if part of it had not been used as building land. Moreover, the quality of that land has increased. In the long term governments have allowed more and more land to be used for building purposes as populations have increased.

The supply of labour

It is a mistake to assume that the supply of labour in an economy is given by the numbers of people in work. The total supply can be increased (or decreased) from this figure in two ways. Firstly, in an economy there is a large pool of people at present not in work who could be persuaded to work if wages were high enough. Secondly, the existing workforce could work harder in terms of overtime or increased productivity. A large number of factors affect the number of people available for work at any given wage rate. These include:

1 The benefits available for not working. If unemployment benefits rise, then some workers may prefer to be unemployed rather than to have a job. Equally a rise in pensions may persuade some workers to retire early. A grant to sixth former students would persuade some school children to stay on at school.

economies over the past 50 years. However, neo-classical economists argue that the supply curve of labour eventually becomes backward sloping. In Fig. 29.2, as wage rates increase up to W_2, the worker wishes to work longer hours. At a wage rate of W_1, for instance, the worker is prepared to work L_1 hours. At the increased wage rate of W_2 he is prepared to work L_2 hours. However, L_2 is the maximum number of hours that the worker is prepared to work. If wage rates rise further, say to W_3, then the worker prefers to worker fewer hours (L_1) and take more time off for leisure activities. This is because at certain levels of income (income equals the wage rate times the number of hours worked), extra leisure becomes worth more to the worker than the extra goods and services that his extra pay could provide. In all Western economies, there has been a gradual reduction over the past 50 years in the number of hours worked and an increase in the number of days' holiday taken. A common feature of many trade union demands in an annual round of pay negotiations is not only extra money, but also a shorter working week and extra holiday entitlements.

An aerial view of the City of London. Why are land rents so high in the City?

2 The alternatives available to working. If, for instance, the number of women having children rises, then some of those women will prefer to stay at home to look after their child.

3 The total size and composition of the population. If, as happened between 1950 and 1964, the birth rate in the UK rises this results in an increase in the numbers of people seeking jobs 16 years later. The fall in the birth rate in the 1920s and 1930s meant a smaller number of those in the working population than would otherwise have been over the next 60 years.

4 The pecuniary rewards to work. If for instance, real wages rise, then paid work becomes relatively more attractive than other activities such as housework, child minding or leisure. Increased real wages are a major determinant of the large increases in the number of females wishing to work in developed

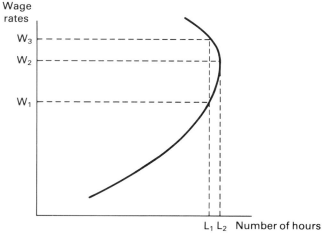

Fig. 29.2

5 Non-monetary factors. All other things being equal, workers will demand higher wages for jobs which are dirty, dangerous, have long or unsocial hours of work, or which are boring or dehumanising.

Of equal interest is the supply of labour to any particular market. High levels of unemployment may exist in an economy whilst at the same time there may be labour shortages in particular markets. The supply of labour to any particular market is dependent upon the following:

1 The numbers of potential workers in the economy with the right talent, skills, training and capability for the job. A very large proportion of the working population could become road sweepers. Very few could become brain surgeons. In other words, at any given wage rate, the supply of road sweepers far exceeds the supply of brain surgeons. In some industries, the supply is so limited that wages can be very

high indeed. Good pop stars and footballers are two examples. The Government can increase or decrease the potential supply to any market through its training policies. For instance if the Government closes down large numbers of teacher training colleges, then this will automatically limit the supply of teachers onto the market.

2 The willingness of workers to move geographically. Regional unemployment has been a feature of all industrialised economies. Certain regions of a country have a higher rate of unemployment than others

Data 29.2

Goodbye to the 'cornflake family'

John Gapper

The last few months have seen a stream of initiatives by British companies to attract and retain women. Midland Bank plans to set up 300 workplace nurseries; Boots, the retail chemist, is introducing job sharing for junior managers; Royal UK, an insurance company, is giving bonuses to mothers who return to work within a year.

The immediate reason for the renewed interest in working women is that economic growth has created skilled labour shortages, on top of the demographic fact of falling numbers of young people – the traditional source of recruits – up to 1995. Women are being cast in their traditional role as a reserve army of labour.

But something deeper is also happening. Not only do women form 80 per cent of the projected rise in the workforce up to 1995, but the long-term shift in Britain's industrial structure towards service employment favours them.

The effect on the sexual balance of employment has been marked. Women have taken most of the jobs created in

Britain this decade. Of jobs created between June 1983 and March 1988, 740,000 went to women working part-time and 550,000 to women working full-time, while male part-timers grew by only 230,000 and male full-timers fell by 100,000.

Women are also coming to think of themselves once more as workers. Although women dominated industries such as brewing and textiles in Britain in the 17th century, there was a sharp decline in women's participation rates during the 19th century – in particular because of social hostility to married women taking paid employment.

Married women's participation rates in peacetime remained low until the 1950s, despite the acceptance of young women doing jobs such as nursing. Now, however, according to the Government survey Social Trends, only 45 per cent of working age women consider that women with children under the age of five ought not to work, compared to 78 per cent in 1965.

Some things have not changed. Although men may approve of women

working, emancipation does not extend to domestic responsibilities. Housework is mostly still performed by women – in 88 per cent of households they do most washing and ironing, and in 72 per cent they do most cleaning. They also take far greater responsibility for child care.

Combined with the comparatively poor public provision of child care for working mothers in Britain, the effect has been to push many women into part-time work. Sixty-five per cent of women workers are married, and 45 per cent work part-time. By comparison, in France, only 23 per cent of women workers were part-timers in 1986.

The need to attract women will require many employers to change both the terms on which they offer work, and the payments made for particular skills.

Ms Joanna Foster, who chairs the Equal Opportunities Commission, believes many companies suffer from organising work according to the needs of "the cornflake family" of television advertisements, with two children, a mother who stays at home and a working father. "Most women work part-time because it is the only way they can balance their lives," she says.

The Financial Times. 20.2.89

1 Outline the changes in the supply of labour in the UK described in the article.

2 Using diagrams, explain how UK employers could change the supply of labour in the 1990s.

because many workers in those regions are unwilling to move to another in search of jobs. There are a number of reasons for this. Firstly, workers are reluctant to move from places where they have strong family and community ties. Secondly, knowledge of jobs in other regions may be very limited. This is particularly true of less skilled, low paid jobs. Thirdly, institutional factors, such as great difficulty in getting reasonable local authority housing accommodation, may discourage workers.

3 The willingness of workers to move from industry to industry. An out-of-work steel worker may not consider jobs in anything but heavy industry, since he believes that his skills are only suited to that. On the other hand, firms may actively discourage workers from broadening their work horizons by their recruiting policies of only taking workers with the 'right' sort of industrial experience. Trade unions or professional associations may act so as to limit the supply of labour to an industry. This is considered in more detail in Chapter 15.

It is often argued that levels of taxation have an important effect upon incentives to work. The standard argument is that increasing tax rates will reduce the willingness of workers to work. The proposition needs to be defined more carefully.

What is meant by a reduction in incentives to work? It could mean that fewer of the potential labour force want jobs. It could mean that existing workers refuse to undertake overtime, work extra days, etc. Or it could refer to the fact that workers refuse promotion because the extra monetary rewards are not sufficient to outweigh the disadvantages of extra responsibility, moving house, etc. Higher personal taxation could affect any of these three categories. However, a number of counter arguments can be put. Firstly, people work for reasons other than money. They enjoy their jobs. It gives them prestige, status, stimulation, a social atmosphere. A budding manager would surely not work less hard if an extra 2p were put on standard rate income tax. On this argument small losses in extra taxation would affect incentives to work, but the effect would be negligible. Secondly, workers may decide to work harder after a tax increase in order to maintain their standard of living. A worker may have become accustomed to living on £170 a week and have many fixed commitments. In these circumstances he is unlikely to work shorter hours or risk his chances of promotion by working less hard.

Neo-classical theory argues that if all workers were identical, then all wage rates would be equal. Market forces would ensure that firms offering less than this wage would find it impossible to attract workers, whilst firms offering above average wages would be besieged by potential applicants and would in consequence lower the wage rate for the job. However, not all workers are identical. It is because of this that wage differentials arise.

The supply of capital

Any economy can devote its scarce resources to the production of either consumption goods or capital goods. The decision to produce one necessarily involves the decision not to produce the other. In an economy with no foreign trade, consumers and governments who do not spend all of their income must save it. Those savings are then channelled into investment, additions to the total stock of capital.

Hence, what determines the level of saving in the economy must equally determine the supply of capital. Neo-classical economists argue that saving is determined by the rate of interest. The higher the rate of interest, the higher the level of savings. So the supply of capital must be determined by the rate of interest.

In Fig. 29.3, the upward sloping supply curve of capital is shown. Increases in interest rates, say from r_1 to r_2, result in higher levels of savings from S_1 to S_2 and thus higher investment. Higher investment leads to an increased stock of capital.

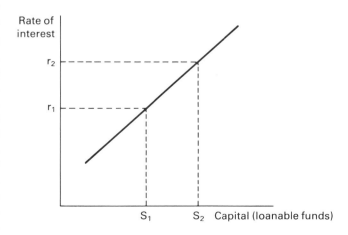

Fig. 29.3

The supply of entrepreneurship

In return for risking his capital and for organising factors of production, the entrepreneur is rewarded by profit. The popularity of the entrepreneur has risen since the 1970s. It is not that there are necessarily more entrepreneurs about, but rather that economists and governments have become disillusioned with the oligopolistic sector of the market, for two main reasons. Firstly, there has been a growing feeling that the entrepreneur is the standard bearer of genuine competition in the market. Secondly, the oligopolistic sector of the market has been blamed for failing to provide enough jobs in the economy. The small scale entrepreneur is seen as far more likely to provide new jobs in the market than the large capital-intensive firm.

The supply of entrepreneurship to the market is dependent upon levels of profitability. The higher the level of profitability, the more workers will turn into entrepreneurs. For instance, if it becomes apparent that health food shops are making large profits, workers will be tempted into risking their capital and setting up in business as owners of health food shops.

One way of raising the real level of profitability is to make the opportunity cost of entrepreneurship less attractive. If workers find it difficult to undertake paid employment, then becoming an entrepreneur will become more attractive. In deepening

---

Data 29.3

The folk heroes of today

Charles Batchelor

Britain has created an enterprising business community from fairly barren soil over the past decade. New businesses are being set up at the rate of 200,000 a year; more than 100 new venture capital companies have sprung up and management buy-outs have emerged as a popular method of revitalising tired businesses.

"Entrepreneur; Eight British Success Stories of the 1980s" by Paul Burns and Tony Kippenberger traces the histories of 14 businessmen and women who between them have started eight very successful businesses.

Readers might be tempted to attribute their success to government programmes to help small firms, to changes in the tax regime, to the establishment of the USM. But most of the entrepreneurs would have achieved their goals irrespective of these measures, the authors conclude.

So what makes for success? The authors point to vision, perseverance, a willingness to take risks and a good business idea, but show that there is no set formula. The backgrounds of the chosen entrepreneurs provide no clue to their ultimate success. Only three (Richard Gabriel of Interlink Express, a parcels delivery company, and the two Sock Shop founders) had self-employed parents. The others had either working class or professional backgrounds.

Many people dream of starting up on their own but most need a trigger to get them to act. David Bruce, founder of Bruce's Brewery, grew frustrated with his career prospects with one of the large brewers. Bob Payton, (the American founder of the My Kinda Town chain of restaurants), faced the prospect of being transferred back from London to New York to a job he did not want.

Perhaps the most intriguing aspect of success is the personal qualities that are needed. Stamina and the ability to work long hours appear to be an important ingredient. This is allied with tenacity. Gray worked on her business idea for seven months before she got backing, while Robert Wright, founder of Connectair, a commuter airline, spent 18 months seeking support.

The products with which these entrepreneurs made their money were by no means revolutionary. They were just sufficiently innovative to differentiate them from the competition. Interlink Express made imaginative use of information technology to speed up parcels delivery. Sock Shop was based on the simple idea that there would be demand for specialist shops selling socks and tights.

The Financial Times. 31.1.89

---

1 *What is an entrepreneur?*
2 *To what extent can government policy create an enterprise culture in an economy?*

recession, as more and more workers are made redundant, it is perhaps not surprising that the number of new firms being set up is likely to increase. Equally, under such conditions the number of firms going bankrupt is also likely to increase!

Another factor which affects real profitability is the level of taxation on profits. The higher the tax rate, the lower will be the level of after tax profits, and the lower the supply of entrepreneurship to the market. However, this need not necessarily be the case. Higher taxation may encourage an increase in entrepreneurship. Existing entrepreneurs may feel that they need to risk more capital and work even harder following a tax rise in order to maintain levels of profitability. This mirrors the argument presented concerning the effect of taxation on wages.

Terms for review

factors of production

marginal revenue product

mobility of labour

incentives to work

entrepreneurship

Summary

Neo-classical theory argues that the reward to each factor of production—rent for land, wages for labour, interest and profits for capital and entrepreneurship—is determined by the demand and supply of each factor. The demand curve is the marginal revenue product curve of that factor. No simple theory of supply exists. However, the supply curve of a factor is in general upward sloping.

Essay questions

1 What factors determine the wages of (a) plumbers and (b) doctors.

2 What determines the supply of labour in an economy? What effect would you expect (a) an increase in child benefits and (b) a fall in the real value of unemployment benefit to have on the supply of labour?

3 What is meant by an 'entrepreneur'? What effect would you expect a deep recession to have on the supply of entrepreneurship?

30

Factors of production—the classical and neo-Keynesian approaches

Ricardo's theory of economic rent

David Ricardo, a classical economist of the early nineteenth century, was interested in why land rents increased. He argued that the agricultural land of the time in England was in fixed supply. If the land were not used for agriculture it would have no alternative use. Thus the supply of such land was perfectly price inelastic, as in Fig. 30.1. Whatever the rent paid to landlords, the same amount of land would be supplied. So if the demand curve for land were D, then landlords would earn a rent of OFBA. If population increased and the demand for food went up, then the demand for land would increase too, say to D'. The rent received by landlords would consequently increase to OECA. Ricardo predicted that as population increased, rents would rise. Land-owners, therefore, would be better off despite not having 'worked for' or 'earned' that increase.

Ricardo's theory can be generalised to deal with all factors of production. **Economic rent** is defined as the payment to a factor of production over and above that which it would receive in its next best use. In the case of Ricardo's agricultural land, it had no alternative use and therefore all the payment for

the use of the land was economic rent. However, it i more likely that land did have alternative uses ever in Ricardo's time. It could, for instance, have bee used for hunting or for industrial purposes. In tha case, the economic rent paid for the land was th difference between the price paid for its agricultura use and what would have been paid for its use say a hunting land.

A top fashion model. Do all models earn economic rent.

Rent

E — — — — — C

F — — — — — B

O — — — — A — — Agricultural land

S

D'

D

Fig. 30.1

To take another example, if a pop star earns £1 million a year, and in his next best occupation he could have earned £10 000 a year, then his economic rent is £990 000. The £10 000 is called his transfer earnings. Transfer earnings are the payments which a factor would have been able to obtain in its next best use. Another way of looking at it is to say that the pop star would have been prepared to be a pop star at any income greater than £10 000 a year. Therefore, transfer payments represent the minimum amount of payment which a factor needs to keep it in its present use. At a payment of less than £10 000 a year the pop star would do better to change his job to his next best occupation. Economic rent can thus be defined as any payment greater than transfer earnings.

In Fig. 30.2, ordinary demand and supply schedules have been drawn for a factor of production. The equilibrium payment is OP, and OQ units of the factor are employed. The last unit employed, the Qth unit, receives just that payment necessary to keep it in that employment. However, the Cth unit of production is willing to be employed for only OB of payment. But it is being paid the same as all the units employed, that is OP. Hence BP represents its economic rent. The combined economic rent for all the units of production employed up to Q is therefore represented by the shaded area APE. The transfer earnings are represented by the shaded area OAEQ. Total payment to the units is OPEQ (the quantity employed times their price).

It should be noted that economists use the word 'rent' in a different way from its normal usage.

The theory of economic rent has certain implications for government policy. A government may

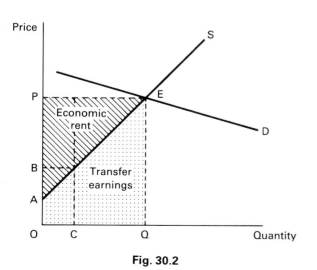

Fig. 30.2

Data 30.1

Strike at Vauxhall

Brian Groom

The ghost of hot wage autumns past was abroad in a tree-lined park beside Vauxhall's Luton car plant yesterday morning, when nearly 7,000 workers voted by about three to one to strike from Friday night over a 7.7 per cent pay offer covering 14 months.

Even if last-minute peace efforts delay or avert a national strike by the company's 14,500 manual workers, they have clearly regained their bargaining strength. Vauxhall's surge to a 14.5 per cent UK car market share from 11.7 last year and 8.5 per cent in 1981—partly because of the Cavalier—has given them power.

The offer, like last year's 8 per cent deal, is among the highest in industry. A strike would not only set back Vauxhall's recovery, it would also severely dent its record on working hours lost through disputes. These have been negligible for the past two years, but in 1979 27 per cent were lost.

Comparing motor industry pay is difficult because of the variable bonuses paid by most companies. According to Incomes Data Services, Vauxhall's current range of weekly basic rates of £95.36-£122.66 compares with Ford's £102.84-£132.80, BL's £90-£118.35, and Talbot's £92.12-£124.20.

Vauxhall bonuses have recently ranged from £0.75p a week to £16.40; BL's from £10.80 to £30; and Talbot's were about 10 per cent of basic earnings. Ford pays an attendance allowance of between £6.59 and £8.53.

Some of the old attitudes were in evidence at Luton yesterday. One worker who favours a strike, asked if he was worried about its effect on Vauxhall's recovery, said: "Ain't bothered mate. We got what we want."

The Financial Times. 29.9.83

1 *Are Vauxhall workers able to earn economic rent?*

judge that it is unacceptable for the owners of a factor of production to make large gains simply because of relatively high levels of demand. It may therefore decide to tax these relatively high earnings. The theory of economic rent suggests that these factors will continue in their present use so long as the tax is not greater than the economic rent being earned by the factor. Consider a land site in the middle of a big city. Let us suppose that in its present use as office accommodation it earns a rent of £2 million a year. If it were in its next best use, say warehousing, it would earn half that, £1 million a year. In this case the Government can tax the landowner up to £1 million before the landowner will consider transferring its use. Another example would be a North Sea oil field. In any one year the operators of a certain field may need to earn £200 million to maintain production and to be prepared to undertake further exploration. If the field yields £400 million then the Government may tax the company up to £200 million without affecting the company's decision to exploit the field and to develop others.

Neo-Keynesian analysis of the capital market

Neo-Keynesians have rejected the neo-classical theory of marginal productivity. They prefer to look back to the writings of the original classical economists such as Ricardo and Adam Smith in order to construct their theories of determinants of factor prices.

In the 1950s, certain neo-Keynesian economists started to argue that the neo-classical analysis of the capital market was fundamentally wrong. Neo-classical economists argue that as interest rates rise, the demand for capital goods will fall. In Fig. 30.3, the marginal efficiency of capital schedule is drawn. In any normal price diagram, the price of the product does not determine the quantity of the product. For instance, if the price of a pint of beer increases from 60p to 80p, this does not alter the volume of beer. A pint of beer does not become a gallon of beer when pubs increase their prices!

Capital is arguably different as, unlike beer, it is impossible to measure it in volume terms. It makes sense to say that 1 million barrels of beer were sold last month. It makes no sense to say that 1 million units of capital were sold to British industry last

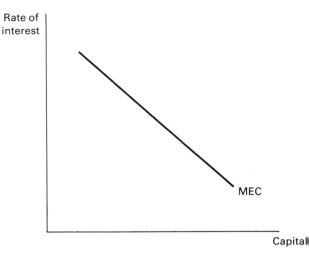

Fig. 30.3

month. This is because each unit of capital is different, varying from a simple hammer, to a large factory, to 60 shop counters for a new department store. So economists have always tended to measure the volume of capital in money terms. Last month's investment is not recorded as 1 million units of capital, but as say £3 000 million.

Neo-classical economists argue that 'net present value' techniques need to be used to calculate the total stock of capital in an economy. This is where the present value is calculated by considering the future income to be generated and converting it to one present value by using a rate of discount or interest. So in order to calculate the stock of capital in any economy, the economist needs to use a rate of interest. The higher the rate of interest, the lower is the net present value of the stock of capital.

A demand or supply curve for a product is drawn on the assumption that the price and quantity of the product are two distinct entities. But in the case of capital, the rate of interest determines the value of the quantity of capital. So it is not possible in the case of capital to draw demand and supply curves. If we did, we would be involved in circular reasoning; this is because a fall in the rate of interest would not only increase investment demand, according to marginal revenue product theory, but would also change the value of capital, according to net present value methods.

The neo-Keynesian conclusion is that the neo-classical theory of capital is fundamentally wrong

They argue that the nation's stock of capital is determined not by price (the rate of interest) but by income. The existing stock of capital is historically given. New capital or investment is determined by whether or not investors think they need new investment to produce extra output. Firms will invest if orders exceed maximum possible production at a price which covers cost-plus-mark-up. This view, that investment is determined by changes in income, is known as the accelerator principle (see Chapter 8).

Neo-Keynesian analysis of the labour market

Neo-Keynesians argue that the majority of output in a developed economy is produced in the 'planning sector' of the economy, where firms are large and markets are oligopolistic in nature. Firms in the planning sector have sophisticated employment practices. The norm is that a minority of workers work for a lifetime in the firm. However, this minority fills all the decision-making posts in the firm. They also represent over 50% of the wages bill because the majority of workers such as cleaners and catering staff are low paid, low skilled and often part-time. The minority face a clear career structure within the firm. Appointments to jobs are made almost entirely from within the firm. Recruits only come in at the bottom of this career ladder as trainees. This has very important implications for wage determination.

1 The firm represents a near monopoly employer for its career employees. This is because other firms within the industry are also operating similar employment practices. So there is no free market for such workers. Workers can of course change jobs, but their transfer earnings are very low. For instance, a typical thirty-five year-old bank manager would find it very difficult to find another job outside his bank at anything near the wage he was currently receiving.

2 The workforce represents a near monopoly supply of labour to the firm. This is because the policy of firms is to hire workers only at the trainee stage. If there is a shortage of certain groups of workers, younger workers are promoted more rapidly than they would otherwise have been. If there are too many workers of a certain sort, promotion is curtailed and workers might be encouraged to seek early retirement or be retrained to undertake other functions. Sacking workers is a policy of last resort. The very survival of the firm would have to be at risk to warrant such a measure.

3 Wage structures are carefully laid down and change only rarely. Differentials between workers are calculated according to longstanding ideas of their worth rather than any pressure from current free market forces. For instance, the sixteen-year-old recruit with five 'O' levels receives one-third of the salary of a middle-ranking manager who will no longer be promoted. The most highly skilled shop floor worker receives the same as the average salesman for the firm. When it comes to wage bargaining, wage differentials are rarely changed.

4 The level of wages is not fixed by the supply and demand for labour, as both are highly wage inelastic. The bargaining between the two sides represents a power struggle between the owners of capital and the providers of labour. Large pay increases tend to be at the expense of profits. Small pay increases lead to greater profitability. The outcome of wage negotiations is determined by the relative strengths of the two parties. In a recession, with unemployment rising and output stagnating, workers are in a relatively weak position and wage increases tend to be low. In a high growth economy, workers are in a stronger position and wage increases are higher.

5 Trade unions increase the strength of labour in a firm. If there are no trade unions, labour is weak because it faces a monopoly employer. Trade unions help redress the balance, and prevent the exploitation of the workforce by the owners of capital. Without independent trade unions, the workforce is at a severe disadvantage.

So far, we have described the planning sector of the private economy. What of the other sectors? Firstly, the public sector operates in a very similar way to the planning sector. There is a monopoly employer—the Government. The majority of career workers find it difficult to transfer to the private sector because of the specialisation of their skills and the preference of the planning sector to train its own staff. Public sector workers tend to organise into trade unions. The level of wages is determined by the relative power of Government and its employees.

In the market sector of the private economy, however, wages are much more influenced by demand and supply factors. Labour is not effectively unionised and is faced by a large number of potential employers. Workers are highly mobile, able and willing to move from job to job provided by the numerous firms in an industry. Skills required in the market sector are less specialised than those in the planning sector. Indeed the planning sector takes a disproportionate share of workers with formal qualifications, leaving the market sector with a disproportionate share of the unskilled. One unskilled job is much like another and therefore unskilled workers are potentially more mobile than skilled

---

Data 30.2

Pay curb easier under Labour, says study

By Philip Bassett, Labour Editor

TRADE UNION wage mark-up – the differential between union and non-union pay rates – is lower under Labour than Conservative governments, according to a study of union wages over time.

The study of the union wage differential over 30 years provides evidence that incomes policies do work with unions when a friendly government is in office.

The forthcoming report, by Mr Michael Beenstock from the Hebrew University in Jerusalem and Mr Chris Whitbread of the City University Business School looks at data prepared in the London School of Economics on the extent of the union wage differential from 1953 to 1983.

The study does not look especially at the absolute level of the union mark-up – put by most authoritative research now at about 10 per cent – but at its changes over time.

It finds that although there have been short-term fluctuations in the mark-up, it rose over the period. In the mid-50s to mid-60s, the rising trend is not particularly marked, but the differential showed a sharp increase in the period 1967–72.

The study shows that the mark-up trend was flat from 1972–79, followed by another large increase between 1979 and 1980. Since then it has remained at the higher level.

The authors look at a number of factors which affect the union differential, including cyclical economic factors, benefit levels, incomes policies, union density, and the political complexion of the Government.

The rise of about 10 percentage points in union density over the 1950–80 period may have added about 4 percentage points to the union mark-up.

The doubling of real supplementary benefit rates over the period added a further 4 percentage points to the mark-up, while the rise in unemploy-ment added about 9 percentage points.

The authors say that "the mark-up is 5 percentage points higher under a Conservative government than under Labour", and they conclude that "on average, the unions appear to heed Labour calls for restraint more than Conservative ones."

This showed that "trade unions are less militant when their own 'natural' party is in office."

The study concludes that the time-series suggests that in the period under examination, the behaviour of the mark-up suggests that there has been no fundamental change in its own measurement of union power.

The Financial Times. 27.10.88

---

1 *Explain briefly what affects the size of the 'trade union wage mark-up'.*

2 *Using diagrams explain in detail why a rise in unemployment should add to the union mark-up.*

orkers. In the market sector of the private eco-omy the neo-classical theory of the market free wage determination is realistic. But the market sector is only a very small part of any developed economy. So it is not adequate as a general theory of wage determination.

Clearing the labour market

One last point must be made. Neo-classical econo-mists argue that unemployment can be solved by reducing the price of labour. If wages decline, as in Fig. 30.4, from W_1 to W_E, equilibrium is restored in the labour market because $Q_E Q_2$ workers no longer wish to work, whilst firms demand an extra $Q_1 Q_E$ workers.

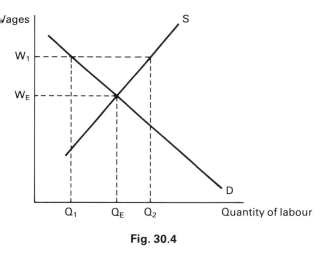

Fig. 30.4

Neo-Keynesians argue that this analysis is mis-leading. They say it is pointless to talk about the total supply of labour in this context because individual labour markets are so fragmented. If the diagram is to be used, the demand and supply curves for labour must be drawn inelastically, as in Fig. 30.5. This is because, at any given national average wage, large rises or falls in wages will have little effect upon firms' or governments' decision to hire or fire labour or upon individuals' decisions to leave or join the labour force. A return to equili-brium from wage rate W_2 would require a massive drop in wages. The experience of the Great Depress-ion of the 1930s showed that falls in wages did not cure unemployment and there is no evidence to suggest that the 1980s will prove any different.

Indeed, falls in wages reduce aggregate demand and thus push the demand curve for labour to the left, resulting in increases in unemployment rather than falls. On the neo-Keynesian view, pricing workers back into jobs by reducing their wages is at best ineffective and at worst reduces the living standards of everyone in the economy. The only way to reduce unemployment is to increase aggregate demand, thus providing new permanent jobs in the economy, and creating a climate in which governments and firms are prepared to invest to provide new work-places for their workforce.

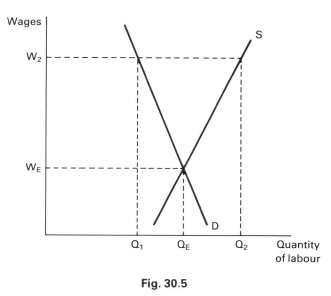

Fig. 30.5

Summary

Economic rent is the payment to a factor made over and above what it could earn in its next best use, i.e. payment over and above its transfer earnings. Neo-Keynesians argue that the stock of capital in an economy cannot be measured and that investment is a function of income and not price. In the labour market, they argue that neo-classical theory only applies to the relatively unimportant market sector of the economy. In the planning sector, monopoly employers face monopoly employees. As a result, wages and levels of employment are determined by the relative bargaining strength of both sides. According to neo-Keynesians, only increasing aggregate demand will clear the labour market.

Terms for review

economic rent

transfer earnings

Essay questions

1 *What do economists understand by 'economic rent'? Can trade unions affect the levels of economic rent earned by labour?*

2 *How are wages determined in (a) the retailing industry and (b) the mining industry in the UK?*

31

The economic problem

Introduction

So far, we have discussed many types of economic problems and possible solutions. In this chapter, we will draw all this together and attempt to find out what is common to these problems. The basic question to be asked is 'What is economics?' Then we will discuss how different types of economy can solve this problem and to what extent they do this efficiently.

A definition of economics

'Economics' has been variously defined. Adam Smith considered it to be an 'inquiry into the nature and causes of the wealth of nations'. Another classical economist, J. S. Mill, defined it as 'the practical science of the production and distribution of wealth'. This concentration on wealth was typical of the concern of classical economists for economic development.

Neo-classical economists, however, were far more interested in studying the interactions of economic units within the economy than in considering the direction of the total economy. The standard modern definition of economics shows this neo-classical bias. In the 1930s, L. Robbins defined economics as 'the science which studied human behaviour as a relationship between ends and scarce means which have alternative uses'. What Robbins was saying was that a problem arises because:

Economic resources are finite. Some resources, such as the air we breathe, are to all intents and purposes infinite. But they are exceptional. Steel, coal, cars, holidays have a finite supply, i.e. they are scarce. Moreover, the total supply of all resources available at any one point in time is finite also. This means that each individual resource has an opportunity cost. If more holidays are produced then fewer cars can be produced. If more hospital care is given, then fewer other goods and services can be produced, and so on.

2 Human wants are infinite. There is no limit to the amount that an individual wants to consume. These economic commodities include not only goods and services but also the amount of leisure time available, the diminution of everyday economic risks, and the quality of the environment in which a person has to live. A society as a whole may choose to devote extra resources to helping poorer countries, or setting up an elaborate scheme of social welfare provision, or sending men into outer space. It is very important to realise here that we are not arguing that the consumption of more and more goods and services will make a person happier. After all, consumers may be misled through the power of advertising and other means of promoting into wanting goods with zero or negative utility. When we say that wants are infinite we mean that human beings, both individually and as a society, will always prefer to allocate a larger bundle of goods and services than a smaller one.

Because resources are scarce or finite, and human wants are infinite, society has to construct economic systems to resolve the resulting conflict. There are three aspects to this conflict:

1 An economic system has to decide **what** to produce. In what proportion will it produce cars, or nuclear bombs, or flower pots?

2 It has to decide **how** to produce its goods and services. In what proportion will it use labour or machines, for instance?

3 It has to decide **for whom** production is to take place. Will 1% of the population take 90% of all production, or will the allocation of production be more equitable?

The economic problem

Each of these choices can be expressed diagrammatically. In Fig. 31.1, a **production possibility frontier** or **boundary** is shown. A production possibility frontier shows combinations of goods which an economy can produce. So in Fig. 31.1 the economy can produce no armaments and OC of all other goods, **or** OE of armaments and OA of all other goods, **or** OD of armaments and OB of all other goods, **or** OF of armaments and no other goods, **or** any other combination on the frontier. The frontier assumes that the economy is at full employment. Production may be within the frontier, e.g. where OD of armaments and OA of all other goods are produced. An economic system needs to decide **what** combination of goods is to be produced, i.e. where it wants to be on or within its production possibility frontier.

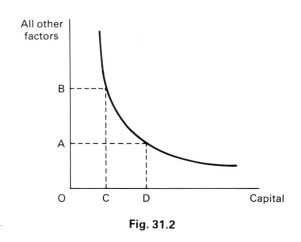

Fig. 31.2

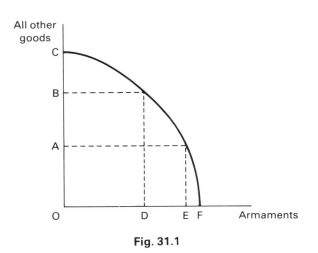

Fig. 31.1

Figure 31.2 shows choices of production techniques. The curve indicates what combination of factors of production is needed to produce one unit of output. For instant, to produce one unit of output, OC of capital and OB of all other factors can be employed, **or** OD of capital and OA of other factors can be used.

Figure 31.3 shows choices about income distribution. On the *x*-axis, income earners are split into decile groups according to their ranking in the income distribution. The decile 0–10 is the bottom 10% of income earners. A distribution such as the one shown by Line 1 gives a far more equal distribution than that shown by Line 2.

The three major types of economic system found amongst developed economies will now be considered in turn. They will then be compared from the viewpoint of efficiency.

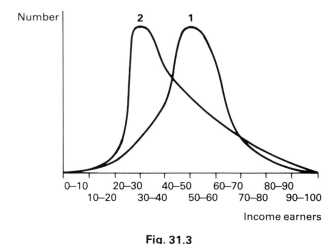

Fig. 31.3

The free enterprise economy

In a pure **free enterprise economy**, all goods and services, apart from pure public goods, are provided via the market mechanism. It is consumers who decide what is to be produced. According to the theory of consumer sovereignty, their spending 'votes' tell producers which goods and services are wanted at a given price and which are not. Firms which make goods that consumers do not want will go out of business. Firms which make goods that are in excess demand will be able to make abnormal profit, resulting in extra production and lower prices.

Data 31.1

Lawson to fight guns before butter argument

Christopher Huhne

The Government's attitude to defence spending was neatly summed up by one of the Cabinet's war veterans during a heated discussion about new equipment. "If I'd had a second class bayonet," he huffed, "I wouldn't be here today."

Second class bayonets—or fewer first class ones—are nevertheless back on the agenda after Mr Michael Heseltine, the Defence Secretary, was bounced last week, much to his annoyance, into accepting £230 million of Treasury cuts only a day after publicly proclaiming the largest sustained increase in British defence spending since the Second World War.

There are plenty of motives for tackling defence spending, not least the substantial evidence that it entails long-term costs in terms of lower investment and growth. But the first reason for Mr Lawson's willingness to grasp the nettle is that the present level and projected increases in defence spending look unsustainable in the face of the Government's commitment to lower budget deficits and lower taxation. Something has to go.

Previous Conservative governments were certainly aware of defence spending's economic consequences, as the statement on defence of 1956 made clear: "The burden of defence cannot be allowed to rise to a level which would endanger our economic future. This burden does not consist only in the effect of high defence expenditure on the general level of taxation, important though that is.

"Defence production falls in the main upon the metal and metal using industries, which supply about half our exports and are of great importance in the re-equipment of British industry."

The economic costs are great, yet Britian's defence spending last year was higher in absolute terms than of any other European ally. It was higher per head. It was higher as a proportion of national income, and it is growing faster. How long can this really go on?

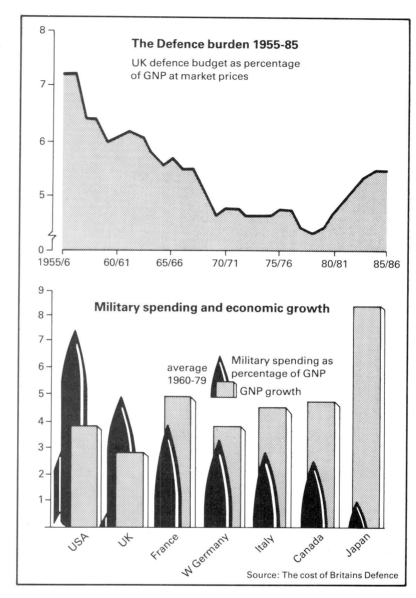

The Defence burden 1955-85
UK defence budget as percentage of GNP at market prices

Military spending and economic growth

average 1960-79

Military spending as percentage of GNP

GNP growth

USA — UK — France — W Germany — Italy — Canada — Japan

Source: The cost of Britains Defence

The Guardian. 14.7.83

1 Using a diagram, explain what an economist would understand by a 'guns before butter argument'.

2 Is there any evidence to suggest that high military spending is associated with low economic growth?

as new firms are attracted into the industry. Note that this assumes that there are no barriers to entry or exit to industries.

The mode of production (how goods and services are produced) is again determined via the market mechanism. Producers will be anxious to attain the least cost means of production available to them. The owners of factors of production will be interested in receiving the highest possible payment for their factors. Both groups are free to obtain the best possible price that they can get in the market place.

Production is generated for the owners of the factors of production. They are the only consumers who can obtain an income. The higher the value of the factor, the more income can be generated and therefore the more spending 'votes' are obtained.

A very small minority of goods and services needs to be provided by the public sector. These 'public goods' would otherwise not be provided if left to the market system.

In practice, there are no pure free enterprise economies anywhere in the world. Economies which approximate nearest to the model might be the USA and Canada. Here, the public sector provides other goods and services apart from pure public goods—education being one example. Incomes are given even to those who own no factors of production, e.g. the handicapped and the old; even if those incomes are very small. Finally, governments are constantly having to police 'free' markets to prevent any increase in the power of oligopolistic and monopoly producers over their markets. Economists such as J. K. Galbraith argue that most markets in the USA are not 'free' and that producers tell consumers what to buy rather than the reverse.

Why are great extremes of poverty and wealth likely to exist in a free enterprise economy?

Data 31.2

Victorian virtues that were vices

C. Gordon Tether

The great 19th century chronicler Charles Dickens must surely be turning in his grave if he can hear the glib talk we are now getting about returning to Victorian values.

As he worked so hard to show, while the Victorian mode of life ensured that the upper crust had never had it so good, it created a veritable economic hell for much of the rest of the community. The "caring society" we have established in its place may have its faults – not least that it is not always caring enough. But that is hardly an argument for turning the clock back.

Many of mankind's traditional vices waxed rather than waned during Victorian times – prostitution, for instance, flourished on a scale that has almost never been equalled before or since. But, what is even more to the point, some of the Victorian period's much vaunted virtues had a strong element of vice in them or acquired it as a result of overzealous applications.

This is particularly true of those who contributed in large measure to the Victorian economic success story. The enthusiasm for making people work harder was responsible for the near-slave conditions in which so much of the work force lived out its lives. The enthusiasm for saving found expression in a determination on the part of employers to reward that workforce in such parsimonious fashion that its incomes were often hardly sufficient to provide families with the bare necessities of life.

In such circumstances, it was hardly surprising that family life became brutalized for a substantial part of the population.

Lesson

As for the greater freedom of choice that this is said to be one of the main purpose of the Tories' Victorianization crusade: there was obviously very little of that for the mass of the population in the last century. So little indeed that Marxist revolutionaries could appeal to the workers with the catch phrase "You have nothing to lose but your chains" without being seen as guilty of perpetrating a gross exaggeration.

The lesson the Victorian experience underlines in no uncertain fashion was not a new one. It is that freedom is relative; that one man's licence is all too often the measure of another's incarceration. We have spent most of the past century striving to create a society of which the nation can be proud. That could never be said of that which characterised Victorian Britain.

The Times. 2.3.83

1 What, in the author's opinion, were the main 'virtues and vices' of the Victorian free market economy?

2 To what extent was there 'freedom of choice' in the Victorian economy?

planned

The command economy

In a pure **command economy**, it is the State which decides what to produce, how to produce it and for whom it is to be produced. In order to do this, the State must have a clear set of objectives. It may decide that its objective is to provide everybody with an identical standard of living. Or its objective may be to devote as large a percentage of resources to military production as possible, given the constraint of keeping the population alive at some minimum standard of living.

The question of what to produce will be limited by the availability of resources and the techniques of production. An economy might not, for instance, be capable of producing 2 million cars and 1 million trucks. Planners will have to decide which is the most important priority of the two and sacrifice production of the least important. Planners will also have to decide which producers are going to be allocated which factors of production. Producers are all owned by the State and are given targets for production, fixed according to the quantity of resources allocated to them. Money will not exist, and consumers will be allocated their share of production probably via a ration book system. Note also that only the State can own factors of production.

As with the pure free market economy, no 'pure' command economy exists in the world today. Economies which approximate most to this ideal type are the USSR and her satellite Eastern European Comecon partners, and China. The bulk of the production side of the economy is run via a command mechanism. Some private producers do exist but are relatively unimportant except in agriculture. Workers, however, are paid in money and are free to buy what they like subject to rationing systems on some commodities and subject to availability of goods. These two provisos in fact severely limit their freedom of choice in the market place.

Data 31.3

Moscow moves on shortages

By Quentin Peel

THE daunting scale of the Soviet Union's drive to overcome consumer goods shortages and details of the crash programme ordered to cope with it have been revealed by Ms Alexandra Biryukova the most powerful woman in the Soviet hierarchy and the deputy premier in charge of light industry.

Almost 300 heavy industry factories – including some from the defence industry, engineering and construction – have been ordered to re-equip for consumer goods production, she said.

Investment in light industry is to be tripled from the present level, to Roubles 20bn (£18bn) in the next five-year plan, with a huge increase in capacity of key sectors, such as furniture production, electrical goods, and automobiles.

But the scale of the expansion is still failing to keep up with the volume of unsatisfied consumer demand, estimated by government statistics at Roubles 70bn.

Nor will the planned expansion come near Western levels of consumer goods output per head of population.

Ms Biryukova, revealed that production of key items, such as televisions, washing machines, household furniture, vacuum cleaners and tape recorders, had already been substantially increased, but shortages in the shops were getting worse.

"All this has failed to relieve the problem," she said. "The supply of goods seriously lags behind the buying power of the population. Many new products are now in short supply, including goods which until recently were plentiful – such as soap and washing powder."

Ms Biryukova spelt out the immediate plans to convert substantial parts of Soviet industry to consumer production. She also revealed that many state enterprises were refusing to accept central state orders to step up output – because it is not profitable enough.

New rules approved by the Council of Ministers will allow factories to keep a higher proportion of their profits if they produce household goods for central government procurement.

She blamed the current crisis on the inability of economic and trade organisations and manufacturing enterprises to study the consumer market and forecast demand.

Furniture was in short supply because the central planners and manufacturers had failed to take account of an acceleration in house building and a trend to build "garden huts and dachas" as second homes.

The Council of Ministers had decided to "reprofile" existing factories to switch to consumer goods production, and almost 300 had been ordered to do so as a first step, she said, including defence manufacturers.

The problem of factories refusing to accept orders for consumer goods meant that state contracts totalling almost Roubles 9bn had been rejected, Ms Biryukova said, accusing the enterprises concerned of "group egoism".

The Financial Times. 14.1.89

1 Using examples from the article, explain the role of planning in a command economy.

2 To what extent can a command economy respond to consumer choice?

The mixed economy

In a mixed economy, the State provides some goods and services whilst the private sector provides other goods and services. The State will provide its services through a planning mechanism. It decides what level of service is needed and then hires factors of production to produce that output. The State may also provide goods or services via the market mechanism. Here, profits are unlikely to indicate how resources are allocated. This is because the state is probably a monopoly producer. The profitability of a state-owned enterprise will therefore be a reflection of the degree to which the enterprise is exploiting its market power and the degree to which it is producing efficiently at lowest cost. In the private sector, goods and services will be provided via the market mechanism. As with a free enterprise economy, consumer spending 'votes' and profits will decide what is to be produced.

The way goods are produced will be dependent upon least cost modes of production. Both private and public sectors should have an interest in keeping costs to a minimum. The owners of factors of production will attempt to hire out their factors for the greatest possible price, although the state may intervene to prevent some factors from earning large payments—much of which is likely to represent economic rent.

The state will distribute many goods and services free of charge. These will include a wide variety of public and merit goods. Other goods and services may be distributed at reduced cost. The state may also redistribute income so that it is not only owners of factors of production who are able to buy goods and services in the private sector of the market. It is still likely to be true, however, that those who own the most valuable factors will gain a larger share of goods produced in the private sector of the economy than those who are relatively poor.

The mixed economy is the dominant economic system in Western Europe today. The degree of 'mixing'—state versus private production—varies but a figure of 40% state to 60% private is not uncommon. A free market economy such as the USA has an approximate 25% state to 75% private mix, whilst a command economy such as the USSR is likely to have a mix of 75% state to 25% private (although figures for the latter are difficult to estimate). A mixed socialist economy, such as Yugoslavia's, is likely to have a larger public sector than a mixed capitalist economy such as the UK's.

An evaluation of different economic systems

The performance of differing economic systems can be evaluated. Several criteria can be used, although ultimately how important a criterion is in relation to others can only be a value judgement.

1 Range of choice The nearer an economy comes to being a free enterprise economy, the greater should be the freedom of choice, both for consumers and for the owners of factors of production. In a command economy, consumers have little choice about what they buy. In part this will be because the State automatically provides many goods and services, and in part because the State is unlikely to produce a wide variety of goods for sale. In a command economy, for instance, it makes little sense to produce 5 different types of car all of the same size and the same engine capacity. In a developed mixed or free enterprise economy, consumers are likely to have such a choice as different firms compete for sales. The owners of factors of production are also likely to have less freedom of choice in a command economy. Labour in particular may have no choice about where it is located. The greater the choice available to individuals, the higher should be the level of economic welfare. This is because individuals can allocate their spending power, or their factors of production, to the use which maximises their utility or welfare.

2 Income distribution A wide range of choice is an advantage to those who are able to exercise that choice. In a free enterprise economy, choice is almost non-existent for many because they have little income to spend and the value of the factors of production they own is low. Only a minority of the population, for instance, have a choice of whether or not to work in jobs requiring two 'A' levels. Only about 10% of the population have a choice about whether to accept a job requiring a degree or not. An insignificant percentage of the population have the choice of whether to become brain surgeons, university professors, or nationalised industry chairmen.

An important dimension of economic performance therefore is the extent to which people are able to exercise genuine choice. In free enterprise economies, large differences in income and wealth tend to appear. The result is that for many in that society, there is no real choice about what job to take or what to consume.

Therefore the degree of choice for them is irrelevant. What is important is the income and wealth distribution of the economy. An improvement in income or wealth is likely to lead to a greater gain in welfare for the less well off in society than an expansion of choice.

Greater equality of income and wealth is one of the most important aims of the command economies of the USSR and China. In a mixed economy, inequality is accepted but extremes of poverty tend to be eliminated through taxation and welfare systems. The degree of equality that will lead to a maximisation of welfare for the economy remains a value judgement.

3 Individual economic security In a pure free enterprise economy, those who fall on bad times, either through their own fault or through pure mischance, obtain the ultimate economic penalty— death through starvation or exposure. In nineteenth century Britain, all too many viewed this as a desirable feature of an economic system. Even today there are many who argue that aid should not be given to poor developing countries suffering famine because 'it will make the population lazy' or 'if they know that we will bail them out every time, they won't bother to work.' In practice, in the USA and Canda there are some safety nets, although they are far from generous, for the poor.

Individual economic security is important because people tend to prefer riskless solutions for their economic lives. They would prefer to live in a society where their income remained the same before and after a severe industrial accident for instance, than one where following the accident they received no income and died as a result. The more an economic system can provide this economic security, the more it will increase welfare. In a command economy, there tends to be more economic certainty than in a free enterprise economy.

4 Economic growth Chapter 11 discussed whether economic growth is or is not desirable. Here we will assume that higher economic growth is more desirable than lower economic growth. Statistics show that there is no correlation between a type of economic system and high economic growth. This is hardly surprising given the complex causes of growth. What can be discussed though, is to what extent particular types of economic system inhibit growth by wasting scarce resources.

In a free enterprise economy, the source of wastage lies in X-inefficiency or organisational slack.

Some economists have argued that in the USA, up to 10% of GDP may be accounted for by these payments over and above what is necessary for the production process. There will also be a misallocation of resources due to the oligopolistic structure of most markets, leading to abnormal profits and high costs associated with wasteful advertising and promotion of products.

In a command economy, wastage occurs in a variety of ways. Firstly the planning bureaucracy is likely to be less efficient at allocating resources than a large number of firms in a market economy. They will find it difficult to react flexibly and quickly to changes in economic conditions. Secondly, if the monetary rewards are the same whatever happens, there will be little incentive to work hard and work well. The results of this are extremely damaging in the USSR. Workers may need to be bribed to do a job well. They may have a job 'on the side' in the black market sector of the economy to which they devote most of their efforts. They may seek to augment their salaries by petty pilfering, accepting bribes etc. This is difficult to eradicate, in part because few property rights exist. People feel that robbing the State, a large anonymous organisation, is not as dishonest as robbing the owner of a small firm. Bureaucratic corruption is a way of life in the USSR today, from window cleaner to top Party bosses.

In a mixed economy, it can be argued that 'bureaucratic inefficiency' exists in the public sector whilst X-inefficiency exists in the private sector. There is no evidence, however, to suggest that state organisations are inherently less efficient than private organisations. For instance, the public sector health service in the UK is probably as efficient as the equivalent private sector service in France or Germany. Privatising the UK health service will not automatically make health care provision more efficient in the UK. Indeed, it may make it less efficient because of the resulting duplication of resources and a growth of X-inefficiency.

5 Unemployment and Inflation High unemployment and inflation are both undesirable in an economy. Both free market and mixed economies have shown greater tendencies to this than command economies. The reason is simple—the operation of thousands of separate markets does not guarantee either full employment or an absence of inflationary pressures. The monetarist–Keynesian debate about the stability of an economy is not important here because even the most extreme monetarist cannot deny that random shocks to the economy can produce temporary unemployment and a rise in prices. In command economies, prices are fixed centrally. Inflationary pressures take the form of lengthening queues for goods and services. Unemployment does not exist because workers are allocated to jobs. What does exist is a large degree of hidden unemployment. Workers are allocated to factories where they are not needed. Factories hoard workers so that the burden of work is not too harsh!

6 Externalities In a pure free market economy, nobody 'owns' the environment. The result is that economic units consume the environment until the point where marginal utility is equal to zero. The result is often ugly towns, polluted waterways, and air full of dangerous substances. In a command economy, bureaucratic inefficiency often leads to as great a disregard for the environment as in a free enterprise system. The USSR certainly cannot claim to be any better than the USA at protecting its environment from man's activities. It is mixed economies which have the best record in this area, in part because there is an acceptance that the State should intervene in the private sector when the private sector is obviously causing environmental damage.

7 Other measures Economic systems could be considered from a number of other viewpoints. One such viewpoint is the extent to which an economy provides the consumer with goods which lead to an increase in welfare. The power of advertising enables private producers in free market and mixed economies to sell many goods which contribute little or nothing to welfare. Equally, the bureaucracies of the command economy often order the production of goods which are of limited interest to their consumers.

Another viewpoint from which economies may be considered is the degree of political coercion needed to ensure the smooth running of the economy. In free enterprise and mixed economies, strong laws about property rights need to be enforced. The operation of these laws tends to favour those with high incomes at the expense of those with low incomes. The command economies of Eastern Europe and the USSR however, are associated with police states. It may be argued that a command economy can only be made to work if the people in it are deprived of most of their political rights.

Specialisation, the division of labour and exchange

Self-sufficiency—one person producing all the goods and services he or she needs—is limited even in the most primitive societies. Production takes place in a co-operative environment where workers specialise in particular tasks. The reason for this is simply that co-operation and specialisation are far more productive than pure self-sufficiency.

Adam Smith, in his book *An Enquiry into the Nature and Causes of the Wealth of Nations*, described the division of labour (specialisation by workers) in making a pin:

'*One man draws out the wire, another straightens it, a third cuts it, a fourth points, a fifth grinds it at the top for receiving the head; to put it on is a peculiar business, to whiten the pins is another; it is even a trade by itself to put them into the paper.*'

By himself, one man might hope to make at best 20 pins per day. But working together a group sharing out tasks between themselves could average 4800 pins a day, a 220-fold increase in productivity. There are a number of reasons why specialisation is more productive than self-sufficiency:

1 Workers can perform those tasks which they are best at doing, either through natural ability or through training.

2 Capital—machines, factories, offices, tools etc.—can be provided to workers cost-effectively; it would be extremely wasteful for instance to provide everybody with a tractor to grow their own food.

3 Workers do not lose time changing from job to job, perhaps having to learn new skills as they change.

4 The most productive land resources can be used. What is as important today is that specialisation also allows the maximum use of knowledge. Technology has become so complex that no person could hope to be able to produce all the goods and services available today.

A very important insight of Economics is that specialisation is beneficial even if some factors of production are better at producing all things than others. Take, for example, two brothers, a plumber and an electrician, who have formed a partnership. Both can do each other's work and the plumber is a much faster worker than the electrician. The plumber can plumb three times as fast as his brother and do electrical work twice as fast. It is not difficult to see that they would be foolish to share out work equally between them. The team will complete the work quickest if the plumber specialises in plumbing because that is what, comparatively, he is best at doing. Only when all the plumbing work is done should he help his brother with electrical work. Similarly, if a doctor is better at clerical work than her secretary it would not make sense, given respective salary levels, for the doctor to spend part of her time being her own secretary. This principle of specialisation in an international context (the theory of comparative advantage) was explained in more detail on pages 166–169.

Our present high standard of living would not be possible without specialisation. But there are limits to the degree of specialisation possible or desirable. Specialisation necessitates exchange. If a worker is going to produce pin heads all day, he needs to know that he will be able to exchange those pin heads for food, clothing and all the other necessities of life. If exchange is to be efficient, there must be a medium of exchange which is widely acceptable and that medium is called money. Markets must also exist where buyers and sellers can come together in order to exchange goods and services. Or there must be some central organisation which allocates production in such a way that workers receive a share of output.

The smaller the market, the less the opportunity for specialisation. For instance, the scope for specialisation is greater in the market for jeans, a standard product selling in large quantities world wide, than in cricket balls, a product which sells in small quantities in a few localised markets. The nature of the tasks performed can also limit specialisation. In theory it might be better for one worker to produce pin heads all day long, but in practice the worker might feel so bored or alienated that his productivity might be higher and the quality of his work better if he were to perform a greater variety of tasks.

It might also be unwise to become too dependent on others. A country specialising in producing ships might suddenly find the market contracting, leaving it with unemployed ship yards and workers, and lower incomes. Or a firm might suffer problems because it buys key components from another firm whose workers have gone on strike.

Summary

The economic problem can be defined as the problem associated with living in a world where human wants are infinite but resources for production are scarce. Any economic system must resolve three resulting problems: What is to be produced? How is it to be produced? For whom is it to be produced? Three main types of economic system exist. In a free enterprise economy, the market mechanism decides how and for whom production is to take place. In a command economy, the State decides. In a mixed economy a mixture of state and private sector provision exists. Economic systems can be evaluated according to numerous criteria including choice, income distribution, individual economic security, growth, unemployment, inflation and externalities.

Terms for review

the economic problem

scarcity

production possibility frontier or boundary

free enterprise economies

planned or command economies

mixed economies

choice

income distribution

division of labour

Essay questions

1 What is understood by the 'economic problem'? How does a free market economy resolve this problem?

2 Can water be said to be 'scarce'?

3 Distinguish between a 'mixed' economy and a 'command' economy. In what ways are these two types of economic system economically inefficient?

32

Economic methodology

Introduction

Economic methodology refers to the way in which economists think and the tools which they use. Throughout this book, economic methodology has been used. The aim of this chapter is to make explicit what has only been implicit throughout this book.

Economics—a science or a study?

It is claimed by many economists that economics is a science. Others claim that to call economics a science is misleading. The study of the behaviour of human beings cannot be a 'science', but only a 'study'.

In order to understand this argument it is necessary to understand what is meant by a 'study' and a 'science'. A study does the following:

1 Gathers facts, for instance that unemployment in the UK in 1983 was 3.1 million.

2 Sorts out and classifies these facts into categories, divisions, etc. For instance, data is gathered which is then classified into 'consumption', 'investment' and 'exports'.

A science does more than this. It goes on to do the following:

3 Builds generalised models or theories to explain existing observations. This book is devoted to explaining such theories.

4 Uses models or theories to predict what will happen in the future.

Can economics explain past events or predict future ones? Some would say no, because human behaviour is unpredictable. It is not possible to predict how one housewife will react to a particular sales promotion. But economic scientists argue that it is possible to predict how one million housewives would react to such an event. Evidence shows, for instance, that supermarket chains which cut prices gain greater market share, all other things being equal. Although it is not possible to predict how one economic unit will react, it is possible to predict the reactions of a large group.

Human behaviour is arguably not entirely predictable, so the social sciences, including economics,

To what extent is the behaviour of an individual unpredictable?

Data 32.1

Co-integration may be more valuable than chaos

From Professor Christopher Gilbert

Sir, Professor David Stout (Letters, May 17) dismisses forecasting in business economics too lightly.

It is fashionable to argue that economies are chaotic. This would imply that very small changes in initial conditions would result in substantial changes after a period of time. Clearly this would make forecasting further ahead than the very near term impossible.

In fact, although economies are very complicated, they do not appear to be chaotic. Indeed, in many cases we may be able to forecast the medium to long term with greater accuracy than the short term.

A topical example is provided by metal prices. These have shown enormous and unpredictable variability over the past 18 months, but in the longer term we know that prices must fall to the level of production costs.

Similarly, in the long term the value of the dollar will be determined by purchasing power parity – but in the short to medium term there can be substantial unforecastable deviations from this level.

These long run relationships, which are entailed by economic theory, require that economic time series exhibit the property of co-integration. I recommend this concept to Professor Stout as of much greater value to business economics than the concept of chaos.

Christopher Gilbert,
Department of Economics,
Queen Mary College, University
of London,
Mile End Road E1

The Financial Times. 22.5.89

1 *Explain the two views of economics put forward in the letter.*

2 *To what extent can economics be a science?*

---

deal in probabilities or likelihoods. If this is correct, economics can only be at best an inexact science. A physical science may forecast an event accurately. An economist will only be able to estimate a result. A problem arises when the man in the street, the industrialist or the Government demands that the economist provide an exact answer to a question such as 'how many people will be unemployed next year?' It is because a precise answer cannot be given to this sort of question that its status as a science continues to be viewed with scepticism.

The inability of economists to agree on which of their theories is correct could support one of a number of arguments. Economics may still be in its infancy. Because we do not yet know enough about how the economy operates, economics cannot yet be accorded the status of a science. It may never possess a body of accepted theory because the evidence needed to validate one theory and refute conflicting theories may be unobtainable. It is true that economists find exceptional difficulty in obtaining accurate raw data for much of their work. Or, because human behaviour is unpredictable, economists may never be capable of producing valid theories.

5 Lastly, a science tests models to see whether they are true or false.

Some sciences are 'experimental'—that is, it is possible to set up an experiment (sometimes involving control groups) to test a theory. However, not all sciences can be experimental. Astronomers, for instance, cannot set up experiments in interstellar space to test their theories. Economists too find that most of their theories cannot be tested under laboratory conditions. This is because the numbers of people involved are too large, or because it would be unethical or irresponsible to conduct the experiment or most importantly, because it is impossible to keep all other factors constant which would otherwise affect the variables in the experiment. An experiment to test the proposition '6 million unemployed in the UK would bring inflation down to zero' would not only be unethical but would be impossible to prove or disprove conclusively. Other factors might affect unemployment and inflation whilst the experiment was taking place and thus invalidate it.

Positive and normative economics

A positive statement is a statement capable of proof or disproof. Examples of such statements are 'inflation is currently running at 10%' or 'if unemployment falls by half a million, inflation will double'. A normative statement is a statement of values. Examples of normative statements are 'a 10% inflation rate is too high' or 'unemployment should be made to fall by half a million'.

Some economists claim that economics should only be concerned with positive statements. They

When you have looked into the abysmal eyes of a hungry child you don't check the protein statistics, nor take refuge in global per capita.

Ritchie Calder

OXFAM

OX 338C/81

Is this photograph making a positive or normative statement?

argue very strongly that, as a science, economics is concerned with constructing theories which are capable of proof or disproof. It is the role of the economist to find out how the economy operates. It is **not** the role of the economist to put forward value judgements. That should be left to the people whom the economist is advising—the industrialist or the politician, for instance.

Another school of thought, going back to Adam Smith, regards economics as the study of 'political economy'. These economists see economics as not only concerned with facts and testable theories, but with value judgements. For instance, it is the role of the economist not merely to say that unemployment is 4 million, but to say that it is too high. Because economics deals in value judgements, it is 'political' as well as being 'scientific'. This argument is no different from the one being conducted in physical sciences. Some argue that a nuclear physicist, for instance, should not be concerned with the fact that his work may result in the construction of more efficient nuclear bombs or the building of nuclear power stations which turn out to be highly dangerous. Equally, in biology, issues such as cloning and other forms of genetic engineering raise vast ethical questions. Some argue that it is not the business of the biologist to consider the ethical implications of his or her scientific work.

What is certainly true is that the distinction between positive and normative economics is not so distinct as it might at first seem. Consider the following 'positive' argument:

1 Trade unions bring members out on strike in the UK every year.
2 Strikes result in lost production for firms.
3 Lost production for firms results in lower national income.
4 Conclusion: trade union strikes cause national income in the UK to be lower than it would otherwise be.

Each of the stages of this argument can be tested empirically. The conclusion is a 'positive' one in that it is capable of proof or disproof. The conclusion is correctly drawn from the three preceding statements. Yet many British people would read the conclusion as a normative statement. This is because they would reword it in their minds to read:

'Trade unions can be blamed for strikes which damage the British economy.'

301

Data 32.2

Tax system reform

By Philip Stephens

A CALL for a radical shift in the way the Government taxes income and wealth to encourage enterprise and the growth of ownership was made yesterday by Dr David Owen, the SDP leader.

In a lecture on reshaping the tax system, Dr Owen said a shift towards an expenditure tax where "we tax spending but exempt saving" was central to the future of public policy towards property, land and inheritance.

He said a broad-based system of taxation, in which all reliefs were removed and rates reduced, had been shown to be politically impossible to achieve.

In those circumstances the Government should acknowledge its economic role in encouraging all forms of savings – for productive investment, for social housing, for rent, for educational investment, and for infrastructure investment.

Dr Owen said there was nothing wrong, distorting or discriminating in itself in the provision of tax relief for mortgage interest payments.

He said it was a legitimate aim of government policy to encourage home ownership.

The distortion arose because the Government discriminated between types of saving. Exemptions should therefore be extended to give basic rate income tax relief on all types of saving.

The change would result in a further narrowing of the tax base but that would be offset by the introduction of a life-time expenditure tax. The object would be to enable people to accumulate wealth during their lifetime but to tax inherited wealth, gifts and any savings realised in order to fund spending.

Making it easier for individuals to build up wealth would be an essential component in meeting the challenge of a growing population of retired and a shrinking number of people of working age.

At the same time, heavier taxation of inheritances and gifts – based on taxing the recipient rather than the donors – would be entirely consistent with a policy designed to encourage enterprise.

At present the very rich had become wealthy by inheritance, which was at odds with the notion that was at the heart of market economics – that wealth should be a reward for effort.

The Financial Times. 20.4.89

1 To what extent can positive and normative economics be distinguished? Use examples from the passage to illustrate your answer.

'Blame' and 'damage' both carry normative messages. Many positive statements are not perceived by most hearers as being positive—they are interpreted in a normative fashion.

The argument itself is heavily value-laden. There is no mention of **why** trade unions bring members out on strike. This lack of interest in the motivation of trade union activities is a value judgement. Moreover, there is no mention of the extent to which strikes cause a loss of national income. Most readers would automatically infer from this argument—an argument which is repeated again and again in British newspapers, on television, and in Parliament—that the loss of national income was significant. The argument is true but without significance if the loss of income were, say, only 1p per year per head in the UK. Many supposedly positive statements are, in practice, normative because of what has been omitted from the statement.

Adam Smith and other classical economists did not conceal the fact that they were interested in economics because of the support it would give to their beliefs concerning how governments should run the economy. The title 'political economy' expressed their view of the discipline. Some economists today argue that Adam Smith was right in seeing economics as inextricably bound up with value judgements. Other economists argue that positive and normative economics can be clearly distinguished. It is the task of the economist to investigate the positive aspects of the discipline in a scientific manner. Normative aspects are the concern of the individual and there can be no valid 'discussion' between economists about individual value judgements.

Economic modelling

Throughout this book, models and theories have been put forward without too much explanation as to what constitutes a **model** or **theory**. Models and theories have been treated as if they were identical, whereas in fact they are distinct. All models are theories, but loosely formulated theories are not models.

An example of a theory would be that consumers buy more goods as their income increases. For this theory to become a model, the relationship between consumption and income would have to be more definitely specified. A mathematical presentation, for instance, stating that:

$$C = £100 + 0.5Y$$

would turn this theory of the consumption function into a model.

Models need not be expressed mathematically. However, the precision of mathematical language means that in practice the vast majority of models are specified mathematically. Apart from the precise nature of specification, models and theories are identical, and throughout the rest of this chapter we will use 'model' and 'theory' as if they were interchangeable terms.

A definition of a model is that it is a simplification of reality. A model picks out certain aspects of what it is trying to describe. This means that it must omit other aspects. Most models described in this book have been positive models—that is, they have attempted to describe and explain the economy as it actually is.

The accelerator theory, for instance, argues that investment is a function of past changes in income. Proponents of this theory are not saying that past changes in income are the only determinant of investment. What they are saying is that past changes in income are the major determinant of investment. Other factors, such as the rate of interest, do affect investment, but they either complicate the model unnecessarily without changing its basic predictions, or are not important enough to include in the model.

Some models in economics are normative in nature. A normative model is one which attempts to describe some ideal situation. For instance, the model of perfect competition is a positive model in the sense that it attempts to describe how certain markets operate in the real world. It is also a normative model because it is used to describe how a market should operate. Proponents of free market economies, for instance, argue that it is a role of government to make markets conform to the perfectly competitive model because this will improve welfare and efficiency in the economy as a whole.

Simplifying reality has its advantages and disadvantages. One advantage is that the more simplified the model, the easier it is to understand and to work with. For instance, the model which argues that 'price and quantity demanded are inversely related' is easily comprehensible even to primary school children. Complicating the model by arguing that 'income, as well as price, might affect the quantity demanded' poses problems which even many 'A' level candidates cannot grasp.

The major disadvantage of simplifying reality is that the model may distort reality because of what is omitted. Returning to the accelerator theory, it could be said to distort reality if 51% of investment were determined by past changes in income, but 49% were determined by interest rate levels. This is because, although past changes in income are the most important determinant of income, changes in interest rates are in practice almost as important. A better theory would combine both factors. On the other hand, if interest rates only caused 5% of investment, and 95% was explained by the accelerator theory, then it is arguably justified to ignore interest rates. Ultimately, no model can describe reality perfectly because the model would need to be as complex as reality itself—the model would be a perfect reconstruction of reality.

A good positive model has a number of features:

1 It should be able to describe or explain past events to an acceptable degree of accuracy.

2 It must be able to predict what will happen in the future, given sufficient data.

3 It must be internally consistent—that is, the various parts of the theory must follow on logically from each other.

4 The assumptions of the model should be clearly stated and should be realistic.

5 The model should be as simple as possible and should yield powerful conclusions.

6 It should be formulated so that it can be proved or disproved by recourse to evidence.

Many models do not possess all of these characteristics. The monetarist–Keynesian debate would not exist if either macro-economic model could completely explain past events and predict future events. Models which appear in textbooks have a sufficiently long existence to be internally consistent, but new models produced by academic

Data 32.3

Why forecasters keep their fingers crossed

Ralph Atkins

In the bowels of Her Majesty's Treasury, the offical computer model of the economy, if not in disgrace, can hardly claim to have had a glorious year.

In an age of sophistication, forecasts have become dependent on thousands of calculations, equations, endogenous (from inside the model) and exogenous (determined outside it) variables, identities (pseudo or real) and logarithms galore. There is an element of human fudge in forecasts, but the computers do the groundwork. The problem is that the predictions are still seldom right.

Unlike say physicists, economists appear unable to use computers with any precision. The difficulties are twofold:

● First, big industrial economies have proved too complex for economists to understand completely. Even relatively straightforward questions, such as what determines how much consumers spend in shops, are matters of much debate.

Frequently, different sectors of the economy interact in an unpredictable fashion. And responses to changes or shocks (perhaps caused by events elsewhere in the world) are subject to time lags of indeterminate length. If economists cannot agree about how an economy works, it is hardly surprising that attempts to model it on computers are imperfect.

● Second, the information is poor. UK economic statistics are notorious for their inaccuracy. Figures for the growth of gross domestic product last year, in particular, have been subject to ridicule as the various measures available have told different stories.

Monthly data are often revised and changes in trends are rarely spotted until two or three months later.

City economists rely more on spreadsheets to project trends forward and take account of special factors in particular months. When forecasting a year ahead, the performance of City analysts is on a par with that of the Treasury. At least, they are all more or less equally wrong.

Kevin Gardiner, UK economist at Warburg Securities, believes that forecasting trade figures is a hazardous business. He says, "You know what you think the bottom line is over the year as a whole and then you look at the most recent month's numbers and whether you expect things to diverge. You add in any special factors, do a lot of rounding and cross your fingers."

The Financial Times. 14.3.89

---

1 To what extent are the economic models described in the passage 'good' models?

---

economists are often attacked on their logic and mathematics. The theory of perfect competition, as a positive model, is often criticised for having totally unrealistic assumptions. Neo-classical demand theory is criticised for having powerful assumptions which yield such weak conclusions that they are of little use in the real world of decision-making. Again, marginal utility theory is a poor theory because it has been impossible to prove or disprove.

The degree to which any of these aspects of a 'good' model is important depends upon what use the model is to be put to. An excellent predictor of Christmas is an increase in the money supply. Yet somebody who was not familiar with Christmas might construct a model which showed increases in the money supply causing Christmas. This model would be an excellent predictive model, but would be a totally false construct of reality. Modern macroeconomic models of the economy are designed primarily to predict future events. The equations which are used serve that function rather than attempting to explain reality. It is likely, but it is not necessarily true, that models which accurately describe reality will predict well.

Models can incorporate a number of different features. One very important feature is time. Models which have no time element are called **static** models, whilst **dynamic** models incorporate a time element. An example of a dynamic model is the accelerator theory. The simple Keynesian multiplier model, on the other hand, is static. Static models are easier to work with than dynamic models. Dynamic models, however, are likely to be more realistic.

Another distinction is between **partial** and **general** models. Rather like the model/theory distinction, this distinction is rather loose. A partial model is one which includes only a few variables. A general model includes many variables. But there is no magic number which distinguishes 'few' from 'many' variables. An example of a partial model could be the market for council housing. An example of a general model could be the market for all housing. Partial models have the advantage of being simpler to use and to understand. General models are likely to give a closer description of reality.

An **equilibrium** model is one which assumes that equilibrium will be restored following a change in variables in the model. A definition of equilibrium is a situation where there is no tendency to change. Equilibrium can also be said to apply to a situation where expectations or plans are being realised. In the circular flow of income model, for instance, a change in an injection (i.e. a situation where plans are not going to be realised) leads to a move from one equilibrium position to another. In fact, all static models are equilibrium models because they deal with comparisons of two equilibrium situations. A disequilibrium model considers movements from one disequilibrium point to the next. The cobweb theorem is a disequilibrium model because it attempts to chart movements along a disequilibrium path.

Models may be categorised according to whether they are **macro-economic** models or **micro-economic** models. Macro-economic models deal with the economy as a whole. Micro-economics is concerned with the behaviour of individual markets. For instance, the Keynesian consumption function is a model which attempts to predict how much all consumers in an economy will consume. The equivalent micro-economic theory—for instance, marginal utility theory—attempts to explain how individual consumers allocate their consumption.

Models may incorporate **stock** concepts or **flow** concepts or both. A flow concept is one which involves a time element. For instance national income is a flow concept because income is earned over time. A stock concept is one which can be measured at a point in time. The wealth of an individual can be measured at a point in time.

Summary

In this chapter, we considered the extent to which economics may be called a science. It was pointed out that economics is never likely to provide accurate forecasts of future events in the way that physics can. The extent to which the lack of precision of economics is acceptable or unacceptable largely determines the degree to which it can be considered a science. The positive/normative debate was then considered. Economists who view economics as a science tend to argue that positive economics alone is worthy of consideration by economists. An economic model was defined as being a simplification of reality. The simpler the model, the easier it was to work with, but also the farther away from reality it moved. The criteria for a 'good' model were outlined. Features of models, such as dynamic/static were reviewed.

Terms for review

economic science

positive and normative economics

political economy

economic models and theories

static and dynamic

partial and general

equilibrium and disequilibrium

stocks and flows

Essay questions

1 What is an economic model? Illustrate your answer using a macro-economic model of income determination.

2 To what extent can economics be considered a science?

3 What is meant by 'positive economics'? To what extent is the theory of perfect competition a positive model of the firm?

Index to charts

Page reference numbers for the charts of the UK economy.

balance of payments
    Balance of trade   156
    Current balance   156, 171
    Invisible trade   156
    Net transactions in UK external assets and liabilities   156
    Reserves, gold and foreign currency   156
    Visible exports: by trade area 1966 and 1987   174

consumption
    Change in consumer's expenditure (at 1988 prices)   51
    Change in expenditure on durable goods (at 1988 prices)   51
    Distribution of consumers' expenditure 1963 and 1982   45

demand for money
    Change in the demand for money (change in M_3)   30

disposable income
    Change in personal disposable income (at 1988 prices)   51

earnings
    change in average earnings   121

exchange rates
    Sterling effective exchange rate (1985 = 100)   157
    Sterling exchange rate: US dollars   157

imports
    Change in import prices   121

inflation
    Inflation: Retail price index, percentage change   56, 91, 109, 119, 121, 125

investment
    Change in gross domestic fixed capital formation (at 1985 prices)   103, 150
    Gross domestic fixed capital formation by asset 1965 and 1988   59
    Gross domestic fixed capital formation: Plant and machinery (at (1985 prices)   64
    Gross domestic fixed capital formation: Total (at 1985 prices)   64

money
    Change in money stock (M_1)   17, 125
    Change in money stock (M_2)   17, 125
    Change in money stock (M_3)   17, 43, 125, 150
    Change in money stock (M_4)   17
    Change in money stock (M_5)   17
    Special deposits, end of year   43

national income
    Change in gross domestic product at factor cost (at current prices)   30
    Change in gross domestic product at factor cost at (1985 prices)   64, 91, 103, 131, 150

profits
    change in gross trading profits of companies and financial institutions   121

public sector
    Public sector borrowing requirement   43
    Public sector borrowing requirement (at 1985 prices)   103

rate of interest
    British government securities long dated (20 years): percentage yield average of working days   23, 30
    Building Societies: interest rate on ordinary shares last Friday of the year   23
    Industrial securities: debentures: average yield   64
    London clearing banks deposit account (7 days notice) rate of interest   23, 51, 56
    Treasury bill yield: last Friday of the year   23, 43

saving
    Personal saving: as a ratio of personal disposable income 1971–1986   53
    Personal savings ratio (personal saving as a percentage of personal disposable income)   56, 103

stock
    Stock changes: Changes in the value of the physical increase in stocks and work in progress (at 1985 prices)   150

terms of trade
    Terms of trade (1985 = 100)   171

unemployment
    Unemployment by duration: UK   131
    Unemployment UK, per cent   119, 131, 150

vacancies
    Unfilled vacancies, per cent   119, 131

Index

References to the text are given in normal type. References to the main themes of the data are given in bold.

abnormal profits   228, 242, 245, 247, 250, 261, 263, 264, 271, 272, 290, 296
absolute advantage   166
absorption approach to the balance of payments   155, 158
accelerator   63–65, 145, 285, 303
ad valorem taxes   73
advertising   **271**, 93, 238, 256, 259, 289, 297
   informative advertising   270
   persuasive advertising   270
   and efficiency   270–272, 296
Affluent Society, The   88
aggregate consumption   45
aggregate demand (or aggregate expenditure)   **104**, 99–100, 107–115
   control of   178–181
   and devaluation   158–159
   and employment   135
   and equilibrium income   99–100, 111–115
   and import controls   190
   and inflation (see demand-pull inflation)
   and interest rates   107–108, 159
   and the money supply   107, 110, 183–184
aggregate supply   108–115, 118, 158–159, 178
agriculture   204, 205–206, 242, 252, 270, 282
   cobweb theorem   202, 204, 305
   Common Agricultural Policy   205
   and income stabilization   206–207
   and price stabilization   205–206
agricultural development (see rural development)
aid to developing countries   **198**, 196–198, 200, 296
aims of economic policy   177
allocation of resources   272, 289–290
   and economic systems   290–297
animal spirits   62
anti-monopoly legislation   262
assets
   bank assets   18–19
   financial and physical assets   31–33, 183, 184
assumptions in model building   303–304
assurance   53
automatic stabilizers   180
autonomous expenditure   97
average cost   221, 228, 241
   long run   220–221, 226–227
   short run   220–221, 226–227
average product   226, 275
average propensity (see propensity)
average revenue (see revenue)

backward sloping supply curve   277
balance of payments   **153, 156, 190**, 121, 151–165, 177, 196
   absorption approach   155, 158
   balance of trade   151
   current account   151, 154–160, 177
   disequilibrium   154–160
   gold and foreign currency reserves   151, 153, 155, 156, 158, 161, 162, 163, 188
   invisible trade   151
   surpluses   154–155
   transactions in external assets and liabilities   152, 153, 154, 155, 159
   visible trade   151
   and monetary policy   35–36
   and the trade cycle   143
balanced budget   179, 180
balanced budget multiplier   179–180
bank multiplier   19–21, 38
Bank of England (see central bank)
Bank Rate   36–37
banks
   accounts   15

reserve assets   19–21, 37, 38
   and the creation of money   18–21, 41–42, 178
barriers to entry and exit   **239**, 238–239, 242, 245, 248, 250, 252, 261–263, 271, 292
barriers to trade (see import controls)
barter   14
base period   26–27
basic human needs approach   194, 200
Baumol W.   232
behavioural theories   234, 255–256
'Big Bang'   182
bills of exchange   25, 26
birth rate   199
black economy   **84**, 21, 85
black market   296
bonds   **40**, 24–5, 36, 38–39
   and the demand for money   31
boom   141, 144, 255
branded goods   235–236, 245, 248, 252
Brandt Report   196
Bretton Woods system   162
budget
   balanced budget   179, 180
   budget deficit   179, 180
   budget surplus   179
budget line   215–217
building cycle   143
building societies   41–42, 53, 108
business cycle (see trade cycle)

Cambridge Economic Policy Group (CEPG)   190
canons of taxation   74–75
capita, per   94
capital   59–60, 230, 274
   demand for capital   275–276, 284–285
   human capital   87, 193
   marginal efficiency of capital   60–63, 108, 284
   social capital   197
   supply of capital   279
   working capital   59
   and growth   88, 90
capital account on the balance of payments   151–152, 177
capital consumption or depreciation   58, 59, 82–84
capital expenditure   67
capital gains taxation   73
capital market   284
capitalist economies (see free market economies)
cartels   **207**, 206
   and efficiency   263–264
Carlyle T.   1
cash ratio   19, 38
ceiling in the trade cycle   146
central bank   20–21, 23
   and exchange rate policy   151, 158, 160–163
   and monetary policy   36–41
central planning   293–294
centrally planned economies (see command economies)
certificate of deposit   25
Chamberlain E. H.   245
characteristics of products   235–236
cheque   15
choice   173, 189, 266, 294
circular flow of income   79, 97, 145, 180, 195
   equilibrium   99–101
class structure   91
classical economics   1, 2
   comparative advantage   166–169
   economic rent   282–284
   economics   289
   model of the economy   107–115

Index

political economy 302
  unemployment 132–140
cobweb theorem 202, 204, 305
collective consumption (or public) goods 67–71, 290, 292
collusion 252
Comecon 294
command economies **294**, 293–294, 295–297
commercial bills 25
Common Agricultural Policy 205
common external tariff 173
Common Market (see European Community)
communist economies (see command economies)
comparative advantage **167, 168**, 166–170, 171, 174, 297
competition (see market sector, monopolistic competition, monopoly, oligopoly, perfect competition, planning sector)
competitiveness 121, 171, 174, 178, 188, 190
complementary goods 204
consols 25
constant prices 26–27
constant returns to scale 223
consume (see propensity to consume)
consumer behaviour 211–218
consumer durables 46, 59
consumer rationality 218, 271
consumer sovereignty **258**, 256, 267, 290
consumption, consumption function **49, 51**, 45–51, 53, 58, 107, 303, 305
  measured consumption 46, 48
  permanent consumption 46, 48
  propensity to consume 46–51, 98–99, 179, 180
  and the trade cycle 141
contractual savings 54
corporate taxation
  and growth 90
corporations 232
Corset 39–41
cost-benefit analysis 270
cost of living 95–96
cost-plus pricing 231, 252, 254, 285
cost–push inflation **121, 123**, 120–122, 126, 159, 186
costs **220, 222**, 6, 219–229
  allocation of costs 236
  average cost 221, 228, 241
  fixed cost 219–221, 228, 230, 241
  imputed costs 219
  long run cost 220–221, 226–227
  marginal cost 221, 228, 241
  opportunity cost 29, 154, 169, 219
  short run cost 220–221, 230, 241
  total cost 221, 228
  variable cost 219–221, 230, 241
  and advertising 270–271
  and efficiency 260–261, 270–271
  and monopolistic competition 245–248
  and monopoly 250–251
  and oligopoly 248–250
  and perfect competition 242–245
  and the planning sector 252–254
countervailing power 256
creation of money 18–21, 38, 41–42, 178
credit 49
credit creation 18–21, 41–42, 178
credit controls 39–40
credit creation 18–21, 38, 41–2, 178
credit multiplier 18–19, 19–21, 38
credit policy 39–40, 177, 184–185
cross-elasticity of demand 10
cross-subsidisation 236
crowding-in 105
crowding out 105, 180–181
currencies (see exchange rates)
currency control (see exchange control)
current account
  balance of payments 151, 154–160, 177
  bank 15
current expenditure 67
current prices 26–27
customs union **174**, 173
cycles (see trade cycles)

cyclical unemployment 130
debentures 25
debt crisis **198**, 200
decreasing returns to scale 223
deflation 141, 159, 179
deflationary gap 103–105, 180
demand **5, 8, 12**, 3–5, 7–13, 201–210, 211–218, 304
  aggregate demand (see aggregate demand)
  demand for factors of production (see under each factor)
  derived demand 274
  elasticity of demand (see elasticity)
  individual demand 201–202
  market demand 201–202
  shifts of demand 4–5
  and marginal revenue product 275–276
demand deficient unemployment 130
demand for money **30**, 29–33, 107–108, 114, 124, 143, 158, 181
demand management 178, 180
demand-pull inflation 118–120, 125, 158, 181, 186
demarcation 88
denationalisation (see privatisation)
deposit
  certificate of deposit 25
  sight deposit 15
  time deposit 15
depreciation
  capital consumption 58, 59, 82–84, 219
  of the exchange rate (see devaluation)
depression 130, 141, 144, 149
  Great Depression 1, 97, 103, 133, 135, 162, 178, 287
derived demand 274
devaluation **189**, 155–159, 160, 162, 188
developed countries 193
developing countries (DC's) 193
development economics 193–200
diminishing marginal utility 211–214
diminishing returns 226–227, 275
directors, role in the firm 232
"dirty" float 162
discounting 284
diseconomies of scale 223–226
disintermediation 40
disposable income 48, 49
dissaving 46, 54
distribution of income and wealth 49–51, 72–73, 76–77, 94, 95, 116, 118, 194, 266–267, 290, 295–296
  functional distribution 274
  personal distribution 274
distributive efficiency 260
disutility 211
dividends 186–187
division of labour 297–298
Domestic Credit Expansion (DCE) 36
dual economies 193, 196
duopoly 252
durable goods 46, 59
dynamic analysis 202, 304–305

economic development **195, 197, 198**, 193–200
  (see also growth)
economic efficiency (see efficiency)
economic integration **174**, 173–175
economic rent **283**, 282–284, 295
economic security 296
economic systems 289–298
economic theory 1–2, 299–300, 302–305
economic welfare 92–96, 154, 171, 172, 173, 189, 197, 198, 265–266, 272, 295–297
economics
  normative **302**, 301–302, 303
  positive **302**, 301–302, 303
economies
  command 293–294, 295–297
  dual 193, 196
  free enterprise or market economies 76, 290–292, 295–297, 303
  mixed economies 295–297
economies of scale **225**, 223–226, 260–261

308

economists (see classical, Keynesian, monetarist, neo-classical and neo-Keynesian economics)
education
  and growth 87–88
efficiency
  allocative efficiency 260, 261–272
  distributive efficiency 260
  economic efficiency **262, 264, 267, 269, 271**, 182, 240, 260–273
  productive efficiency 260–261, 266, 271
elasticity **12**, 9–12
  cross-elasticity of demand 10
  determinants 13
  formula 10
  income elasticity of demand 10
  price elasticity of demand, 10, 13, 235–236
  price elasticity of supply 10
  and advertising 271
  and the balance of payment 155–158
  and the demand for money 32
  and the labour market 275
  and monopolistic competition 246–247
  and oligopoly 248, 250
  and perfect competition 243
  and revenue 11–12
  and taxation 208–209
employment **104** (see full employment and unemployment)
endogenous variables 41
entrepreneurship **280**, 75, 181–182, 191, 255, 274
  supply 280–281
entry barriers (see barriers to entry)
equilibrium
  balance of payments 154–155
  consumer equilibrium 213
  full employment equilibrium 103–105, 110–115
  market equilibrium 7–9, 202, 204
  model 305
  output of the firm 241–242
  price 7
  price of factors of production 274
eurobond 25
European Community (EC) **174**, 173, 205
  Common Agricultural Policy 205
  common external tariff 173
  customs union 173
  European Court 264
  European Monetary System (EMS) 163
excess demand 118, 120, 125
exchange 297
exchange controls 160, 172, 188
exchange rate **154, 157, 161, 163, 164, 189**, 152–164, 177, 184
  Bretton Woods system 162, 163
  crawling peg 163, 164
  "dirty" float 162
  fixed exchange rates 161–162
  floating exchange rates 160–163
  forward currency markets 160
  gold standard 161–162
  managed float 162
  policy 188–189
  wide band system 162–163
  and devaluation 155–159
  and economic welfare 95, 160
  and monetary policy 35–38
exogenous variables 41
expectations-augmented Phillips curve 127, 138
expenditure 82, 99–100
  planned expenditure 99–101
export-led growth 195–196
exports (see balance of payments and international trade)
  and the circular flow of income 97–106
external economies of scale 226
externalities **269**, 268, 270, 297

factor cost 82
factor endowments 87
factors of production 86, 255, 274–288, 293, 295
  factor shares in national income 274
  (see also land, labour, capital, entrepreneurship)
final value 82

financial economies 224
firms (see costs, directors, goals, monopolistic competition, monopoly, nationalised industries, oligopoly, perfect competition, planning sector, shareholders, supply)
fiscal policy **181, 183**, 177, 178–182, 184, 188
first world countries 193
Fisher I.
  and the Quantity Theory of Money 21
fixed capital formation 82
fixed cost 219–221, 228, 230, 241
fixed exchange rates 161–162
floating exchange rates 160–163
flows 305
foreign aid **198**, 196–198, 200, 296
foreign exchange (see exchange rate)
foreign exchange reserves 151, 153, 155, 156, 158, 161, 162, 163, 188
foreign trade (see international trade)
formal sector 194
forward currency market 160
fourth world 193
free enterprise or market economy **293**, 76, 290, 292, 295–297, 303
free rider problem 71
free trade 171–173, 182, 189
free trade area 173
freedom of entry and exit (see barriers to entry and exit)
frictional unemployment 130, 132, 177
Friedman M. 48, 49, 50, 51, 118, 123, 127, 137, 143, 145
fringe benefits (see perks)
full employment 103–104, 109, 110–115, 118, 120, 126, 135, 158–159, 179, 184, 290
functional distribution of income 274
fundamental or persistent disequilibrium 154–155
funding 38

gains from trade 166–169
Galbraith J. 88, 252, 256, 270, 292
General Agreement on Tariffs and Trade (GATT) 189
general models 305
General Theory of Employment, Interest and Money, The 1, 97, 135
General Theory of the Second Best 266
Giffen good 217
gilts or gilt-edged stock or government stock or bonds 25, 36, 38–39, 219
goals of firms 230–234, 268
gold and foreign currency reserves 151, 153, 155, 156, 158, 161, 162, 163, 188
gold standard 161–162
government (see public sector)
Great Depression 1, 97, 103, 133, 135, 162, 178, 287
Green Revolution 195
gross domestic fixed capital formation 83
  (see also investment)
gross domestic product 82
gross investment 58, 88
gross national expenditure 82, 84
gross national income 82, 84
gross national product 82, 84
growth, economic **89, 90, 91, 92, 94, 95, 181, 291**, 86–96
  and the balance of payment 159
  and development economics 193–200
  and the distribution of income 76
  and economic integration 174–175, 189–191
  and government policy **68**, 177–191
  and import controls 173
  and investment 88, 90, 178
  and welfare 92–96, 296

Hecksher–Ohlin theory 169
hidden economy 85
high powered money 19–21, 108
hire purchase controls 39–40
homogeneous goods **237**, 159, 169, 235–237, 242, 245, 264
horizontal summing 201, 245
hot money 154
household behaviour (see consumer behaviour)
human capital 87, 193

Index

Hume D.   1
hyperbola   11
hyperinflation   118

identity   21
imperfect competition (see monopolistic competition and oligopoly)
import controls   **172**, **191**, 172–173, 189–191, 196
import licences   173
import substitution   195–196
imports (see balance of payments and international trade)
   and the circular flow   98–102
   and inflation   119, 122, 162
imputed costs   219
incentives   75, 181–182, 279, 281
incidence of taxation   **209**, 207–209
income (see also national income)
   circular flow of income   79, 97, 99–101, 145, 180, 195
   disposable income   48, 49
   distribution of income   49–51, 72–73, 76–77, 94, 95, 116, 118, 194, 266–267, 274, 290, 295–296
   measured income   50
   permanent income   48, 49
   transitory income   49–50
   and the demand for money   30–33
   and investment   63–65, 145, 285, 303
   and saving   53–57
income effect   216–217
income elasticity of demand   **12**, 10
income stabilization schemes   195–196
income tax   73
incomes policies (see prices and incomes policies)
increasing returns to scale   223
index numbers   26–27
indexation   118
indifference theory   214–217
indirect taxation   73
indivisibilities   225
induced withdrawals   98
industrial relations
   and growth   88
industrialisation
   and developing countries   196
industry
   structure of industry   235
inefficiency (see efficiency)
   X-inefficiency   225, 255–256, 260, 267, 296
inelastic (see elasticity)
inequality (see distribution of income)
infant industry   **191**, 190–191
inferior goods   3, 217
inflation   26–27, 108–115, 116–128, 296–297
   cost-push inflation   **121**, **123**, 120–122, 126, 159, 186
   costs of inflation   **117**, 116, 118
   demand-pull inflation   **119**, 118–120, 125, 186
   hyperinflation   118
   imported inflation   119, 122, 162
   monetarist theory of inflation   **124**, **125**, 122–124
   Quantity Theory of Money   21–22
   slumpflation   119
   stagflation   119
   and devaluation   158–159
   and government policy   177–191
   and savings   56–57
   and the trade cycle   143
   and unemployment   125–127, 135, 138–140
inflationary gap   103–105, 120, 158, 179
infrastructure   69
injections   97–106
   planned injection   100
innovation (see technology)
   and efficiency   270
innovation cycle   143
institutional shareholders   274
integration   **174**, 173–175
interest (see also rate of interest   274
   interest rate policy   29–40
internal economies of scale   223–226
internalising an externality   268, 270

international liquidity   162
International Monetary Fund (IMF)   36, 155, 162
international trade (see also balance of payments)   35–36, 151–175
inventory cycle   146–147
investment   **59**, **61**, **63**, **64**, **100**, 53, 58–66, 112–113, 114, 178, 188, 195, 254, 256, 279, 284
   accelerator theory   63–65, 145, 285, 303
   gross investment   58, 88
   marginal efficiency of capital theory   60–63, 107, 108, 204
   net investment   58, 59, 88
   overseas investment   154–155, 172
   private sector investment   59–60
   public sector investment   60
   and the balance of payments   152, 154–155, 172, 184
   and the circular flow   97–106
   and economic development   196
   and growth   88, 90, 178
   and import controls   190–191
   and the trade cycle   141
invisible trade   151

J-curve   157–158, 160
Jarrow March   136
Jobcentres   137

Keynes J. M.   1, 97, 101, 118, 135
Keynesianism   1
   aggregate supply curve   108–109, 114–115
   balance of payments   159, 160
   consumption function   48–51, 114
   credit policy   184
   demand for money   29–33
   demand management   178
   devaluation   159, 188
   economic development   195
   fiscal policy   178–182
   income determination   97–106
   inflation   118–122, 186–188
   import controls   190–191
   investment   62, 63–65
   monetary policy   42–43, 183, 184
   money supply   42–43
   multiplier model   98–99
   Phillips curve   126
   savings   54–55
   supply side economics   178
   trade cycle   145–147
   unemployment   130, 135
"kinked" demand curve   248, 250
knowledge, perfect   239–240, 241, 242, 270
Kondratiev   147–149
Kuznets S.   147

labour (see also full employment, unemployment, wages)
   derived demand for labour   274
   division of labour   297
   factor of production   274
   labour market   **278**, 132–135, 285–287
   labour mobility   132, 137, 175, 279
   supply of labour   276–279, 285–287
   and economic rent   282–284
   and incentives   75, 181–182, 279, 281
Lancaster K.   266
land   86–87, 274, 276, 282
law of diminishing marginal utility   211–212
law of diminishing returns   226, 275
leakages (see withdrawals)
Leibenstein   255
leisure   277
lender of the last resort   23
less developed countries (LDC's)   170, 193
Lewis A.   193, 194
liabilities
   bank   18–19
limited companies   232
Lipsey R.   266
liquidity
   international   162

liquidity preference schedule 31–32, 34
liquidity trap 31, 32
living standards (see also economic welfare) **95**, 121, 194, 293
Local Authority stocks 25
long run 220–221, 226–227, 231
long wave trade cycles 147–149

M_0, M_1, M_2, M_3, M_4, M_5 definitions 16
macro-economic demand schedule 108
macro-economics 1, 304, 305
managed float 162
managerial economies 223
managerial theories of the firm 228, 231–233, 254–255
margin 1
marginal cost (see cost)
marginal cost pricing 265–266
marginal efficiency of capital 60–63, 107, 108, 284
marginal product **275**, 226, 284
    marginal physical product 275
    marginal revenue product 275–276
marginal propensity (see propensity)
marginal revenue (see revenue)
marginal utility theory 211–214, 304
mark-up 252, 261, 271
market economies 76, 290–292, 295–297, 303
market demand curves 201–202
market mechanism 201–210
market prices 82
market sector 252, 256, 286–287
market system 260
marketing economies 224–225
markets **8, 12**, **201**, **207**, 9, 202
    equilibrium 7–9, 202, 204
Marshall-Lerner condition 157–160
Marxist economics
    and development 195, 196
maturity 24, 25
measure of value 14
medium of exchange 14, 16
mergers policy 262
merit goods **72**, 71–72
methodology 299–305
microchips 147–149
micro-economics 1, 305
Mill J. S. 289
Minimum Lending Rate 36
miracle economies 86, 93
mixed economies 295–297
mobility of labour 132, 137, 175, 279
models **304**, 1–2, 299–300, 302–305
monetarism 1–2
    consumption function 48–52
    credit policy 184
    crowding out 180–181
    demand for money 29–32
    devaluation 188
    fiscal policy 180–182
    income determination 107–115
    inflation 122–124
    monetary policy 43
    money 43
    natural rate of unemployment 126–127, 137–139
    Phillips curve 126
    prices and incomes policies 186
    Quantity Theory of Money 21–22
    saving 55
    supply side economics 178, 181–182
    transmission mechanism 143–145, 183–184
monetary base 16, 20
monetary base control 38–39
Monetary History of the United States 143
monetary policy **37, 39, 40, 42, 43, 185**, 34–43, 177, 183–186
    and the balance of payments 35–36
    and exchange rates 35–36
    and interest rates 34–35
money **15**, 14–18
    broad 16
    creation 18–21, 41–42, 178

demand for money 29–33, 107–108, 124, 243
functions of money 14–15
high-powered money 19–21, 108
narrow 16
Quantity Theory of Money 21–22, 122
velocity of circulation of money 21–22, 122
and the trade cycle 143
money illusion 127, 135
money multiplier 19–21, 38, 109–110
money supply **17, 20**, 14–22, 41–43, 180, 183, 184, 186, 188, 304
    money supply definitions 16
    and the balance of payments 35–36
    and the trade cycle 143–145
    and the transmission mechanism 143–145, 181
monopolistic competition **247**, 245–248
    and efficiency 245–247
    and equilibrium 260–261, 265
Monopolies and Mergers Commission 262
monopoly 235, 250–251, 292
    equilibrium 250
    natural monopoly 261
    and efficiency 260–261, 262, 265, 266, 272
    and innovation 270
    and the labour market 285
    and price discrimination 250–251
monopsony 252
mortality rate 199
multinational companies 175, 198–199, 230
multiplier
    balanced budget multiplier 179–180
    bank or credit or money multiplier 19–21, 38
    real or Keynesian multiplier **100, 101, 103**, 98–100, 102, 105, 107, 135, 147, 179, 180, 305
multiplier-accelerator model 145–146
multi-product firms 236

National Debt 36, 37, 179
national expenditure (see aggregate demand and national income)
national income 274 (see also circular flow of income and income)
    equilibrium national income 99–105, 111–115, 126
    growth of national income 86–96
    measurement **81, 83, 84**, 79–85
    real and money national income 93
    and economic welfare 92–96
    and the Quantity Theory of Money 22
    and the trade cycle 141–149
nationalised industries (see also public sector efficiency) 262
    pricing 265–266
natural monopolies 261
natural rate of unemployment 123, 126–127, 137–140
neo-classical economics 1–2
    consumer sovereignty 256
    demand 211–218
    economic integration 174
    economics 289
    factors of production 274–281
    firm 230, 241–251, 254, 255, 256, 261, 263–264
    full employment 97
    investment (marginal efficiency of capital theory) 60–63
    labour market 132–135, 137, 287
    marginal cost 228
    marginal cost pricing 265–266
    profits 272
    savings 54, 56
    price determination 3–13, 201–210
    unemployment 132–135, 287
neo-Keynesian economics
    factors of production 284–287
    the firm 231, 252–254, 261
    marginal cost 228
net investment 58, 59, 88
net national income 84
net present value 264
net property income from abroad 82
New Industrial State, The, 256
newly industrialised countries (NIC's) 193

Index

nominal value 24–25
non-durable goods 46
non-exclusion 69, 70
non-human wealth 49
normal profit 228, 241
normative economics 301–302, 303
North Sea oil
  and taxation 284
notes and coins 15

Ohlin B. 169
oligopoly (see also planning sector) **237, 249,** 235, 248–250,
  280, 285, 292, 296
  and efficiency 260–261, 262, 265, 267, 272
  and innovation 270
  and the "kinked" demand curve 248, 250
open market operations 38
opportunity cost **291,** 29, 154, 169, 219, 228, 280, 289
optimum output 245, 260, 261
Organisation of Petroleum Exporting Countries (OPEC)
  205–206
organisational slack (see X-inefficiency)
output (see national income)
overhead costs (see fixed costs)
overseas investment 154–155, 172

paradox of thrift 101
partial model 305
per capita measurement 94
perfect competition **243,** 242–245, 248, 275, 303, 304
  assumptions 242
  short run and long run equilibrium, 242–245
  and efficiency 260–261, 263, 265, 266, 270, 272
  and innovation 270
perfect knowledge 239–240, 241, 242, 270
perfectly elastic and inelastic 10–11
perks 233, 254
permanent consumption 46
permanent income 48, 49, 55
permanent income hypothesis 48, 49, 55, 195
personal disposable income 48, 49
personal distribution of income 274
Phelps A. W. 125
Phillips curve **139,** 125–128, 138–140, 179, 186
planned economies (see command economies)
planned expenditure 99–100
planning sector 252–254, 256, 259, 270, 285, 286
political economy 301, 302
poll tax 73
population 175, 199–200, 277
positive economics **302,** 301–302, 303
poverty 76–77 (see also development economics)
precautionary demand for money 30
preference similarity theory 170
present value 264
price
  cost-plus pricing 231, 252, 254, 285
  discrimination 250–251
  price elasticity of demand 10, 235–236
  price elasticity of supply 10
  nationalised industry pricing 265–266
  price stabilisation schemes 205–206
  price taker 242, 243, 252
  price theory **5, 8, 12, 201, 207, 209,** 3–13, 201–210
prices and incomes policy 127, 186–188
private cost 266, 268, 270
private sector 67
  efficiency 182
privatisation 182, 226–168
product differentiation (see branded goods)
production
  factors of production 86, 255, 274–288
production possibility frontier or boundary 290
productivity 120, 188, 190
profit **5,** 81, 122, 186–188, 189, 219, 228, 274, 276, 280–281, 285,
  295
  abnormal profit 228, 242, 245, 247, 250, 261, 263, 264, 271,
   272, 290, 296

normal profit 228, 241
retained profit 90, 254
  and economic development 196
  and economic efficiency 182, 296
  and wages 285
profit maximisation 233, 254
  short run 230, 241–242, 250
  long run 231, 242, 254
profit satisficing 233, 234, 254, 255
progressive taxation 73–74, 76
propensity to consume **51,** 46–51, 98–99, 179, 180
propensity to import 98–99, 180
propensity to save 54–57, 98–99, 180, 195
propensity to tax 98–99, 179, 180
property income from abroad 82
property tax 73
proportional taxation 73
protectionism **172,** 171–173, 189
public corporation (see nationalised industries)
public expenditure (see public spending)
public goods 67–71, 290, 292
public limited companies 232
public sector 67–78
  and efficiency 182, 296
  and wages 285
public sector borrowing requirement (PSBR) **43, 103,** 112, 178,
  179, 181, 184
  and monetary policy **43,** 36, 37
public sector debt repayment (PSDR) 179
public spending **68, 70, 72,** 67–73, 177–185
  and the circular flow 97–106, 112

Quantity Theory of Money 21–22, 114, 122
quota 172, 177

Radcliffe Committee Report 42–43
rate of discount 284
rate of interest **23, 24,** 22–23
  real rate of interest **27,** 116
  and the balance of payments 159–160
  and consumption 49, 107–108
  and the exchange rate 153–154, 184
  and government policy 184
  and investment 60–63, 107–108, 184
  and monetary policy 34–39, 183
  and the PSBR 36
  and the trade cycle 143
rate of return 219
rates 73
real values 255, 281
real wage unemployment 132–135
recovery 141
rectangular hyperbola 11
redemption 24
redistribution of income 73–74, 76–77, 116, 118, 266–267
reflation 190
regional policy 175
regional unemployment 130, 175, 278
regressive taxation 73–74, 76
rent 274
  economic rent **283,** 282–284, 295
reserve asset ratio 19
reserve assets 19–21, 38
reserve ratio 19–20, 38
reserves, gold and foreign currency 151, 153, 155, 156, 158, 161,
  162, 163, 188
resources, allocation 272, 289–297
Restrictive Practices Court 264
restrictive trade practices 263–264
Retail Price Index (RPI) 46
retained profit 90
returns
  law of diminishing returns 226–227, 275
returns to scale 223–226
revaluation (see also devaluation) 157
revealed preference theory 217–218
retaliation 173, 190
revenue 228, 241, 247–248

and elasticity 11–12, 206–207
and monopolistic competition 245–248
and monopoly 250–251
and oligopoly 248–250
and perfect competition 242–245
and taxation 208
"revised sequence" 256
Ricardo D. 169, 171, 282, 284
risk 219, 228, 274, 280–281
and interest rates 22
Robbins L. 289
rural development 196

sales maximisation 232–233
satisficing 233, 234, 254, 255
saving, saving function **53, 55**, 49, 53–57, 58, 279
propensity to save 54–57, 98–99, 180, 195
and the circular flow 98–102
scale economies (see economies of scale)
scarcity 289
Schumpeter J. 147, 149, 270
Schwartz A. 143
science **300**, 299–301
seasonal unemployment 130, 177
second best, general theory of 266
second world 193
sector
market 252, 256, 286–287
planning 252–254, 256, 259, 285, 286
private 67, 182
public 67–78, 182, 285, 296
sectoral unemployment 130
separation of ownership and control 232
shareholders 232–233, 254, 255, 274
shifts in demand curves 4
short run 220–221, 226–227, 230
sight deposits 15
Simon H. 234, 255
simplification in model building 303
slump 130, 141
slumpflation 119
Smith A. 1, 3, 74, 166, 284, 289, 301, 302
snake (see European Monetary System)
social capital 193
social costs **269**, 266, 268, 270
social wage 77
sovereignty, consumer 256, 267, 290
Special Deposits 39
specialisation 169, 172, 174, 297–298
speculative demand for money 31
spillovers (see externalities)
stabilisation
income 206–207
price 205–206
stagflation 119
standard for deferred payment 14–15
standard of living **95**, 121, 194, 293
static 202, 304–305
stock
company stocks 25
government stock 25, 219
local authority stocks 25
stock appreciation 81–82
Stock Exchange 25, 53, 61, 62, 182
stocks
and the trade cycle 141, 143, 146–147
stocks and flows 305
stocks and work in progress 82
store of value 14
structural unemployment 130
subsidies 184, 191, 208, 265
and national income measurement 83
subsistence economy 85, 194
substitute goods 6, 13, 204
Supplementary Special Deposits 39–41
substitution effects 216–217
supply **5, 12, 231**, 6, 7, 201–210
aggregate supply 108–115, 118, 158–159, 178

elasticity of supply 10
individual supply 201–202
market supply 201–202
shifts in supply 6
short run supply 230, 254
and the market sector 252
and perfect competition 243–245
and the planning sector 254
supply of factors of production 276–287
capital 279
entrepreneurship 280–281
labour 276–279, 285–287
land 276
supply side of the economy **183**, 108–115, 118, 120, 178, 181–182
supply side policies 115, 181–182

take-overs 226, 233
tariffs (see also import controls) 172, 173, 177
tastes 4
taxation **70, 74, 75**, 73–77, 177
ad valorem taxes 73
allocative effects 75–76
canons of taxation 74–75
direct and indirect taxation 73
incidence of taxation **209**, 207–209
income taxes 73
progressive, regressive and proportional taxes 73–74, 76
property taxes 73
tax avoidance 85
taxes on capital 73
unit tax 73
and the circular flow of income 98–102
and economic development 195
and economic rent 284
and growth 90
and incentives 75, 181–182, 279, 281
and investment 62
and supply 6, 207–209
technical economies 223
technological gap theory 170
technology 6, 62, 88, 90, 147–149, 170, 194, 221, 254, 266, 270
technostructure 256, 259
terms of trade **171**, 170–171
theory economic 1–2, 299–300, 302–305
General Theory of the Second Best 266
third world 193
thrift, paradox of 101
tied aid 197
time
long run 220–221, 226–227, 231
short-run 220–221, 226–227, 230
very long run 221
time deposits 15
total (see under each term)
trade
gains from trade 166–169
international trade (see international trade)
terms of trade 170–171
and protectionism 171–173, 189
trade bills (see commercial bills)
trade creation 173
trade cycle **142, 146, 148, 150**, 130, 141–149, 184, 255
trade diversion 173
trade gap 196
trade unions 112–113, 121, 122, 123, 133–34, 137, 188, 277, 279, 285, 301–302
trading surplus 81
training 278
and growth 88
and unemployment 118
transactions
and Quantity Theory of Money 21–22
transactions demand for money 29–30
transfer earnings 283, 285
transfer payments 72–73, 76–77, 81
transitory income 49–50
transmission mechanism 123, 143, 145, 161, 183, 184
Treasury Bills 26, 36

Index

Treaty of Rome   264
trickling down   193

U-shaped cost curve   226
uncertainty   30, 252
underdeveloped economy   193
underemployment   194
undistributed profit (see retained profit)
unemployment   **131**, **134**, **137**, 108–115, 129–140, 277–278, 296–297, 300, 301
   classical unemployment   132–140
   cost of unemployment   129
   cyclical unemployment   130
   demand deficient unemployment   130
   frictional unemployment   130, 132, 177
   hidden unemployment   130, 132, 297
   Keynesian unemployment   130
   natural rate of unemployment   123, 126–127, 137–140, 182
   real wage unemployment   132–135
   regional unemployment   130, 175, 278
   seasonal unemployment   130, 177
   sectoral unemployment   130
   structural unemployment   130
   voluntary unemployment   **134**, 133
   and government policy   177–191
   and inflation   125–127, 135, 138–140
   and the Phillips curve   **139**, 125–127, 138–140, 179, 186
   and the trade cycle   141
unions (see trade unions)
unit elasticity   10–12
unit of account (see measure of value)

utility   211–218, 254, 255, 289, 297
   diminishing marginal utility   211–214

vacancies   131
value added   82
value judgement   301–302
value added tax   73
variable cost (see cost)
velocity of circulation of money   **114**, 21–22, 114, 122
very long run   221
visible trade   151

wages   274, 277, 285
   and the Phillips curve   125–127
wants   287, 297
war loan   25
wealth (see capital)
   and consumption   49–51
   and saving   56–57
Wealth of Nations, The   1, 166
Weber M.   88
welfare   92–96, 154, 171, 172, 173, 189, 197, 198, 265–266, 272, 295–297
Williamson   233, 254
withdrawals   97–106
   planned withdrawals   101
work schemes   132
working capital   59
working week   277

X-inefficiency   **255**, 225, 255–256, 260, 267, 296